C000128967

EVICTIONS

Graham Foundation / MIT Press Series in Contemporary Architectural Discourse

Achtung Architektur! Image and Phantasm in Contemporary Austrian Architecture
Eeva-Liisa Pelkonen

Inside Architecture
Vittorio Gregotti

Evictions: Art and Spatial Politics
Rosalyn Deutsche

EVICTIONS

ART AND SPATIAL POLITICS

ROSALYN DEUTSCHE

Graham Foundation for Advanced Studies in the Fine Arts
Chicago, Illinois

THE MIT PRESS
CAMBRIDGE, MASSACHUSETTS
LONDON, ENGLAND

Publication of this book has been supported by a grant from the Graham Foundation for Advanced Studies in the Fine Arts.

Page 284 reproduces the jacket design by Victoria Wong from *Variations on a Theme Park: The New American City and the End of Public Space*, edited by Michael Sorkin. Copyright © 1992 by Michael Sorkin. Reprinted by permission of Hill and Wang, a division of Farrar, Straus & Giroux, Inc.

This book was set in Bembo by Graphic Composition, Inc., and was printed and bound in the United States of America.

Library of Congress Cataloging-in-Publication Data

Deutsche, Rosalyn.
    Evictions : art and spatial politics / Rosalyn Deutsche.
      p. cm.
    Includes bibliographical references and index.
    ISBN 0-262-04158-8 (hb : alk. paper)
    1. Public space. 2. Public art. 3. Space (Architecture) 4. City planning. I. Title.
NA9053.S6D48   1996
711′.13—dc20   96-15527
                                                            CIP

For Robert Ubell

Contents

ACKNOWLEDGMENTS

I feel very fortunate in having had so much help writing this book.

First, I would like to thank the people who invited me to write the articles and deliver the talks that were the original versions of these essays—Douglas Crimp, Irit Rogoff, Brian Wallis, Philomena Mariani, Neil Smith, Michael Dear, Mark Wigley, and Richard Ingersoll. I am also grateful to the editors of the journal *October* for making a space for my work on art and urbanism.

Work on the final essay was supported by a grant from the Graham Foundation for Advanced Studies in the Fine Arts, which also assisted in the publication of the book.

My thanks to Jennifer Berman for tracking down and collecting the photographs. Thanks also to Roger Conover, Matthew Abbate, and Yasuyo Iguchi at the MIT Press and to Lois Nesbitt for her constructive copyediting.

I am particularly indebted to my students at several universities, with whom I first discussed many of the ideas in these essays and who responded with interest and challenging questions.

Thomas Keenan and Bruce Robbins were very generous in reading and commenting astutely on portions of the final manuscript.

For various kinds of help over the last decade and during the preparation of this book, I would like to thank Robert Benton, Marielle Cohen, Marion Cohen,

Beatriz Colomina, Douglas Crimp, Hans Haacke, Thornton Hayslett, Jennifer Hayslett-Ubell, Frances Katz, Thomas Keenan, Silvia Kolbowski, Laura Kurgan, Ernest Larsen, Doreen Massey, Elizabeth Miller, Sherry Millner, Meaghan Morris, Matt Mungan, Linda Nochlin, Abigail Solomon-Godeau, Renee Shanker, Lynne Tillman, Anthony Vidler, Jane Weinstock, Mark Wigley, and Krzysztof Wodiczko. I deeply appreciate the wisdom and compassion of Deborah Tanzer. Robert Ubell has sustained me in ways that I cannot even begin to measure. This book is dedicated to him with love.

The essays collected here were written over a period of ten years on topics ranging from public art and homelessness to the repression of feminism in critical theories of public space. With the exception of "Agoraphobia," which was written especially for this book, they have been published previously. While they have been revised and, in a few cases, expanded for this volume, their arguments are unchanged. The essays remain marked by the circumstances in which they were produced, as conditional interventions in historically specific—and ongoing—cultural debates. Each essay can be read independently, but together they form a single project that explores connections among contemporary art, space, and political struggles.[1] The essays discuss diverse spaces—cities, parks, institutions, exhibitions, artworks, disciplines, identities. I am concerned not only with the struggles taking place inside these spaces but with the less visible and therefore more pressing struggles that, I argue, produce and maintain all spaces.

The essays enter and question a particular interdisciplinary space—a discourse that combines ideas about art, architecture, and urban design, on the one hand, with theories of the city, social space, and public space, on the other. In shorthand, I sometimes call this interdisciplinary field "urban-aesthetic" or "spatial-cultural" discourse. While this discourse is not new, its present intensity and ubiquity are. It has attracted considerable attention since the early 1980s. Why, my essays ask, has it become so popular, so rapidly, in so many different arenas—the academy, the art world, urban planning, mass media, municipal documents, social movements—and among so many disparate political groups, from neoconservative policy intellectuals to leftist cultural critics? What political issues are at stake in the discourse about art and space? What political relationships organize the space of the discourse?

My answers to these questions are various and provisional. While the focus on urban-aesthetic discourse unites my essays, it also periodically disrupts their continuity. The discourse itself is neither monolithic nor static but, on the contrary, takes different forms and is capable of growing and changing. New alliances between urban and aesthetic disciplines were forged during the years in which I wrote these texts, and the imperative of responding to these shifting formations prompted revisions in my own thinking, encouraging me to call into question my earlier premises and to enlarge my critique of "spatial politics" so that it extends to the space of politics itself. *Evictions* documents these transformations.

The book is divided into three interconnected sections that represent three stages of my involvement in debates about art and social space. The first section analyzes the mutually supportive relationship that developed in the 1980s between aesthetic ideologies and an oppressive program of urban restructuring. The opening essays draw on critical spatial theory, especially neo-Marxist geography, to contest mainstream and conservative ideas about art, the city, and public space. The second section criticizes an alliance that has formed between prominent urban and cultural scholars who use critical spatial theory for quite a different purpose—to ground an account of postmodern culture that shores up traditional left political projects and rejects new kinds of radical political philosophies, social movements, and aesthetic practices, including new feminist theories. The final section returns to the question of public space raised early in the volume. These last essays explore contemporary aesthetic debates about the meaning of the term *public* but rethink the question of public space from the feminist and radical democratic perspectives adopted in the second section.

As a whole, the book argues that the dominant paradigm of urban-aesthetic interdisciplinarity and the most influential radical critiques of that paradigm—

although they both mobilize a democratic rhetoric of "openness" and "accessibility" and rise to the defense of public space—are structured by exclusions and, moreover, by attempts to erase the traces of these exclusions. Exclusions are justified, naturalized, and hidden by representing social space as a substantial unity that must be protected from conflict, heterogeneity, and particularity. *Evictions* takes account of specific exclusions in urban-aesthetic discourses to expose the authoritarian strategies that construct unitary images of social space. In the end, I contend that conflict, far from the ruin of democratic public space, is the condition of its existence.

The essays in the first section, "The Social Production of Space," were written between 1985 and 1988. I first became interested in art and spatial politics in the early 1980s when I observed the coincidence of four phenomena in New York City: massive urban development, intensification of official rhetoric about new public spaces, an explosion of interest in the aesthetics of urban planning, and a sharp increase in public art commissions. What, I wondered, is the relationship among these urban and aesthetic events? The opening essays examine different aspects of art's social function in contemporary urbanism and question the dominant model of urban-aesthetic discourse that was then—and, to a great extent, still is—used to explain this function. Promoting the participation of art and architecture in urban redevelopment projects, this model neutralizes the political character of both art and the city. It couples an aesthetic ideology positing that art and architecture transcend social relations with an urban ideology that presents the spatial organization of cities as the natural product of biological, social, or technological evolutions undergone by a supposedly organic society. These concepts sanction art's role in the urban environment as beneficial while legitimating existing urban conditions as inevitable.

My essays counter this urban-aesthetic alliance by combining critical ideas about the social construction of "art" with perspectives, taken from critical urban studies, on what Henri Lefebvre calls "the production of space"—a phrase coined to signify that the organization of the city and of space in general is neither natural nor uniformly advantageous. Space is, rather, political, inseparable from the conflictual and uneven social relations that structure specific societies at specific historical moments. This section examines the involvement of aesthetic practices in what urban theorists call "the politics of space," including struggles over public space.

"Krzysztof Wodiczko's *Homeless Projection* and the Site of Urban 'Revitalization'" investigates the role played by architecture, urban planning, park design, and historic preservation in obscuring the conflictual character of urban redevelopment. Focusing on New York's Union Square Park, an example of a new public space whose wholesale transformation was engineered under the banners of historical continuity and return to tradition, I investigate the city's campaign to restore the park's historical monuments. The monuments exemplify the kind of "outdoor art" sponsored by late nineteenth-century municipal beautification movements, and I compare the part played by these movements in shaping the industrial city to the role of contemporary aesthetic disciplines in organizing postindustrial space.

In exploring these processes, I first had to understand the significance of urban redevelopment and its residential component, gentrification. What was their relationship to another urban event—the sudden appearance of large numbers of homeless people on the streets of New York? Earlier, I had coauthored an article investigating links between the gentrification of New York's Lower East Side and the widely celebrated growth of what was then called the "East Village art scene." The article placed gentrification within broader processes of global sociospatial restructuring.[2] Now, aided by critical urban theory, I extended the analysis. Instead of celebrating redevelopment as a "revitalizing" and "beautifying" process, I view it as the historical form of late-capitalist urbanism, facilitating new international relations of domination and oppression and transforming cities for private profit and state control. The mechanism of redevelopment, I argue, destroys the very conditions of survival—housing and services—for residents no longer required for the city's economy. The emergence of a large population of homeless residents is redevelopment's most visible symptom.

This analysis disputes the idea that new public spaces and homelessness are two discrete phenomena, an image that makes people without homes appear to introduce conflict into public space. Instead, I claim that homeless people and public spaces are integrally linked, dual products of the spatioeconomic conflicts that constitute contemporary urban restructuring.

Interwoven with this analysis is a critique of the depoliticized aesthetics instrumental in portraying redevelopment as the preservation of tradition. Juxtaposing these aesthetic concepts with a different kind of aesthetic practice, I explore a public project about homelessness proposed for the Union Square monuments by the artist Krzysztof Wodiczko. I was first inspired to write my essay about Union Square after seeing Wodiczko's *Homeless Projection: A Proposal for the City of New York,* which I interpreted as a confrontation with the official Union Square redevelopment program. While the promoters of Union Square redevelopment used the square's historical monuments to advertise the benefits of redevelopment, Wodiczko appropriated the sculptures to create a counterimage of redevelopment. Employing slide projections that transformed the gentrified statues into homeless people, he forced the monuments to testify to the sociospatial conflicts that they were being employed to conceal. Against the city's official restoration program, Wodiczko disclosed the social divisions—and the social groups—expelled when historical monuments are presented as symbols of social cohesion. Wodiczko's project thus contests the neutralizing concepts of "historic preservation" and "contextualism" that dominated architecture, public art, and urban planning in the 1980s. In my reading, this contestation is a true act of restoration. For this book, influenced by new ideas about rights, I have elaborated on the portion of the Union Square essay in which I analyze Wodiczko's *Homeless Projection* as an attempt to create a democratic public space in the public spaces of the redeveloped city.

"Uneven Development: Public Art in New York City" expands the analysis introduced in the Union Square essay. I criticize the widespread tendency in art and urban discourse of the 1980s to celebrate what was called the "new public art." In contrast to an earlier conception of public art as "art in public places," the new public art was touted as "socially responsible," "site-specific," and "functional" because it helped design, and so contributed to the "beauty" and "utility" of, its newly redeveloped urban sites. "Uneven Development" questions the social function of redevelopment itself and its functionalist rhetoric. Excavating the history of Battery Park City in Lower Manhattan as a case study of the marriage of redevelopment and the new public art, the essay employs Henri Lefebvre's analysis of spatial contradictions and his critique of urban planning to argue that a genuinely responsible public art must, in Lefebvre's words, "appropriate" space from its domination by capitalist and state power. In the tradition of radical site-specific art, public art must disrupt, rather than secure, the apparent coherence of its new urban sites. Defending the democratic potential of site-specificity against its depoliticization by conservative forces, I explore parallels between critical treatments of space in aesthetic and urban theory. Using a work by Krzysztof Wodiczko as an example once again, I suggest that Lefebvre's appropriation of space is similar to the reorganizations of space undertaken by certain site-specific artists. For both, public space is not a preconstituted entity created for users; it arises only from a practice (or counterpractice) of use by those groups excluded from dominated space.

"Representing Berlin" was completed before the Union Square and Battery Park City essays but after I had begun to investigate the intersection of contemporary urban and aesthetic discourses. The essay applies this investigation to modern art history, demonstrating how the discipline's traditional isolation from urban scholarship, coupled with its empiricist bias and idealist presuppositions, set the stage for the neutralization of urban sites in 1980s art discourse. The essay, extended for this book, was first presented at a symposium organized in 1985 by the London Royal Academy of Arts in conjunction with the exhibition "German Art in the 20th Century." The exhibition represented expressionism as the national artistic style of modern Germany and associated it with the country's liberation from Nazi and foreign domination. In this way, it also invented a pedigree for German neoexpressionist painting that had emerged in the late 1970s and early 1980s. But to many critics neoexpressionism was neither new nor emancipatory. Rather, it embodied a regression to conventional artistic forms and ideals of aesthetic autonomy—ideals that had recently been challenged by new contextual art practices governed by the principle that an artwork's meaning is socially constructed and inseparable from the historical conditions of its existence.

"Representing Berlin" contributes to the critique of neoexpressionism's retreat from the social, as exhibited in expressionist paintings of the city. In "Krzysztof Wodiczko's *Homeless Projection*" and "Uneven Development," I relate critical spatial strategies deployed in postmodern art to critical theories of space in urban studies. I argue that both disciplines emphasize the social production and therefore the mutability of spatial arrangements. "Representing Berlin" makes a complementary point. In expressionist "city paintings," traditional notions about the autonomy of aesthetic space cannot be dissociated from traditional ideas about urban space. Both sets of ideas support existing urban conditions by making them appear natural and inevitable. The reciprocity between aesthetic and urban ideologies is exemplified in the art-historical category "urban expressionism," commonly thought to have originated in Berlin. Examining the dual claim that expressionism is a quintessentially "urban" style and that Berlin is an "expressionist city," I trace the history of urban expressionism from its invention in Berlin in the early twentieth century to its revival in the late 1970s by promoters of German neoexpressionism. I contend that urban expressionism combines mutually sustaining urban and aesthetic discourses to perform two depoliticizing roles: Berlin emerges as the exemplar of an urban condition understood as universal and transhistorical, and expressionism appears as the epitome of art's capacity to transcend social life.

"Representing Berlin" also contains interpretations of two artworks by Louise Lawler and Hans Haacke that present alternative, politicized ways of engaging urban contexts. Unlike the new public art, these works do not collaborate in the design of the redeveloped city. Unlike neoexpressionist city painting, they do not seek to transcend urban social conditions. On the contrary, they draw attention to those conditions. But they do not reduce art's social meaning to a simple reflection of "external" social reality, a model that leaves art per se politically neutral. Instead, they employ spatial tactics developed in postmodern art—site-specificity, institutional critique, critiques of representation—to reveal the social relations that constitute both aesthetic and urban spaces.

In 1971, nearly a decade before the expressionist revival, Haacke produced two works that in retrospect can be seen as forerunners of site-specific art that addresses both urban and aesthetic sites.[3] Haacke's works, created for his upcoming exhibition at New York's Guggenheim Museum, exposed the covert operations of New York's real-estate industry, which shapes the use and appearance of urban space. But Haacke's "real-estate pieces" posed a powerful threat to one of New York's most prestigious aesthetic spaces. After seeing plans for the works, the Guggenheim's director canceled Haacke's exhibition. This incident is the topic of "Property Values: Hans Haacke, Real Estate and the Museum." The essay was written in 1985 for the catalogue accompanying what became, given the Guggenheim cancellation, Haacke's first one-person show in a New York City museum. The Guggenheim's director argued that the "specificity" of the real-estate pieces was incompatible with the museum's identity as an aesthetic domain standing above social conflicts. I contend that this censorship shows how the museum's presumed autonomy is actually a contingent relationship of exclusion—the museum is endowed with a universal aesthetic essence by repressing the social conflicts that constitute its very conditions. Drawing analogies between the fetishization of city and museological spaces, "Property Values" reevaluates the Guggenheim episode in light of the collaborative relationships between art institutions and New York real estate in the 1980s.

The book's second section, "Men in Space," responds to new problems raised by a form of urban-aesthetic interdisciplinarity generated by an influential group of neo-Marxist geographers and cultural critics. The alliance between the two disciplines was anticipated in Fredric Jameson's well-known 1984 essay, "Postmodernism, or, the Cultural Logic of Late Capitalism." The alliance was launched decisively in 1989 when two critical geographers, David Harvey and Edward Soja, published books about postmodernism, marking the entry of urban studies into debates about postmodern culture. Jameson's and Harvey's critique of contemporary culture, like the essays in the first section of my book, is based on theories about the social production of space. But instead of drawing parallels between critical spatial theories and critical postmodern art, these writers employ politicized spatial discourse to define postmodern art forms as an escape from politics. I argue that Harvey and Jameson enlist the social production of space discourse to protect the space of traditional left political projects, based on ideas of social totality, against the challenges posed by new political practices built on partial critiques and aims. While the texts in "The Social Production of Space" draw upon critical urban geography to intervene in aesthetic discourses that legitimate the capitalist production of space, the "Men in Space" essays examine the politics of radical geography's construction of spatial politics. Using ideas about representation generated by cultural theory, they criticize geography's own production and maintenance of a masculinist space. Written between 1990 and 1993, the essays present a feminist contestation of this space.

The title essay of the section, "Men in Space," appeared soon after the publication of Harvey's and Soja's books. It links these books to the work on art and the politics of space by cultural critics Jameson and T. J. Clark. I argue that what unites these scholars in a new interdisciplinary formation is their rejection of issues of sexuality and gender and their marginalization of feminist social analysis. "Men in Space" asserts that the repression of feminism is a structural, not an incidental, element of the group's foundationalist social theory and unitarian epistemology. These writers conceive of society as an impartial totality integrated by an economic foundation. They believe that a single antagonism—class—embodies the antagonistic character of the social totality. Consequently, only one theory—Marxism—can adequately account for social relations of subordination. My essay uses feminist ideas about the politics of images to challenge these claims. While authors like Clark measure artistic images of the city against an external urban reality, feminist theories treat visual images as themselves social relations—representations producing meanings and constructing identities for viewing subjects. "Men in Space" suggests that the image of a coherent social space perpetuated in the new urban-aesthetic discourse is a fantasy that harbors its own spatial politics. Elevating the subject of the image to a vantage point from which he can supposedly "see" the social totality, it relegates different perspectives to subordinate or invisible positions.

"Boys Town," a critique of Harvey's *The Condition of Postmodernity,* elaborates on the analysis begun in "Men in Space." The earlier article originally appeared in an art magazine while "Boys Town" was written first as a lecture and then as an essay for an audience of geographers and urban scholars, obligating me to survey the history and key issues of contemporary art that I felt Harvey had distorted or ignored. This interdisciplinary responsibility gave me an opportunity to demonstrate how the very postmodern art practices that Harvey condemns as nonpolitical—critiques of visual representation—offer an important political challenge to his social theory, which he models on vision.

"Boys Town" examines the spatial politics implicit in Harvey's contention that postmodernism's valorization of "fragmentation" and difference conceals the totality of late-capitalist space and therefore jeopardizes the possibility of emancipatory struggles. For Harvey, new intellectual currents that start from different points of social analysis or that identify new objects of political study are complicit with capitalism's concealment of social reality. I argue that when Harvey claims to perceive an absolute basis of social unity, he must refuse to acknowledge the political contribution of art informed by feminist theories of representation. For feminists have analyzed the foundationalist image of society as a fiction of subjects driven by a desire to disavow their own partial and fragmented condition.[4]

"*Chinatown*, Part Four? What Jake Forgets about Downtown" responds to two articles by urban spatial theorists: Mike Davis's "*Chinatown*, Part Two? The 'Internationalization' of Downtown Los Angeles" and Derek Gregory's "*Chinatown*, Part Three? Soja and the Missing Spaces of Social Theory." My *Chinatown* essay explores the references to film noir and descriptions of urban scholars as hard-boiled detectives currently popular in critical urban discourse—especially in Davis's *City of Quartz*, a cultural history of Los Angeles. Why, I ask, do neo-Marxist urban scholars, who completely detach the study of space from questions of sexuality, so readily compare their work with noir—a genre that links the dangers of the city with the sexuality of femmes fatales? I suggest that the absence of questions of sexuality in urban discourse is the first clue to their presence.

The essay argues that urban theory's invocation of noir to support its claim to objectivity and to reinforce its avoidance of issues of subjectivity demonstrates urban theory's resistance to contemporary cultural criticism and is, moreover, a symptom of its underlying preoccupation with sexuality. Treating urban studies not as a discourse that simply explains culture but as itself a form of culture, "*Chinatown*, Part Four?" uses ideas about noir developed in feminist film theory to interrogate the field's objectivist claims. Contemporary spatial theory, the essay concludes, does not, as its practitioners who cite noir assume, simply penetrate deceptive appearances to uncover urban reality. Rather, it too is a spatial production: it sets up, and simultaneously detaches itself from, images of the city and of space that define a masculine subject.

∽

The final section, "Public Space and Democracy," goes back to questions about public art and public space raised in the first part of the book—questions that have become more prevalent among art, architecture, and urban critics in the 1990s. What does the term *public* mean now? The concluding essays reconsider this question in light of the ideas about foundationalism, subjectivity, and sexual difference explored in the previous section. They do not abandon the earlier critique of bourgeois concepts of the public—notions that protect the exclusionary rights of private property and legitimate state control of urban spaces—although, with the help of theorists of radical democracy, they problematize this critique. They continue to stress the importance of disputing conservative ideas of democracy that, in defending public space as a universal realm to be shielded from politics, attempt to rally popular consent to authoritarian forms of power. But these essays also question the authoritarianism of certain leftist redefinitions of public space as a "public sphere"—the very domain of democratic politics.

In "*Tilted Arc* and the Uses of Democracy," I use the notorious controversy over the removal of Richard Serra's *Tilted Arc* (1981) from Manhattan's Federal Plaza in 1989 to examine contemporary aesthetic debates about the meaning of public space. The essay, written as a review of a book documenting the *Tilted Arc* incident, concentrates on the rhetoric of democracy mobilized by opponents and supporters of Serra's sculpture. Both sides, like all defenders of public space, presented themselves as promoters of democracy. I defend Serra's left-wing advocates against the charge of elitism leveled against them by neoconservatives, who, in a textbook example of what Stuart Hall calls "authoritarian populism," used the *Tilted Arc* debate as an opportunity to endorse cultural privatization and to justify state censorship of critical art in the name of the people's right to public space. I also support what I consider to be the democratic possibilities of site-specific art against conservative definitions that make site-specificity consistent with the concealment, rather than the questioning, of power in public art's urban sites. But "*Tilted Arc* and the Uses of Democracy" also argues that, faced with an onslaught of conservative democratic rhetoric, the sculpture's defenders made few efforts to articulate concepts of democracy, public art, or public space in more radical directions. I link this failure to the left's reluctance to abandon myths of the "great artist"—now reincarnated as "the exemplary political artist"—and its continuing attachment to vanguardist attitudes as incompatible with democratic principles as are conservative notions of democracy. I conclude that art critics who want to defend public space should take a harder look at the question of democracy.

"Agoraphobia" takes up this question, placing aesthetic debates about public space within the context of broader struggles over the meaning of democracy. While some of the ideas in this essay were introduced in an earlier article, I have expanded and restructured them into a virtually new text that examines conservative, liberal, and leftist redefinitions of the term *public*. The essay has two principal objectives. First, it brings new theories of "radical and plural democracy" to bear on current thought about what makes art public. Although public art discourse has so far paid little direct attention to these theories, the issues they raise are already present at the very heart of controversies over aesthetic politics. I then intervene in a particular controversy, disputing a suggestion made by certain leftist critics that art informed by feminist ideas about subjectivity in visual representation is irrelevant, even a danger, to art's participation in what these critics call public space. I argue that feminist critiques, which explore the public rather than private nature of vision and subjectivity, are crucial to the growth of a different and, to my mind, more democratic public space.

Over the last decade, radical cultural critics have counteracted neutralizing conceptions of the public by defining public space as a public sphere—an arena in which citizens engage in political activity—and by redefining public art as work that enters or helps create such a space. But the question of the meaning of the public is not settled by equating public space with political space. Rather, a new question arises: Which politics?

I approach this question by comparing two critical concepts of the political public sphere. One is based on a strict division between an abstract, universalist public and a private arena of conflicting, partial interests. Champions of this concept treat public space as a realm of social plenitude that has declined—even vanished—in a "postmodern" epoch of conflict, heterogeneity, and particularity. A contrasting position holds that a unitary public space is not "lost," but is, instead, what critic Bruce Robbins (borrowing from diverse theorists of the public) calls a "phantom." In this view, the singular public space is a phantom because its claim to be fully inclusive has always been an illusion. What is more, the very notion of an undivided social space is irremediably deceptive, constituted by disavowing plurality and conflict.

The struggle between these competing conceptions of public space is rephrased in current debates about art's publicness. Some critics call for the recovery of an artistic public sphere modeled on Enlightenment ideals of a political public. In this unified public space, impartial citizens rise above particularity and conflict, dedicating themselves to reaching consensus about the common good through the exercise of reason. In contrast, art informed by feminist critiques of vision implicitly casts doubt on the citizen of the classical public sphere by exposing how the impartial subject is a masculinist fiction whose wholeness is secured by mastering difference and otherness. I liken this art to critiques of modern political theory undertaken from the point of view that the modern idea of the citizen must be reworked if democracy is to be extended. These critiques hold that the impartial citizen, far from an autonomous being, is constructed by the very object from which he claims detachment: he can develop only in the presence of "society" set up as an object that, unified by an absolute foundation, itself transcends partiality—a complete totality. From the standpoint of radical democracy, however, this image of society is incompatible with democratic values. For, as the political philosopher Claude Lefort proposes, democracy is invented when references to an unconditional basis of social unity are abandoned. Without an underlying positivity, society cannot be internally complete. Rather, its identity becomes an enigma and is therefore open to limitless debate—a debate that is coterminous with public space.

I conclude that art critics who advocate a return to the ideal of a unitary public sphere try to recuperate the masculinist subject and, in so doing, hide from the very openness of public space that they ostensibly champion. To this end, they cast art informed by feminist critiques of subjectivity into privacy, dismissing it as inimical to political public space. The eviction of feminist critiques from the artistic public sphere has something in common with all of the evictions explored in this book. It seeks to protect a space—in this case the space of politics—whose coherence, it is imagined, precedes representation. In my final essay, "Agoraphobia," I argue that this search can lead in authoritarian directions. When space is pictured as a closed entity, conflicts—and social groups associated with conflict—appear as disturbances that enter space from the outside and must be expelled to restore harmony. Against nostalgic images of space that externalize and delegitimate conflict, "Agoraphobia" stresses the importance of remembering that we cannot recover what we never had. Social space is produced and structured by conflicts. With this recognition, a democratic spatial politics begins.

I

The Social Production of Space

In *The City Observed: A Guide to the Architecture of Manhattan,* Paul Goldberger concludes his historical survey of Union Square with the following observation:

> For all that has gone wrong here, there are still reminders within the
> square itself of what a grand civic environment this once was. There
> are bronze fountains and some of the city's finest statuary. The best of
> the statues are Henry Kirke Brown and John Quincy Ward's eques-
> trian statue of Washington, with a Richard Upjohn base, and Karl
> Adolf Donndorf's mother and children atop a bronze fountain base.
> There is also an immense flagstaff base, 9½ feet high and 36 feet in
> diameter, with bas-reliefs by Anthony de Francisci symbolizing the
> forces of good and evil in the Revolutionary War; *even if a derelict is
> relieving himself beside it, it has a rather majestic presence.*[1]

This use of a homeless person as a foil for the aesthetic merits of a sculptural base
and for the nostalgic visions evoked by civic monuments will hardly surprise anyone familiar with Goldberger's apologies for the luxury condominiums, lavish corporate headquarters, and high-rent office towers that proliferated in New York
City throughout the 1980s. Goldberger was then senior architecture critic of the

New York Times and, like his account of the Union Square monuments, his journalistic appraisals of the decade's profitable new buildings remained indifferent to urban social conditions, divorcing them from the circumstances of architectural production. Goldberger never mentioned the fact that the architects of New York's construction boom not only scorned the glaring need for new public housing but relentlessly eroded the existing low-income housing stock, thereby destroying the conditions of survival for hundreds of thousands of the city's poorest residents. Detaching himself from questions of housing and focusing on what he deemed proper architectural concerns, he also impeded the more basic recognition that the destruction of low-income housing was no accidental by-product of the decade's architectural expansionism but was, along with unemployment and cuts in social services, an essential component of the economic imperatives that motivated the new construction in the first place.

But the architecture discourse exemplified by Goldberger's journalism obscures the urban context most effectively not when it turns its back on the city altogether but when it professes "social responsibility" in the form of a concern for the city's physical environment. Intermittently, for instance, Goldberger addressed the substantial threat that the construction of the 1980s posed to New York's light, air, and open space. To meet this threat, however, he espoused a concept of urban planning that, far from offering a solution, was itself a considerable part of the city's social problems.[2] Asserting that the critical factors in development projects are the size, height, bulk, density, and style of buildings in relation to their immediate physical sites, Goldberger disregarded architecture's political and economic sites. True, he conceded in passing that "architecture has now come to be a selling point in residential real estate as much as it has in commercial."[3] But this recognition did not prevent him from aiding the destruction of housing and communities by aestheticizing the real-estate function of current construction much as he did the commercial function of the early twentieth-century skyscraper.[4] In short, he made common cause with contemporary development for the rich and privileged using the same rationale that authorized his description of the sculptural treasures of Union Square: celebration of the essential power and romance of, in the first case, the skyscraper, and, in the second, the historical monument.

The City Observed appeared in 1979, only a few years before "derelicts," along with other members of a "socially undesirable population,"[5] were evicted from Union Square by a massive program of urban redevelopment. Like all such episodes in the most recent New York real-estate boom, this one forcibly "relocated" many of the area's lower-income tenants and threatened others with a permanent loss of housing. The publication of Goldberger's guide coincided with the preparatory stage of the redevelopment plan, and the book shares prominent features of the planning mentality that engineered Union Square redevelopment and of the public relations campaign that legitimated it: aesthetic appreciation of the architecture and urban design of the neighborhood coupled with sentimental appeals for the restoration of selected chapters of the area's history.

The thematic resemblance between the book and the planning documents is no mere coincidence. It vividly illustrates how instrumental aesthetic ideologies can be for the powerful forces determining the use, appearance, and ownership of New York's urban spaces and for the presentation of their activities as the restoration of a glorious past. For Goldberger, "Union Square's past is more interesting than its present. Now the square is just a dreary park, one of the least relaxing green spaces in Manhattan."[6] Invariably, the reports, proposals, and statements issued by New York's Department of City Planning, the City Parks Commission, and municipal officials about the various phases and branches of Union Square redevelopment also reminisced about the square's glorious history and lamented its sharply contrasting present predicament. As one typical survey put it: "For the most part, the park today is a gathering place for indigent men whose presence further tends to discourage others from enjoying quiet moments inside the walled open space."[7] These texts paid no attention to the future of Union Square's displaced homeless. Neither did they consider the prospects for new homeless people produced by the mass evictions and increase in property values caused by redevelopment. Instead, they conjured a past that never existed. Narratives recounting vaguely defined historical periods stressed the late-nineteenth-century moment of

Union Square's history, when it was first a wealthy residential neighborhood and then a fashionable commercial district, part of the increasingly well known (thanks to a wave of museum exhibitions, media reports, and landmark preservation campaigns) "Ladies' Mile."[8] Redevelopers were most eager to revive this presumably elegant and genteel era, and aesthetic discourse helped them construct a distorted architecture and design history of the area, offering reassuring illusions of a continuous and stable tradition symbolized by transcendent aesthetic forms. The history of Union Square, it is said, lies before our eyes in its architectural remains. Using the same methods that smoothed the way for the design and execution of redevelopment, reconstructed histories such as Goldberger's take readers on a tour of the area's buildings, monuments, and "compositions."[9]

Krzysztof Wodiczko's *Homeless Projection: A Proposal for the City of New York* interrupts this "journey-in-fiction."[10] Using the same terrain and the same "significant" architectural landmarks, Wodiczko's public artwork takes a radically different position within the politics of urban space. Its form: site-specific, temporary, collaborative with its audience; its subject matter: the capitulation of architecture to the conditions of the real-estate industry; the content of its images: the fearful social outcome of that alliance. These qualities render *The Homeless Projection* useless to those forces taking possession of Union Square in order to exploit it for profit. They militate also against the work's neutralization by aesthetic institutions. Instead of fostering an unreflective consumption of past architectural forms to oil the mechanism of urban "revitalization," the project identifies the system of economic and political power operating in New York beneath what the artist once called "the discreet camouflage of a cultural and aesthetic 'background.'"[11] Eroding the aura of isolation that idealist aesthetics constructs around architectural forms, *The Homeless Projection* also—by placing those forms within a broad and multivalent context—dismantles the even more obscurantist urban discourse that relates individual buildings to the city construed only as a physical environment. Wodiczko's project reinserts architectural objects into the surrounding city understood as a site of economic, social, and political processes. Consequently, it contests the belief that monumental buildings are stable, transcendent, permanent structures containing essential and universal meanings. *The Homeless Projection* proclaims, on the contrary, the mutability of their language and calls attention to the changing uses to which they are put as they are continually recast in new historical circumstances and social frameworks.

While the architecture and urban discourses circulating in journalism such as Goldberger's and in the documents produced by New York's official urban-planning professionals manufactured an aesthetic disguise for revitalization, *The Homeless Projection* dramatically interferes with that image, restoring the viewer's ability to perceive the connections that these discourses sever or cosmeticize— the links that place the interrelated disciplines of architecture, urban design, and, increasingly, art in the service of the financial forces that shape New York's built environment. Further, the clear ethical imperative behind the work's intervention in contemporary urban struggles contrasts sharply with the dominant architectural system's preferred stance of "corporate moral detachment."[12]

Wodiczko entered the arena of New York housing politics when he mounted an exhibition in a New York art gallery. *The Homeless Projection* exists only as a proposal first presented at 49th Parallel, Centre for Contemporary Canadian Art, in the winter of 1986. Consisting of four montaged slide images projected onto the gallery's walls and a written statement by the artist distributed in an accompanying brochure, the proposal outlined a plan for the transformation of Union Square Park. Wodiczko's exhibition coincided with the unfolding of the redevelopment scheme that was actually transforming Union Square, opening several months after the completion of the first phase of the park restoration—the ideological centerpiece and economic precondition of the district's revitalization. Such drastic changes in the built environment are engineered by institutionalized urban planning. "What has been of fundamental importance," writes a critic of the history of town planning, "is the role of the project, that is of imagination."[13] These projects mobilize vision and memory. No matter how objectifying their language, they are, by virtue of their selective focuses, boundaries, and exclusions, also ideological statements about the problems of and solutions for their sites. Since *The Homeless Projection*'s potential location was a target of the pervasive and calculated urban process of redevelopment, Wodiczko's photographic and textual presentation in a space of aesthetic display—the art gallery—recalled the visual and

Krzysztof Wodiczko, *The Homeless Projection: A Proposal for the City of New York,* 1986, Abraham Lincoln Monument, Union Square Park (photo courtesy Krzysztof Wodiczko and Galerie Lelong).

Krzysztof Wodiczko, *The Homeless Projection: A Proposal for the City of New York,* 1986, Lafayette Monument, Union Square Park (photo courtesy Krzysztof Wodiczko and Galerie Lelong).

Krzysztof Wodiczko, *The Homeless Projection: A Proposal for the City of New York,* 1986, Mother and Child Fountain, Union Square Park (photo courtesy Krzysztof Wodiczko and Galerie Lelong).

Krzysztof Wodiczko, *The Homeless Projection: A Proposal for the City of New York,* 1986, George Washington Monument (photo courtesy Krzysztof Wodiczko and Galerie Lelong).

written forms of city planning. Like the official proposals generated by the teams of engineers, landscape architects, designers, demographers, sociologists, and architects who shaped Union Square's renovation, Wodiczko's presentation envisioned alterations to its prospective site and set forth the principles and objectives governing the proposal. Unlike such documents, however, *The Homeless Projection* offered no suggestions for enduring physical changes to the area under study. Instead, the artist disclosed a plan to appropriate temporarily the public space of Union Square Park for a performance in the course of which he would project transient images onto the newly refurbished surfaces of the four neoclassical monuments that occupy symmetrical positions on each side of the park. Yet impermanence is not the only quality distinguishing Wodiczko's proposal from official projects. There is another, more crucial difference between the two: mainstream planning claims that its proposals will restore a fundamental social harmony that has been disrupted while Wodiczko's project illuminates the prevailing social relations of domination and conflict that such planning both facilitates and disavows.

THE IMAGE OF REDEVELOPMENT

The Homeless Projection was a proposal for a work to be situated in Union Square, but the work's subtitle, "A Proposal for the City of New York," suggests that Union Square was only a determinate location of an urban phenomenon extending far beyond the immediate area. Indeed, the transformation of Union Square from a deteriorated yet active precinct consisting of a crime-ridden park, low-rent office buildings, inexpensive stores,[14] and single-room occupancy hotels into a luxury "mixed-use" neighborhood—commercial, residential, retail—was only an individual manifestation of an unprecedented degree of change in the class composition of New York neighborhoods. The concluding phases of these metamorphoses—following the preliminary and calculated stages of abandonment, neglect, and deterioration—were identified in the early 1980s by a constellation of inaccurate, confusing, and distorting terms. Overtly falsifying was the overarching rubric "revitalization," a word whose positive connotations reflect nothing other than "the sort of middle-class ethnocentrism that views the replacement of low-status groups by middle-class groups as beneficial by definition."[15] "Revitalization" conceals the very existence of those inhabitants already living in the frequently vital neighborhoods targeted for renovation. The term most routinely mobilized to designate urban changes was "gentrification," which, coined in London in the 1960s, does suggest the class interests at work in the process. In New York, however, the term was used primarily in a celebratory spirit, and, in any case, it misidentifies the gentrifying classes as a landed aristocracy.

Where explanations of revitalization and gentrification existed at all, they were generally formulated out of the concepts, values, and beliefs espoused by the financial institutions, politicians, corporations, real-estate developers, landlords, and upper-middle-class residents who benefited from the process. At their most self-serving—and in the form most widely disseminated in the mass media—such accounts repressed the social origins, functions, and effects of gentrification, presenting it as the heroic act of individuals. "When an area becomes ripe for gentrification," New York's former housing commissioner explained,

> a condition that cannot be rigorously identified in advance but seems to depend on the inscrutable whims of an invisible hand, the new purchasers face monumental tasks. First the building must be emptied. Then layers of paint must be scraped from fine paneling; improvised partitions must be removed; plumbing must be installed and heating ripped out and replaced. Sometimes the new buyers spend years under pioneering conditions.[16]

Not all descriptions were so blatantly misleading. But those that specified or even criticized gentrification's social effects tended to be superficial, impressionistic, or eclectic rather than grounded in an understanding of the specific factors governing patterns of urban growth and change.

By the middle of the decade, however, some efforts had been made to "identify rigorously" the structural elements that prepare the ground for gentrification and to ascertain precisely whose needs regulate the restructuring of urban space within which gentrification was playing a leading role. These new theories were based on the premise that the physical form of the cityscape is inseparable from the specific society in which it develops. The wholesale reorganization of urban space represents, then, no mere surface phenomenon. It is part of a full-scale social restructuring. In 1984, trying to place gentrification within the context of this broader restructuring, Neil Smith and Michele LeFaivre developed a "Class Analysis of Gentrification."[17] By contrast with notions of "inscrutable whims" and "invisible hands," the authors examined a systematic combination of economic processes—a devalorization cycle of declining real-estate values—through which inner-city neighborhoods have been historically developed into deteriorated areas in order to create the necessary conditions for gentrification. Taking place within the wider periodicity of capitalist expansion, the devalorization cycle—consisting of new construction, landlord control, blockbusting, redlining, and abandonment—produces a situation in which a developer's investment can yield a maximum profit. Profit maximization depends on the existence of a substantial gap between the current capitalization of real estate in a specific location and the potential return on investment: "When this rent gap becomes sufficiently wide to enable a developer to purchase the old structure, rehabilitate it, make mortgage and interest payments, and still make a satisfactory return on the sale or rental of the renovated building, then a neighborhood is ripe for gentrification."[18]

By the authors' own admission, their analysis of the devalorization cycle is schematic. It must be adjusted to accommodate variations among development procedures in diverse cities and to account for such variables as conflicting capital interests, state interventions, and the emergence of community movements. Nonetheless, the analysis destroys the myth that arbitrary, natural, or individual actions produce neglect and abandonment, which are then "corrected" by gentrification. Rather, abandonment and gentrification are tied together within the logic of an economic system, demonstrating that they are integrally linked products of specific decisions made by the primary actors in the real-estate market—financial institutions, developers, government, landlords.

Smith and LeFaivre's description of the real-estate devalorization cycle stresses the commodity function of city neighborhoods under capitalism. The authors emphasize commodification even more strongly when they place gentrification within the larger transformations taking place in central cities. In so doing, they closely follow the detailed study of capitalist urbanization made by David Harvey, a geographer who has tried to understand the factors propelling the flow of capital into the built environment of the city during particular economic periods.[19] Harvey applies to urban processes Marx's critique of the contradictions of capitalist accumulation and a Marxist analysis of the ways in which capitalism attempts to ensure its own survival. He thus emphasizes capitalism's tendency toward overaccumulation, a crisis that occurs when the production of capital in certain sectors of the economy exceeds opportunities to employ it at the average rate of profit. Manifested in falling rates of profit, overproduction, surplus capital, surplus labor, or greater exploitation of labor, overaccumulation crises can be temporarily solved by switching investment into other sectors of the economy. Harvey views extensive investment in the built environment as a symptom of such crisis—"a kind of last-ditch hope for finding productive uses for rapidly over-accumulating capital."[20] Because real-estate investment entails long-term, large-scale projects, the (short-lived) success of the attempt requires the mediation of financial and state institutions.

Smith and LeFaivre bring Harvey's conclusions to bear upon contemporary central-city development and gentrification, which they see as a component of capital's strategy of switching investments. To counteract falling rates of profit, capital moves into areas such as real estate and construction. Describing gentrification as "the latest phase in a movement of capital back to the city,"[21] the authors argue persuasively against the prevailing idea that gentrification is a spontaneous "back-to-the-city" movement on the part of individuals suddenly eager for the excitement of cosmopolitan life.

But the use of city neighborhoods as commodities to be exploited for profit is only one of their purposes in a capitalist economy. Neighborhoods have also traditionally provided the conditions for reproducing labor power. For Smith and LeFaivre, gentrification represents the definitive replacement of the latter function by the neighborhood's service as a commodity: "The economic function of the neighborhood has superseded the broader social function."[22] Yet gentrification is itself a means for reproducing labor power. In 1980s New York, the tension between the two uses may well have signaled internal capitalist conflicts between those interests that required the conditions to maintain the labor force—lower paid and part-time service workers in particular—and those that could profit from the destruction of those conditions. Gentrification is, then, a specific historical instance of a more general contradiction between the imperatives of accumulation and reproduction in the late-capitalist city. In 1984, writing about the new commercial art scene then unfolding on New York's Lower East Side, Cara Gendel Ryan and I situated gentrification within the shifts taking place in the composition of the late-capitalist labor force.[23] Citing heavy losses in manufacturing jobs in New York City, unemployment in the industrial sector due to automatization of labor, and the concomitant steady growth in jobs in the financial, business, and service sectors, we reasoned that gentrification was a crucial part of a strategy for restructuring the nation's workforce. Coupled with the loss of blue-collar jobs and cuts in basic services, it has helped impoverish and disperse the traditional, now largely redundant workforce and has allocated urban resources to fulfill the needs of the city's corporate workers.

Changes in the nation's labor force were conditioned and modified by a global reorganization of labor that had accelerated since the 1970s. Global restructuring has had profound ramifications for urban spatial organization on a variety of levels. As a system for arranging production on a global scale, the new international division of labor entails the transfer by multinational corporations of labor-intensive and productive activities elsewhere, often to third-world countries, and the intense concentration of corporate headquarters in a few international centers. Enhancing flexibility and control over vastly extended operations, strategies are formulated, managerial decisions made, and financing administered from the global cities. To qualify as such an international center of business a city must possess, first, a high proportion of headquarters of corporations doing the majority of their business in foreign sales, and, second, a centralization of international banks and international corporate-related services: law, accounting, and advertising firms.[24] By the late 1970s in the United States only New York and San Francisco had emerged as such international centers where "even the international activities of firms headquartered outside these cities were increasingly linked to financial institutions and corporate services within them."[25] But in addition to transforming relationships among international and national cities, the new international division of labor affects the workforce within the corporate center itself. These centers present limited opportunities for blue-collar jobs, further "'marginalizing' the lower class which has traditionally found job mobility extremely difficult."[26]

As an arm of broader governmental policy, urban planning in New York City began in the 1970s to focus on the needs of the city's new economy—its corporate-linked activities and workers—and on maximizing real-estate profits. Simultaneously, it engineered the dispersal of that "immobile" population with no place in the restructured economy. Bureaucratic procedures and planned development programs executed the task. Union Square revitalization was such a program. The close correspondence between its evolution and the unfolding of broad economic trends is clear. In 1976 the area became the object of City Planning Commission attention, and in 1984 the final redevelopment plan was approved. During these years New York lost more than 100,000 blue-collar jobs and gained over twice as many in the finance, insurance, and other business industries. These changes, which had been accelerating since the 1950s, were reflected in the Union Square area. That period, especially the phase between 1970 and 1980, saw an exodus of light-manufacturing companies from the district's lofts, which were subsequently converted to more profitable residential and commercial uses compatible with the city's new economic base. Although it is difficult to furnish accurate figures for Union Square itself, since the area includes portions of four separate census tracts, the neighborhood's middle-class residential population substantially increased. By the early 1980s, 51 percent were employed in the service industries and 43 percent in wholesale and retail businesses, while other employment sectors showed "less growth."[27] The disparity in employment possibilities indicates that New York's period of economic prosperity and resurgent business expansion was, in truth, an era of intense class polarization. According to a report prepared by the Regional Plan Association and based on 1980 census data, 17 percent of the New York area's upper-income households accounted for more than 40 percent of the area's total income, while 42 percent—those with incomes under $15,000—accounted for only 14 percent of that income.[28] (By 1983, in New York City itself, those with incomes under $15,000 constituted over 46 percent of the population.[29]) The report surmised that "the economic outlook for hundreds of thousands of poorly educated, low-income residents throughout the New York area, stretching from Trenton to New Haven, is growing more bleak."[30]

The objectives and effects of New York's redevelopment programs can be accurately assessed only within the framework of this larger urban development. The City Planning Commission, however, did the opposite. During this period, it started to constrict its vision by employing a strategy that the Board of Estimate would eventually codify under the name "contextual planning." Further, the commission pinpointed this time of extreme class polarization, wrenching economic restructuring, and social dislocation of the poor—most evident in the forced mobility of people without homes—as the moment when the city finally began to be conserved, stabilized, and protected from radical change as well as from the radical impositions of modernist architectural concepts. Advised by the architects, urban designers, planners, and engineers who staff the Department of City Planning, the commission modified its zoning regulations, bureaucratic methods, and physical design orientations to "guide" development by the principle of responsiveness to the needs of particular city environments. It pursued a design path directed toward the historic preservation of existing circumstances. With relief, one architect and urban planner for the city praised the preservationist outlook:

> The urban aesthetic of associational harmony is reasserting itself under the banner of *cultural stability.* The mercurial rise to prominence and power of the urban preservationist movement has helped to fuel this change in direction. Preservation of both our most valued urban artifacts, whether they be the conventionalized row houses of Brooklyn Heights or the sumptuous dissonance of the New York Public Library is an important, if not vital, contribution to our sense of emotional well-being.[31]

This redevelopment—the resurgence of tradition and the emergence of a restricted and spectacularized notion of cultural preservation—helped smooth over violent disturbances in the city's social life.[32]

From its inception, Union Square redevelopment was conceived and executed under the aegis of historic preservation, restoration of architectural tradition,
and reinforcement of the existing urban context. These concepts dominated public
discourse about the redevelopment scheme and the narrower aspects of the
decision-making process. The four bronze monuments in Union Square Park—
refurbished and rendered newly visible—incarnate the attempt to preserve traditional architectural appearances in order to deliver Union Square into the hands
of major real-estate developers and expedite luxury development. In fact, the patriotic statues became a useful symbol to the proponents of revitalization as early as
1976, when the Department of City Planning received a $50,000 "City Options"
grant, part of a New York City Bicentennial Project, from the National Endowment for the Arts. The grant was "to produce designs that would improve city
life." After consulting with the community board, elected officials, businessmen,
"civic leaders," and other city agencies, the planning department published a report
entitled *Union Square: Street Revitalization,* the first exhibit in the case history of
Union Square redevelopment. This report became the basis for the *Union Square
Special Zoning District Proposal,* originally released in November 1983, revised in
June 1984, and, after passing the city's review procedure, adopted later that year.
The final redevelopment plan fulfilled the primary goals and followed many of
the specific recommendations outlined in *Union Square: Street Revitalization.* In
applying for the City Options grant, the planning department selected four "historic" neighborhoods as the object of its study and design proposals. Its ambition,
the application stated, was preservation: "Cities contain many centers and communities rich in history and a sense of place. We seek to develop prototypical techniques by which the particular character of these areas can be reinforced so as to
assist in their preservation through increased safety, use and enjoyment."[33] Among
the strategies developed to "capitalize on existing elements worthy of preservation"[34] was the first suggestion for improving the park: "Restore the center flagpole, a memorial to the 150th anniversary of the United States, which features the
Declaration of Independence engraved in bronze."[35]

The cover of *Union Square: Street Revitalization* capitalized on another Union
Square monument and patriotic event, reproducing an engraving from a
nineteenth-century copy of *Harper's Weekly* captioned "The Great Meeting in

Union Square, New York, To Support the Government, April 20, 1861." The print depicts a crowd of New Yorkers gathered at the base of the colossal equestrian statue of George Washington, now ceremonially located at the southern entrance to the park but then situated on the small island at the park's eastern perimeter. The illustration evokes a brief time during the Civil War when Union Square became a meeting place for a public believed to be unified by nationalist sentiment. Loyal citizens repeatedly rallied around the Washington statue listening to speeches by Mayor Opdyke and letters of endorsement from the governor, president, and other officials. Newspapers describe the patriotic, unified spirit of these crowds:

> The great war-meeting at Union Square effectually removed the false impression that the greed of commerce had taken possession of the New York community, and that the citizens were willing to secure peace at the sacrifice of principle. . . . The patriotism of the citizens was also indicated by the wrath which that meeting excited at the South. The Richmond *Dispatch* said: "New York will be remembered with special hatred by the South, for all time." [36]

The name of the square, originally referring only to its physical position at the juncture of Broadway and the Bloomingdale Road, was now imbued with connotations of national unity and shared history, dreams that, it was hoped, had come true as a result of the war.[37] The placard with the word *union* occupying dead center of the *Harper's Weekly* print affirms these sentiments.

The survival of this myth of unity helped repress beneath lofty ideals of communal harmony the more disquieting memories of the conflicts that characterized modern urban society, conflicts visible in Union Square itself. Union Square Park, for instance, was the scene of some of America's earliest labor demonstrations, including the New York segment of the first May Day celebration in 1886. Class divisions would conspicuously reemerge in the 1930s when the square became the customary New York site for communist rallies and militant demonstrations by the unemployed and homeless. In *Union Square,* published in 1933, "proletarian novelist" Albert Halper used the park's heroic monuments to highlight

Cover of *Union Square: Street Revitalization*

the contradictions between, on the one hand, idealized representations symbolizing spiritual ideas and the presence of a protective and reassuring authority, and, on the other hand, the current realities of starvation and police brutalization of demonstrators. Halper described Donndorf's mother-and-children fountain on the square's west side—where it still stands—as "a dreamy piece of work" facing Broadway right near the "free Milk for Babies Fund hut."[38] With similar irony, he juxtaposed the "big history" represented by the great men and deeds memorialized in the park's other statues with the historical class struggle, whose skirmishes were then being waged within the square itself.

But the original intentions behind such monuments, when they were erected in American cities in the late nineteenth century, actually corresponds more closely to their later use by the apparatus of Union Square redevelopment. As Christine Boyer argues, neoclassical imitations of Greek and Roman sculptures were designed to conceal social contradictions by uplifting "the individual from the sordidness of reality" through the illusions of order, timelessness, and moral perfection that neoclassicism was supposed to represent.[39] Although never comprising a planned or unified sculptural program, the Union Square monuments exemplify the type of strategically positioned sculpture promoted by the nineteenth-century municipal art movement—copies of Parisian copies of Greek and Roman landmarks of art and architectural history. Decontextualized, invested with new meanings about America's emerging economic imperialism and national pride, they were products of the decorative offshoot of the municipal art movement, itself part of a widespread attempt in the late nineteenth and early twentieth centuries to create order and tighten social control in the American city.[40] Inspired by fears of the unplanned chaos of urban industrialization, squalor and disease in the slums, extensive immigration, and a wave of labor disturbances, the notion of urban planning and design as an instrument that could counteract these threats appeared in nascent form among civic art crusaders. Their activities are, then only one aspect of the effort, as David Harvey describes it,

> to persuade all that harmony could be established around the basic institutions of community, a harmony which could function as an antidote to class war. The principle entailed a commitment to community improvement and a commitment to those institutions such as the Church and civil government capable of forging community spirit. From Chalmers through Octavia Hill and Jane Addams, through the urban reformers such as Joseph Chamberlain in Britain, the "moral reformers" in France and the "progressives" in the United States at the end of the nineteenth century, through to model cities programmes and citizen participation, we have a continuous thread of bourgeois response to the problems of civil strife and social unrest.[41]

As part of this network, municipal art advocates sought to generate a sense of order and communal feeling through spatial organization and decorative beauty.

They targeted public open spaces, such as Union Square Park, as prime locations for shaping the desired community, a public realm of cohesive values formed through moral influence. "Modern civic art," wrote Charles Mulford Robinson, one of its foremost supporters, "finds in the open space an opportunity to call [the citizens] out-of-doors for other than business purposes, to keep them in fresh air and sunshine, and in their most receptive mood to woo them by sheer force of beauty to that love and that contentment on which are founded individual and civic virtue."[42] New York's municipal art specialists consistently lamented that Union Square was a missed opportunity for such civilizing missions.

They were fortunate, however, that the square existed at all. One of the few public squares provided in the 1811 Commissioner's Map that established the rectilinear grid plan for "upper" Manhattan above Washington Square, Union Square almost failed to materialize. In 1812 it was recommended that plans for the square be dropped since they would require the use of land and buildings with high real-estate values. Although the project survived these threats and finally opened to the public in 1839, greatly enhancing land values in the immediate vicinity, civic art reformers regretted that the park was never properly utilized to create a physically—and therefore socially—cohesive public space. One critic proposed that it be turned into the civic center of New York.[43] Another suggested that a proper and elaborate sculptural program be organized there around the theme and images of liberty secured by the War of Independence. "Could anything influence more forcibly the national pride of our coming generations?"[44] Public statues, embodying social ideals, would, it was hoped, "commemorate in permanent materials the deeds of great citizens, the examples of national heroes, the causes for civic pride, and the incentives to high resolve which are offered by the past."[45] As instruments for the pacification of an unruly populace, the sculptures, like the street layouts devised by the municipal art movement, "searched not to transform the contradictions between reality and perfection but for the norms that moral perfection must follow."[46] Indeed, when Robinson, who codified municipal art concepts, turned his attention to conditions in the metropolitan slums, he ignored the problem of poverty itself, declaring, "With the housing problem civic art, its attention on the outward aspect of the town, has little further to do."[47]

———

Blinding itself to the most troubling facts of urban life, separating the city's social structure from its "outward aspect," the municipal art movement only contributed to the persistence of the housing problem. By the 1980s, the uses of New York's civic sculptures—and of the architectural and urban design system that they represent—had everything to do with the housing problem. This is amply confirmed by the fate of the Union Square monuments. Surely, the appearance of a nineteenth-century American imitation of a Roman equestrian statue on the cover of a late-twentieth-century city-planning proposal for redevelopment during a period of fiscal crisis demonstrates the extreme pliability of the monument's meanings and functions. Yet the architects of redevelopment (and the copywriters of real-estate advertisements) used the sculpture to shore up the illusions of cultural stability, historical continuity, and universal values connoted by such architectural forms. They thus denied that their own acts of preservation are ideologically motivated, shaped by particular investments, presenting preservation as, instead, a neutral deed of cultural rescue.[48] With the title "Union Square: Street Revitalization" unfolding across them, the nineteenth-century print and the George Washington monument were appropriated to embody an idea of urban redevelopment as restoration. The "union" placard promised that coherence and harmony in the public realm would adhere to the Union Square created by the redevelopment project. Similarly, the monuments themselves, their dirty images cleaned up, layers of grime and graffiti removed from their surfaces as part of the park renovation, were enlisted to project an image of redevelopment as an act of benign historic preservation. Suffusing all official accounts of Union Square's metamorphosis, this became the classic image of gentrification, securing consent to and selling the larger package of redevelopment. The aesthetic presentation of the physical site of development is, then, indissolubly linked to the profit motives impelling Union Square's revitalization.

But this image of redevelopment can be contested by reconstructing the steps taken by the city to create the new Union Square. The fact that the first visible sign of change in the area arrived in the form of the park renovation reinforced the perception of Union Square redevelopment as a beautification program. Media reports, too, focused on the park for almost a solid year before there was any public indication of more comprehensive activities. The sequence in which events were reported and in which changes became visible mirrored the terminological inaccuracies surrounding urban restructuring. Mistaking the new residents of "new" neighborhoods for a lost aristocracy, for example, the term *gentrification,* like the park renovation, participated in the nostalgia that prevailed during the Reagan years for genteel and aristocratic ways of life, a sentiment fully exploited and perpetuated by prestigious cultural institutions. The term also yields erroneous perceptions of inner-city change as the rehabilitation of decaying buildings. Redevelopment, by contrast, involves rebuilding, usually after buildings have been razed and sites cleared. In these aggressive acts, the power of the state and corporate capital is more obvious.

In Union Square, the illusion that the park restoration preceded redevelopment plans produced an equally distorted picture. The actual narrative differed considerably from surface impressions. Documents generated during the process indicate the extent to which planning in the area was part of the comprehensive policy adopted by city government following New York's fiscal crisis. The initial survey of Union Square, financed by the City Options grant, took place at a time when austerity measures had been imposed on city residents. *Union Square: Street Revitalization* completely embraced the popular explanations offered by politicians and financiers about the origins of the fiscal crisis—overborrowing, corruption, greedy workers and welfare recipients—and accepted the "solutions" justified by these explanations—cuts in basic services and deferred wage increases.[49] The report asserted that "public financing of new [housing] projects must be ruled out" in the development of Union Square's housing "frontier."[50] In its place, private development of housing, as well as of office and retail space, became a panacea. Hopefully, efforts might be made to "enlist the real-estate industry in effort [sic] to market new or rehabilitated housing units."[51]

The report's seemingly neutral, descriptive language concealed its own role in executing a brutal solution to a problem larger than Union Square's deterioration: the incompatibility of the city's new economy and its traditional workforce. The solution lay in "attempting to get rid of the poor and take away the better situated housing stock to reallocate to the workers needed by corporate New York."[52] The same year that *Union Square: Street Revitalization* appeared, Roger

Starr, the city's housing and development administrator during the fiscal crisis, advocated the "resettlement" of residents no longer needed in the corporate-oriented economy. Referring to deteriorated neighborhoods that, he hoped, would be vacated by such "relocation," Starr asserted that "the role of the city planner is not to originate the trend of abandonment but to observe and use it so that public investment will be hoarded for those areas where it will sustain life."[53] Using Starr's "empirical" methods, the planning department complied with his prescription. Redevelopment, then, was hardly a matter of the city enlisting the real-estate industry to fulfill the needs of residents. Rather, real estate and other capital interests enlisted city government to supply the conditions to guarantee their profits and reduce their risks.

The extent of the city's intervention in the housing market on behalf of corporate profits emerges in its clearest outlines in the 1983 proposal for redevelopment. The *Union Square Special Zoning District Proposal* acknowledges that "Manhattan-wide market changes in the manufacturing, commercial, and residential sectors"[54] had brought about changes in the population and land uses of its wider study area: the territory bounded by Twelfth Street to the south, Twentieth Street to the north, Third Avenue to the east, and Fifth Avenue to the west. The proposal points out, however, that Fourteenth Street and Union Square proper had benefited little from prevailing trends in the area. This pivotal center needed infusions of government support. "The Square continues to have a poor image,"[55] the report maintains, affirming that a principal barrier to development were the "social problems" plaguing Union Square Park, particularly its use by a "socially undesirable population (e.g., drug peddlers)."[56] By this time, however, the park had been "fenced off for reconstruction,"[57] a project that had been publicly announced in 1982.

The obstacle that the park's image represented had already been anticipated in the 1976 study. But the full force of the city's class-biased response to the problem and of its rationale for current urban policy is demonstrated by a difference between the 1976 and 1983 documents. In 1976, the surveyors concluded that "high income households . . . are more likely to be attracted to the Upper East Side or other established prestigious neighborhoods"[58] than to the shabby area around Union Square. Admittedly, the report contains no suggestions for providing low-income housing but does make some pretense of formulating strategies for furnishing moderate-cost housing. The later proposal disregards both. By 1983, the implications of the original report had become clearer and hardened into policy. At the very moment when services to the poor were cut and the assumption made that no thoughts of public financing of housing could even be entertained, the government, acting through the Parks Commission and Planning Department, was directing its funds toward subsidizing the rich.

The $3.6 million restoration of the park constitutes such a public subsidy. Both the 1973 and 1983 Union Square plans indicate the degree to which the success of redevelopment depended on cleaning up the park's image and transforming it into an external housing amenity. An indication of the accuracy of this prediction is the fact that by the time the restoration was planned and publicized, and, significantly, during the preparation of the final planning department proposal, the destiny of the area's most important development parcel—the entire city block occupied by the abandoned S. Klein department store—was being decided. In July 1983 a two-year option to buy the property had been acquired by William Zeckendorf, Jr., New York's most active real-estate developer, particularly in speculation in poor neighborhood lots that were to become catalysts for gentrification. The planning department map labels the property the "S. Klein/Zeckendorf Site." Zeckendorf intended to develop it for luxury commercial and residential use, but his plans depended on the subsequent fulfillment of various city plans. One plan, however, was already under way as the hindrance that the park's image represented to gentrifying groups was being removed. The restoration of the park can, then, only be viewed as that crucial stage of gentrification in which the poor are dislodged in order to make a neighborhood comfortable for high-income groups.

Typically, this stage of displacement is sanctioned under the auspices of crime prevention and the restoration of order. The park, in other words, was being reclaimed from thieves and drug dealers. This goal, paramount in determining the urban design principles that governed the park's renovation, also reveals the limits of the program of historic preservation and of the attempt to create a continuity between past and present. While existing nineteenth-century structures—the park's monuments—were refurbished and sham ones—lights and kiosks—constructed, the park was also bulldozed in preparation for the first phase of its "restoration" to its "original" condition. Phase I thoroughly reorganized the park's spatial patterns to permit full surveillance of its occupants. This change was accomplished through design precepts aimed at creating "defensible space." Oscar Newman, who popularized this phrase, considers "defensible" that space which allows people to control their own environments.[59] But the phrase comes closer to describing the application of the disciplinary mechanism that Foucault termed "panopticism" to state-controlled urban surveillance. By producing defensible space, architects and urban designers become agents of the discreet and omnipresent disciplinary power "exercised through its invisibility; at the same time it imposes on those whom it subjects a principle of compulsory visibility."[60] Grounded in ideas of natural human territorial instincts, defensible space assigns architecture the role of policing urban space:

> Architectural design can make evident by the physical layout that an area is the shared extension of the private realms of a group of individuals. For one group to be able to set the norms of behavior and the nature of activity possible within a particular place, it is necessary that it have clear, unquestionable control over what can occur there. Design can make it possible for both inhabitant and stranger to perceive that an area is under the undisputed influence of a particular group, that they dictate the activity taking place within it, and who its users are to be. . . . "Defensible space" is a surrogate term for the range of mechanisms—real and symbolic barriers, strongly defined areas of influence, and improved opportunities for surveillance—that combine to bring an environment under the control of its residents.[61]

That the private corporate and real-estate interests represented by the new Zeckendorf Towers, its future residents, and other beneficiaries of Union Square redevelopment would exercise "unquestionable control" over the public space of Union Square Park was assured by a few decisive changes in the park's physical appearance and circulation system. An open expanse of lawn with two walkways cutting directly across the park replaced the original radial pattern of six paths converging on a circle in the park's center; a pathway encircling the park's periphery provided the major circulation route; trees were removed and thinned out; and removal of walls and trees created an open plaza at the park's southern entrance. According to the police department in Saint Louis, this is the precise configuration of a safe park because it permits "natural" surveillance from a long periphery that can be easily patrolled.[62] A statement by the design office of the New York City Parks Commission applauded the success of Phase I:

> With design emphasis on improved accessibility, visibility and security to encourage its optimal use, the park has once again recaptured its importance as a high quality open space amenity for this community. Since Phase I began, the area around the park has changed quite dramatically. It is felt that the park redesign has contributed greatly to the revitalization of the Union Square area, and regained the parkland so needed in this urban environment.[63]

The manipulation of New York's high level of street crime has proved instrumental in securing public consent to redevelopment and to a planning logic of control through the kind of spatial organization exemplified by Union Square Park's sophisticated new security system. On April 19, 1984, at the inaugural ceremony for the restoration, the existing landscape had already been demolished. Mayor Koch told an assembled crowd: "First the thugs took over, then the muggers took over, then the drug people took over, and now we are driving them out."[64] To present the developers' takeover as crime prevention, however, the social and economic causes of crime were repudiated as thoroughly as the causes and aims of redevelopment were obscured. Koch, for example, wholeheartedly endorsed the resurgence of biological determinist ideas about the origins of "predatory street crime." Reviewing *Crime and Human Nature,* a book by sociobiologists James Q. Wilson and Richard J. Herrnstein, in the neoconservative *Policy Review,* Koch reiterated the authors' explanations of street crime in terms of biological and genetic differences that produce unreformable delinquents.[65] He then used these explanations to justify New York's methods of crime control and its continuing

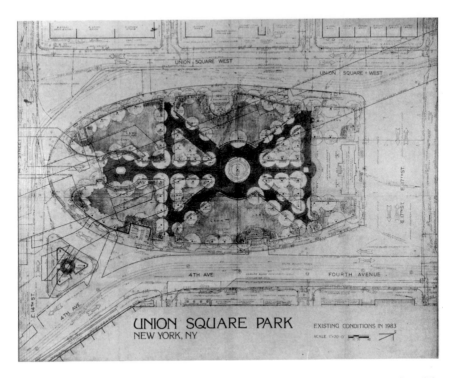

Union Square Park, architectural drawings. Existing conditions in 1983 (left); proposed modifications (right).

attack on the poor: higher levels of indictments and convictions of felons, an increased police force, the imposition of criminal law for purposes of "moral education,"[66] and, by implication, redevelopment projects that, employing architecture as a disciplinary mechanism, transform city neighborhoods into wealthy enclaves in order to facilitate the movement of "undesirables" and "undesirable market activities"[67] out of the immediate vicinity.

These tactics of urban restructuring are not entirely new. Neither is the erasure of the less appealing signs of restructuring nor the disavowal of its social consequences. Over a hundred years ago, Friedrich Engels described similar procedures for transforming the city to meet the needs of capital. At that time, disease, even

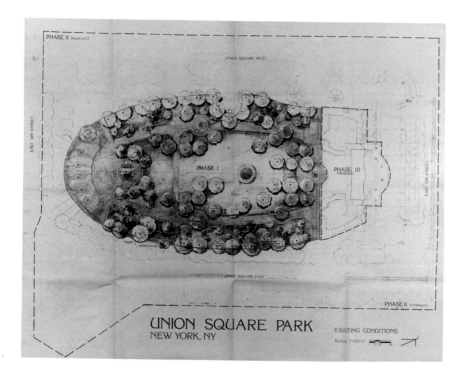

more effectively than crime, legitimated the violent dislocation of the poor. Engels refers to this process by the word *Haussmann,* appropriating the name of Napoleon III's architect of the reconstruction of Second Empire Paris:

> By "Haussmann" I mean the practice, which has now become general, of making breaches in the working-class quarters of our big cities, particularly in those which are centrally situated, irrespective of whether this practice is occasioned by considerations of public health and beautification or by the demand for big centrally located business premises or by traffic requirements, such as the laying down of railways, streets, etc. No matter how different the reasons may be, the result is everywhere the same: the most scandalous alleys and

lanes disappear to the accompaniment of lavish self-glorification by the bourgeoisie on account of this tremendous success, but—they appear again at once somewhere else, and often in the immediate neighborhood.[68]

About the housing question, Engels continues: "The breeding places of disease, the infamous holes and cellars in which the capitalist mode of production confines our workers night after night, are not abolished; they are merely *shifted elsewhere!*"[69]

That bourgeois solutions only perpetuate urban problems is indicated by the growing numbers of homeless who live no longer inside Union Square Park but on the surrounding streets and sidewalks. Furthermore crime has, in the words of the *New York Times,* "moved into Stuyvesant Square," only a few blocks away, having "migrated from nearby areas that have been the focus of greater police surveillance."[70] Parks Commissioner Henry J. Stern concurs: "It's clear some of the problems of Union Square Park, and maybe Washington Square Park, have migrated to Stuyvesant Square."[71] By subsuming all of New York's social ills under the category of crime, the rationale for revitalization reproduces and heightens the problems of poverty, homelessness, and unemployment. Simultaneously, it attempts to eradicate their visible manifestations. Embodied in the restored park and its monuments, architectural efforts to preserve traditional appearances also hide the proof of rupture.

THE HOMELESS PROJECTION: COUNTERIMAGE OF REDEVELOPMENT

"Behind the disciplinary mechanisms," writes Foucault, "can be read the haunting memory of 'contagions,' of the plague, of rebellions, crimes, vagabondage, desertions, people who appear and disappear, live and die in disorder."[72] Similar repressions inhabit the controlled urban space that Wodiczko selected as the site of *The Homeless Projection.* Wodiczko's project encourages a critical public reading of this Haussmannian arena of beautified surfaces, suppressed contradictions, and relocated problems. If, as I suggested earlier, the form of the proposal that Wodiczko exhibited at 49th Parallel at once uses and comments on the presentational conventions of contemporary city planning, the project's realization as a performance in Union Square would have critically scrutinized—re-presented—the city environments that such planning produces. For this performance, Union Square would have provided a fully equipped, carefully arranged, and strategically located theater of urban events. This "fake architectural real estate theater," as Wodiczko describes it, was built by a series of well-calculated strategies in an urban revitalization campaign. Carried out in the name of history—the Zeckendorf Towers were advertised as "The Latest Chapter in the History of Union Square"—that campaign tried to consign its own brutal history to oblivion.

Using the Union Square site, still haunted by memories of recent changes and marginalized city residents, *The Homeless Projection* conjures the memories of alterations and social conflicts from the very spaces and objects designed to exorcise them. To awaken these memories, Wodiczko planned to take advantage of the park's physical configuration and the spectacle created by its restoration. The plentiful lamps—reproductions of nineteenth-century Parisian streetlights—and the platform on which the park is elevated—a legacy of alterations to the Fourteenth Street subway station in the 1930s—furnished a public stage accessible to a ready-made city audience. The setting included tangible reminders of social restructuring in the park's spatial reorganization: redirected pathways, newly sodded lawns, thinned-out foliage. Since Wodiczko's work inserts the park restoration into the context of more extensive architectural activities, the signs of urban change that by 1986 surrounded the park would have completed his set, although most were not yet in existence when the proposal was first designed. Scaffolding, cranes, exposed building foundations, demolished structures, fenced-off construction areas, and emptied buildings attested to the large-scale restructuring of the city. They juxtaposed signs of destruction with the signs of preservation in the park itself. The huge, luxury Zeckendorf building rising across the street—"The Shape of Things to Come," as its billboard announced—indicated the principal beneficiaries of this activity.

In addition to lighting, stage, audience, and sets, Union Square Park provided Wodiczko with actors in the shape of the park's figurative monuments. Wodiczko's temporary appropriation of the statues prompted an awareness of the role they were already playing in New York's gentrification. Evoking memories different from those that the monuments were originally meant to conjure and from those that the restorers hoped to elicit, *The Homeless Projection* probed the less exalted purposes that underlie seemingly reverential acts of faithful preservation. Sculptures once placed in open spaces in the hope of pacifying city residents were manipulated by Wodiczko to construct and mobilize a public, "restoring" the space as a site of public debate and criticism. Using the monuments in their contemporary incarnation—mediums for repressing the changed conditions of urban life—Wodiczko converted them into vehicles for illuminating those conditions. In this way, he planned to make the city's built environment into a type of Brechtian theater about which Walter Benjamin observes: "To put it succinctly: instead of identifying with the characters, the audience should be educated to be astonished at the circumstances under which they function." [73]

Despite energetic attempts by the mass media, the city, real-estate promotions, and segments of the cultural establishment to present the bronze statues as representatives of eternal values—aesthetic and moral—the monuments have indeed been recast in compromising situations and positions. Haphazard from its inception, the Union Square sculptural program is generally taken to symbolize liberty and individual freedom, an interpretation originating in the nineteenth century when commentators noted that two of the sculptures fortuitously share a common subject: heroes of the French and American democratic revolutions. The George Washington statue was erected in 1856 and, although it adopts the codes of Roman imperial sculpture, is habitually described as a symbol of the freedom secured by the War of Independence. Standing now on the park's eastern edge, Lafayette, by Frederic August Bartholdi, sculptor of the Statue of Liberty, was presented to New York in 1873 by the city's French residents as a memorial to French-American relations. Inscriptions on the statue's base commemorate two instances of such solidarity: mutual inspiration and support during the American Revolution and sympathy extended by the United States to France during the difficult period of the Franco-Prussian War and the Paris Commune, the latter an urban revolution for which the monument apparently has no sympathy to offer. The remaining nineteenth-century statues—Abraham Lincoln, erected three years after the death of the Civil War president, and the fountain located on the western side of the park, a "heroic bronze group" of a mother and children—do not strictly conform to the Revolutionary War theme but can be readily assimilated into the general patriarchal program and atmosphere of eclectic classicism. As the author of the Emancipation Proclamation, Lincoln contributes to the motif of liberation from tyranny. But on July 4, 1926, Tammany Hall greatly strengthened the sculptural program's thematic coherence by donating a huge flagpole base that was placed at the center of the park. The base solidified the topos of freedom, displaying the full text of the Declaration of Independence, a relief depicting a struggle against evil, a quotation from Thomas Jefferson encircling the base, and a plaque stating, "This monument setting forth in enduring bronze the full text of the immortal charter of American liberty was erected in commemoration of the 150th Anniversary of the Declaration of Independence."

Originally, the park's six pathways converged on the flagpole base. Now this tribute to freedom is stranded in the middle of a broad expanse of lawn designed to render the public accessible to surveillance and to prevent illicit activities at the park's center—the most distant point from the perimeter policing. The monument's changed position suggests that the enduring principle that it now commemorates has little to do with what it ostensibly honors: the democratic revolution's establishment of the right to freedom. Rather, the flagpole base memorializes the interests historically protected by principles of individual liberty: the freedom of private property, in this case, the unfettering of the financial forces in whose interest the park renovation was largely undertaken. The meaning of the sculpture's metamorphosis—an example of what Wodiczko terms architecture's "real-estate change"—was confirmed when the park monuments were presented in the Zeckendorf Towers sales office, which opened in the spring of 1986. Framed photographs of the statues were displayed among a group of pictures representing Union Square's history and showing the park's mounted police as a backdrop for a model of the new condominiums, whose prices approach half a million dollars. That a substantial number of apartments were sold in the first week of business fulfills the prophecy of a 1984 *Times* editorial that, urging support for Union Square redevelopment, seconded the City Planning Commission's faith that "the location

Zeckendorf Towers Sales Office, 1986.

of the public square and its handsome lines and *great statuary* will attract investment from builders." [74]

Still, the dogma persists that monumental architecture can survive changes in both the immediate context of its display and the broader contingencies of history with its dignity and power intact. Successful monuments, we have recently been told, transcend the "trivialities" of commercialism. This assertion is grounded in the same aestheticist premises as the belief that successful monuments transcend the "trivialities" of social conditions such as poverty and homelessness. It is not unexpected, then, that Paul Goldberger, who elevated the Union Square flagpole base above the "degrading" action of "a derelict," seven years later, during New York's bicentennial celebration, rhapsodized the "essential dignity" of the Statue of Liberty. Unfortunately, Goldberger's defense was not prompted by a desire to fortify the monument's original message against contemporary waves of anti-immigrant sentiment and attempts to enact repressive legislation against Hispanics and Asians in the United States. Rather, he applauded the Statue's ability to rise above such issues and fulfill a monument's "fundamental" role in the urban environment: "The city that is too large and too busy to stop for anyone seems, through this statue, to stop for everyone. Suddenly its intense activity becomes background, and the statue itself becomes foreground: we cannot ask of a monument that it do anything more."[75]

With remarkable clarity, Goldberger inadvertently summarizes not the actual effects of monuments but the ideological operations of his own idealist aesthetic and urban principles. Stretching the tenet of aesthetic autonomy to include the city that surrounds the individual monument, he fetishizes the urban environment at the level of its physical appearance. He thus describes the Statue of Liberty's compositional relationship, by virtue of its permanent position in New York Harbor, to a city which, through that relationship, is rendered more physically coherent. But Goldberger himself, utterly neutralizing and restricting the notion of context, uses architecture to push into the background, to blur, the city's "intense activity"—its social processes, its intense real-estate activity.

The Homeless Projection, by contrast, treats architecture as a social institution rather than as a collection of beautiful or utilitarian objects and addresses urban space as a terrain of social processes. It uses the Union Square monuments neither to depreciate the significance of the city's activities nor to minimize the meaning of its individual architectural objects. Instead, the work foregrounds their constitutive relationship. Wodiczko planned to project onto the surfaces of the four figurative monuments in Union Square Park—representatives of architecture's attempt to "preserve its traditional and sentimental appearances"[76]—photographic images of the attributes of New York's homeless population, the group most noticeably dispossessed by such preservationism. Magnified to the scale of the monuments, though not heroicizing or representing homeless people themselves, the images would have remained, as they did in the gallery installation, unchanged throughout the artist's performance. The images show various characteristics of homeless people: their costumes and equipment; their means of travel occasioned by enforced mobility; and the repertoire of gestures that they adopt to survive and to secure an income on the streets. Far from transcending the "trivial" facts of city life, Wodiczko's monuments are forced to acknowledge the social facts they have helped produce.

The Homeless Projection's images are of, precisely, trivial objects: a shopping cart, a wheelchair, a can of Windex. And while these monumentalized commonplace items clash absurdly with the heroic iconography of the neoclassical statues, they also seem oddly at home there. Wodiczko gives his altered monuments an appearance of familiarity by seamlessly joining the images to the statues' own forms and iconography. He might, for example, superimpose a photograph of a human hand over a statue's bronze one so that the projected image merges imperceptibly with the sculpted figure's anatomy. As in surrealist montage, however, the appearance of continuity only makes the presence of the new material more startling. Disengaging spectators from their customary disregard of the monuments and from the seduction attempted by the restoration program's new presentation, attitudes that isolate the monuments from surrounding conditions, *The Homeless Projection* allows viewers to perceive the sculptures only in relation to those conditions.

The artist ensures this primary reading by means of the images' iconography coupled with montage techniques—the formal relationships that Wodiczko establishes between image and architecture. His careful accommodation of an unchanging image to the appropriated surface of an existing architectural structure has a twofold effect. First, it focuses the viewer's attention on the structure—on the monument's physical stability as well as its mythical symbolic stability. One becomes aware of the image of inevitability and power that the monument itself normally projects. At the same time, Wodiczko's projection uses the structure's own formal and iconographic codes to undermine its seemingly unshakable homogeneity and authoritative permanence. Manipulating the structure from within, the montage symbolically moves the object so that its actual instabilities can be perceived. The congruence between image and architecture is crucial since it renders the projection more astonishing as excluded material—the evidence of homelessness—returns within the vehicle of its repression—the architecture of redevelopment. An evicting architecture becomes an architecture of the evicted. The surprise engendered by this uncanny impression alters the viewer's relation to urban objects. For if dominant representations imprint their messages on receivers by inviting immediate identification with images so "natural" they seem uncoded, Wodiczko's transformed images have the opposite effect: impeding both the monuments' messages and the viewer's identification with authoritative images, they foster a creative consumption of the city. Wodiczko's works are, then, projections onto projections.

But *The Homeless Projection* does not simply interrupt the monuments' speech. It does so precisely by extending, deepening, and radicalizing the statues' own messages. Wodiczko's images of the tokens of homelessness depict the current oppressive outcome of conflictual private property relations. The images are, however, integrated into architectural and urban forms symbolizing social unity, the common interest of the people supposedly represented by the democratic state. The projection thus highlights a seeming contradiction between the state's claim to represent the common good and its support of economic domination. This contradiction is enshrined in the Union Square monuments in both their present incarnation and their original form. As monuments to the democratic revolutions of the late eighteenth century, the statues not only commemorate social unity. They also celebrate "the rights of man," which, inaugurated by those revolutions, proclaim the individual freedoms guaranteed by the democratic state. Wodiczko's projection suggests that there are good reasons to question the political function of these twin aspects of the state: on the one hand, the state represents an ideal, universal realm elevated above the conflicts of civil life and, on the other hand, it is the guardian of the rights of man. Karl Marx, for one, famously argues that precisely the dual character of the bourgeois concept of the state makes capitalist relations of oppression and exploitation appear inevitable.[77] The real goal of the bourgeois state, he claims, is to naturalize and therefore justify social conflict. The democratic revolution, writes Marx, brought the modern state into existence by separating the state and civil society. Shattering civil society into a depoliticized realm of atomized individuals and of material life, the revolution simultaneously constituted the state as a domain of harmony transcending the particularities and strife of civil life. Marx reasons further that people in bourgeois society are likewise split in two. As citizens, endowed with civil rights, they live an abstract life as communal beings. But the rights of man—human rights—are the "rights of the *member of civil society,* i.e., of egoistic man, of man separated from other men and from the community."[78] The practical consequence of human rights is to ensure the freedom of private property by protecting the self-interest of each individual against any concern for the social good. For Marx, the bourgeois notion of "political emancipation," the granting of civil rights, implies that people can only be freed from this conflict abstractly, through citizenship in the state. Consequently, individualistic man, the bearer of the rights of man, emerges as "real man." The idea of political emancipation thus presupposes the necessity of private property and precludes the abolition of economic conflict, which, safeguarded in the form of human rights, the bourgeois state is instituted to protect.

We may disagree with Marx's wholesale dismissal of human rights as mere bourgeois delusion. There is another way to think of rights. Criticizing Marx's analysis of the rights of man, the political philosopher Claude Lefort presents a different theory of democracy.[79] Lefort argues that the split between state and civil society did not take place, as Marx thought, with the democratic revolution but earlier, during the monarchy. At stake in Lefort's "correction" of Marx's history is not chronological accuracy but the meaning of democracy. According to Lefort, Marx's failure to investigate the alteration represented by developments during the monarchical period made him unable to perceive the *different* alteration brought about by the emergence of the bourgeois state. As a consequence, Marx saw only one aspect of the democratic revolution and could not appreciate the significance of the political revolution that destroyed absolutism, a destruction that occurred with the Declaration of the Rights of Man. For Lefort, the democratic revolution inaugurated a change in the meaning of rights coextensive with equally radical mutations in the meanings of society and of power. Under the monarchy, the meaning and unity of society appeared to rest upon an absolute basis—a transcendent foundation that was embodied in the figure of the king and from which the state derived its power. With the fall of the monarchy, the origin of social unity and of power resides, as the Declaration of the Rights of Man states, in "the people." The declaration refers power to the people, but the democratic act deprives "the people" of a fixed source of meaning. They, too, have no substantial identity. The democratic revolution consists, then, of the disappearance of certainty about the meaning of society, which legitimates debate about the question of social unity. The meaning of society is decided within the social itself but is not immanent there. Rather, uncertainty about foundations authorizes democratic debate and questioning of power.

Lefort agrees with Marx that the Declaration of the Rights of Man was made in the name of human nature, but because right is deprived by the democratic revolution of an absolute foundation, it, too, is relocated from a transcendent realm to a space within society. Rights become an enigma. Against Marx, Lefort argues that the democratic revolution actually reduces the source of rights not to nature but to the human utterance: it is the essence of rights to be declared. And since neither rights nor "the people" who declare them are given entities but emerge only with the declaration, rights do not, as Marx thought, testify to man's separation from man but to the social interaction implicit in the act of declaring. The human subject as the bearer of rights is not an autonomous but a radically contingent being.

Still, Lefort is careful to point out that what Marx failed to see in the rights of man does not negate what he did see. Defending democracy, in other words, is no reason for dismissing Marx, who "was perfectly correct to denounce the relations of oppression and exploitation that were concealed behind the principles of freedom, equality, and justice."[80] Marx's insight can, then, illuminate both the social functions performed by Union Square's statues in the redevelopment process and the nature of the challenge raised by Wodiczko's *Homeless Projection*. Like the bourgeois state, the public monuments can only symbolize communal harmony and universal good if the sphere of economic conflict—real estate, in this case—is constituted as a private domain dissociated from public life. But precisely this rigid separation of public and private spheres also enabled the monuments to serve as the guardians of real estate. By causing the effects of the private economic sphere

---

to reappear within the public monuments and thus threatening the security of the public/private divide, *The Homeless Projection* revolutionizes the statues, which, in their altered state, are forced to acknowledge their own contradictions and repressions.

But what if, following Lefort, we also find something in the idea of human rights that Marx did not find? What if we see not only a "false" freedom through which the bourgeois state guarantees the rights of private property but also the possibility, inaugurated by the democratic invention, of social groups raising demands for freedoms—for rights—that challenge the omnipotence of state power and the exclusions of property? What if we define public space as the space where society constitutes itself through an unending declaration of rights that question and limit power? *The Homeless Projection* might then be read as a symbolic declaration of new rights—for homeless people. Infiltrated with Wodiczko's images, the statues issue a demand for the legitimacy of homeless residents as members of the urban community, a demand raised against the legitimacy of state power to exclude them—from Union Square, from the city, from society itself. Transformed into the medium of such a demand, the Revolutionary War monuments become a commemoration of the democratic revolution, whose most radical act in Lefort's view was to make it possible to question the basis of power. Temporarily, that is, the statues metamorphose into the public monuments, and Union Square into the democratic public space, that they are officially proclaimed to be. For Wodiczko's project takes account of the exclusions that create the social unity that the monuments supposedly represent and thereby subjects the foundation of that unity to democratic contestation. *The Homeless Projection* thus extends the very revolution that Union Square's sculptural program ostensibly memorializes but whose most radical messages it evades.

To facilitate what I have interpreted as a democratic questioning of social unity, Wodiczko manipulates the statues' own language, breaking up its apparently unitary and stable meanings. He transforms the classical gestures, poses, and attitudes of the sculpted figures into the gestures, poses, and attitudes currently adopted by people begging on the streets: George Washington's left forearm presses down on a can of Windex and holds a cloth, so that the imperial gesture of his right arm is transformed into a signal made by the unemployed to stop cars, clean windshields, and obtain a street donation. Lincoln's stereotypically "proud but humble" bearing is reconfigured, through the addition of a crutch and beggar's cup, into the posture of a homeless man soliciting money on a street corner. A bandage and cast change Lafayette's elegant stance and extended arm into the motions of a vagrant asking for alms, and the mother sheltering her children metamorphoses into a homeless family appealing for help. In addition, Wodiczko projected a continuously fading and reappearing image onto the Lincoln monument: an emptied building with a partially renovated facade.

This "style" of building—conspicuously empty despite an equally visible need for housing—was a familiar New York spectacle throughout the 1980s. Its surface, like the surface of the monuments, had been partially restored as part of a presentation to encourage neighborhood speculation. Fissuring the surfaces of the Union Square monuments—the images of gentrification—with images of the vacated building and of the mechanisms by which the homeless survive, *The Homeless Projection* concretizes in a temporary, antimonumental form the most serious contradiction embodied in New York architecture: the conflict between capital's need to exploit space for profit, on the one hand, and the social needs of the city's residents, on the other. Mapping these images onto the monuments in a public square, Wodiczko forces architecture to reveal its role as an actor in New York's real-estate market. Wodiczko's intervention in the space of Union Square revitalization thus addresses the single issue most consistently ignored by the city throughout the long and complicated course of redevelopment: displacement. During *The Homeless Projection,* and afterward in viewers' memories, the Union Square monuments, diverted from their prescribed civic functions, would have commemorated this urban event—mass evictions and development-produced homelessness.

Real-Estate Aesthetics

Indifference to and concealment of the plight, even the existence, of displaced residents was predictable. To foster development, the city encouraged a suppression of data on displacement and homelessness. While *The Homeless Projection* places this issue at the center of urban life, official architecture and urban disciplines took part in its cover-up in Union Square. To appreciate fully the extent of this repudiation, it is necessary to understand the crucial role played by "contextual aesthetics" during a key phase of revitalization.

Government subsidies to real-estate developers are not limited to direct financial outlays or to tax abatements and exemptions. Benefits also accrue from the city's administration of institutional allowances for building, especially through its bureaucratic procedures and zoning regulations. Union Square development depended on a specialized proceeding through which the planning commission permits zoning constraints to be waived or altered. The vehicle for this alteration is the "special zoning district" defined in the planning department dictionary as a section of the city designated for special treatment "in recognition of the area's unique character or quality."[81] Permitting changes in the use, density, or design of buildings in the specified area, the creation of a special zoning district is commonly portrayed as a flexible response to "perceived needs."[82] Commentators frequently demonstrate this flexibility by comparing it to the rigidity of the 1961 Zoning Resolution, whose rules the special zoning district has, since the 1970s, tended to modify or circumvent. Champions of the special district start from the premise that the 1961 zoning code is grounded in the principles of European modernist architecture of the 1920s; they then characterize it as "utopian," "antitradition," "antiurban," and "unresponsive to context." Casting support of the special zoning district as a "critique of modernism" and conflating urban and aesthetic problems, advocates present current manipulations of land-use regulations to aid redevelopment as responsiveness to the environment and the social needs of city residents. The following assessment of the problems justifying the use of the special zoning district typifies this logic:

> Less than ten years after the adoption of the 1961 Zoning Resolution, disaffection with the results of the utopian vision set in. . . . The prevailing view was that the new zoning was incompatible with the best efforts of architects and urban designers to produce high-quality architecture and good city form. This belief, while most often heard from architects and urban designers was also expressed with great regularity

by the developers, bankers, and community representatives, and other professional, lay, and governmental constituencies. They posited that zoning was legislating esthetics, and that a single vision was too restrictive, leaving little room for genuine architectural design quality. The result is a cookie-cutter building that is ugly and sterile, set in an ill-considered and barely usable public open space that is often neglected, or used by the seedier elements of New York's street-corner society. These same buildings appear to be insensitive to the existing buildings around them, creating dissonance in urban form.[83]

The special zoning district is treated, then, as a means to conserve tradition, restore coherence and stability, and ensure architectural diversity. But it serves other functions as well.

The Zeckendorf Company's plans in Union Square depended on the creation of a special district for sites fronting directly on the park. After purchasing the option to build on the Klein site, Zeckendorf announced that the realization of his project, which was itself crucial to the area's redevelopment, was contingent on the rezoning already proposed by the planning department. The zoning change would increase the allowable density for buildings around the square, providing additional space bonuses for the Klein property in return for the developer's renovation of the Fourteenth Street subway station. The 1983 summary of the planning department's two-year study undertaken to "guide" redevelopment so that it would reflect the "existing urbanistic context" set out the rationale for the special zoning district.[84] In recognition of Union Square's architectural uniqueness and to foster "compatibility between any new construction and the existing significant architectural buildings,"[85] the proposal not only suggested increased density allowances for new buildings to match those of the late-nineteenth- and early-twentieth-century structures. It also created special "bulk distribution regulations": plazas or ground-floor setbacks were prohibited (the park made plazas unnecessary), and the facades of all buildings on the square had to be built to the property line and to rise straight up for a minimum of eighty-five feet. A system of mandated setbacks and a restriction on towers within one hundred feet of the square would, according to the proposal, ensure light and air.

Zeckendorf's architects had already designed his mixed-use building to conform to these contextualist principles. Four seventeen-story apartment towers would rise from a seven-story base occupying the entire building site. They would begin at a point farthest from the park and terminate in cupolas to "echo" the historic tower of the Con Edison building behind them. According to Zeckendorf, the building plan addressed "the concerns we've heard from the community about not overshadowing the park and fitting in with the rest of the structures there."[86] The key point of the zoning rationale and of Zeckendorf's compliance was the contention that the new buildings would not merely harmonize with the existing environment but also recapture its history as an elegant neighborhood. As a *New York Times* editorial put it:

> To understand fully what the rescue of Union Square would mean, the observer has to imagine how it once resembled London's handsome Belgravia and Mayfair residential districts. By insisting on the eight-story rise directly from the sidewalk, the planners hope that modern apartment house builders will produce a contemporary echo of the walled-in space that gives the small squares of London and America's older cities their pleasing sense of order and scale.[87]

Before ultimate approval (with slight modification) in January 1985, both the rezoning proposal and the design of the Zeckendorf Towers had to pass through a public review process. Over a period of seven months, each project was debated at public hearings, first before the community boards, then before the City Planning Commission, and finally before the Board of Estimate. The city and the developer submitted obligatory, highly technical environmental impact statements in which they were required to show "the potential environmental effects of a proposed action on noise level, air and water quality and traffic circulation."[88]

The supreme measure of the city's alignment with corporate interests in the area is the failure of any of its reports to mention the socioeconomic impact of the redevelopment plan on the area's low-income population. Displacement of residents, the most obvious effect of the literal demolition of housing as well as the more extensive effect of revitalization—raised property values—was virtually un-remarked in the hundreds of pages generated throughout the planning and review processes. The unquantifiable numbers of homeless people who, according to the New York State Department of Social Services, "find shelter out of the public view"[89] in city parks were driven from the newly visible Union Square, their num-bers increased by those made homeless by the larger redevelopment plan.

Also not mentioned in the city's reports was the single-room-occupancy hotel that stood on the Klein site. Its demolition was the precondition of the Zeck-endorf project, and its address, 1 Irving Place, is now that of the luxury towers. Similarly, the planning department surveyors who in the proposal applauded the increasingly residential character of the neighborhood due to middle-class loft con-versions and who examined the quality of existing residential buildings, failed to survey the thirty-seven single-room-occupancy hotels and rooming houses in the area around the special district, buildings containing six thousand housing units for residents on fixed or limited incomes.[90] Yet the relationship between current levels of homelessness and single-room-occupancy displacement in New York City was well known:

> This shrinkage of housing options is nowhere more visible than in the long-time staple housing source for low-income single persons—the single-room-occupancy (SRO) hotel. Across the country the number of units in SROs is declining. In some areas they are being converted to luxury condominiums, while in others they are abandoned by own-ers unable to afford taxes and maintenance costs. In New York City, SROs have disappeared at an alarming rate. Because of this—and other forces at work—it is estimated that as many as 36,000 of the city's most vulnerable residents, the low-income elderly, now sleep in the streets.[91]

Although the number of lower-priced SRO units in New York declined by more than 60 percent between 1975 and 1981,[92] the burden of surveying the area and determining the effects of Union Square redevelopment on the occupants of these dwellings fell to the housing advocates who argued against development plans at the Board of Estimate hearing. The environmental impact statements ignored the impact of both primary displacement—the direct consequence of the demolition of the SRO on the Zeckendorf site—and the more significant secondary displacement—the displacement caused by higher rents, enhanced property values, real-estate speculation, legal warehousing, and, temporarily, illegal conversion of neighborhood rooming houses.[93]

Throughout, this concealment was facilitated by appeals to aesthetic contextualism and by the cultural sentiments informing all three phases of Union Square revitalization: the park restoration, creation of the special zoning district, and approval of the Zeckendorf project. Although traveling under the sign of contextualism, the architects and designers who minutely calculated the physical effects of rezoning and of the towers on the shadows and air in Union Square or judged the project's aesthetic effects on the cornice lines of the square's other buildings exemplify what Ernest Mandel calls the "real idol of late capitalism"—"the 'specialist' who is blind to any overall context."[94]

During the same period, the ranks of the city's technocrats swelled to include artists, critics, and curators who were asked to fulfill the task, spelled out at the time in a Mobil advertisement, of encouraging residential and commercial real-estate projects and revitalizing urban neighborhoods. One example of cooperation with these corporate demands by sectors of the art establishment is public art placed in redeveloped spaces and applauded as socially responsible because it contributes, functionally or aesthetically, to the so-called pleasures of the urban environment. Such work is based on the art-world equivalent of official urban planners' constricted version of contextualism. Knowing the social consequences of this contextualism underscores the urgency of creating alternative art practices such as *The Homeless Projection,* whose reorientation of vision disturbs the tightly drawn borders secured by New York's contextual zoning.

The true issue is not to make beautiful cities or well-managed cities, it is to make a work of life. The rest is a by-product. But, making a work of life is the privilege of historical action. How and through what struggles, in the course of what class action and what political battle could urban historical action be reborn? This is the question toward which we are inevitably carried by our inquiry into the meaning of the city.

—Raymond Ledrut, "Speech and the Silence of the City"

BEAUTY AND UTILITY: WEAPONS OF REDEVELOPMENT

By the late 1980s it had become clear to most observers that the visibility of masses of homeless people interferes with positive images of New York, constituting a crisis in the official representation of the city. Dominant responses to the crisis took two principal, often complementary, forms: they treated homelessness as an individual social problem isolated from urban politics or, as Peter Marcuse contends, tried "to neutralize the outrage homelessness produces in those who see it."[1] Because substantial efforts to deal with homelessness itself would have required at least a partial renunciation of its immediate causes—the commodification of housing, existing employment patterns, the social service policies of today's austerity state—those committed to preserving the status quo tried, instead, through strategies of isolation and neutralization, to cope with the legitimation problems that homelessness raises.

Exemplary of the "social problem" approach is a widely circulated report issued in June 1987 by the Commission on the Year 2000. Obedient to its governmental mandate to forecast New York City's future, the panel described New York as "ascendant," verifying this image by pointing to the city's "revitalized" economy and neighborhoods. Conspicuous poverty and patent stagnation in other neighborhoods nonetheless compelled the commission to remark on the unequal character of this rise: "We see that the benefits of prosperity have passed over hundreds of thousands of New Yorkers."[2] But the group's recommendations—prescribing the same pro-business and privatizing policies that are largely responsible for homelessness in the first place—failed to translate this manifest imbalance into a recognition that uneven economic and geographical development is a structural, rather than incidental, feature of New York's present expansion. The panelists' own expansive picture required, then, a certain contraction of their field of vision. Within its borders, social inequities appear as random disparities and disappear as linked phenomena. An optical illusion fragments the urban condition as "growth"—believed to occur in different locations at varying paces of cumulative development but ultimately to unfold its advantages to all—emerges as a remedy for urban decay, obscuring a more integrated economic reality that is also inscribed across the city's surface. For in the advanced capitalist city, growth, far from a uniform process, is driven by the hierarchical differentiation of social groups and territories. Residential components of prosperity—gentrification and luxury housing—are not distinct from, but in fact depend upon, residential facets of poverty—disinvestment, eviction, displacement, homelessness. Together, they form only one aspect of the city's comprehensive redevelopment, itself part of more extensive social, economic, and spatial changes, all marked by uneven development. Consequently, redevelopment proceeds not as an all-embracing benefit but according to social *relations* of ascendancy, that is, of domination. Consensus-oriented statements such as *New York Ascendant* disavow these relations, impressionistically offering proof of growth side by side with proof of decline; both acquire the appearance of discrete entities. But today there is no document of New York's ascendancy that is not at the same time a document of homelessness. Municipal reports, landmark buildings, and what we call public spaces are marked by this ambiguity.

Faced with the instability pervading New York's urban images, the second major response to homelessness—the neutralization of its effects on viewers—attempts to restore a surface calm that belies underlying contradictions. To legitimate the city, this response delegitimates the homeless. In the spring of 1988 Mayor Ed Koch demonstrated the neutralizing approach while speaking, fittingly, before a group of image makers, the American Institute of Architects (AIA), convened in New York to discuss (even more appropriately) "Art in Architecture." Answering a question about Grand Central Terminal—landmark building and public place—Koch, too, emphasized the dual significance of New York's urban spaces by directing his listeners' attention to the presence of the homeless people who now reside in the city's train stations:

> These homeless people, you can tell who they are. They're sitting on the floor, occasionally defecating, urinating, talking to themselves many, not all, but many—or panhandling. We thought it would be reasonable for the authorities to say, "You can't stay here unless you're here for transportation." Reasonable, rational people would come to that conclusion, right? Not the Court of Appeals.[3]

The mayor was denigrating the state court's reversal of an antiloitering law under which police would have been empowered to remove the homeless from transportation centers. Even had police action succeeded in evicting the homeless, it is doubtful that it could have subdued the fundamental social forces threatening the station's appearance as an enduring symbol of New York's beauty and efficiency. Deprived of repressive powers, however, Koch could protect the space only by ideological means, proclaiming its transparency, in the eyes of reasonable people, to an objective function—transportation.

To assert in the language of common sense that an urban space refers unequivocally to intrinsic uses is to claim that the city itself speaks. Such a statement makes it seem that individual locations within the city and the spatial organization of the city as a whole contain an inherent meaning determined by the imperative to fulfill needs presupposed to be natural, simply practical. Instrumental function is the only meaning signified by the built environment. This essentialist view systematically obstructs—and this is actually its principal function—the perception that the organization and shaping of the city as well as the attribution of meaning to spaces are social processes. Spatial forms are social structures. Seen through the lens of function, spatial order appears instead to be controlled by natural, mechanical, or organic laws. It is recognized as social only in the sense that it meets the purportedly unified needs of aggregated individuals. Space, severed from its social production, is thus fetishized as a physical entity and undergoes, through inversion, a transformation. Represented as an independent object, it appears to exercise control over the very people who produce and use it. The impression of objectivity is real to the extent that the city is alienated from the social life of its inhabitants. The functionalization of the city, which presents space as politically neutral, merely utilitarian, is then filled with politics. For the notion that the city speaks for itself conceals the identity of those who speak through the city.

This effacement has two interrelated functions. In the service of those groups whose interests dominate decisions about the organization of space, it holds that the exigencies of human social life provide a single meaning that necessitates proper uses of the city—proper places for its residents. The prevailing goals of the existing spatial structure are regarded as, by definition, beneficial to all. The ideology of function obscures the conflictual manner in which cities are actually defined and used, repudiating the very existence of groups who counter dominant uses of space. As the urban critic Raymond Ledrut observes, "The city is not an object produced by a group in order to be bought or even used by others. *The city is an environment formed by the interaction and the integration of different practices.* It is maybe in this way that the city is truly the city."[4]

Ledrut's definition of the city as the product of social practice, negating its hypostatization as a physical entity, strongly opposes the technocratic definition of the city as the product of experts. The city, Ledrut insists, is not a spatial framework external to its users but is produced by them. These competing definitions are themselves a stake of political struggle. Deceptively simple, Ledrut's formulation

has far-reaching implications. Not only does it explicitly acknowledge the participation of diverse social groups in the production of the environment, it argues
against an environment imposed from above by state institutions or private interests, dictated by the necessities of control and profit but legitimated by concepts
of efficiency and beauty. Describing the city as a social form rather than as a collection and organization of neutral physical objects implicitly affirms the right of currently excluded groups to have access to the city—to make decisions about the
·spaces they use, to be attached to the places where they live, to refuse marginalization. It refers to a concrete social reality suppressed by dominant urban spaces,
sketches the terms of resistance to those spaces, and envisions the liberation of the
environment in what Henri Lefebvre calls a "space of differences."[5] In place of the
image of the "well-managed city," it proposes the construction of a "work of life,"
suggesting that such a vital work is extinguished by discourses that separate people
endowed with "eternal" needs from an environment supposedly built to meet
them. It restores the subject to the city. The struggle to establish the validity of
Ledrut's definition of the city is, then, irrevocably fused to other controversies
about the city's form and use. "The definition of urban meaning," Manuel Castells
maintains, describing the inscription of political battles in space,

> will be a process of conflict, domination, and resistance to domination,
> directly linked to the dynamics of social struggle and not to the repro-
> ductive spatial expression of a unified culture. Furthermore, cities and
> space being fundamental to the organization of social life, the conflict
> over the assignment of certain goals to certain spatial forms will be
> one of the fundamental mechanisms of domination and counter-
> domination in the social structure.[6]

Koch's assignment of a directing purpose—transportation—to Grand Central Terminal in order to prevail over what he portrayed as a parasitic function—
shelter for homeless people—encapsulates this means of domination. First, it se-
questers a single place from broader spatial organization. But the real efficacy of
the functionalization of the city as a weapon in struggles over the use of urban

space rests on its ability to deny the reality that such struggles produce spatial organization in the first place. Yet the presence in public places of the homeless— the very group Koch invoked—represents the most acute symptom of a massive and disputed transformation in the uses of the broader city during the 1980s. Far from a natural or mechanical adjustment, this reorganization was shaped in all of its facets by prevailing power relations. It included the transformation of New York into a center for international corporations and business services with attendant changes in the nature of employment. The shift of manufacturing jobs elsewhere, frequently overseas, was accompanied by a loss of traditional blue-collar jobs and the rise of poverty-level wages in low-echelon service-sector or new manufacturing jobs. By the close of the decade, even mass-media analyses routinely noted this change as a cause of homelessness, although they usually viewed it as a technological inevitability. Since, under capitalism, land and housing are commodities to be exploited for profit, the marginalization of large numbers of workers engendered a loss of housing for the poor as New York devoted more space to profit-maximizing real-estate development—high-rent office towers, luxury condominiums, corporate headquarters—that also provided the physical conditions to meet the needs of the new economy. Today's homeless, therefore, are refugees from evictions, secondary and exclusionary displacement—the conversion of their neighborhoods into areas they can no longer afford.[7] More broadly, the homeless are products of wage and property relations and of governmental policies allocating spatial resources to the uses of big business and real estate while withdrawing them from social services such as public housing. The homeless were also produced by technical decisions of state and municipal planning agencies about land uses, decisions that increasingly reinforced an economically and racially segregated spatial structure by directing low-income groups toward the city's periphery. To elucidate the specific historical, rather than mythical, reasons for today's homeless residents, the homeless should, more accurately, be called "the evicted." Koch's attempt, exemplified in his address to the architects' convention, to extract New York's urban spaces from the very social relations that create them further marginalizes the poor. Having first been expelled from their apartments and neighborhoods, they are now denied, by means of what the French Situationists termed "a black-mail of utility,"[8] a right to the city at all.

Exhortations to the authority of objective use are considered in Situationist pronouncements to be one of two mechanisms shielding the capitalist conquest of the environment from challenge. The other is aesthetics, which the Situationists characterized, along with urban planning, as "a rather neglected branch of criminology."[9] Their appraisal is still pertinent for New York, where notions of beauty and utility furnished the alibi for redevelopment. Under this protection, the conditions of everyday life for hundreds of thousands of residents have been destroyed. The reciprocity between discourses of beauty and utility is illuminated by the fact that Koch's question and answer session at the AIA convention replaced, at the last minute, a prepared speech that he was to deliver not on the well-managed city, but on the beautiful one. The substitution does not indicate a reversal of priorities. Both urban images are equally instrumental for the redevelopment process. In the name of needs and corresponding functions, Koch engaged in narrow problem solving about the uses of public spaces. His espousal of the city that speaks for itself permitted a remarkable silence about the incompatibility of true functionality and a social system in which production "is accomplished not for the fulfillment of needs in general, but for the fulfillment of one particular need: profit."[10] Indeed, as Jean Baudrillard warns, "any system of productivist growth (capitalist, but not exclusively) can only produce and reproduce men—even in their deepest determinations: in their liberty, in their needs, in their very unconscious—as productive forces."[11] Within such a system, if a person "eats, drinks, lives somewhere, reproduces himself, it is because the system requires his self-production in order to reproduce itself: it needs men."[12] In bourgeois society, when people such as today's homeless are redundant in the economy—or needed to cheapen labor costs—they are converted from residents of the city into predators on the "fundamental" needs of New Yorkers. No longer required as productive forces, the homeless themselves have no requirements.

The stunning reversals enacted in the name of utility—invoking to demonstrate natural needs the very group whose existence testifies to the social mediation of needs—also take place in the name of beauty. The mayor's prepared speech on the government's relation to aesthetics celebrated the city's preservation of historical landmarks, architectural heterogeneity, and neighborhood context, mobilizing a protectionist discourse of permanence and continuity under whose aegis patterns of development progressively threatened historical action, diversity, and entire communities with elimination. Such inversions are possible because commitments to beauty and utility, presupposed to lie outside sociomaterial conditions, present themselves as incontrovertible evidence of public accountability. As further proof of the advantages of New York's "ascendancy," Koch's planned speech stressed his administration's interest in the aesthetics of the city—its revitalization of the municipal art commission, programs of flexible zoning regulations, planning controls, design review panels, and public art. "Once again," the speech asserted, "public art has become a priority."[13]

REDEVELOPING "THE PUBLIC"

It is not difficult to understand why an increase in public art commissions accompanied New York's ascendancy. As a practice within the built environment, public art participates in the production of meanings, uses, and forms for the city. In this capacity, it can help secure consent to redevelopment and to the restructuring that constitutes the historical form of advanced capitalist urbanization. But like other institutions that mediate perceptions of the city's economic and political operations—architecture, urban planning, urban design—it can also question and resist those operations, revealing the suppressed contradictions within urban processes. Since these contradictions stamp the image of the city with a basic instability, public art can be, in an Althusserian sense, a "site" as well as a "stake" of urban struggle.

It is also predictable that, along with demonstrations of the new city's beauty and utility, intensified talk of "the public" went hand in hand with the accelerating privatization and bureaucratization of land-use decisions in New York. Wholesale appropriations of land by private interests, massive state interventions that deterritorialize huge numbers of residents, and inequitable distribution of spatial resources by government agencies insulated from public control: these acts governing New York's landscape require a legitimating front. Citing "the public," whether attached to art, space, or any number of other objects, ideas, and practices, is one means of giving the uneven development of New York democratic legitimacy.

Discourse about "the public" is frequently cast as a pledge made by the principal actors in the real-estate market—developers, financial institutions, landlords, corporations, politicians—to rescue, for New Yorkers, a significant quantity of "public space" from the ravages of "overdevelopment." Routinely, for instance, public areas, paid for with public funds, furnish private redevelopment projects with the amenities necessary to maximize profits.[14] In other cases, city regulations require corporations to build privately owned atriums or plazas in exchange for increased density allowances. The resulting sites are designated "public" spaces. These phenomena mirror each other as facets of the privatization of public space. They represent individual answers to the problems faced by municipal governments confronted with the need to facilitate capital accumulation and still maintain responsiveness to residents' demands for participation in decisions about the uses of the city. Private public space is widely celebrated as an innovative partnership between the public and private sectors—erroneously supposed to be distinct spheres. Such an alliance, we are told, if extended to the configuration of the entire city, would benefit all New York residents. Yet under current circumstances, the provision of space for "the public" attests to the wholesale withdrawal of space from social control. Clearly, the local state can meet with only limited and precarious success in harmonizing its goals of meeting capital's demands and maintaining democratic legitimacy since the two goals are, objectively, in conflict. Not surprisingly, therefore, New York's new public spaces, materializations of the attempt to reconcile these goals, are the objects of contests over uses and are, moreover, hardly designed for accessibility to all. Rather, through a multitude of legal, physical, or symbolic means, they permit access by certain social groups for selected purposes while excluding others.

When disputes do arise that threaten to expose the political implications of such exclusions, rhetoric about "the public" justifies particular exclusions as natural. Because "the public" is defined either as a unity or, what amounts to the same thing, as a field composed of essential differences, dilemmas plaguing the use of public spaces can be attributed to the inevitable disruptions attendant on the need to harmonize the "natural" differences and diverse interests characteristic of any society. Heightened diversity is viewed, even further, as a distinctive feature of

modern urban life, whose problems, in turn, are understood to result from a supposedly inevitable technological evolution undergone by human society. Neutralizing concepts of diversity are wielded to defeat genuine diversity and to
depoliticize conflicts. "The public," employed as an imprecise and embracing
rubric, substitutes for the analysis of specific spatial contests, ascribing discord to
quasi-natural origins. Exclusions enacted to homogenize public space by expelling
specific differences are dismissed as necessary to restore social harmony. The discourse of the public thus disavows the social relations of domination that such
expulsions make possible.

Exclusions and homogenization, undertaken in the name of the public, characterize what the German filmmaker Alexander Kluge calls the "pseudo-public
sphere," his term for the public sphere that Jürgen Habermas has famously theorized as a category of bourgeois society. Kluge and Oskar Negt describe a series of
permutations undergone by the bourgeois public sphere, especially its transformation in the interests of maximizing profits. But, according to Negt and Kluge, the
bourgeois—or, as variously labeled, the representative, classical, or traditional—
public sphere was a pseudo-public sphere from its inception. Although idealized
by Habermas as a spatiotemporal terrain where citizens participate in political dialogue and decision making, the bourgeois public sphere for Negt and Kluge actually represses debate. This repression originates in the strict demarcation drawn in
bourgeois society between the private and public realms. Because economic gain,
protected from public accountability by its seclusion within the private domain,
actually depends on publicly provided conditions, the bourgeois public sphere was
instituted as a means for private interests to control public activity. But since capitalism requires the preservation of the illusion that an absolute boundary divides
the public and private realms, the contradictions that gave birth to the public
sphere are also perpetuated and "reconciled" in its operations. Conflicts are homogenized by transmuting differential interests into an abstract equality supposedly
based on universal reason and by privatizing whole realms of social life. The homogenization of divergent concerns can, however, only be effected through exclusions: "A representative public sphere is representative insofar as it involves
exclusions." It "only represents parts of reality, selectively and according to certain

value systems."[15] Negt and Kluge describe how, increasingly, the pseudo-public sphere has yielded to a public sphere that is privately owned, determined by profit motives, and characterized by the transformation of the conditions of everyday life into objects of production. Within this public sphere—which Negt and Kluge, unlike Habermas, do not measure against a supposedly lost ideal—"the public" is defined as a mass of consumers and spectators.[16] Against both the pseudo- and private public spheres, grounded in relations of exclusion, homogenization, and private property, Negt and Kluge envision the construction of an oppositional public sphere, an arena of political consciousness and articulation of social experience that challenges these relations.

Recently artists and critics have sought to initiate such a challenge within art practice by constructing what is sometimes termed a cultural or aesthetic public sphere. The idea that art cannot assume the existence of a public but must help produce one and that the public sphere is less a physical space than a social form nullify, to a considerable extent, accepted divisions between public and nonpublic art. Potentially, any exhibition venue is a public sphere and, conversely, the location of artworks outside privately owned galleries, in parks and plazas, or simply outdoors hardly guarantees that they will address a public. While in these ways the concept of a public sphere shatters the category of public art, it also raises serious questions for art conventionally so categorized and, especially, for work commissioned to occupy New York's new public spaces. Given the proliferation of pseudo- and private public spaces, how can public art counter the functions of its "public" sites in constructing the city?

We can at least begin to answer this question by discarding the simplifications that pervade mainstream aesthetic discourse about the public. Rather than a real category, the definition of the public, like the definition of the city, is an ideological artifact, a contested and fragmented terrain. "'The public,'" as Craig Owens observes, "is a discursive formation susceptible to appropriation by the most diverse—indeed, opposed—ideological interests."[17] But crucial as this perception is, significant challenges to dominant interests will continue to elude us unless this basic understanding prompts further inquiries into the precise identity of those interests and the concrete mechanisms through which they exercise power. Unless we seriously respond to Owens's subsequent question—"Who is to define, manipulate and profit from 'the public'?"[18]—critical interventions will remain inchoate and directionless. A principal issue confronting all urban practices is the current appropriation of public space and of the city itself for use by the forces of redevelopment. Public art shares this plight. Although its current predicament is not without historical precedent—most notably in late-nineteenth-century civic beautification and municipal art movements—the complexities of the present moment necessitate a new framework for analyzing the social functions of public art.

PUBLIC ART AND ITS USES

Most existing aesthetic approaches can neither account for current conditions of public art production nor suggest terms for an alternative, possibly transformative practice. Even when familiar with issues of the public sphere or informed by sophisticated materialist critiques of aesthetic perception, they are generally formulated with little knowledge of urban politics. Needless to say, traditional art-historical paradigms cannot illuminate the social functions of public art—past or present—since they remain committed to idealist assumptions that obscure those functions. Maintaining that art is defined by an independent aesthetic essence, prevailing doctrines hold that while art inevitably reflects social reality, its purpose is, by definition, the transcendence of spatiotemporal contingencies. Conventional social art history provides no genuine alternative. Frequently attracted to the study of public art because of what they perceive as its inherently social character, social art historians (in keeping with the discipline's empiricist biases) confine themselves to describing either the iconography or the historical "context" of individual works, restricting meaning to the work's overt subject matter and relegating social conditions to a backdrop. Such scholars thus preserve the dissociation of art—ontologically intact—from discrete social "environments" with which art merely "interacts." In addition, art history mystifies the social environment just as it does the work of art. With few exceptions, art-historical discussions of the city are based on notions of the city as a transhistorical form, an inevitable product of technological evolution, or an arena for the unfolding of exacerbated individualism.[19]

More importantly, the current role of public art in urban politics raises questions about some critical perspectives. Beginning in the late 1960s, contemporary art and criticism challenged modernist tenets of aesthetic autonomy by exploring art's functions in mutable social circumstances. Artists initiated this critique by shifting attention away from the "inside" of the artwork—supposed in modernist doctrine to contain fixed, inherent meanings—and focusing instead on the work's context—its framing conditions. Site-specificity, an aesthetic strategy in which context was incorporated into the work itself, was originally developed to counteract the construction of ideological art objects, purportedly defined by independent essences, and to reveal the ways in which the meaning of art is constituted in relation to its institutional frames. Over the years, in what is now a familiar history, site-specificity underwent many permutations. Most fruitfully, artists extended the notion of context to encompass the individual site's symbolic, social, and political meanings as well as the discursive and historical circumstances within which artwork, spectator, and site are situated. Insofar as this expansion stressed the social and psychic relations structuring both artwork and site, exclusive concentration on the physical site often signaled an academic fetishization of context at the aesthetic level. But critical site-specific art, as distinguished from its academic progeny, not only continued to incorporate context as a critique of the artwork but attempted to intervene in the site. The newly acknowledged reciprocity between artwork and site changed the identity of each, blurring the boundaries between them, and paved the way for art's participation in wider cultural and social practices. For public art, the objective of altering the site required that the urban space occupied by a work be understood, just as art and art institutions had been, as socially constructed spaces.

One of the more radical promises of public art that attempted to defetishize both art and urban space was that artists and critics would articulate their aesthetic opposition to the spaces of art's reception with other forms of social resistance to the organization of the city. Taking such a step does not mean, as some realist or "activist" positions imply, that art must relinquish its specificity as a political practice. It does, however, entail the recognition that an artwork's identity is always modified by its encounter with its sites. It is, for example, insufficient to support site-specificity by simply stating, as some critics have done, that a work like Richard Serra's *Tilted Arc* (1981) intervened in the city in order to redefine space as the site of sculpture.[20] The significance of the intervention also depends on how art is redefined in the process. Because *Tilted Arc* did not address the stakes of redefining the city, it exhibited a combination of specificity and generalization symptomatic of the split it maintained between critical aesthetic issues and critical urban problems. On the one hand, the sculpture was undoubtedly wedded concretely to its site: it established itself in relation to the surrounding architecture, engaged and reoriented existing spatial patterns, invited viewers into the space of the work, and traced the path of human vision across the Federal Plaza. Perhaps, as Douglas Crimp argues, setting up *Tilted Arc* as an example of radicalized site-specificity, the work metaphorically ruptured the spatial expression of state power by destroying the plaza's seeming coherence.[21] It might also, as Crimp less speculatively suggests, have revealed the condition of alienation in bourgeois society. These are the most provocative claims that have been made for *Tilted Arc* as a practice that confronted the material conditions of art's existence. Although they identify a radical potential for public art, they tend, as an interpretation of Serra's work, toward exaggeration. For *Tilted Arc* still floated above its urban site. The lingering abstraction of the sculpture from its space emerges most clearly in the attitude of the work and its supporters toward urgent questions about the uses of public space.

Indeed, "use" was elevated to a central position in the debates about public art generated by the hearings convened in 1985 to decide whether Serra's sculpture should be removed from its site.[22] The proper use of the site became a banner under which crusades against the work were conducted. Supporters countered with alternative uses. *Tilted Arc*'s most astute defenders problematized the assumptions about utility that justified attacks on the sculpture, challenging, as does the work itself, simplistic or populist ideas about natural, self-evident uses. Yet in proposing aesthetic uses for the space, isolated from its social function in specific circumstances, supporters substituted one ideological conception of use for another, perpetuating, as did the work's detractors, a belief in essential, noncontingent uses of space. Moreover, the notion that *Tilted Arc* bestows on the Federal Plaza an aesthetic use simply available to all ignores questions recently posed in a multitude of disciplines about differences among users and, further, about the users' role in *producing* the meanings of their environments. Phenomenological readings, placing subjective experience of space outside the sociomaterial conditions of the city, fail to take into account that the primary object of their study is already ideological. "The situation of man confronting the city," writes Raymond Ledrut, "involves other things than schemas of perceptive behavior. It introduces ideology." [23]

Precisely because the ideology of spatial use was never introduced, critical discussions about *Tilted Arc*, despite the prominence accorded to questions of use, remained aloof from the most crucial public issues about the uses of space in New York today: conflicts between social groups about uses; the social division of the city; and which residents are forcibly excluded from using the city at all. These issues occupy the heart of urban politics. They were also the hidden agenda of neoconservative assaults on *Tilted Arc*, which, represented as an impediment to the uniformly beneficial uses of public space, became a foil against which to measure the supposed usefulness of other kinds of public art that celebrate and perpetuate the dominant uses of space. Yet these questions remained unexcavated during the hearings because, confined within the boundaries of critical aesthetics, critical discourse about the sculpture failed to consider the function of public art in contemporary urbanization—the spatial component of social change. While the *Tilted Arc* debate frequently included complex materialist critiques of art's production and of aesthetic perception, it nonetheless obstructed interrogation of the conditions of production of New York's urban space.

Opening this question requires that we dislodge public art from its ghettoization within the parameters of aesthetic discourse, even critical aesthetic discourse, and resituate it, at least partially, within critical urban discourse. More precisely, such a shift in perspective erodes the borders between the two fields, revealing crucial interfaces between art and urbanism in public art. The need for criticism to conceptualize this meeting ground is especially urgent now since neoconservative forces are performing that task in order to promote a type of public art that complies with the demands of redevelopment. "In fact," to cite just one journalist who has set forth the "new criterion" for public art, "public art needs to be seen as a function not of art, but of urbanism. It needs to be thought of in relation to, rather than insulated from the numerous other functions, activities and imperatives that condition the fabric of city life."[24] The problem we face, then, is not so much the absence of any consideration of the city in current accounts of public art but rather that these accounts perpetuate mythologizing notions about the city. Typically, they claim both to oppose cultural elitism and to remain committed to artistic quality, a claim that parallels the assertion that the redeveloped city provides quality public space. Journalists thus promote a type of public art that is fully incorporated into the apparatus of redevelopment. My desire to approach contemporary public art as an urban practice is motivated by the imperative, first, to respond to concrete events changing the function of public art and, second, to contribute to the formation of a counterpractice. A counterpractice must, however, possess an adequate knowledge of the dominant construction within which it works. In the case of public art, it depends on a critical perception of the city's metamorphosis and of the role that public art is playing within it.

When Mayor Koch's speechwriters for his talk before the American Institute of Architects stated that "once again, public art has become a priority," they were drawing attention not only to an increase in the number of public art commissions but also to enhanced support for a qualitatively different kind of public art. Even though their reference to art was part of a speech on aesthetics—the beautiful city—it could equally have supported the mayor's later remarks about utility—the well-managed city. For the "new public art" illustrates the marriage of the two images in the redevelopment process.

In the eyes of proponents, what distinguishes the new public art and renders it more socially accountable than the old is precisely its "usefulness." "What is the new public art?" asked an art journalist in one of the earliest articles reporting on the new phenomenon: "Definitions differ from artist to artist, but they are held together by a single thread: *It is art plus function,* whether the function is to provide a place to sit for lunch, to provide water drainage, to mark an important historical date, or to enhance and direct a viewer's perception."[25] From this indiscriminate list of functions it is difficult to ascertain precisely how the new public sculpture differs from previous types. Nineteenth-century war memorials, after all, commemorate important events, and *Tilted Arc,* against which the new art defines itself, directs a viewer's perception. Yet advocates do specify, no matter how vaguely, a quality that distinguishes the new public artists: "All share a dedication to extra-aesthetic concerns. Use—not as in criticality but as in seating and tables, shade and sunlight—is a primary issue."[26] And, "We are putting function back into art again."[27] Again, "This architectural art has a functional basis. Unlike most traditionally modern works of painting and sculpture, which modern artists were careful to define as 'useless' in comparison to other objects of daily life, recent architectural art is often very much like a wall, a column, a floor, a door or a fence."[28] Scott Burton, whose work—primarily furniture designed for public places—epitomizes the phenomenon, repeatedly declared that "utility" is the principal yardstick for measuring the value of public art.[29]

The new art, then, is promoted as useful in the reductive sense of fulfilling supposedly essential human and social needs. Just as Koch designated Grand Central Terminal a place for travel, this art prescribes places in the city for people to sit, to stand, to play, to eat, to read, even to dream. Building on this foundation, the new art claims to unify a whole sequence of divided spheres, offering itself as a model of integration. Initially polarizing the concerns of art and those of utility, these artists then transcend the division by making works that are both art and usable objects. Through this usefulness, moreover, art is supposedly reconciled with society and with the public benefit. Use, we are told, ensures relevance: "As an artist working toward the social good, [the public sculptor] produces works that are used by the populace, that inhabit its plazas, that are part of its plans for urban design and economic redevelopment—works that rapidly leave the environment of art to enter the realm of artifacts."[30] Just as function is limited to utilitarianism, social activity is constricted to narrow problem solving so that the provision of useful objects automatically collapses into a social good. "The social questions interest me more than the art ones," says Burton, describing his furnishings for the Equitable Assurance Building, a structure whose function in raising real-estate values Burton fails to examine. "I hope that people will love to eat their lunch there."[31] He continues, "Communal and social values are now more important. What office workers do in their lunch hour is more important than my pushing the limits of my self-expression."[32]

The conflation of utility with social benefit has a distinctly moralistic cast: "All my work is a rebuke to the art world,"[33] Burton states. Critics agree: "[Scott Burton] challenges the art community with neglect of its social responsibility. . . . Carefully calculated for use, often in public spaces, Burton's furniture clearly has a social function."[34] All of these purported acts of unification are predicated on prior separations and thus conceal underlying processes of dissociation. Each element of the discourse about the new public art—art, use, society—first isolated from the others, has individually undergone a splitting operation in which it is rationalized and objectified, treated as a nonrelational entity: art possesses an aesthetic essence; utilitarian objects serve universal needs; society is a functional ensemble with an objective foundation. They all surmount specific histories, geographies, values, and relations to subjects and social groups, and all are reconstituted as abstract categories. Individually and as a whole, they are severed from social relations, fetishized as discrete objects. This is the real social function of the new public art: to present as natural the conditions of the late-capitalist city into which it hopes to integrate us.

The supreme act of unification with which the new public art is credited, however, is its interdisciplinary cooperation with other professions shaping the physical environment: "The new public art invariably requires the artist to collaborate with a diverse group of people, including architects, landscape architects, other artists and engineers. So far, most of the public artists have had few problems adjusting to the collaborative process; indeed, many have embraced it with enthusiasm."[35] Another critic writes: "Few might have guessed that these collaborations would so seriously affect the art, design and planning professions in such a short time."[36] Yet given that the new public art rallies all of the notions that currently inform redevelopment, it is hardly surprising, if not in fact completely predictable, that such work would be rapidly incorporated into the process of designing New York's redeveloped spaces. Presented as beautiful, useful, public, and expertly produced, the work advertises these new environments as images of New York's ascendancy. Indeed, the rise of collaborative public art accompanied the acceleration of urban redevelopment almost from its inception. In 1981 John Beardsley concluded his survey of "community-sponsored" art projects, *Art in Public Places,* by observing a recent shift in artistic attitudes. "A new kind of partnership is emerging between contemporary artists and the nation's communities," he explained in a chapter entitled "New Directions: Expanding Views of Art in Public Places," "with the result that artists are increasingly involved in significant development efforts. In part, this is a consequence of new initiatives within cities. As an element of major building programs in the last decade and a half, some have sought the participation of artists in developing innovative solutions to public design problems."[37]

Public art collaborations emerged in the late 1970s and grew to such an extent that a decade later they dominated accounts of public art. "This is a season," wrote Michael Brenson in 1988, "that is bringing the issue of artistic collaboration to a head. Over the past few years a great deal of hope has been invested in the partnership between sculptors and architects, and between sculptors and the community. There is a widespread feeling that this is the future for public sculpture and perhaps for sculpture in general."[38] The consistent invocation of "the community" in passages such as these typifies the terminological problems pervading discussions of public art and endowing the new public art with an aura of social accountability. That Beardsley's book consistently describes government-funded art as community-sponsored is especially ironic since the "new initiatives within cities" and "major building programs" that he cites as the impetus for collaborations frequently comprise state interventions in the built environment that destroy minority and working-class communities, dispersing their residents. "Community" conjures images of neighborhoods bound together by relations of mutual interest, respect, and kinship; "community-sponsored" implies local control and citizen participation in decision making. But it is community, as both territory and social form, that redevelopment destroys, converting the city into a terrain organized to fulfill capital's need to exploit space for profit. If anything, clashes, rather than agreement, between communities and state-imposed initiatives are likely to characterize urban life today.

Inaccuracies of language, demonstrating indifference to urban politics, resemble other distortions pervading discourse about public art collaborations, confusing the terms of aesthetic politics as well. Just as these misrepresentations appropriate urban discourse, they use the vocabulary of radical art practice to invest the recent marriage of art and urban planning with a social justification. The new public art is deemed "anti-individualist," "contextualist," and "site-specific." Collaborative artists frequently voice a lack of concern with private self-expression and thereby express their opposition to the autonomy and privilege of art. As part of urban design teams, they also reject notions of public art as "decoration" because, as they contend, they are not merely placing objects in urban spaces but creating the spaces themselves. If writers such as Beardsley single out new initiatives within cities as one factor contributing to the growth of public art collaborations, they find a second crucial factor in developments within contemporary art itself: "In part, [the shift to public art partnerships] follows as well from the increasingly interdisciplinary character of contemporary art. . . . There is a pronounced shift in these projects from the isolated object to the artwork integrated with its environment and from the solitary creator to the artist as a member of a professional team."[39]

Clearly, the new public art is born of recent tendencies within urbanism and art practice. To say so tells us very little. Genuine explanation depends on understanding the nature of each of these developments and their interaction. The new art's promoters misconstrue both sources of the new public art. The difference between their version of site-specificity and its original meaning is obvious and needs only to be summarized here.

The commitment to developing an art practice that neither diverts attention from nor merely decorates the spaces of its display originated from the political imperative to challenge the apparent neutrality of those spaces. Contextualist art intervened in its spatial environment by making the social organization and ideological operations of that space visible. The new public art, by contrast, moves "beyond decoration" into the field of spatial design in order to create, rather than question, the coherence of the site, to conceal its constitutive social conflicts. Such work moves from a notion of art that is "in" but independent of its spaces to one that views art as integrated with its spaces and users but in which all three elements are independent of urban social relations. Simply combining twin fetishisms, this public art is instrumental for redevelopment. One critic, specifying "a right way and a wrong way to insert art in public places," describes a collaborative art project in New York that, she believes, exemplifies the right way because it represents the gentrification of site art—it's been successfully, even brilliantly, tamed, its sting removed. You can sometimes miss the good old days when artists were fierce individualists wrestling the wilderness to its knees, like Dan'l Boone with the bear; the "otherness" of art out on the American desert touched some mythic nerve. But times have changed. The two traditions—the gentrified and the wild—can't be mixed.[40]

This statement constructs false dualisms that displace important differences. What has been eliminated from the new "site-specific" art is not "individualism" as opposed to teamwork but rather political intervention in favor of collaboration with dominant forces. The measure of just how depoliticized this art has become— and how political it actually is—under the guise of being "environmentally sensitive" is the author's presumption that gentrification is a positive metaphor for changes in art practice. As anyone truly sensitive to New York's social landscape realizes, her prior description of gentrification as the domestication of wild frontiers profoundly misapprehends the phenomenon. Gentrification only appears to result from the heroic conquest of hostile environments by individual "pioneers." In truth, as Neil Smith writes, "It is apparent that where the 'urban pioneers' venture, the banks, real-estate companies, the state or other collective economic actors have generally gone before. In this context it may be more appropriate to view the James Rouse Company not as the John Wayne but as the Wells Fargo of gentrification."[41] The depiction of gentrification—a process that replaces poor, usually minority, residents of frequently well-established neighborhoods with middle-class residents—as the civilization of wild terrains is not only naive about economics. It is ethnocentric and racist. The use of this conceit in art criticism epitomizes the arrogance of an aesthetic discourse that claims to respond to urban environments but lacks any commitment to comprehend them.

Instead, absorbing dominant ideology about the city, proponents of the new public art respond to urban questions by constructing images of well-managed and beautiful cities. Theirs is a technocratic vision. Insofar as it discerns a real problem—the loss of people's attachment to the city—it reacts by offering solutions that can only perpetuate alienation: the conviction that needs and pleasures can be gratified by expertly produced, professionally "humanized" environments. The incapacity to acknowledge that the city is a social rather than a technical form renders this vision helpless to explain a situation in which the same system that produces, for profit and control, a city dissociated from its users, today, for the same reasons, literally detaches people from their living spaces through eviction and displacement. Faced with such circumstances, the technocratic view is left with limited options: encouragement of these actions; disavowal; dismissal of homelessness as an example of how the system fails rather than, more accurately, how it currently works. The belief that homelessness represents such an isolated social "failure" can generate a resigned abandonment of the most troubling facts of city life, justifying support for the use of the city for economic growth, modified, perhaps, by degrees of regulation. One urban designer, dedicated to institutionalizing urban design as a technical specialty and arm of public policy, freely acknowledges, for instance, that gentrification and historic preservation displace "earlier settlers" in city neighborhoods. He even suggests measures to "mitigate the adverse effects of social change in historic districts" but succinctly concludes that "the dynamics of real estate in a private market always mean that someone profits at someone else's expense. On balance, the preservation and restoration of old neighborhoods has to be considered valuable for the economic health of a city, even if there is hardship for individuals."[42]

Confident that the dominant forces producing today's city represent the collectivity—while members of displaced social groups are mere individuals—and equally confident, despite references to "social change," that such forces are immutable, interdisciplinary urban design teams—which now include public artists—fashion the mental and physical representations of New York's ascendancy. To do so, they must suppress the connection between redeveloped spaces and New York's homelessness.

THE SOCIAL USES OF SPACE

Public artists seeking to reveal the contradictions underlying images of well-managed or beautiful cities also explore relationships between art and urbanism.

Their interdisciplinary ventures differ, however, from the new collaborative and useful ones. Instead of extending the idealist conception of art to the surrounding city, they combine materialist analyses of art as a social product with materialist analyses of the social production of urban space. As a contribution to this work, urban studies has much to offer since it explores the concrete mechanisms by which power relations are perpetuated in spatial forms and identifies the precise terms of spatial domination and resistance. Since the late 1960s, the "social production of space" has become the object of an impressive body of literature generated by urbanists in a variety of fields: geography, sociology, urban planning, political economy. Critical spatial theories share a key theme with critical aesthetic thought, and the two have unfolded along a similar trajectory. Initially, each inquiry questioned the paradigm dominating its respective discipline. Just as radical art practice challenged formalist dogma, radical urban studies questioned mainstream ecological perspectives on urban space.[43] "The dominant paradigm," writes sociologist Marc Gottdiener,

> loosely identified as urban ecology, explains settlement space as being produced by an adjustment process involving large numbers of relatively equal actors whose interaction is guided by some self-regulating invisible hand. This "organic" growth process—propelled by technological innovation and demographic expansion—assumes a spatial morphology which, according to ecologists, mirrors that of lower life forms within biological kingdoms. Consequently, the social organization of space is accepted by mainstreamers as inevitable, whatever its patterns of internal differentiation.[44]

The ecological perspective describes forms of metropolitan social life in terms of the adaptation of human populations to environments in which certain processes remain constant. Employing biologistic analogies, this view attributes urban growth patterns to laws of competition, dominance, succession, and invasion and thus explains the morphology of the city as the outcome of seminatural processes.[45] Even when the ecological legacy of environmental determinism has been complicated or discarded altogether, prevailing tendencies within urban studies continue to view space as an objective entity and to marginalize the role of the wider social system in producing urban spatial form. But just as critical art practice in the late 1960s and 1970s sought to defetishize the ideological art object, critical urban studies did the same with the ideological spatial object—the city as an ecological form. The two inquiries investigated the ways in which social relations produce, respectively, art and the city.

Having insisted, however, on the relationship between society and art, on the one hand, and society and space, on the other, both critiques rejected the idea that this relationship can be reduced to simple reflection or interaction. If formalism could reenter aesthetic discourse in the notion that art inevitably mirrors society, so idealism could return to spatial discourse in the formulation that space mirrors social relations. But "two things can only interact or reflect each other if they are defined in the first place as separate," observes Smith. "Even having taken the first step of realization, then, we are not automatically freed from the burden of our conceptual inheritance; regardless of our intentions, it is difficult to start from an implicitly dualistic conception of space and society and to conclude by demonstrating their unity."[46] Indeed, by means of such separations, not only are space and art endowed with identities as discrete entities, but social life appears to be unsituated, to exist apart from its material forms. Space and art can be rescued from further mystification only by being grasped as socially produced categories in the first instance, as arenas where social relations are reproduced, and as themselves social relations.

Framing my remarks about kindred developments in two distinct fields is a belief that they share a common purpose. Both attempt to reveal the depoliticizing effects of the hegemonic perspectives they criticize and, conversely, share an imperative to politicize the production of space and art. These similar goals do not merely offer an interesting academic parallel. Nor, as in standard conceptions of interdisciplinarity, do they simply enrich each other. Rather, they converge in the production of a new object—public art as a spatial activity. Understanding the fusion of urban space with prevailing social relations reveals the extent to which the predominant tendency within public art to design the landscape of redevelopment fully implicates art in contemporary spatial politics.

———

Such a statement only makes sense, however, in light of a theory of spatial organization as a terrain of political struggle. Urban studies, far from a monolithic discipline, is characterized by debates on "the politics of space" far too complex to receive justice within the scope of this essay.[47] Still, it is necessary to outline, however briefly, why space is on the political agenda today as it has never been before. Henri Lefebvre, who coined the phrase "the production of space," attributes the significance of space, at least in part, to changes in the organization of production and accumulation under late capitalism. New spatial arrangements assure capitalism's very survival. Because, according to Lefebvre, production is no longer isolated in independent units within space but, instead, takes place across vast spatial networks, "the production of things in space" gives way to "the production of space."[48] Due to this growth of space and to revolutions in telecommunications and information technology, "the planning of the modern economy tends to become spatial planning."[49] Lefebvre's premise has some clear implications. Individual cities cannot be defined in isolation from their relationships with other places, relationships that take place within and across various geographic levels: global, regional, urban. The spatial restructuring of New York can be comprehended only within a global context that includes the internationalization of capital, the new international division of labor, and the new international urban hierarchy.[50] Cities such as New York occupy the upper ranks of this hierarchy. They are centers for decision making and administrative control of finance capital and global corporations. Productive activities and low-level clerical jobs are exported, permitting savings on labor costs along with enhanced flexibility and control. But the corporate center itself emerges not only through global restructuring but through a restructuring within the city. New concentrations of luxury housing, office buildings, and high-status entertainment and recreational facilities serve the new workforce and destroy the physical conditions of survival for blue-collar workers. This restructuring is paradoxical, entailing simultaneous deindustrialization and reindustrialization, decentralization and recentralization, and internationalization and peripheralization. Crucial to understanding the character of New York, however, is the insight that within the finance and service center, as on the global level, individual spaces have no intrinsic substance: their character and condition can be explained only in relation to other city spaces.

To a great extent, specific spatial relations within the city correspond to the broader circumstances of accumulation under advanced capitalism. Today, accumulation occurs not by absolute expansion but through the internal differentiation of space. It is, then, a process of uneven development. The idea that uneven spatial development is "the hallmark of the geography of capitalism"[51] combines insights of geography with a long and embattled tradition within Marxist political economy. Theorists of uneven development explain capital accumulation as a contradictory process taking place through a transfer of values within a hierarchically unified world system. "In this whole system," writes Ernest Mandel,

> development and underdevelopment reciprocally determine each other, for while the quest for surplus-profits constitutes the prime motive power behind the mechanisms of growth, surplus-profit can only be achieved at the expense of less productive countries, regions and branches of production. Hence development takes place only in juxtaposition with underdevelopment; it perpetuates the latter and itself develops thanks to this perpetuation.[52]

Urban geographers and sociologists routinely include uneven development among the features distinguishing the production of late-capitalist space. Smith has extensively analyzed it as a structural process governing spatial patterns at all scales. His work can help us comprehend the spatial restructuring of New York in the 1980s since it explains phenomena such as gentrification and redevelopment as manifestations of the broad, yet specific, underlying process of uneven development affecting land use in the city.

Smith theorizes two factors responsible for uneven development at the urban scale. Following David Harvey, he applies to explanations of urban space theories maintaining that overaccumulation crises prompt capital, in an attempt to counteract falling rates of profit, to switch its investment from crisis-ridden spheres of the economy into the built environment. Gentrification and redevelopment represent this attempt. But uneven development in the city arises not only in response to such broad economic cycles but also because of corresponding conditions within metropolitan land markets. According to Smith, the profitability of investment in the built environment depends on the creation of what he calls a "rent gap."[53] The rent gap describes the difference between the current and potential value of land. The devalorization of real estate, through blockbusting, redlining, and abandonment of buildings, creates a situation in which investment by real estate and finance capital for "higher" land uses can produce a profitable return. Redevelopment is the consequence of both the uneven development of capital in general and of urban land in particular. Whether or not one agrees that the creation of a rent gap is sufficient to produce redevelopment, Smith's thesis discloses the concealed relation between processes such as gentrification and those of abandonment. The decline of neighborhoods, rather than being corrected by gentrification, is in fact its precondition. But the theory of uneven urban development also helps us understand the construction of the image of the redeveloped city. To portray redeveloped spaces as symbols of beneficial and uniform growth, declining spaces must be constituted as separate categories. Growth as redifferentiation is disavowed. Consequently, the repressed "other" of spaces of ascendancy has a concrete identity in the city's deteriorating areas and in the immiseration of residents.

Uncovering the economic determinations of spatial redifferentiation in New York does not, however, illuminate the operations of space as a determining weight on social life or as ideology. For Lefebvre, advanced capitalism creates a distinctive and multivalent space that "is not only supported by social relations, but . . . also is producing and produced by social relations."[54] Capitalist space or what Lefebvre calls both "abstract space" and "dominated space" serves multiple functions. It is, at once, a means of production, an object of consumption, and a property relation. It is also a tool of state domination, subordination, and surveillance. According to Lefebvre, abstract space possesses a distinctive combination of three qualities: it is homogeneous or uniform so that it can be used, manipulated, controlled, and exchanged. But within the homogeneous whole, which today spreads over a vast area, it is also fragmented into interchangeable parts, so that, as a commodity, it can be bought and sold. Abstract space is, further, hierarchically ordered, divided into centers and peripheries, upper- and lower-status spaces, spaces of the governing and the governed. All three features of abstract space require that space be objectified and universalized, submitted to an abstract measure. Abstract space can function as a space of control because it is generalized from specificity and diversity, from its relation to social subjects, and from their specific uses of space.

Above all, numerous contradictions haunt this space. As a global productive force, space is treated on a universal scale, but it is also, in Lefebvre's words, "pulverized" by relations of private property and by other processes that fragment it into units. For Lefebvre, this contradiction corresponds to the basic contradiction of capitalism outlined by Marx between the forces of production—the socialization of geographical space, in this case—and the social relations of production—the private ownership and control of space. But Lefebvre's universalization-pulverization contradiction also represents a conflict between the need to homogenize space so that it can serve as a tool of state domination and to fragment space so that it can facilitate economic relations.

But while abstract space homogenizes differences, it simultaneously produces them. Lefebvre's account of this contradiction is compelling: while capitalist space tends toward the elimination of differences, it does not succeed in its homogenizing quest. As the globalization of space creates centers of decision making and power, it must expel people: "The dominant space, that of the spaces of richness and power, is forced to fashion the dominated space, that of the periphery."[55] Relegating groups of people and particular uses of space to enclosed areas outside the center produces what Lefebvre calls an "explosion of spaces." As abstract space imposes itself on the social space of everyday life, a multitude of differences appear. "What is different," writes Lefebvre, "is, to begin with, what is *excluded:* the edges of the city, shanty towns, the spaces of forbidden games, of guerrilla war, of war."[56] The spread of abstract space continuously heightens the contradiction between the production of space for profit and control—abstract space—and the use of space for social reproduction—the space of everyday life, which is created by but also escapes the generalizations of exchange and technocratic specialization. Abstract space represents, then, the *unstable* subordination of social space by a centralized space of power. This constitutive instability makes it possible for users to "appropriate" space, to undo its domination by capitalist spatial organization. This activity, an exercise of what Lefebvre refers to as "the right to the city,"[57] includes the struggle of expelled groups to occupy and control space.

Lefebvre's intricate formulations about the preeminence of space in social conflicts have provoked extensive criticism, including charges of "spatial fetishism," "vagueness," and "reproductionism," especially from orthodox Marxists. Lefebvre first became familiar to English-speaking readers through Manuel Castell's *The Urban Question* in which the author opposed Lefebvre in a debate on the theory of space.[58] Although Castells later returned to many of Lefebvre's ideas, which by that time had been embraced by numerous Anglo-American urbanists, Lefebvre's emphasis on social reproduction makes him vulnerable to criticism from leftist critics who continue to privilege production as the determining base of social life and therefore as the fundamental location and objective of emancipatory struggle. In addition, Lefebvre's rejection of reformist measures to ameliorate urban problems coupled with his refusal to propound doctrinaire solutions frustrate both liberal critics and those leftists searching for a single explanatory factor or a preconceived model of alternative spatial organization. For Lefebvre, however, the model is itself the tool of technocratic spatial knowledge that, producing repetition rather than difference, helps engineer the production of abstract space. One principal value of his critique is precisely that it does not prescribe a new orthodoxy of urban planning. Moreover, for Lefebvre meaning is not fixed in objective economic structures but is continuously invented in the course of what Michel de Certeau calls "the practice of everyday life"—the use and undoing of dominated space by those it excludes.[59] Lefebvre's analysis of the spatial exercise of power as the conquest of differences, while thoroughly grounded in Marxist thought, rejects economism and opens the possibility of advancing the analysis of spatial politics into feminist, anticolonialist, and radical democratic discourse. Even if one disagrees with his humanist belief in a previously integrated social space, Lefebvre has, more thoroughly than anyone of whom I am aware, theorized how the organization of urban space functions as ideology. He thus provides a starting point for cultural critiques of spatial design as an instrument of social control.

For Lefebvre, space is ideological because it reproduces prevailing social relations and because it represses conflict. Abstract space gives rise to, and is produced by, contradictions, but spatial organization is also the medium through which contradictions are contained. "One of the most crying paradoxes of abstract space," writes Lefebvre, "is that it can be simultaneously the birthplace of contradictions, the milieu in which they are worked out and which they tear up and finally, the instrument which allows their suppression and the substitution of an apparent coherence. All of which confers on space a function previously assumed by ideology."[60] Professions such as urban planning and design—and, now, public art—assume the job of imposing such coherence, order, and rationality on space. They can be regarded as disciplinary technologies in the Foucauldian sense insofar as they attempt to pattern space so that docile and useful bodies are created by and deployed within it. In performing these tasks, such technologies also assume the contradictory functions of the state. Called upon to preserve space for the fulfillment of social needs, they must also facilitate the development of an abstract space of exchange and engineer the space of domination. Consequently, urban practitioners who view planning as a technical problem and politics as a foreign substance to be eliminated from spatial structures are involved in, and simultaneously mask, spatial politics.

The contours of New York's redevelopment cannot be conceptually manipulated to fit exactly within the mold of Lefebvre's description of late-capitalist space. Yet his concept of abstract space, coupled with that of uneven development, helps clarify the terms of urban spatial struggle. Materialist analyses of space enable us to evaluate the effects of cultural practices, such as the new public art, which are engaged in that struggle on the side of real estate and state domination. They also suggest ways in which public art can enter the arena of urban politics to undermine that domination, perhaps facilitating the expression of social groups excluded by the current organization of the city. Participation in urban design and planning enmeshes public art, unwittingly or not, in spatial politics, but public art can also help appropriate the city, organized to repress contradictions, as a vehicle for illuminating them. It can transform itself into a spatial praxis, which Edward Soja has defined as "the active and informed attempt by spatially conscious social actors to reconstitute the embracing spatiality of social life."[61] Against aesthetic movements that design the spaces of redevelopment, interventionist aesthetic practices might—as they do with other spaces of aesthetic display—redesign these sites. For if official public art creates the redeveloped city, art as spatial praxis approaches the city in the cautious manner of the cultural critic described by Walter Benjamin. Confronted with "cultural treasures"—"documents of civilization"—Benjamin's critic unveils the barbarism underlying their creation by brushing their history "against the grain."[62] Likewise, we can brush New York's spatial documents of ascendancy against the grain, revealing them to be documents of homelessness. First, however, it must be acknowledged that they have a history.

THE SOUL OF BATTERY PARK CITY

"In Battery Park there was nothing built—it was landfill—so it was not as if there was a history to the place. This was a construction site."[63] The sentiment that New York's waterfront development lies not only on the edge of the city but outside history is widespread, here voiced by a public artist who recently cooperated as part of an urban design team creating a "site-specific installation"[64] called South Cove, a park located in a residential area of Battery Park City. South Cove is only one of several collaborative "artworks" sponsored by the Fine Arts Committee of the Battery Park City Authority, the state agency overseeing what has become "the largest and most expensive real estate venture ever undertaken in New York City."[65] The elaborate art program, whose ambition matches the scope of the real-estate program, "will be," most critics agree, "New York's most important show-case for public art."[66] As a massive state intervention in New York redevelopment and, concurrently, exemplar of the governmental priority now accorded public art, Battery Park City elicits virtually unanimous accolades from public officials, real-estate and business groups, city planners, and art and architecture critics alike. The apotheosis, individually, of urban redevelopment and of the new public art, it also seals their union. Dominant aesthetic and urban discourses dissemble the nature of the alliance. Typical of the art world's role in this process is John Russell's response to the unveiling of designs for a major Battery Park City art collaboration—the public plaza of the World Financial Center, the project's commercial core. Commenting on the interaction between art and urbanism represented by this event, Russell starts by defining the essence of Battery Park City as aesthetic—the encounter between land and water:

Battery Park City is just across the water from the Statue of Liberty, as everyone knows, and it therefore occupies a particularly sensitive position. In every great city by the sea there comes a moment at which land meets with moving water. If the city is doing a good job, whether accidentally or by grand design, we feel at that moment that great cities and the sea are predestined partners. Their interaction can turn whole cities into works of art.[67]

Having intimated that maritime cities are shaped by transcendent forces, Russell invents romantic precedents for Battery Park City, first in a lineage of seaside cities—St. Petersburg, Constantinople, Venice—and then in the great painting, music, and literature that they inspired. But the meaning of Battery Park City is determined less by its natural topography—land meeting water—than by cultural discourses, including ideas drawn from art history about the nature of another encounter—that between art and the city. Art history has several traditional ways of describing this relationship. The city can be a work of art. The city, or the experience of the city, influences the subject matter and form of works of art. And, of course, there are artworks situated in the city—public art. Russell mobilizes all three categories, beginning, as we have seen, with the first. But he also implies that Battery Park City's natural destiny to be an aesthetic object generates reciprocal possibilities for revitalizing art as well. Fulfilling its task of effecting the city's metamorphosis into an artwork, art itself will be transformed: "What [the Battery Park City Fine Arts Committee] did was to redefine the respective roles of architect, art and landscape designer in the planning of large-scale building projects. Instead of being assigned pre-existing spaces in which to present works of art, the artists are to function from the outset as co-designers of the spaces."[68]

With this assertion, Russell enters the discourse about public art. Celebrating the "new notion of public art," he describes the new art as work that is immersed in, rather than aloof from, metropolitan life: "The general thrust of the plan was away from the hectoring monumentality of 'public sculpture' and toward a kind of art that gets down off the pedestal and works with everyday life as an equal partner."[69] But because Russell has already defined Battery Park City as itself a work of art in an aestheticist sense—as, that is, essentially independent of social life—he in fact frees the new public art to do exactly the opposite of what he claims: to ignore the city's social processes and their effect on the everyday life of residents. The purported metamorphosis of Battery Park City and, by extension, of all New York into an artwork conceals the city's social metamorphosis. If, then, the new art relinquishes its status as an aesthetic object isolated from "life," it does so only to confer that mystifying status on Battery Park City itself.

Similar mystifications pervade descriptions of all facets of Battery Park City. Surpassing even the usual promotional enthusiasm with which the mass media announce the progress of New York real-estate developments, articles and speeches about the completion of Battery Park City treat it as a symbol of New York's rise from "urban decay," "urban crisis," and "urban fiscal crisis." Battery Park City exemplifies multiple victories—of public policy, public space, urban design, and city planning.

> The phoenix-like rising of their [major corporations'] collective new home [Battery Park City] is demonstrating that predictions of lower Manhattan's demise were unduly hasty—like forecasts for other downtowns across the nation.[70]

> For this is the real significance of Battery Park City—not the specific designs of its parks or its buildings, good though they are, but the message the large complex sends about the importance of the public realm.[71]

> Battery Park City . . . is close to a miracle. . . . It is not perfect—but is far and away the finest urban grouping since Rockefeller Center and one of the better pieces of urban design of modern times.[72]

> A major governmental success and an example of what government can do.[73]

In short, an "urban dream"[74] and, in Governor Mario Cuomo's succinct assessment, "a soaring triumph."[75]

The project's physical foundation on a manufactured landfill generates still other optimistic tropes. Battery Park City is fresh, untrodden territory unencumbered by historical fetters and past failures, a glittering token of New York's ability to reverse deterioration, an emblem of hope. Ironically, the image bestowed on land that has been *literally* produced figuratively severs the space from the social processes that constituted it. Such conceits inadvertently convert Battery Park City's imaginary landfill into a palpable symbol not of the city's triumph but rather of the mental operation that fetishizes the city as a physical object. The landfill bespeaks the triumph of the technocratic city produced by powers that surpass people. From the project's inception, it was described as the creation by urban professionals of a "community." It provides, according to one planning critic, "the urban functions and amenities—shops, restaurants, schools, parks, rapid transit, utilities, public and recreational facilities—that make a real community."[76] "We see plan making and implementation," reads the master plan, "as interrelated parts of the same process: successful city building."[77] So attenuated are the bonds tying the landfill to its social foundations that, unsurprisingly, Battery Park City almost speaks for itself, stressing its origins in a technical achievement: "It is what it calls itself: a city. It begins by making its own land."[78]

Of course, Battery Park City does have a history. It did not spring full-blown from the water nor, as public relations accounts present it, from the imagination of such "visionaries" as Governor Nelson Rockefeller and Mayor John Lindsay, who then bequeathed their "dreams" to Governor Cuomo and Mayor Koch. It emerged, instead, from a series of conflicts over the use of public land and especially over the socioeconomic composition of city housing. Successive alterations in architecture and design comprise another historical dimension of the project. Intersecting these narratives, Battery Park City in its nearly complete present form synchronically occupies a key position in New York's historically constituted structure of spatial relations. Long overdue, an exhaustive critique of Battery Park City has yet to be undertaken. Here, I want to retrieve enough of the project's history so that we can see the ways in which art and design intervened at a critical moment of the project's unfolding. Restoring the housing question to representations of Battery Park City is crucial, since Battery Park City's design collaborations conceal the ramifications of this issue by placing political questions outside the province of beauty and utility. The organization of housing provision vividly embodies the political contradictions of contemporary urbanization. As the central expenditure of low-income families, housing most acutely reflects New York's social polarization. Withdrawal of housing from poor and minority residents forcibly denies them a right to the city. To illuminate Battery Park City's role in the development and distribution of housing is, then, to apprehend the project as a graphic emblem not of New York's triumph but of its uneven development.

When, in May 1966, Governor Rockefeller first proposed Battery Park City as a "new living space for New York" and part of his overall program for Lower Manhattan redevelopment, the plan included 14,000 apartments: 6,600 luxury, 6,000 middle-income, and 1,400 subsidized low-income units.[79] Mayor Lindsay also wanted to develop Lower Manhattan, but solely for high-income residents. On April 16, 1969, Rockefeller and Lindsay presented a compromise plan allocating only 1,266 out of 19,000 units to the poor.[80] About 5,000 middle-income units were included, with the remaining apartments earmarked for luxury use. Charles J. Urstadt, then chairman of the Battery Park City Authority, speaking as the state's mouthpiece and anticipating protest against the small proportion of low-income housing, announced that the housing mix was "not immutable."[81] Indeed, in the political climate of the late 1960s numerous liberal groups demanded greater proportions of low-income housing in Battery Park City in exchange for their support of Lindsay's reelection that year. Manhattan borough president Percy E. Sutton, calling the proposed development the "Riviera on the Hudson,"[82] stated that "it will use scarce public land resources and public powers to benefit mainly groups and social classes fully capable of meeting their housing needs without public aid."[83] More radical elements—tenant groups in particular—also voiced opposition. Yet Lindsay believed, as expressed in the 1969 Plan for New York City, that New York had to remain a "national center" in order to ensure the city's overall prosperity. "He saw preservation and enhancement of the central areas for the elite as crucial to the whole future of the city."[84] Placing low-income housing in Battery

Park City was, in Lindsay's words, "equivalent to putting low-income housing in the middle of the East Side of Manhattan."[85] Nonetheless, Lindsay needed the support of liberal Democrats, and in August he reversed his stand, asking that two-thirds of Battery Park City's 15,000 apartments be built for low- and middle-income tenants.[86] At a City Planning Commission hearing, a Lindsay aide stated that the mayor believed that "the social benefits to be gained from having an economically integrated community in lower Manhattan far outweigh 'the financial burdens.'"[87] Two months later, the Board of Estimate approved the revised Battery Park City plan, although representatives of the East Side Tenants Council and City Wide Anti-Poverty Committee on Housing still protested the liberal decision, arguing that "the low-income New Yorker who most needs new housing was being forgotten by the Battery Park City planners."[88] Several months earlier, Jack Rand of the East Side Tenants Council had charged in a letter to the *New York Times* that the authority was discriminating between Manhattan and Brooklyn in the distribution of low-income housing.[89]

Under the legal arrangements for the approved plan, the city of New York, owner of the land, would lease it under the terms of a Master Lease to the Battery Park City Authority, which would control its development. The Master Lease went into effect in June 1970. The authority planned to issue tax-exempt bonds to finance the project, with payment on the bonds to be made out of the revenues generated by development. The authority also intended to select private developers to build all of Battery Park City's housing, but, because of construction and housing market conditions, developers were unwilling to assume the risks involved without government support. The city moved to provide it. In 1972, "a consensus developed that several provisions in the original Master Lease . . . would be cumbersome, time-consuming or overly costly in the execution of the physical construction of the project, or would impede the marketability of the completed facilities and the administrative operations of the Authority."[90] Thus, the City Planning Commission and the Board of Estimate endorsed changes to "eliminate or modify the inevitable conditions."[91] These changes reduced the proportion of low-income housing to approximately twelve percent. Thirty percent of the units were to be luxury and fifty-six percent middle-income. But even the changed proportions do not indicate the full extent of the authority's class-biased action. Officially designated limits for establishing low-, middle-, and luxury-income housing eligibility always demand scrutiny, since, for one thing, housing costs increase, and, for another, income standards are constantly adjusted. By 1972, as sociologist Maynard T. Robison points out, "the cost of 'middle-income' housing was such that its residents would be quite well off."[92] Amendments that year to the Master Lease also eliminated the requirement that each of Battery Park City's residential buildings reflect the income mix of the entire project. This meant that low-income housing could be segregated.

Between 1972, when the first Battery Park City bonds were issued, and 1979, a year before the first payment on the bonds came due, the proposed housing mix remained stable but little progress was made on implementing the project. Site development on the ninety-one-acre landfill continued. Various construction deals were worked out, only to collapse. Robison, who has extensively investigated the unfolding of Battery Park City from its inception until 1979, attributes the lack of activity to two interrelated factors. First, he believes, all of the principal actors in the Battery Park City project—government officials, financial institutions, real-estate developers—wanted to build a luxury district for corporate and real-estate investment. The site, however, presented several obstacles impeding demand for expensive housing in the area: surrounded by unattractive and decaying terrain, it had no park, stores, restaurants, or entertainment and recreational facilities. The question for the major groups involved in Battery Park City was, it seems, not whether the public sector should encourage the privatization of the city by subsidizing the rich and guaranteeing business profits but "how to do so in the face of pressure to use public resources and the site to benefit groups other than the elite."[93]

By 1979, the turning point in Battery Park City's evolution, the answer had appeared in the form of the "fiscal crisis." Sanctioned by orthodox explanations of the mid-1970s crisis in New York's public finance, the state ultimately transferred Battery Park City's spatial resources to the private sector. Leasing the land to private developers, the authority sought to attract them through substantial tax abatements, exemptions, and financial incentives to use Battery Park City for office towers and luxury condominiums. The authority also undertook the task of site development for these projects, creating parks and other amenities to convert the area into an elite district as quickly as possible. In 1979 the immediate fiscal problem facing the Battery Park City Authority was the likelihood that, because it had not yet generated sufficient revenues, it would have to default on the first payment of principal—due November 1, 1980—of its outstanding bonds. City and state officials, developers, and urban planners agreed that Battery Park City's "failure" resulted from the project's overly ambitious conception and from New York's current fiscal troubles.[94] A "workout" plan, they believed, must be informed by knowledge of "the city's tough urban realities."[95] Thus, Battery Park City's situation assumed, just as the fiscal crisis itself did, an aura of inevitability that fostered acceptance of inequitable solutions.

Crises in public finance are not caused by inexorable economic laws, however, but by specific economic relations. Critics of conventional definitions of urban fiscal crisis stress varying alternative explanations, but, in general, they position it within the broader economic crises of capitalist countries.[96] Local crisis is inseparable from larger crises of the public sector during which social services are cut back in order to aid business. Some economists analyze urban fiscal crisis as a reflection of the inability of municipal governments to raise revenues in a new era of capital mobility and flexible accumulation. City governments, reacting to forces that are to a considerable extent outside their control, adopt policies oriented toward attracting private investment. Peter Marcuse, emphasizing the uses of "urban fiscal crisis" as a concept, points to two constituent factors.[97] The first is the problem inherent in capital accumulation, which, to counteract falling rates of profit, constantly seeks to cheapen labor costs and automate production. To accomplish these goals, capital shifts locations. The state, however, must bear the social costs of capital mobility: infrastructure provision, facilities for the working population, the redundant workforce left behind when businesses move elsewhere. Consequently, Marcuse identifies a real tendency to crisis within the economic and political systems but suggests that there is also a *fraudulent* crisis that justifies government policies transparently serving private interests. Both the real crises and the fraudulent one, however, should be perceived as processes in a particular social system, not as the natural result of inevitable economic forces. In this sense, the dominant construction of the category "urban fiscal crisis" is ideological. It presents crises as natural and then uses that naturalizing premise to justify transferring resources to the private sector and withholding them from the services most needed by the poor. It thus perpetuates the conditions that it purports to explain and vividly demonstrates the unequal weight of public and private interests in municipal finance policies.

In 1979 the ideology of crisis justified such inequitable measures in Battery Park City, aimed at providing the project's "last chance." [98] To rescue Battery Park City, a new legal framework, financial scheme, and master design plan were adopted to "make something useful" out of the site. [99] Principally, the goal was to attract private financing. To do so, the new plan provided substantial tax abatements and other financial incentives and relocated Battery Park City's commercial zone, previously relegated to the landfill's southern end, to a central location. The plan eliminated all subsidized low-, moderate-, and middle-income housing as well.

To facilitate these changes, the new plan also included an altered legal arrangement, a variant of a widespread strategy by which government encourages the private sector and cushions it from direct public control. According to an agreement worked out between the administrations of Governor Hugh Carey and Mayor Koch, the state used its power of condemnation to bring the Battery Park City land under the direct ownership of the state Urban Development Corporation. In this way, the city yielded much of its legal control over the project. Indeed, the purpose of the maneuver was "to free the project from the welter of city regulations." [100]

But what, in this case, is meant by "the welter of city regulations?" The shift of legal ownership of Battery Park City from the city government to a state authority actually ensured, under the guise of antibureaucratic efficiency, that developers would be liberated, as far as possible, from the constraints imposed by existing democratic procedures for regulating land-use and planning decisions in New York: community board reviews, public hearings, and City Planning Commission approval. Authorities—public corporations empowered to issue bonds in order to undertake economic activity—are one of the few popularly accepted forms by which the United States government engages in economic ventures. As Annmarie Hauck Walsh concludes in an exhaustive study of government corporations, they are largely protected from public accountability. Justified by the claim that their quasi-independent status makes them less vulnerable to political influence, authorities are in reality less accessible to government regulation, community interests and local pressures. Removing Battery Park City from city ownership helped remove it from the demands to which municipal government is especially sensitive. "Hybrid creatures," says Walsh, authorities are "corporations without shareholders, political jurisdictions without voters or taxpayers."[101] An interrogation of the authority form of public business cannot be separated from other questions about decision making and resource allocation since, organized and run according to business principles, authorities frequently undertake projects on the basis of financial viability rather than public service. Financing through the bond market—with its attendant imperatives to guarantee the security of bonds and, further, to make them profitable on the secondary market—also affects the type of enterprises promoted by authorities. The significance of these criteria can be grasped in the fact that in May 1980, following the adoption of the new Battery Park City Plan, Standard and Poor, a leading financial rating agency, granted Battery Park City's new bonds the highest possible credit rating, thus assuring their successful sale.[102] Indeed, the new plan predicted financial results so successfully that later in the same year, Olympia and York Properties was conditionally approved as developer of Battery Park City's entire commercial sector. Eventually, the commercial structures materialized, aided by tax advantages and low-interest loans, as the World Financial Center. By April 1982, Battery Park City had become New York's "newest prestige address."[103] "As a result of economic forces no one could have foreseen," the New York Times reported, "luxury-level housing for upper-middle income or higher-income people is at present the only kind that can be built."[104]

The Battery Park City scheme released physical planning and land-use decisions from "bureaucratic" entanglements only to submit them to the control of a technocracy amenable to redevelopment—New York's urban design professionals. Urban designers had, in fact, been welcomed into New York City government as agents of public policy in the late 1960s, exactly when Battery Park City was first proposed. Alexander Cooper Associates, an urban design firm that later, in the 1980s, engineered major redevelopment projects in New York and New Jersey, prepared the third component of the Battery Park City "workout," the project's new master plan, complying with the mandate to make the project "more attractive for investment and responsive to current planning approaches."[105] The draft plan outlined the basic design that ultimately determined Battery Park City's final form. Earlier, both principals of the firm, Alexander Cooper and Stanton Eckstut, had been leaders of Mayor Lindsay's Urban Design Group. In 1971, Cooper served as executive director of the Urban Design Council, precursor of the Urban Design Group of which Cooper was, for a time, also director. It is a measure of the extent to which planning and aesthetic discourses block comprehension of the urban social context that in 1969, during the height of agitation for low-income housing in Battery Park City, the mayor's Urban Design Council, along with the Municipal Art Society, endorsed the strongly contested Battery Park City plan without mentioning the housing controversy at all.[106]

More than ten years later, designers again marginalized housing as an issue in "successful city building" when they devised Battery Park City's master plan. Directing the appearance, use, and organization of Battery Park City land, the discourse about design and the actual spaces that the planners produced also assumed the task of rewriting the site's history, not so much concealing social reality as transposing it into design. For if Battery Park City's plan became a medium for evacuating history as action and conflict, it did so by reinventing history as spectacle and tradition. Thus, in 1979, the moment when Battery Park City changed most definitively and when New York entered its accelerated phase of restructuring, development proceeded under a master plan stressing continuity, permanence, and invariance. Just when decisions about land use became increasingly privatized and were withdrawn from public control, designers resurrected talk about public space in a form that represses its political implications. Just when Battery Park City was given over to the needs of profit, ensuring not only that low-income housing needs would be unmet but also that more people would become homeless through raised property values in the city, emphasis intensified on designed spaces that would allegedly fulfill essential human needs. With the construction of Battery Park City as the epitome of abstract space—hierarchical, homogeneous, fragmented—designers mobilized a discourse about diversity, history, and site-specificity. Early in the process, the Battery Park City Authority incorporated public art into the master plan: in 1982, "as part of its commitment to good design," the authority established the Fine Arts Program "to engage artists in the planning and design of the community's open spaces."[107] Besides South Cove Park, collaborative ventures between artists, architects, and landscape architects now include the plaza of the World Financial Center, the South Gardens, and West Thames Street Park. Numerous other "public" works were selected because they are considered to be "sensitive," if not intrinsic, to their sites.

The 1979 master plan discarded the original futuristic plan for Battery Park City, which had been adopted, with Lindsay's support, in the late 1960s. Replacing the old arrangement, which emphasized Battery Park City's architectural disjunction from the rest of Manhattan, the Cooper-Eckstut design, labeled "A Realist's Battery Park City,"[108] aimed to integrate Battery Park City—physically, visually, functionally—with New York, making it a supposedly organic extension not only of adjacent neighborhoods in Lower Manhattan but of the rest of the city. The layout extended—and slightly reoriented in the direction of the water—Manhattan's rectilinear grid, subdivided the land into smaller development parcels, and relocated the commercial area. Further, the plan emphasized the use of traditional architectural elements and street furniture for the waterfront esplanade and other public spaces, objects copied from past structures in old New York neighborhoods—Central Park, Gramercy Park, Madison Avenue, and the Upper West Side—to confer the status of tradition. "We wanted to make it look as though nothing was done," explained Eckstut.[109] In addition, the new plan created a system of conventional blocks to allow developers to take on small parcels and established flexible controls that do not prescribe final designs for individual buildings. All of these features were adopted to assure, within the framework of an intensified redevelopment program, the diversity and sense of historical memory that mark a city produced over time. History, then, was to be simulated in a compressed time frame and diversity isolated in physical style and in the realm of historic "preservation."[110] In city planning rhetoric, "history" became so malleable that the notion that Battery Park City has no history was exchanged for the notion that Battery Park City has always existed.

The Cooper-Eckstut plan, sanctioned by fiscal crisis ideology, stated unequivocally that "the mechanism for providing large numbers of subsidized middle- and moderate-income housing—as originally envisioned—does not now exist. . . . The State is not in a position to sponsor moderate-income housing and there is no technique for meeting the needs of this income group."[111] Low-income housing received no mention, despite the designers' contention that a revised plan could "pursue a planning concept more in keeping with development realities . . . without sacrificing the amenities that make the project desirable."[112] When Governor Cuomo took office in 1983, however, he voiced concern about the fact that public land was being given over on a grand scale to luxury housing and commercial development. According to Meyer S. Frucher, president of the Battery Park City Authority, the governor told him to give the project "a soul." The soul, which Cuomo has since defined as Battery Park City's "social purpose," materialized in 1986 in the form of the Housing New York Corporation, a state agency empowered to issue bonds backed by Battery Park City revenues in order to finance the provision of low- and moderate-income housing in New York City. The first phase of the plan, which contributed its funds to Mayor Koch's program to rehabilitate city-owned properties, consists of the renovation of 1,850 apartments in Harlem and the South Bronx, with one-third of the units reserved for the homeless. Battery Park City's "soul," offered as proof of the benefits of public-private partnership, has also been loosely extended as a rubric under which all of the project's "public" benefits—its art and open spaces—are grouped. No doubt the government agencies and officials most deeply implicated in Battery Park City would like people to view the "soul" of the project as, indeed, its animating principle. Yet even without examining the details of the city's housing plan—what percentage of the units will actually serve the homeless, how they will be run and maintained, whether as part of cross-subsidy programs they will, primarily, encourage redevelopment—several realities frustrate this contention. First, it begs the question of whether low- and moderate-income housing should be provided by channeling public resources toward large-scale redevelopment. Since redevelopment, as part of broader restructuring, produces homelessness, no matter what palliatives are administered to mitigate and push out of sight its worst effects, we are being asked to believe that the housing crisis can be cured only by publicly encouraging its causes. Second, the assertion that the Battery Park City plan is a triumph for the public sector places the government squarely in support of the spatial relations that the plan reinforces—luxury enclaves in the city center shielded from areas for the poor and minorities on the periphery. Such an assertion supports the idea that public resources should be directed toward the production of New York as a segregated city.

It is, of course, true, as one expert observed about Battery Park City's low- and moderate-income housing program, that "advocates of low-income housing will take housing wherever and however they can get it."[113] But this should not obscure, through either resignation or a false sense of victory, the realization that the Battery Park City program confirms not the triumph of public policy but rather the manner in which New York's preeminent space of wealth, power, and decision making has been forced to fashion the dominated spaces, too, thus corroborating Lefebvre's description of the contradictions of capitalist space. In keeping with Lefebvre's evaluation of urban planning, the spatial design of Battery Park City suppresses this contradiction by substituting an image that presents the area's abstract space as natural, traditional, diverse, and, moreover, functionally integrated with the entire city. Public art collaborations and the discourse that validates them also assume these tasks. Paramount among their methods is the assertion that the spaces they produce are useful. "It seems," says a public artist at Battery Park City, "that there are archetypal needs that are met regularly in different cultures—needs for protected spaces, places of distraction. I am interested in poking at these potent situations and trying to find ways of creating equivalents within our own context."[114] The humanist myth rehearsed in this statement about universal conditions and needs aims, as Roland Barthes observed more than thirty years ago, "to suppress the determining weight of History: we are held back at the surface of an identity, prevented precisely by sentimentality from penetrating into this ulterior zone of human behavior where historical alienation introduces some 'differences' which we shall here quite simply call 'injustices.'"[115]

Surely, within what the artist calls "our own context"—New York's social polarization, uneven development, and homelessness, all exemplified by Battery Park City—to posit that a "need for protected spaces" is *met* in Battery Park City can only perpetuate such injustices. To recognize this operation, however, art discourse must renounce its own humanist myths and acknowledge its own specificity within historical sites. For the weight of Battery Park City's past, as well as its current position within the urban structure, enables us to "know very well," just as Barthes knew about the character of work in capitalist society, that shelter in New York "is 'natural' just as long as it is 'profitable.'"[116] Suppressing this realization, Battery Park City's "soul"—its public art and spaces—mentally released through universalizing notions about beauty and utility, from the material conditions of the project's existence, performs the function of myth. Like the other portion of the "soul"—the low-income housing physically removed from Battery Park City—it attempts to reconcile conflicts arising between the belief that the city should serve social needs and the experience of New York's domination by business and real estate. It is hardly surprising, then, that accounts of the useful public art at Battery Park City fail to comment on major transformations in the project's social uses. No matter how much it speaks of the space's coherence, then, this art fractures the social picture. For, apparently integrated and diverse, Battery Park City is homogenized and hierarchized. Represented as harmonious, it conceals domination. "Historical," it rejects time, converting the past as a product of social struggle into interchangeable fragments of the city's architectural remains. "Public," it transforms public space into places where selected New Yorkers are permitted to do what a *New York Times* editorial called "their public thing."[117] In the end, Battery Park City's art and design do try to integrate the area with New York but with a redeveloped New York—ghettoized and exclusionary.

A Beautiful and Useful Weapon

In the winter of 1987–88, Mayor Koch ordered that homeless people living in public places must be examined by authorities and, if judged mentally incompetent, forcibly hospitalized. Coinciding with these events, which occurred in the

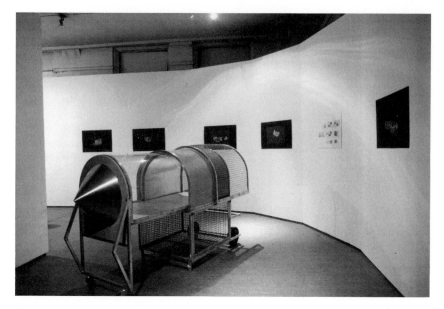

Krzysztof Wodiczko, installation of the Homeless Vehicle at the Clocktower, New York, 1988 (photo courtesy Krzysztof Wodiczko).

middle of a season that is always the most difficult for people without homes, the Clocktower, a city-owned exhibition space in Lower Manhattan, presented a proposal for a public artwork called the *Homeless Vehicle Project*.[118] The exhibition consisted of several elements combined in a presentation that reproduced the traditional format in which urban planning and architecture proposals are unveiled to the public. The show's nucleus was a prototype of a stark, industrial-looking object—a vehicle designed by the artist Krzysztof Wodiczko in consultation with several homeless men. Constructed of aluminum, steel mesh, sheet metal, and Plexiglas, the vehicle's purpose is to facilitate the existence of one segment of the evicted population: individuals who live on the streets and survive by collecting, sorting, storing, and returning cans and bottles to supermarkets in exchange for deposits. The homeless vehicle would enable this group of residents to circulate more easily through the city, a mobility necessitated by their lack of permanent housing and their mode of subsistence. Besides easing the job of scavenging, the cart offers a degree of shelter. Engineered so that it can expand or fold into a variety of positions, it furnishes minimal facilities for eating, sleeping, washing, defecating, and sitting. Sketches of the vehicle demonstrating different aspects of its operation were displayed at the Clocktower along with the model. Also shown were preliminary drawings revealing alterations made by the artist at various stages of the vehicle's evolution as he responded to comments and requests from the consultants.

In a separate area of the gallery, Wodiczko simulated an outdoor urban landscape by projecting onto the walls slides depicting public spaces in New York City: Tompkins Square, City Hall Park, and the area directly outside the Municipal Building. Using montage techniques, he infiltrated the city spaces with ghostly images of the vehicle being maneuvered through these urban spaces by its potential users. The images were enlarged from sketches and their spectral appearance is the result of two technical procedures: the drawings were printed white on black, and, blown up, their outlines became slightly blurred. By visualizing the vehicle in municipal spaces, the projected images thematically related homelessness to the action and inaction of local government, accusing the city not only of failing to cure the problem but of producing it. But Wodiczko's slides also associated homelessness with more dispersed apparatuses of power in the city. The proposal adopted the conventional form of architecture, city planning, and urban design proposals: the visual projection of proposed objects and spatial alterations onto an image or model of the existing urban context. Generally, such projections show the positive, benign, or, at the very least, unobtrusive effect of the proposed changes on the potential sites. Modifying this convention and creating images that merge physical and social sites, Wodiczko's slide presentation both commented on and established its difference from the official role that environmental disciplines play in New York today. These disciplines—examples of what Lefebvre calls "traditional spatial knowledge"—engineer redevelopment, eject people from their homes, and banish the evicted. At the same time, they suppress the evidence of rupture by assigning social functions and groups to designated zones within a seemingly organic spatial

Slide projections of the *Homeless Vehicle Project* at the Clocktower, New York, 1988 (photos courtesy Krzysztof Wodiczko and Galerie Lelong).

hierarchy. Wodiczko's presentation, by contrast, symbolically lodged the homeless in the urban center, concretizing the memory of social disruption and envisioning the impact of the evicted on the city.[119] Taped conversations between Wodiczko and people without homes about the vehicle's design played continuously during the exhibition, and the gallery distributed a text containing transcripts of the conversations and an essay about the project coauthored by Wodiczko and David V. Lurie.

Dictated by the practical needs and direct requests of men who live and work on the streets, the *Homeless Vehicle Project* implicitly expressed support for people who, deprived of housing, choose—against official coercion—to resist being relegated to dangerous and dehumanizing shelters. The homeless vehicle, in no way offering itself as a solution, nonetheless challenged the city's solution: the

proliferation of a shelter system not simply as a temporary adjunct to but in lieu of substantive construction of decent permanent housing. Questioning government housing and shelter policies does not obviate the need for advocates to support, under crisis conditions, the construction of low-income housing "wherever and however they can get it." It simply means that advocacy of housing and even shelters must be framed within a critique that also voices the terms of substantive change—social ownership of housing, opposition to the privileges of private property—and discloses how policies offered as solutions frequently exacerbate or merely regulate the problem. Currently, government stresses "temporary" shelters that, given the lack of new public housing construction, tacitly become permanent. Alternatively, government manufactures cumbersome financing schemes by which a grossly inadequate number of low-income units are provided without direct public expenditure, as a means of facilitating redevelopment and, frequently, for private gain. At the same time, the city continues to channel large subsidies to business

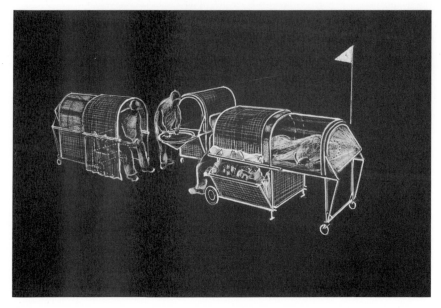

Krzysztof Wodiczko, design and drawing of the Homeless Vehicle, 1987 (photo courtesy Krzysztof Wodiczko).

and developers, thus disavowing and perpetuating the relationship between home-lessness and the city's economic transformation.

Described by one critic as "an insidious form of institutionalized displace-ment purporting to be humane while incarcerating thousands whose only 'crime' is poverty," [120] the shelter system is, however, not only necessitated by restructuring and real-estate development but itself participates in New York's spatial division into core and peripheral areas. By increasing the visibility of the evicted who, in reality, already inhabit urban space, the homeless vehicle dramatizes the right of the poor not to be isolated and excluded. Heightened visibility, however, is only the necessary, not the sufficient, condition for this dramatization. Indeed, visibility can also be used, as it is by conservative urban critics, to strengthen demands for the removal of the evicted. But the homeless vehicle represents the evicted as

Krzysztof Wodiczko, Homeless Vehicle Prototype, 1988 (photo courtesy Krzysztof Wodiczko and Galerie Lelong).

active New York residents whose means of subsistence is a legitimate element of the urban social structure. It thus focuses attention on that structure and, altering the image of the city, not only challenges the economic and political systems that evict the homeless but subverts the modes of perception that exile them.

The homeless vehicle is, then, both a practical instrument and a symbolic utterance. There is no contradiction between these identities. One of the vehicle's practical functions is, after all, precisely to give a voice to—to gain social recognition for—people without homes. But by openly combining practical and rhetorical functions, Wodiczko's vehicle speaks to a question central to debates among the homeless and their advocates and faced by all cultural practices addressing New York's environment: How is it possible to recognize and respond to homelessness as an emergency situation without fostering, as do some proposals designing

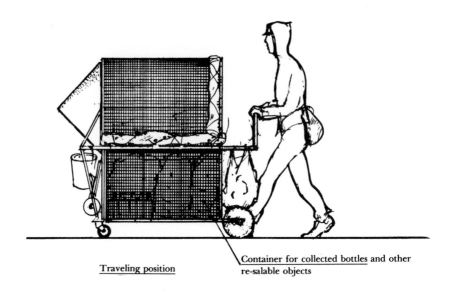

Traveling position

Container for collected bottles and other re-salable objects

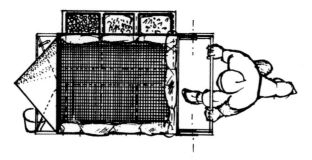

Krzysztof Wodiczko, design and drawings of the Homeless Vehicle, 1988.

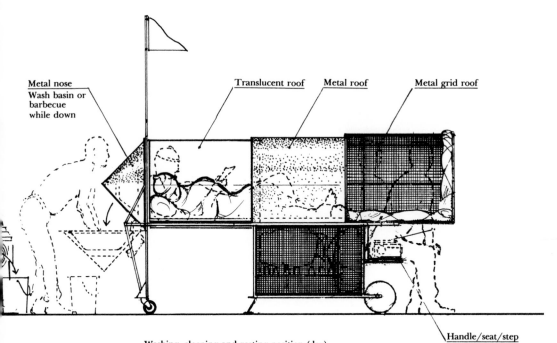

Metal nose
Wash basin or
barbecue
while down

Translucent roof   Metal roof   Metal grid roof

Washing, sleeping and resting position (day)
Metal nose operates as emergency exit,
storage for basin and other objects and tools, or, when open, as
basin or barbecue

Handle/seat/step
in sitting position

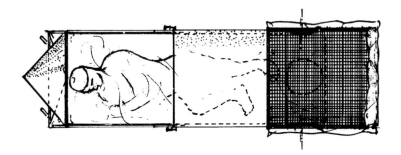

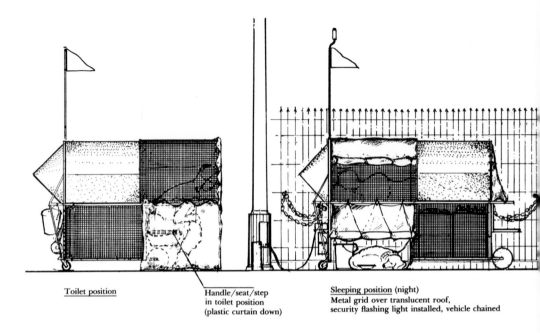

Toilet position

Handle/seat/step
in toilet position
(plastic curtain down)

Sleeping position (night)
Metal grid over translucent roof,
security flashing light installed, vehicle chained

equipment for the homeless, an acceptance of the current situation and a concealment of its causes? One answer is that as art refers to a practical function, it must
also reveal its status as a signifying object, thereby stressing that no element of the
built environment performs a function that is simply natural and prior to representation. Functions are socially produced, often by the very objects that seem merely
to fulfill them. Indeed, if practical plans to help the homeless survive on the streets
do not call attention to the social construction of their own function—and do not
identify the forces producing homelessness—they are likely, no matter how well
intentioned, to become vehicles of the functionalist rhetoric that legitimates
redevelopment.

Openly cooperative, of course, are those plans sponsored by redevelopment
associations themselves, groups who proffer charitable projects as evidence of redevelopment's benefits or of corporate philanthropy. A proposal sponsored by the
Community Redevelopment Agency (CRA) of Los Angeles and exhibited in 1986
at New York's Storefront for Art and Architecture's "Homeless at Home" exhibi-

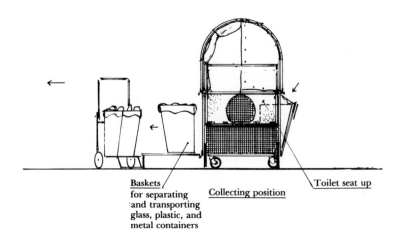

Baskets
for separating
and transporting
glass, plastic, and
metal containers

Collecting position

Toilet seat up

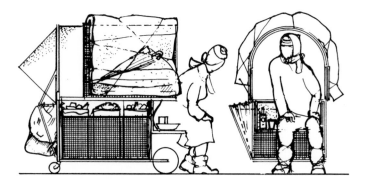

Resting position while traveling and collecting

tion epitomizes this tactic.[121] Observing that Los Angeles's Skid Row lies within the CRA's 1,500-acre Central Business District Redevelopment Project, the CRA announced a plan to direct a portion of the tax revenues generated from the new development and from rising property values toward programs to aid the inhabitants of Skid Row, "recognizing," as the proposal's text put it, "that skid rows will

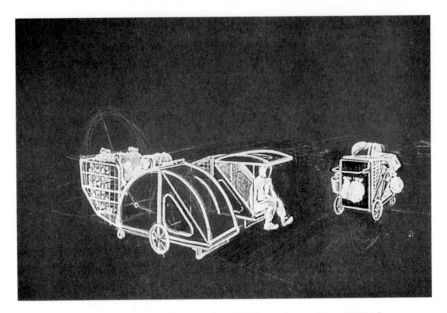

Krzysztof Wodiczko, initial design for Homeless Vehicle, resting position, 1987 (photo courtesy Krzysztof Wodiczko).

always exist" and seeking to "reduce the impact of Skid Row on the adjacent downtown area." Primarily, these projects try to shelter the redeveloped city from the adverse effects of the homelessness it causes and, simultaneously, to counteract the system's legitimation crisis by presenting homelessness as a transhistorical problem.

The *Homeless Vehicle Project* also proposes a way to alleviate some of the worst aspects of evicted people's lives. But in so doing, it strengthens, rather than reduces, their impact on the central business district. The project's critical force springs from the interaction between its practical and signifying purposes, a reciprocity concretized in the design of the vehicle, which, on the one hand, recalls Bauhaus functionalism and, on the other, resembles a weapon. The vehicle thus becomes a tool used against the apparatus of redevelopment. Instead of rendering the homeless invisible or reinforcing an image of them as passive objects, the homeless vehicle illuminates their mobile existence. Instead of severing or cosmeticizing the link between homelessness and redevelopment, the project visualizes the connection through its intervention in the transformed city. It facilitates the seizure of space by homeless subjects rather than containing them in prescribed locations. Instead of restoring a surface calm to the "ascendant" city, as reformist plans try to do, it disrupts the coherent urban image that today is constructed only by neutralizing homelessness. Consequently, the homeless vehicle legitimates people without homes rather than the dominant spaces that exclude them, symbolically countering the city's own ideological campaign against the poor. In a minor, yet exemplary, gesture in this crusade, Mayor Koch, as we have seen, tried to eject the homeless from Grand Central Terminal by aiming against them the weapon of functionalism. The terminal's objective function, he insisted, is to serve the needs of travel, and it is impeded by the stationary homeless. The homeless vehicle retaliates by announcing a different function for the urban environment: the fulfillment of the travel needs of the evicted. It foregrounds a collateral system already built by these residents to support their daily lives. Yet the vehicle does not simply pit one use or group against another. It subverts the rhetoric of utility, silencing the city that seems to speak for itself—the instrumental city—by disrupting the city's silence on the subject of social needs. For the homeless vehicle's function, far from general or inevitable, is clearly a socially created scandal. The work strikes at the heart of the well-managed city, an image that today functions for the needs of profit and control.

At Battery Park City, collaborative public art helps create this image under the guises of utility, beauty, and social responsibility—of forging a rapprochement between art and life. But the homeless vehicle, too, is useful and collaborative. A skilled professional has applied sophisticated design principles to an object of everyday life that, intruding upon space, practices a mode of urban design. But these superficial similarities underscore profound differences. Responding to an emergency, the homeless vehicle is quick and impermanent. Implicit in its impermanence is a demand that its function become obsolete and a belief in the mutability of the social situation that necessitates it. Battery Park City appears to stabilize this situation, but such stationary and monumental spaces become the target of the Homeless Vehicle. While Battery Park City art employs design to enforce dominant social organization, the homeless vehicle uses design for counterorganization, rearranging the transformed city. The shelter system, peripheralization of low-income housing, deterritorialization of the poor—these aspects of contemporary spatial relations are fashioned by Battery Park City art that, producing the privileged spaces of the central city, retains its own privilege as an object outside the political realm. It converts social reality into design. The homeless vehicle, a vehicle for organizing the interests of the dominated classes into a group expression, employs design to illuminate social reality, supporting the right of these groups to refuse marginalization.

In the essay accompanying the exhibition of the *Homeless Vehicle Project,* Wodiczko and Lurie stress the significance of collaborative relationships between professional designers and the vehicle's users: "Direct participation of users in the construction of the vehicle is the key to developing a vehicle which belongs to its users, rather than merely being appropriated by them." [122] Countering the technocracy of design, they seem to allude to the difference between a vehicle planned specifically by and for the evicted and the adaptation by the evicted of supermarket shopping carts. Only through the collective production of objects by their users, Lurie and Wodiczko suggest, might people resist domination. Yet the homeless vehicle's substitution of an actively produced object for an appropriated one suggests the need for a more sweeping change—the production by users of their living space. Just as the project negates the abstraction of function from specific social relations, it challenges the abstraction of the city from its inhabitants. At the same time, however, the vehicle suggests that even under current circumstances production is not confined to those who manufacture the city but includes those who use and appropriate it.

Appropriating the space of the city—reclaiming space for social needs against space organized for profit and control—and diverting it, in a manner similar to what the Situationists called *détournement,* from its prescribed functions, the homeless vehicle responds to ordinary needs and horrifying realities yet, in a mixture of fantasy and reality that some critics find "disturbing," offers a vision of the emancipation of the environment. "In order to change life," writes Lefebvre, "society, space, architecture, even the city must change."[123] Such a possibility will, of course, not be realized in isolated acts of *détournement*. Still, by upholding the "right to the city," the *Homeless Vehicle Project* corroborates Ledrut's definition of the city ("an environment formed by the interaction and the integration of different practices") and thus anticipates the construction not simply of beautiful or well-managed cities—they are, after all, only by-products—but of a "work of life." Through this imaginative act, the project contributes as well to the construction of an oppositional public sphere that counters the dominant relations organizing public space. The production of such a public practice cannot, in fact, be separated from the production of New York City as a living work. Yet the *Homeless Vehicle Project* also testifies to the degree of knowledge about urbanism and to the astuteness, even stealth, of operation required by public art if it is to accomplish these goals. For, given its reliance on corporate and civic approval, public art, like New York itself, will no doubt develop unevenly.

In 1985, the large survey exhibition "German Art in the 20th Century" opened at the Royal Academy of Arts in London.[1] On the threshold, visitors found themselves face to face with two canvases painted by Ernst Ludwig Kirchner on the eve of World War I—*Berlin Street Scene* (1913) and *Friedrichstrasse, Berlin* (1914). The effects of the encounter were, of course, not uncalculated. This immediate confrontation with Kirchner's impassioned city paintings—and with the prostitutes they depict—solicited the audience to accept a version of German art history institutionalized at the Royal Academy as a chronicle of the durability of expressionism: its emergence in the early twentieth century, suppression by the Nazi regime, and postwar, post-occupation resurfacing. The exhibition plan conformed to this tripartite chronology. Expressionist works dominated, filling numerous galleries at the beginning and end of the show. Sandwiched between these flourishing epochs were, first, an artistically fallow fascist period, then a Cold War interlude of "Parisian-style abstraction." "German Art in the Twentieth Century" thus set up a stark opposition—expressionism versus both fascist and foreign oppression—that defined expressionism as Germany's national artistic style and equated it with individual and collective salvation.

But, like all historicist continuities, this representation of modern German art as part of an unfolding, if periodically repressed, romantic continuum is

Ernst Ludwig Kirchner, *Berlin Street Scene*, 1913
(Brücke Museum, Berlin).

Ernst Ludwig Kirchner, *Friedrichstrasse, Berlin*, 1914
(Staatsgalerie Stuttgart).

founded on its own repressions, consigning to a separate domain the art practices
that rupture its coherence. The exhibition's subtitle, "Painting and Sculpture 1905–
1985," marks such a repression. With a single categorical stroke, it limits twentieth-
century German art to traditional aesthetic media and so excises the revolutionary
photomontage production of Berlin dada as well as John Heartfield's photomontages for *AIZ—Arbeiter Illustrierte Zeitung* (Workers' Illustrated Newspaper). This is
no trivial exclusion. Dada artists used photomontage largely to repudiate expressionism's subjectivist forms of social protest, forms historically invested in the medium of painting. For dadaists, expressionism was a "sentimental resistance to the
times," "a moral safety valve," part of Germany's "spirit business," and therefore "a
compensatory phenomenon."[2] "Engulfed in esthetically surpassing the world,"[3]

expressionism ensured the continuation of oppressive social conditions *in* the world. But, as Raoul Hausmann wrote, the term *photomontages*—designating works composed of ready-made, mechanically produced images and typography that were cut up and reassembled, works using mass-media photographs to shatter the media's own messages, arousing viewers from passive aesthetic contemplation, encouraging collective reception, and reaching out to new audiences through new channels of distribution—"translated our aversion to playing artist."[4]

Heartfield, during his dada period, also tied expressionism to bourgeois ideology; later, his photomontage campaign against fascism, conducted on the covers and in the pages of *AIZ,* linked Nazism to the logic of capitalism. His work was explicitly antiexpressionist *and* antifascist. Its presence at the Royal Academy would have seriously disrupted an art-historical narrative that polarizes expressionism and Nazism, associating expressionism's survival with the country's liberation. The decision to include only art that conforms to conventional modes of aesthetic production and reception cannot be dismissed, then, as a practical response to the inevitable pressures of curatorship, permitting, as one organizer explained, "the concentration and concision necessary to the exhibition."[5] Neither can it be neutralized as a vagary of individual taste nor exalted as a liberty taken in the name of cultural pluralism. It was, rather, a defensive operation launched against the very perception by the museum public of the troublesome material that formed the exhibition's structuring absence.

The restriction of German art to painting and sculpture served still other ends that, like the thesis of the triumph of expressionism, were foreshadowed by the Kirchner street scenes at the entrance. Because Heartfield and the dada movement that spawned his work were centered in Berlin, their removal made it possible to associate Berlin primarily with expressionism, even to suggest that Berlin is an "expressionist city." Dada's absence cleared the stage for an uncontested dialogue between mutually supportive aesthetic and urban discourses that, respectively, define expressionism as a transcendent artistic style and Berlin as a mythical metropolis.

Indeed, in placing Kirchner's icons of *Brücke grosstadt*—"big-city"—painting at the origin of a remodeled tradition of modern German art, the curators positioned urban expressionism as Germany's consummate artistic achievement and

Berlin as its privileged location. Implying a natural bond between the two, the exhibition's opening foretold its end—the galleries of canvases by neoexpressionist painters credited with rediscovering Germany's national artistic heritage in West Berlin decades after the end of World War II. As "German Art in the 20th Century" moved inexorably toward its close, it thus attempted to fulfill yet another agenda: to furnish the most lavish pedigree to date for German neo- or, as some critics called it, pseudo-expressionism of the 1980s.[6]

In this respect, the Royal Academy exhibition crowned and also signaled the demise of a legitimating process begun in the late 1970s. At that time, a common strategy for endowing "the new German painting" with the authority of artistic tradition consisted of categorizing its various branches on the basis of such standard art-historical criteria as geographic location, chronological period, group identity, iconography, and style. The resulting typologies invariably reserved a category for a group of paintings that were not only produced in Berlin but, it was claimed, "represented" Berlin and, more broadly, the "urban situation." Labeling this work "urban," supporters tried to invest it with social relevance even as they resurrected a concept of the urban as vague and regressive as the aesthetic ideas that the painting embodies. That such claims were made at a moment when new urban conflicts had erupted in Berlin, as they had in other Western cities, compels one to question how this alliance of urban and aesthetic thought defined the social process of urbanism and the space of that process, the city.

Why were we routinely asked to believe that Rainer Fetting's oil painting of van Gogh standing in front of the Berlin Wall is a significant, indeed emblematic, depiction of Berlin in the 1980s?[7] On what grounds was Fetting's image of the artist's romantic alienation and not, say, Hans Haacke's multimedia installation *Broadness and Diversity of the Ludwig Brigade* elevated to this position? Haacke's work, after all, addressed political, economic, and cultural issues specific to its Berlin site. Why—to raise even more complex questions—was Rainer Fassbinder's play *Garbage, the City and Death,* which addressed alliances between real-estate speculators and city government, prevented from opening in Frankfurt due to alleged anti-Semitism while canvases of mythologized street figures presented in the form of primitivist stereotypes were internationally celebrated as representations of ur-

Rainer Fetting, *Van Gogh und Mauer*, 1978.

ban reality? What institutional events and art-historical discourses produced these constructions? Whose interests in contemporary urban struggles do they ultimately serve?

Helke Sander, in her 1977 film *Die allseitig reduzierte Persönlichkeit—REDUPERS* (The All-round Reduced Personality—REDUPERS), tells the story of a group of women who are producing a photographic documentary about West Berlin. "What the women see," Sander later explained,

Helmut Middendorf, *Electric Night,* 1981.

who don't view reality through ideological blinders—does not serve
to uphold the existing image of Berlin. West Berlin is different from
other cities, among other things because a wall leads around it, and
because an elaborate system of ideological interpretations has been developed for the special status of Berlin. This is what the women realize
after reflecting on their encounter with the city.[8]

Stressing the historical features that distinguish Berlin from other cities, most notably its division by the Wall, Sander's film also suggests that Berlin is internally
fissured by other differences and social antagonisms. The experience of the city
varies, for instance, with the gender of its residents. In striking contrast to Sander's
insistence on Berlin's differences and therefore on its historical and ideological
specificity, celebrants of the city's 1980s art scene asserted that circumstances in
Berlin typify a universal, though intensified, urban experience. Insisting that Berlin
symbolizes something called "the urban condition," they concluded in turn that

neoexpressionism quintessentially embodied that condition because of its intrinsic connection to the archetypal modern city.

Far from an essential bond, however, this link was forged discursively. It was reinforced throughout the 1980s by a series of exhibitions in London and Berlin, of which "German Art in the 20th Century" could be considered the culmination. The trajectory of these exhibitions reveals permutations in the organizers' principles, changes that end in reversal: having started out with a purported commitment to art practices that question aesthetic neutrality, the curators retreated, following the political tenor of the period, to an uncritical affirmation of art's autonomy and redemptive powers. Yet one element remained constant. The Berlin site, common to strongly contrasting, even opposing, art practices, was used to support both positions. It thus gave an appearance of continuity to what was actually a capricious exhibition history.

In 1979, the Whitechapel Art Gallery presented "13° E: Eleven Artists Working in Berlin," one of a number of London events devoted that year to contemporary art in Berlin. The Whitechapel show coincided with, and declared its firm opposition to, an exhibition of contemporary German critical realism and German art of the 1920s being held at the Institute of Contemporary Arts under the title "Berlin: A Critical View." The Whitechapel catalogue attacked what it called the "official" standing of critical realism, manifested in the Berlin Senate's financial support of the ICA show and its refusal of funds for the Whitechapel event. Judging by the number of international exhibitions and publications that followed, the Whitechapel show introduced a pertinent topic.[9] Nicholas Serota, the Whitechapel's director, maintained in his catalogue introduction that "13° E: Eleven Artists Working in Berlin" intended to explore what it means to represent Berlin. The show was prompted, he wrote, by interest in "the work of artists using art as a means of social enquiry or political struggle,"[10] and the artists were chosen because their work addressed social questions and the conditions of artistic production in West Berlin. The title of Christos Joachimides's lengthy catalogue essay, "The Strain of Reality: West Berlin and the Visual Arts 1963–1978," promised that the text would examine relationships between the city's social reality and its art. Instead, platitudes about Berlin's isolation and hazy references to numerous West

German "crises" provided a backdrop for a simple enumeration of artists and events.

No doubt Joachimides seemed a logical choice to "establish a context" for the art displayed at the Whitechapel since the gallery's director envisioned the show as "extending the discussion begun in the important manifestation *Art into Society—Society into Art* organized by Christos Joachimides and Norman Rosenthal at the ICA in 1974."[11] Committed to investigating the ideological functions of German art, "Art into Society" had brought together the work of seven German artists who were testing new strategies of aesthetic intervention in economic and political conditions. Participants challenged the modernist precept that art, by definition, transcends the contingencies of social and historical life. But they also rejected the notion that art's social meaning can be reduced to its depiction or reflection of strictly external social realities—an idea that leaves art itself politically neutral.

Hans Haacke's contribution to "Art into Society," *Solomon R. Guggenheim Museum Board of Trustees* (1974), was based on the premise that the meaning of a work of art does not derive from a property intrinsic to the work but is formed in relation to the work's framing conditions—the modes of its presentation, its institutional supports (see pages 184–190). The idea that art's significance is not absolute but contingent on its presentational contexts simultaneously challenges the idea that art institutions are neutral. Not only are these institutions themselves historically contingent, but they construct what they seem merely to present. They are social institutions.

With *Guggenheim Board of Trustees,* Haacke helped develop a new kind of artwork that incorporates art's institutional contexts into the work itself, thereby giving literal form to the idea that the identity of an artwork is inseparable from the conditions of its existence. The Guggenheim piece was a forerunner of what would become known as "institutional-critical" art, which both uses and subverts the presentational apparatus to uncover the social relations that structure apparently neutral aesthetic spaces. The seven brass-framed panels that compose the Guggenheim piece are ironic imitations of a single element of this presentational apparatus—the list of members of a museum's board of trustees and their prestigious affiliations. Ostensibly, trustee lists exhibit the museum's organizational structure;

in turn they might be exhibited to museumgoers in the form of plaques or institutional reports. They confer an aura of high purpose on the museum's activities and at the same time create an exalted image of the trustees—images that depend on the doctrine that art itself embodies transcendent values. Haacke's work interfered with the museum's self-presentation. It appropriated the list of the Guggenheim's trustees and, like the museum, exhibited it to the public, but for entirely different purposes: *Guggenheim Board of Trustees* questions the purity of the institutional guardians of culture and casts doubt on art's autonomy. The first panel simply reproduces the Guggenheim's own list. Subsequent panels rearrange and expand the data contained in the Guggenheim list, infiltrating it with precisely the kind of information that inventories of trustees exclude and that, more broadly, museological discourse relegates to a realm outside art altogether. For instance, Haacke included information about the oppressive, sometimes violent, economic and political dealings of the corporations with which the Guggenheim's guardians were affiliated. Allowing such material to appear through the very vehicle of its repression—the apparatus of the art institution—Haacke's work reframed the museum. *Guggenheim Board of Trustees* encouraged viewers to challenge the museum's fictional closure, to question art's purported independence from social life, to perceive that the celebrated autonomy of high culture is a socially constructed relationship of exclusion, and, more concretely, to interrogate the hidden links between economic power and "the institutions, individuals and groups who share in the control of cultural power."[12]

Other artists in "Art into Society—Society into Art" stressed the importance of rejecting traditional modes of art production, distribution, and reception. As a whole, the exhibition registered the artists' desire to investigate the historical rather than essential, the social rather than individual, conditions of art and to expose the mechanisms of power operating behind the art institution's facade of aesthetic neutrality.

Given Serota's statement that "13° E: Eleven Artists Working in Berlin" hoped to extend the concerns of "Art into Society—Society into Art," it is surprising that the Whitechapel show gave such a prominent position to what the catalogue called "a new form of expressive figurative painting in Germany."[13] For this new painting and its validating criticism embraced the very ideas so emphatically rejected by the earlier exhibition, attempting to resuscitate the full idealist mythology of studio production—individual creation, originality, universality—and to resurrect the authority of traditional art institutions—gallery and museum. This contradiction notwithstanding, an awareness of neoexpressionist painting was cited as a major factor motivating the Whitechapel show, which, in fact, introduced German neoexpressionism to London. As the introduction claimed, "the moment . . . was propitious." [14] Since the Whitechapel project made no attempt to theorize the relationship between art and social conditions in Berlin but simply linked the two by association, it imparted an aura of political engagement to the work in the exhibition. The Berlin site was used to secure a place for the new German painting as part of a socially radical art practice to which the exhibition was ostensibly dedicated. This claim was furthered by positing a unity to the diverse works at the Whitechapel, based on their distance from critical realism. Opposing the rigidity of that style and, moreover, of the Berlin Senate, the Whitechapel exhibition announced its commitment to personal freedom, freedom from government control, and a freedom embodied, by extension, in the new Berlin painting.

By 1981 "expressive" painting had apparently won the contest to represent Berlin. In London it was ensconced at the Royal Academy as part of an international blockbuster, "The New Spirit in Painting." The following year, Joachimides and Rosenthal curated the huge "Zeitgeist" exhibition at the Martin-Gropius-Bau in Berlin, now with the enthusiastic patronage of the Berlin senator for science and cultural affairs as well as numerous other governmental agencies and corporations. "Zeitgeist" dispensed with any pretense of diversity. The show consisted almost entirely of expressionist works. The history of these two exhibitions is familiar and does not need to be rehearsed here. It is important to note, however, that "Zeitgeist"'s curators asserted more vigorously than ever that an essential relationship tied the art on view to the exhibition's location. "Is it merely a coincidence that Berlin is the site of this event," Joachimides mused, "or are there inner affinities to the art of which [sic] ZEITGEIST is showing?" [15] Yes, he responded, there is indeed such an affinity, but he shifted its basis from that proposed in the earlier shows. No longer was the bond between the art and the city formed by the artists' inquiries into Berlin's social conditions. On the contrary, it was generated by their retreat from those conditions:

> Outside, an environment of horror, made up of the German past and present. Inside, the triumph of autonomy, the architectural "Gesamt-kunstwerk" which in masterly and sovereign manner banishes reality from the building by creating its own. . . . For us the question is how does an autonomous work of art relate to the equally autonomous architecture and to the sum of memories which are present today.[16]

Berlin is thus transformed into the eternal site of art practices that are independent of "reality." Under the banner of representing Berlin, Joachimides supported the notion, only recently challenged in contemporary art practice, that the aesthetic is a sphere divorced from the social.

Sheltered within the Martin-Gropius-Bau were canvases by a group of artists known variously as "the violent painters," "painters of the new vehemence," or, simply, "the boys from Moritzplatz." In 1977, the artists who formed the group's nucleus—Rainer Fetting, Helmut Middendorf, Salomé, and Bernd Zimmer— opened the Berlin cooperative Galerie am Moritzplatz, where they held their first solo exhibitions as well as numerous collective shows. In 1980, the Haus am Waldsee in Berlin featured their work in an exhibition entitled "Heftige Malerei" (Violent Painting), and under this heading the group soon gained international recognition as leading contributors to the German renaissance of painting.

Like other renaissance men, the Moritzplatz boys tried to establish a continu-ity between their work and German artistic tradition, turning in particular to pre-war *Brücke* expressionism. Appropriating the earlier movement's iconography, they filled their paintings with variations on standard *Brücke* motifs—anxiety-ridden

artists with models, primitivized nudes, tribal figures and artifacts, Berlin streets—
and updated the *Brücke*'s cafe, circus, and cabaret scenes with images of contemporary "subcultural" entertainment spots—discotheques and music clubs. They also
adopted the high-contrast color, spatial dislocations, distortions of scale, harsh
brushwork, and primitivizing style of *Brücke* painting, repeating the painterly codes
of "spontaneous," "unmediated" expression. They placed themselves, then, within
national and local traditions—German painting in prewar Berlin.

Art historians and critics embellished these fictions, applauding the artists for
rediscovering German modernism following its eclipse first under the Nazi regime
and then under years of American cultural dominance. Fragile threads of supposedly uninterrupted continuities were unearthed. K. H. Hödicke, the Moritzplatz
painters' teacher, provided one coveted linkage. As a third-generation Expressionist, Hödicke had studied with the last of the original Expressionists, Max Pechstein
and Karl Schmidt-Rottluff, at the Hochschule der Kunste in Berlin.[17] Filtered
through this history, Berlin emerged as a city in which expressive painting had
never died and, consequently, as a place where the sovereign self celebrated in
expressionism also remained eternally alive. Descriptions of Berlin as "a painterly
city" became commonplace.

These postwar histories were highly selective—ignoring major developments in German twentieth-century art antagonistic to expressionism—or confus-
ingly pluralistic—identifying "trends" without theoretical distinction. Superficial
and misleading dichotomies between, for instance, abstraction and figuration or
intellect and emotion obstructed recognition of more significant differences in
postwar art practice. Alternative approaches were readily available, however. In
1977 Benjamin Buchloh had analyzed European art differently, proposing that the
most radical development in European art discourse of the 1960s was a shift from
aestheticism to a consideration of the historical, social, and political circumstances
that condition modes of artistic production and perception.[18] Buchloh, focusing
on the politicized practices of the 1960s and 1970s, theorized a change in concepts,
categories, relationships, and methods of art—from a formalist paradigm to one of
historicity. This new dimension of inquiry, he argued, "demanded from the critical
viewer a different kind of opening up of traditional fields of vision."[19]

Recourse to authority and tradition inevitably reversed this direction. The new German painters were placed within a historical continuum by shutting out materialist inquiries and freely discarding the critical dimensions of recent art. Because revisionist accounts attempted to recover a national artistic experience as a natural cultural reservoir from which to draw inspiration, it was not surprising that they marginalized twentieth-century art practices that questioned the belief in unmediated experience or the tenet that meaning is fixed, transcendent, and directly available in works of art. Such marginalizations, accomplished equally through omission and incorporation, included the absence of any serious consideration of the implications of Berlin dada and Heartfield, the exclusion of overtly politicized practices such as that of Haacke, as well as the inappropriate assimilation of the contemporary work of such artists as Gerhard Richter and Sigmar Polke to a German painting represented as monolithic. Descriptions of recent German art frequently conflated heterogeneous movements. Perhaps the crudest, though by no means unusual, example of this strategy is the work of one German promoter of Moritzplatz painting who grouped the movements of the late 1960s and early 1970s—minimalism, conceptualism, critical realism—under a single unifying characteristic: emotional distance from subject matter.[20] This appraisal made it possible to characterize violent painting's retreat into subjectivism and emotionalism as a radical gesture.

For the violent painters, however, tradition was most consistently invented in the subject of the "big city," a theme with which, it was claimed, they were deeply involved. Supporters depicted the painters' "savage" brushstrokes, "hallucinatory" colors, "expressive" distortions, and iconography as fundamentally "urban." Their use of figurative imagery was cited as evidence of the artists' willingness to confront concrete reality. Fetting and Middendorf, to situate themselves within a lineage of big-city painters, produced hectic, *Brücke*-influenced street scenes while Zimmer painted nature scenes intended to express the notorious antiurban longings of the city dweller. Writers absorbed this work into an art-historical category—urban expressionism—and identified it with the most famous examples of this work: Kirchner's Berlin street scenes executed between 1913 and 1915 and generally considered the artist's mature contribution to German culture. Art journals and catalogues routinely related the Moritzplatz group to Kirchner. Hödicke was extolled for reaching back to Kirchner, "newly discovering the city as artistic Muse" and imparting this source of inspiration to his students who, dubbed "children of the big city," were named Kirchner's legitimate heirs.[21] The rubrics "urban expressionism" and "*Grosstadt* painting" not only offered violent painting a safe niche in German artistic tradition; they helped define it as an art of social critique, a reflection of social conditions, and an act of social protest.

But on what premises did art history base its initial claim that urban expressionism is a critical social statement? What beliefs about both art and the city authorized expressionist city paintings to be considered the authentic representatives of the urban experience? And what theory of social life does the category "urban experience" uphold?

Urban expressionism is a subdivision of a broader art-historical discourse about paintings of the modern city. Primarily characterized by the creation of arbitrary, eclectic, frequently whimsical typologies of "city painting," this discourse as a whole, but especially the literature about urban expressionism, consists with few exceptions of efforts to detect in artists' paintings and writings responses to city environments that themselves remain only superficially examined. This exemplifies the empiricist bias of traditional social art history, which assumes that its objects of study—in this case, city painting—are the ground, rather than the effect, of its own disciplinary activity. Opposing what it calls a "formalist" refusal to deal with art's "content" or "context," social art history has frequently been attracted to paintings of the city because it believes that this subject matter is an intrinsically social iconography. Like certain literary scholars, social art historians have assumed that the city is "by any definition, a social image."[22] But because this formulation presupposes the existence of nonsocial images, it repeats the very form/content dichotomy that it sets out to challenge. It simply replaces the formalist model of aesthetic autonomy and transcendence of urban conditions with a model of interaction between two discrete objects: art—itself socially neutral—and its content, the city, which is inherently and properly social.[23] Maintaining a fundamental separation between art and the city—between culture and society—social art history then confines itself to studying how artists react to an urban environment projected as essentially external to painting. According to one historian of city painting who has attempted to classify these reactions in visual images of modern Paris, Berlin, and New York, "One cannot expect those attitudes to be highly precise."[24]

Once dismissed as inevitable, however, the "imprecision" of artists' attitudes toward the city remains uninterrogated. As a consequence, imprecision is repeated at the level of art-historical analysis. In this respect, mainstream social art history resembles mainstream urban sociology. For, as French sociologist Manuel Castells observes, sociology, too, has long been interested in the city. And not only has sociological discourse been imprecise about the city, but, according to Castells, this explains the popularity of the theme: "If there has been an accelerated development of the urban thematic," he writes, "this is due very largely to its imprecision, which makes it possible to group together under this heading a whole mass of questions felt, but not understood, whose identification (as "urban") makes them less disturbing; one can dismiss them as the natural misdeeds of the environment."[25] Imprecision in art-historical literature about the city cannot, then, be treated as inevitable nor as a mere defect in otherwise sound, if underdeveloped, views of the urban, an error that can be corrected by developing more sharply focused empirical categories of "city painting." Rather, as Castells argues, imprecision performs a social function. If we want to understand this function, typologies of city painting need to give way to an account of the cultural production of the category "city painting." For the greater the clarity of types, the more successfully they obscure the fact that the term "city painting" does not transparently describe a purely objective field. It is a discursive construction. Imprecise social analysis is the ideological core, not an accidental by-product, of the discourse about city painting, which defines its objects of study as, on the one hand, the urban environment, divorced from a theory of the city's social production and, on the other hand, city painting, divorced from any theory of the social production and effects of visual representation. Naturalizing conceptions of the city parallel art history's traditional conception of art as the expression of sovereign individuals whose essential selves precede involvement in social life. Both ideas are apotheosized in urban expressionism—the attempt to transform the city subjectively and recover authenticity in what is conceived of as an inevitably alienating urban environment—and both treat urban phenomena in terms of individual experience.

To approach city paintings as products of preexisting individual imaginations, expressions grounded in preexisting experiences, or even as reflections of a preexisting social reality is to deny that the painted city is a representation—a site where images of the city are set up as reality. Treating city paintings as vehicles that simply convey meaning, conventional approaches foreclose questions about the role that these images play in producing meaning—the meaning of the city as well as the experiences and identities of city dwellers. Yet as early as 1973, in a book titled *Progetto e Utopia* and translated three years later as *Architecture and Utopia*, the architecture historian Manfredo Tafuri had offered a different model, interpreting early-twentieth-century paintings of the city as social practices that produce effects.[26] Tafuri drew on Walter Benjamin's essay "On Some Motifs in Baudelaire," which argues that the human perceptual apparatus changes in response to new spatial configurations linked in turn to socioeconomic changes. Benjamin developed a theory that establishes relationships among various social, economic, and spatial phenomena that for him characterize modernity: the experience of "shock"; the behavior of people in the urban crowd; the urban morphology set in motion by Haussmann's transformation of Paris; and the capitalist mode of production.[27] For Tafuri, as for Benjamin, the modern city has a specific historical identity; it is "objectively structured like a machine for the extraction of surplus value" and "in its own conditioning mechanisms . . . reproduces the reality of the ways of industrial production."[28] But Tafuri speculated about a topic that Benjamin did not explicitly address: the response of avant-garde art movements to the city as subject matter. Tafuri contended that, starting with the expressionist protest, the early-twentieth-century avant-garde performed a dual function. It invented visual codes to embody urban experience and simultaneously dissociated that experience from its basis in the capitalist mode of production. Tafuri argued further that not only did the paintings' iconography and visual codes block an awareness of the historical specificity of modern urbanism, but these codes were deployed in art objects themselves defined as autonomous. In other words, modernist ideas about the meaning of art played an integral role in an aesthetic procedure that evacuated urban history:

> Free the experience of shock from any automatism; found, on the basis of that experience, visual codes and codes of action transformed by the already consolidated characteristics of the capitalist metropolis (rapidity of transformation, organization and simultaneousness of communications, accelerated tempo of use, eclecticism); reduce the artistic experience to a pure object (obvious metaphor for object-merchandise); involve the public, unified in an avowed interclass and therefore anti-bourgeois ideology: these are the tasks that all together were assumed by the avant-garde of the twentieth century.[29]

Avant-garde aesthetic revolutions generated repeated shocks, but for Tafuri these shocks were anything but autonomous. On the contrary, they echoed the continual technical revolution that is the law of industrial production. Nor, in Tafuri's view, did avant-garde movements passively reflect this law. Continually breaking with the past, the avant-garde helped present it as a natural, not historical, law of development and so actively encouraged adaptation to oppressive social circumstances. First, says Tafuri, expressionism registered trauma as natural and therefore as something that must be endured. Later, the constructivist art of assemblage transformed shock into a whole "new principle of dynamic development."[30] Tafuri described this trajectory: "The picture became a neutral field on which to project the *experience of the shock* suffered in the city. The problem now was that of teaching that one is not to 'suffer' that shock, but to absorb it as an inevitable condition of existence."[31]

Like historians of urban expressionism, Tafuri treated experience as something that simply befalls individuals and is unmediated by representation. Unlike these historians, however, he tied modern urban spatial form to capitalist social structures and, in this way, attempted to historicize urban experience, counteracting the way in which it has been naturalized in modernist painting. True, the idea that urban experience is ultimately determined by relations of production repeats the very essentializing gesture that Tafuri has challenged as ideological. Still, his critique offers a useful starting point for rethinking the discourse about urban expressionism since it does not ask what city paintings express, but, rather, what they do.

Failing to raise this question, art historians of urban expressionism have mythologized the conditions of city life as inevitable and established the universalizing premises later mobilized to support German "violent painting." Urban expressionism, these historians tell us, was inaugurated by the *Brücke* artists' contact with Berlin, where by 1911 the group's principal members lived. "In Berlin," writes Eberhard Roters, "German Expressionism became urban."[32] His account of urban expressionism's birth is typical:

> The Expressionist trend linked up with the rhythm and motoricity of the big city, bringing something new into being—Urban Expressionism. . . . The encounter between the Expressionism of the Brücke artists and big city life was comparable to an effervescent reaction, in which Expressionism lost its innocence. The pathos of Urban Expressionism, an emotion provoked by that mutually influential exchange, reflected an accumulation of values that enhanced emotive elements and combined to generate a highly emotional aura: rhythm, dynamics, motoricity, agitation, tension, ecstasy.[33]

Roters's description hyperbolically outlines some of the principal elements comprising what has become the standard model of urban expressionism: individuals confront an external urban reality and have an experience; the city's essence is its natural dynamism, excitement, and tension; this environment of intensified nervous stimulation produces an urban sensibility or personality in its inhabitants—agitated, neurasthenic, alienated, exhilarated; the heightened emotions produced in the individuals are deposited on the surface of expressionist paintings in the form of intense color, radiating and agitated brushstrokes, and energetic contours that, like a seismograph, register the artist's presence; the paintings thus embody a protest against, and subjective transformation of, an urban experience considered inevitably alienating. Kirchner's street scenes are routinely portrayed in these terms, as a "transcription in painting of ecstatic nervousness . . . like colorful stroke storms that release enormous psychic tensions." [34]

Less ingenuous historians uphold the conventional model of urban expressionism but mobilize "sociological" evidence to confirm the existence of a universal "urban personality." Some have drawn on Georg Simmel's famous 1903 essay, "The Metropolis and Mental Life." [35] Indeed, Simmel's presence haunts most histories of Berlin expressionism; his terminology is echoed, more or less distantly. Consider, for example, Donald Gordon's classic description of Kirchner's street scenes as manifestations of a "metropolitan psyche." [36] Other historians rely explicitly on the "Metropolis" essay to explain human behavior in the modern city and its supposed manifestation in paintings. Invariably, however, writers isolate the essay from the body of Simmel's writings, from its philosophical context, and from the developing field of twentieth-century urban sociology within which it occupies a key position. Uncritical and, as we shall see, highly selective references to Simmel's text have given art-historical accounts an appearance of sociological authority, surrounding them with an aura of social criticism. Yet these accounts actually reproduce uncritical ideas about the city and, moreover, support a mystifying social theory in which the city figures prominently.

"The Metropolis and Mental Life" appeals to historians of expressionism because it defines the urban situation in terms of the individual's confrontation with external society. Simmel's analysis of metropolitan life has been used to support the idea that all forms of expressionism, including New York abstract expressionism, are intrinsically urban. Painterly gestures, assumed to be manifestations of the individual artist's presence, concentrated expressions of his feelings, are described as "solutions" to "the urban problem." A solution, however, depends on—indeed it is built into—how a problem is framed. Art-historical accounts portray the urban problem as the struggle of individuals to resist absorption into a "mass identity." [37] German artists, it is said, "looked for a figure strong enough to refute the banality of mass society." [38] Art history has thus conscripted Simmel to transform the urban problem into a specifically modern form of what expressionist discourse frequently defines as the artist's fundamental problem: the essential battle between free individuals and their subordination by the constraints of a strictly external "civilization."

An essay in the catalogue of a 1977 exhibition about images of the city in early-twentieth-century painting exemplifies how Simmel has been appropriated to establish a point of convergence between kindred concepts of the urban and the aesthetic.

> **'The deepest problems of modern life flow from the attempt of the individual to maintain the independence and individuality of his existence against the sovereign powers of society, against the weight of the historical heritage and the external culture and technique of life.'** And these problems were at their most acute in the modern metropolis. Or so Georg Simmel, the German philosopher and sociologist, argued in an essay of 1903 on *The Metropolis and Mental Life*. He might have added, and on good grounds, that many of the deepest problems of modern art flowed from just this source.[39]

The problem for early-twentieth-century city painters, the text continues, "was to find an image with sufficient force to restore the position of the individual against the modular forms of the city and the routine life of the masses."[40] Moreover, the struggle of the city dweller was one and the same with the artist's struggle: "At the same time there was another and overriding priority, which was to preserve the autonomy of painting against those very forces which the artists felt compelled to acknowledge."[41]

Simmel's analysis of the modern city was considerably more complex than art-historical texts acknowledge. In these texts, "The Metropolis and Mental Life" undergoes the same reductions that it has suffered in mainstream urban sociology. Sociological literature about urban expressionism has so far remained overtly oblivious of the history of urban thought with which it shares so many presuppositions, just as it remains oblivious of the urban thought that challenges these presuppositions. Simmel viewed the modern city as the locus of what he considered the salient characteristic of modern life: increased tension between the inner life of the individual and objective culture. Objective culture is the complex of products and formations external to the self and objectified throughout history. Simmel defined subjective culture as the domain of the individual's assimilation of the objective culture and attributed the dissonance of modern life to an increasing gap between the growth of objective culture and the individual's cultural level. The city is the arena of this clash. Analyzing the mechanisms that city dwellers develop to adapt to their environment, Simmel concluded that the metropolis is the site of an interaction between two kinds of individuality: the full expression in the individual of a "general human quality," on the one hand, and a unique, romantic individualism, on the other. The increase in external stimuli in the city intensifies the individual's emotional life. This intensification, coupled with the unique social relationships that result from the city's spatial distribution and its concentration of large numbers of people creates a crisis for the individual personality. But these distinctively urban features also supply the conditions—the loosened social ties and fragmentation resulting from a vastly broadened social formation—for the full development of individualism.

Still, for Simmel the "metropolitan type" is not simply an effect of the city's size and its large numbers of people. Nor is the city merely the terrain of a timeless struggle between individual and society. The urban personality also develops in response to what Simmel viewed as the specific historical elements of modernity— an advanced economic division of labor and the establishment of a money economy. In a famous passage, which plays a key role in Walter Benjamin's analysis, Simmel describes the urban personality's characteristically "blasé attitude": "There is perhaps no psychic phenomenon which has been so unconditionally reserved to the metropolis as has the blasé attitude." [42] He first attributes this posture of indifference, aversion, and reserve to "the rapidly changing and closely compressed contrasting stimulations of the nerves" experienced in the city, but

This physiological source of the metropolitan blasé attitude is joined by another source which flows from the money economy. The essence of the blasé attitude consists in the blunting of discrimination. . . . This mood is the faithful subjective reflection of the completely internalized money economy. By being the equivalent to all the manifold things in one and the same way, money becomes the most frightful leveler. For money expresses all qualitative differences of things in terms of "how much?" Money, with all its colorlessness and indifference, becomes the common denominator of all values; irreparably it hollows out the core of things, their individuality, their specific value, and their incomparability.[43]

For Simmel, then, several characteristics of the city—size and number of people, preponderance of the "objective spirit," division of labor, and the fact that it is the main seat of the money exchange[44]—fashion the urban personality.

Simmel's description of city life in terms of human adaptation to environmental forces itself has a history. It entered American urban discourse through the work of Robert Park and his student, Louis Wirth, leading figures in the Chicago School of urban sociology. Park had attended Simmel's popular Berlin lectures in 1899 and 1900, and Wirth later described Simmel's "Metropolis and Mental Life" as "the most important single article on the city from the sociological standpoint."[45] But the Chicago School transformed Simmel's writings in two significant ways: they combined his ideas with other intellectual influences, most notably the theories of Charles Darwin, and, partially as a result of adapting their version of Darwinism to urban life, they abandoned Simmel's emphasis on the determining effects of a money economy.

The Chicago sociologists developed a comprehensive urban theory based on human ecology, the social theory that accompanied the institutionalization of sociology as a full-fledged discipline in American universities.[46] Applying a hard-science model to the study of urban social life, the Chicago School forged a concept of "the urban" within an analysis based on a biological analogy. These writers defined their object of observation as the process by which human populations adapt to an external environment, producing an "ecology"—a space internally divided into separate areas forming a functional social system: the city. Adaptation was considered the product of a "human nature" expressed in the city's spatial form. As Park asserted at the beginning of his landmark 1916 essay, "The City: Some Suggestions for the Study of Human Behavior in the Urban Environment," the city "is a product of nature, and particularly of human nature" and, therefore, a "laboratory" for studying human nature.[47] Using Darwin's work to demonstrate that forces analogous to those shaping plant and animal communities also govern the evolution of human communities, Park believed that human nature is manifested in the competition for survival. As the struggle for survival distributes different animal and plant species among different habitats, so in human communities competition gives rise to a division of labor that, in turn, generates the city's spatial organization and land-use patterns. Urban form thus corresponds to an orderly distribution of functions, an "equilibrium" toward which ecological communities aspire.

Ecological systems are, however, never static. According to the urban ecologists, change occurs either in the "normal" course of the community's life or when some new element enters to disturb the status quo. Cyclical and evolutionary, change brings about new stages of adaptation and, while it is continual, tends to reestablish equilibrium. Here, too, biology provided a fertile source of concepts for explaining changing spatial configurations. Urban ecologists regularly described patterns of city growth as the spatial expression of "laws" of competition, extension, concentration, dominance, succession, and invasion.[48] The view of the city as a functional organism and evolutionary unit thus fostered a conception of urban spatial form as the inevitable outcome of growth and progress.[49]

The urban ecologists believed that human beings differ from plants and animals, both in their ability to "contrive and adapt"[50] the environment to their needs and in their possession of a culture. Ultimately, however, culture too is environmentally determined. For within Park's perspective, specific cultures develop only at a point where the biotic struggle for existence has produced different areas within the city in which are located particular functional groups. In these places, which the Chicago School, appropriating a term from plant ecology, called "natural areas," people develop bonds based on common goals and values.

131

While Park and other first-generation members of the Chicago School stressed the differentiation of "socially-cohesive" cultural areas within the city, Park's student Wirth, returning to Simmel, assigned a specific cultural content to the city as a whole. Combining human ecology with Simmel's analysis of the urban personality, Wirth's highly influential 1938 essay, "Urbanism as a Way of Life," formulated a conception of a singularly "urban culture" produced by the city as an ecological form. Wirth defined urbanism as a constellation of traits forming the characteristic style of life in cities. Size, density, and heterogeneity of population determine urban culture or social life and also give rise to a distinctive urban personality: "schizoid," aggressive, individualistic, disorganized. Wirth then interpreted differences among cities in terms of three transhistorical variables. Setting out to pinpoint the essence of "the urban," he constructed his object of study by separating relevant from irrelevant phenomena. "In formulating a definition of the city," he warned,

> it is necessary to exercise caution in order to avoid identifying urbanism as a way of life with any specific locally or historically conditioned cultural influences which, while they may significantly affect the specific character of the community are not the essential determinants of its character as a city.
>
> It is particularly important to call attention to the danger of confusing urbanism with industrialism and modern capitalism. . . . Different as the cities of earlier epochs may have been by virtue of their development in a preindustrial and precapitalistic order from the great cities of today, they were, nevertheless, cities.[51]

Historians of urban expressionism have absorbed in an oversimplified form concepts that until recently dominated sociological ideas about the urban and have thus consistently, if unknowingly, heeded Wirth's advice. There is some irony in their doing so, however, since it distances them from Simmel, the very figure whose ideas they ostensibly embrace. Although art historians invoke Simmel's theory of the metropolis to authorize expressionism as the consummate, aesthetic representative of the urban situation, they nonetheless, like Wirth, marginalize key dimensions of Simmel's thought. For while Wirth insisted that urbanism must not be "confused" with industrialism and modern capitalism, it was, as Peter Saunders points out, "precisely such a confusion that characterized Simmel's approach."[52] Yet, in keeping with ecological tenets, art history has posited a social content to the city understood as a transhistorical form or, what amounts to the same thing, has described modern urban conditions as the inevitable outcome of a quasi-natural, technological progression, thereby perpetuating beliefs in an essentially alienating—hence individuating—city life that engenders an "urban personality." Centered on its exacerbated individualism, the "metropolitan type" has in turn provided the discipline with pseudo-sociological support for its conception of "the artist" as exemplar of the sovereign human self who subjectively transcends social conditions—including the urban condition—an idea that forms the basis of expressionism in art.[53]

In the late 1960s and early 1970s, certain urban scholars extensively criticized ecological interpretations of the city precisely because urban ecology tended to dissociate spatial organization from the specificities of industrialism and modern capitalism. These scholars had their own objections to Simmel. Still, they set out to restore the very confusion in his analysis that, thirty years earlier, Wirth had sought to correct. Motivated in part by ghetto uprisings in U.S. cities and by the growth of urban social movements contributing to the events of 1968 in Europe, urban theorists examined urban ecology as a form of spatial knowledge that supports an oppressive status quo by representing urban conditions and conflicts as natural and universal. Against this "traditional knowledge of space," urban geographers and sociologists developed what Henri Lefebvre calls a "critique of space"[54]—a politicized spatial knowledge that treats existing spatial forms as inseparable from particular social structures and as, therefore, susceptible to change.[55]

In 1973, David Harvey's *Social Justice and the City,* a virtual manifesto of the new urban studies, drew a contrast between Park's and Ernest W. Burgess's ecological image of the spatial organization of American cities and the description of

Manchester given in Friedrich Engels's *Condition of the Working Class in England in 1844.*[56] Focusing on these authors' depictions of impoverished ghettoes, Harvey pointed out that Engels and the urban ecologists describe the same pattern of urban land use and the same tendency toward ghetto formation but explain these phenomena differently. For Engels the "social cohesiveness" of the ghetto does not spring, as it does for the ecologists, from biotic forces of competition producing equilibrium and "natural areas" and from the ineradicable passions of Park's "human nature." It arises instead from the economic inequities that structure industrial capitalism. Echoing Marx, Harvey distinguished the ecological approach, which accepts the inevitability of ghettoes, from a "revolutionary" urban theory whose purpose, he argued, is "to eliminate ghettoes."[57]

A year earlier, Manuel Castells had contended that the Chicago School's "urban culture" is "strictly speaking, a myth, since it recounts, ideologically, the history of the human species."[58] Castells defined "the myth of urban culture" as ideology in Marx's sense of the term: the category "urban culture" expresses the truth that urban life is alienating and at the same time obstructs the ability to recognize and transform the social causes of that truth because it gives urban experience a natural origin—the city construed as an ecological form. "The 'city,'" wrote Castells, "takes the place of explanation . . . of the cultural transformations that one fails to (or cannot) grasp and control. . . . The urban ideology is that specific ideology that sees the modes and forms of social organization as characteristic of a phase of the evolution of society, closely linked to the technico-natural conditions of human existence and, ultimately, to its environment."[59] He concludes: "The social efficacy of this ideology derives from the fact that it describes the everyday problems experienced by people, while offering an interpretation of them in terms of natural evolution, from which the division into antagonistic classes is absent."[60]

Castells's observations about the neutralizing effects of mainstream urban sociology, particularly how its definition of the urban conceals class conflicts, closely recall Manfredo Tafuri's remarks about the effects of twentieth-century aesthetic discourse. Tafuri argued that "the expressionist protest," supported by modernist ideas of aesthetic autonomy, portrayed urban experience as inevitable and, moreover, falsely unified the public "in an avowed interclass . . . ideology." The similarity between the two writers is not surprising. Universalizing categories of the urban and the aesthetic have long been entangled in the discourse of urban expressionism. But just as urban scholars challenged the legacy of urban ecology, so aestheticism has hardly gone unquestioned by contemporary artists and critics. On the contrary, for nearly three decades new theories about the politics of urban space have been matched by new theories about the politics of aesthetic space and by the development of art practices that contest autonomy by exploring the artwork's inseparability from its spatiotemporal contexts.[61]

Yet by the close of the 1970s "new vehemence" painting and the cultural apparatus that validated it as a resurgent urban expressionism had reacted against these parallel shifts in urban and aesthetic spatial thought. In the artistic sphere, neoexpressionists reasserted neutralizing assumptions about art's autonomy and transcendence of social circumstances. At the same time, immediately following the development of new urban conflicts in Berlin, they intensified talk of "the urban" in a form that repressed its political implications. Aspiring to express the urban, they launched a veritable offensive against understanding it, speaking instead about the aggressions that inevitably "take root in the isolation and anonymity of metropolitan life."[62] Resuscitating the discourse of urban expressionism, these artists described Berlin as an "energy field" that generates the "grand gestures, violent colors, aggressive images" of expressionist paintings[63] and revived a primitivist iconography, presenting the city as a scene of "primal" conflicts in paintings promoted as embodiments of sovereign self-expression. The city was repeatedly constructed as a universal, eternal environment where archaic rituals are enacted and where, as one Moritzplatz painter put it, "the unifying element is the self."[64]

Regression to urban ideology was only one aspect of a more comprehensive retreat from historical inquiry that characterized neoexpressionism, a retreat frequently presented as historical investigation and even clothed in a rhetoric of historical justice. Recourse to "the urban experience" to glorify the "violent painters" corresponded to the prevalent contention that other German neoexpressionists were symbolically confronting the problematic weight of German culture and ex-piating the Nazi past. "The new German painters," it was said, "perform an ex-traordinary service for the German people. They lay to rest the ghosts—profound as only the monstrous can be—of German style, culture and history, so that the people can be authentically new. They are collectively given the mythical opportu-nity to create a fresh identity."[65] More than two decades earlier, however, analyz-ing the slogan "coming to terms with the past," Theodor Adorno had questioned this desire to forget German history. "One wants to get free of the past," said Adorno, "rightly so, since one cannot live in its shadow, and since there is no end to terror if guilt and violence are only repaid, again and again, with guilt and violence. But wrongly so, since the past one wishes to evade is still so intensely alive."[66]

Following Adorno, Gertrud Koch later described the popular idea of "work-ing through the past" as "the process of converting fascism and Nazism into myth, which began in the mid 1970s. Part of this remodeling of reality is the extinguish-ing of concrete memories . . . and the displacement of those memories by mythic re-interpretations."[67] According to Adorno, this process only leads us to forget "the continued existence of the objective [economic] conditions that brought about fascism in the first place."[68] Mythic continuities extinguish history, past and present, in several ways. They deny historical transformations. At the same time, as Adorno warned, they disavow the persistence of oppressive social conditions underlying apparent change and liberation. They also mask concrete social con-flicts beneath a seeming coherence.

For advocates of neoexpressionism, "the urban condition" provided such a mythic continuity, with the attendant neutralizations of history. Slipping freely be-tween past and present, neoexpressionists linked Moritzplatz painting to Kirchner's street scenes by scorning the changes that had taken place in the years separating pre–World War I Berlin and the Cold War city of the 1980s. An article in a German magazine typifies this suppression: "No city has more right to talk about paintings since there the tradition of painting was never interrupted even when the word 'painting' seemed to vanish from art history. The reason is that Berlin provides a theme for painting—the urban situation."[69] Yet the topic of this article was a very specific "urban situation": the Kreuzberg section of West Berlin where the Moritzplatz painters lived and worked. While the author viewed Kreuzberg as an unchanging painterly theme—the quintessential "expressionist city"—the area differed significantly from the Berlin of Kirchner's day. According to numerous art publications, Kreuzberg possessed three principal artistic attractions: inexpensive rents for large studio spaces; a tension-filled atmosphere and desolate surroundings that inspire an artistic retreat to an "internal" world of images; and an environment of anonymity that liberates the individual. Exploiting Kreuzberg as a thrilling environment for artists, these descriptions exemplified a disturbing tendency in the international art press of the 1980s to romanticize impoverished urban neighborhoods.[70]

Apologists for violent painting revealed this exploitation most strongly not when they ignored Kreuzberg's social problems but when they cited these problems in order to weave them into the fabric of the neoexpressionist zeitgeist. In one of many tributes to Berlin's new painters, for instance, Wolfgang Max Faust listed "minorities" and "the latent violence produced by the concrete disasters of public housing" as two of the painters' most important "big-city" subjects.[71] Routinely, writers on Moritzplatz painting tried to demonstrate the art's social significance by mentioning certain features of Kreuzberg: it was in direct proximity to the Berlin Wall; it was the home of the majority of Turkish *Gastarbeiter* (guest workers) in West Berlin; and it was the scene of bitter conflicts between an official urban renewal policy and alternative movements such as the squatters. Kreuzberg's historical situation included, then, the Cold War and escalating militarism. Its historical urban condition consisted of rampant real-estate speculation, vast unemployment, and the social and political problems raised in the capitalist center by its longstanding imperialist policies in the south.

At the time, Kreuzberg housed one-third of Berlin's foreign workers, mostly Turks, who comprised thirteen percent of West Berlin's population. This group of foreign workers was first actively recruited by the West German Federal Labor Office in the mid-1950s when Germany had exhausted its own postwar industrial reserve army and began to tap the latent surplus population of southern Europe and, later, Eurasia for labor to fuel the "economic miracle." From inception, the official guest-worker system was an institutionalized program of discrimination, attempting to make the foreign workers mobile, temporary, and silent.[72] Nonetheless, the import of foreign labor created a new population of permanent ethnic minorities in West Germany which, with the advent of economic crisis, became the target of government attempts at repatriation and of assaults by right-wing parties for whom guest workers are useful scapegoats as the cause of Germany's economic problems. Strikingly underrepresented in the developing service sector, these workers became largely dispensable, thus facilitating attempts to export unemployment and other social problems by expelling "foreigners."

Gastarbeiter have, of course, been subject to discrimination in housing and have tended to live in the worst inner-city conditions. Left predominantly to the forces of the housing market, their pressing needs have been manipulated by speculating landlords. In Kreuzberg, for example, when landlords abandoned buildings, stopped services, and forced out tenants in hopes of reaping profits from future reconstruction projects, the landlords could easily rent underserviced apartments to Turkish foreign workers desperate to find temporary quarters anywhere. This desperation was engendered in part by government regulations that frequently made the foreign workers' right to bring their families to West Germany contingent on each worker's ability to provide adequate housing.

In 1979 the complex housing situation in West Berlin that took advantage of foreign workers also produced the squatters movement: organized groups of people appropriated abandoned buildings and cooperatively put them into working order as an alternative to official reconstruction and profitable luxury modernization. Squatters, forming self-help networks and tenants' rights offices, also protested the City Senate's plans to tear down housing and proposed that public funds be allocated to tenants (instead of to landlords) to restore buildings. Implicitly, the squatters defined the Berlin housing question in terms different from those posed in official urban renewal debates. Such debates framed an opposition between the use of existing building stock, on the one hand, and new development, on the other. The squatters intervened by placing this controversy within the context of the city's socioeconomic structure—questioning the rights of privately owned real estate, the commodity form of housing provision, and the allegiances of the state in allocating urban resources. The squatters' movement reached its height in 1981 when the police forcibly evicted occupants in violent confrontations.

Faust was probably referring to guest workers and squatters when he wrote that minorities and the concrete violence of housing struggles were two of Moritzplatz painting's urban subjects. But in what sense can these phenomena be claimed as the theme of, or even as an influence on, Moritzplatz work? In the absence of paintings about these subjects, we can only assume that, for Faust, the expressionist stylistic and iconographic signifiers of violent, "urban" emotion—visible painterly gestures, angular forms, high-contrast color, frenzied figures, anxious expressions, crowded canvases—can be equated with, indeed protest against, specific historical forms of urban social violence. This presumption, that intense emotions are themselves an inherently "big-city subject," repeats the basic tenets of urban expressionism, and Faust's allusions to urban political struggles primarily confirm the notion that violence is an eternal feature of city landscapes.

Laudatory attitudes toward the artists' images of minorities have equally troubling implications. For amid conditions produced by a recent episode of imperialist domination—the situation of guest workers—the new vehemence painters produced images of foreigners that resurrected the conventions of early-twentieth-century primitivism, whose problematic relation to, even legitimation of, modern imperialism had long been questioned in art discourse. Numerous painters appropriated non-Western peoples, described as "different sensuous cultures,"[73] as fantasy images. Fetting's self-portraits as a seminude "Indian," for example, conflated the artist with the "other" in order to protest sexual "repression." Such outdated exoticism in coded representations ultimately subjugated "foreign" groups as mirrors of the painters' own aesthetic regressions.

It was, however, the most unusual feature of Berlin's urban landscape—the Wall enclosing the western part of the city—that figured most conspicuously in Moritzplatz painting and in apologies for the work, where the Wall was routinely converted into a symbol of two universal conditions: urban and artistic. The group's emblem was Fetting's *Van Gogh and the Wall* (1978), a painting that depicts, as one supporter put it, "van Gogh, the incarnation of expressionism . . . transplanted to Berlin, at the symbol of German reality."[74] The Wall thus appeared in this painting as a figure of an ongoing spiritual situation—the heroic disease of artistic alienation exemplified by van Gogh—just as the physical isolation of Berlin served as a metaphor of the artist's romantic isolation. Neoexpressionist discourse regularly transformed the division of the city into a concrete symbol of the supposedly schizoid character of the urban personality or of the urban segmentation of social relations. Withdrawn from the contingencies of history, these divisions, it was held, can be overcome in transcendent and redemptive works of art.

Berlin neoexpressionists complemented their depictions of the Wall with works painted directly on the Wall. These works, supplemented by visiting artists, provoked commentaries that raise significant issues about the intersection of aesthetic and urban politics. The point of intersection is the contested notion of "site-specificity." Initiated in 1982 by Jonathan Borofsky's *Running Man,* executed during the "Zeitgeist" exhibition, the wall paintings by professional artists were confined to the section of the Wall where the institutionalized art world was concentrated—between the Martin-Gropius-Bau and the Künstlerhaus Bethanien. Shortly after these paintings gained notoriety in the mass media, an article in *Art in America* described them as "predominantly Neo-Expressionist," "extraordinary political statements," and "site-specific artworks."[75] A month earlier, another critic had designated Borofsky's paintings "site-specific installations" and nominated them for the position of exemplary public art.[76] Yet the simple juxtaposition of the adjectives *neoexpressionist* and *site-specific* glosses over striking contradictions between the meanings of the two terms and obscures a complex history of aesthetic debates. Precisely because the Wall paintings fit so securely within the parameters of neoexpressionism they failed to confront the specificities of their site. Their embrace of neoexpressionism put them at odds with, rather than placing them within, the tradition of critical site-specificity, a practice that arose in the late 1960s as a challenge to modernist doctrines of aesthetic autonomy and transcendence of social relations. Site-specific art practices demonstrated that art is constituted by— is not independent of—social relations. The painting on the Berlin Wall, by contrast, celebrated the masterful transformation of social life by sovereign subjects and so, no matter how vigorously touted as exemplary public art, remained safely within the boundaries of traditional museological discourse. The inclusion of this work under the rubric "site-specificity" represented, then, an appropriation of radical terminology to bolster the pretensions of work that actually withdrew into a supposedly private realm of timeless meanings, psychological generalities, and self-expression—"an internal world of images"—attempting to transform its specific site into a universal one and to present itself as a spiritual transcendence of the Wall's concrete divisions.

Neutralizing representations of Berlin and of urban space in general did not go unopposed during the heyday of neoexpressionism. Two artworks in particular not only offered politicized counterimages of the city but raised questions about the political functions of "the new painting." At the same time, these works challenged and reconfigured the expressionist model of aesthetic space. The first was exhibited in Berlin, the second in New York. Both were site-specific installations situated in urban neighborhoods that were settings of the expressionist revival.

In 1984, the Künstlerhaus Bethanien, a Kreuzberg gallery located about a hundred yards from the Berlin Wall, presented a work by Hans Haacke titled *Broadness and Diversity of the Ludwig Brigade*. Against conceptions of the Berlin Wall as a structure dividing isolated realms or symbolizing mythical polarities, *Ludwig Brigade* examined the dialectic of the Wall's dividing and connecting functions, treating East and West Germany not as entities but as relationships and demonstrating that their difference was also an interdependence. Investigating the connections between the two Germanies, *Ludwig Brigade* questioned the platitude that art could provide an imaginary and liberating transcendence of the Wall's divisions. Instead, the work made visible the oppressive exchanges already taking place between the Germanies—exchanges facilitated by art and fostered by dominant aesthetic ideas. Revealing both the material unities and the social conflicts evaporated by spiritual visions of wholeness, Haacke's project examined the links between art, on the one hand, and economic and state power, on the other, realms that—like the two Germanies—are conventionally separated. Thus, while some critics extolled the new German painters for spiritually healing symbolic breaches, an aesthetic practice such as Haacke's actually surmounts barriers: the ideological

Hans Haacke, *Broadness and Diversity of the Ludwig Brigade,* installation view at the Künstlerhaus Bethanien, Berlin, 1984 (photo courtesy Hans Haacke).

boundaries drawn around phenomena, giving them an appearance of autonomy that protects them from political interrogation.

Ludwig Brigade incorporated the Berlin Wall into a work that, as Walter Grasskamp has written, "probes with emblematic precision the cultural, political and economic import" of its site.[77] Haacke made the site an integral component of the work by staging a confrontation between his installation and a concurrent art-world event that indeed exemplified the conjuncture of cultural, political, and economic power in Berlin. Two days before the opening of *Ludwig Brigade,* another exhibition opened in the city: a show at the Kunsthalle Berlin presenting the businessman Peter Ludwig's collection of East German art. Jointly sponsored by the State Art Trading Agency of the GDR and the Ludwig Institute for Art of the GDR, the Ludwig exhibition, which had originated at Oberhausen, was entitled

"Durchblick" (Seeing Through). It cast Ludwig in the role of a generous mediator, a builder of bridges, indeed—if one believed the show's title—a visionary who was overcoming decades of painful separation between the two German states. "Durchblick" painted a picture of Ludwig as harmonizing a divided nation through the power of art and the strength of his own aesthetic vision, an image that paralleled the claim that the new German painters reconciled oppositions by artistic means.

Haacke's installation questioned the exact nature of Ludwig's border crossings. Haacke focused on the collector's other activities, particularly his chairmanship of the Leonard Monheim Corporation, a company that then produced chocolates under the brand name Trumpf in both West Berlin and, through special, secretive arrangements, the GDR.[78] *Ludwig Brigade* suggested that Monheim's German-German economic dealings were expedited by the cultural transactions of another enterprise—the Ludwig Foundation for Art and International Understanding—which, among other joint ventures, promoted and purchased East German art. While "Durchblick" implied that Ludwig's aesthetic exchanges penetrated the Wall and rendered it transparent, Haacke revealed that these exchanges reduced the visibility of Ludwig's economic penetrations. Though traveling under the sign of transparency—"seeing through"—Ludwig, backed by the two German states and supported by prevailing discourses about art, emerged in *Ludwig Brigade* as a master of disguise.

Indeed, that is how he appears in the oil painting that forms one of the work's main elements. Across a tall barrier that bisected the gallery and replicated the division of Berlin by the Wall, Haacke set up an encounter between two types of visual imagery associated, respectively, with the socialist East and capitalist West. On one side was Haacke's original painting, a parody of socialist realist art; on the other, an "original" billboard advertising Trumpf chocolates. The painting shows Ludwig, camouflaged as an old-fashioned German chocolate maker,[79] flanked by two women carrying picket signs that protest the Leonard Monheim Corporation's oppressive labor policies: unemployment due to automatization of the Trumpf plant in West Germany (where a large proportion of employees were female foreign workers) and low wages in East Germany that maximize the company's

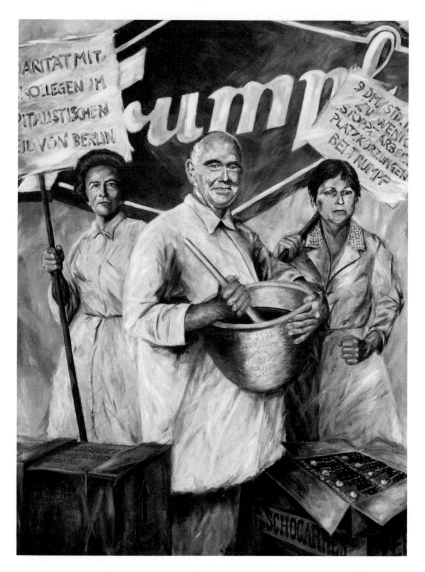

Hans Haacke, *Broadness and Diversity of the Ludwig Brigade,* oil painting, 1984 (photo courtesy Hans Haacke).

Hans Haacke, *Broadness and Diversity of the Ludwig Brigade,* billboard, 1984 (photo courtesy Hans Haacke).

profits. The placards reveal that relations of exploitation also crossed borders. They also call attention to the class divisions concealed by a Cold War rhetoric that portrayed the East/West opposition as the country's sole political division, allowing Ludwig, agent of the conflicts inherent in multinational capital, to present himself as an agent of unification.

The picket signs directly contradict Ludwig's benevolent self-presentation, but Haacke's principal strategy is less direct, an ironic imitation of Ludwig's own deceptions. Ludwig used art as protective coloration to create a philanthropic and amiable image that hid the true nature of his East German presence; Haacke used art to mimic—and unmask—the industrialist's own mimicry.[80] Again like Ludwig, Haacke appropriated art associated with East Germany, parodying the iconographic and compositional codes of socialist realist painting. He posed the two women in his painting as militant workers fighting "the class enemy"—stock figures from the socialist realist arsenal—so that Ludwig, holding a mixing bowl inscribed "People's Owned Enterprise, Candy Factory of Dresden," metamorphoses into the smiling head of a workers' brigade. The painting parodies an agitprop scene that, in a further irony, is dominated by the red and white, diamond-shaped advertising logo for Trumpf chocolates—a corporate trademark camouflaged as a socialist slogan. *Trumpf*, which translates into English as "trump" and is, in both languages, semantically and phonetically akin to "triumph," unfurls like a banner across the top of the canvas. Under this banner, Ludwig masquerades as the friend, not the enemy, of "the people."

Haacke plays on the multiple connotations of the word *trump*, which presides not only over the painting but over the entire work. To a viewer who reads each element of the painting in relation to the others and to the installation as a whole, it becomes clear that in Ludwig's German-German deals, his interests—the interests of capital—rank, like a trump card, above all others. His cultural alliances with the GDR, far from charitable acts of artistic generosity or gestures toward international understanding, emerge as powerful moves in a game of economic domination played within and across the two Germanies. Surrounded by evidence of social conflict, centered beneath the sign of a private multinational corporation yet standing at the forefront of a workers' demonstration, the figure of Ludwig blending ingredients in a bowl mocks the collector's image as the bringer of harmony to a divided people. Furnished with the attributes of an old-fashioned chocolate maker, the leader of Leonard Monheim is obviously trumped up in multiple guises as "a good fellow"—representative of German tradition, unifier, cultural benefactor. Finally, then, he emerges as a double-dealer who, while seeming to liberate Germany from its division and to be a friend of the people—East and West—is a member of an oppressive power.

Haacke's meticulously designed montage also blends together artistic styles associated with the two German states. It imitates the conventions of Soviet-style socialist realism, which became East Germany's official aesthetic after World War II. Yet the work's loose, gestural paint application—classic signifier of free artistic expression—also evokes the liberalization of artistic prescriptions that, beginning in the early 1970s, accompanied the East German art establishment's official proclamation of an era of artistic "broadness and diversity." Caricaturing the Eastern Bloc's sloganeering pronouncements on art's political functions and contrasting this empty rhetoric with Haacke's own critical content, the painting unmasks the lack of any real criticism of the state in socialist art. Haacke's critique is seen most clearly when his painting is placed next to the photograph he used as the source for his Ludwig portrait. Taken at the Oberhausen exhibition, the photo shows Ludwig holding the "Durchblick" catalogue and standing with painter Bernhard Heisig, then a powerful member of the Artists Association of the GDR. Behind the two men is a flattering Heisig portrait of Ludwig. As the literal background for a cultural meeting of the two Germanies, Heisig's ingratiating portrait—utterly remote from a critique of either East German government policy or the capitalist enemy, indeed as strong an advertisement for Ludwig's interests as the Trumpf billboard in Haacke's installation—illustrated the obedience of East German art to the desires of the totalitarian socialist state. "Actually existing socialist art" clearly depended, as Walter Grasskamp puts it, on "politico-economic calculations at higher levels."[81] The thick paint and tactile surface of Heisig's canvas, supposed to stand for artistic freedom, ironically underscored these artistic restrictions, which, of course, directly served Ludwig's objectives.

Since such painterly painting was most familiar to viewers in West Berlin as a hallmark of the neoexpressionist revival, its prominence in Haacke's work encouraged viewers to speculate about further similarities between the two Germanies. On both sides of the Wall, gestural brushwork was being promoted as a sign of loosened repression while supporting, in different ways, existing systems of power. In Western art, the revival of expressionist brushwork was coupled with a resurrection of the oil medium. In a comment that could serve as an illuminating caption to the Oberhausen photograph, Haacke later remarked on the correspondence between the aura of oil painting and that of political power: "The medium as such," declared Haacke, "has a particular meaning. It is almost synonymous with

Bernhard Heisig (left) and Peter Ludwig in front of Heisig's portrait of Ludwig at the opening of "Durchblick," Oberhausen, 1983 (photo Ulrich von Born).

what is popularly viewed as Art—art with a capital A—with all the glory, the piety, and the authority that it commands. Since politicians and businesses alike present themselves to the folks as if they were surrounded by halos, there are similarities between the medium and my subjects."[82] Haacke's painting of Ludwig is itself executed in oil and strategically employs loose brushwork. Placed in a West Berlin gallery as part of an installation about the cultural legitimation of economic and political power, Haacke's choice of style and medium invited two readings. It stressed the role of approved East German art in validating the state and Ludwig's financial dealings, but it also alluded to a complementary role played by the official celebration of self-absorbed romantic individualism in West German art.

Indeed, Ludwig's interests were advanced not only by East German cultural authorities but by the aestheticist ideas informing the new West German paint-ing—which, not surprisingly, the industrialist also collects. For Ludwig's image as the unifier of Germany through cultural exchange can only compel belief if it is presupposed that art possesses the authority to speak in the name of immutable, universal truths and thus transcends the historical conditions of its own production and distribution. Severing the aesthetic from other aspects of the social and dis-avowing the social relations of art itself, this assumption, promoted in the neoex-pressionist return to painting, permitted Ludwig to transpose his financial interests into cultural ones. Neoexpressionist notions that unification is a spiritual operation independent of action in the social world also supported assertions that Ludwig could see through the Wall. But these notions repressed the identity of those forces that, protected by the alibi of art, benefited from such penetration.

It is this dissociative mechanism that *Broadness and Diversity of the Ludwig Bri-gade* "sees through." Encouraging viewers to replace Ludwig's aestheticized vision with a politicized one, Haacke's work invited its audience to consider relationships beyond those suggested in the Ludwig portrait. It asked viewers to observe affilia-tions between the painting and the Trumpf advertisement on the other side of the barrier. Placing the viewer in a space divided between the two images, it chal-lenged the committed spectator to unravel a complex and covert web of contacts among economic, political, and cultural forces in East and West Germany. The work also posed questions about resemblances between the operations of state-controlled art in the East and corporate-controlled culture in the West. And these reflections required viewers to apprehend connections that exist not only between two political systems or two Ludwig factories or even between Ludwig's cultural and economic activities. Viewers also discerned relations between the aesthetic and political domains, worldly relations severed on the register of everyday appearances and in idealist aesthetic thought.

The installation's split format was, ironically, the vehicle for rejoining the aesthetic and political realms. The barrier dividing *Ludwig Brigade* into its "Eastern" and "Western" halves prevented viewers from adopting a centered, detached position from which visually to unify the work. The work's spatial design thus gave literal form to Haacke's rejection of the claim that Ludwig's aesthetic vision could see through the Berlin Wall and unite the two Germanies. More than that, the architecture of Haacke's installation countered the traditional constructions of aesthetic space that authorized Ludwig's claim. In modernist models of disinterested aesthetic vision, the occupant of the centered vantage point escapes immersion in the world because, from this position, he or she can supposedly grasp an image that, itself a self-contained totality, transcends the specific circumstances of its production and reception. In the moment of aesthetic contemplation, viewers are thus propelled outside social space, freed from the contingencies of any particular situation. The idealization of the viewing subject—the possessor, like Ludwig, of a supposedly transcendent aesthetic vision—depends then on a corresponding idealization of the art object—possessor of a transcendent aesthetic essence—and, further, on a disavowal of the dependency. The spatial organization of Haacke's installation disturbed both terms of this mutually guaranteeing relationship. Inseparable from its context, the work simultaneously displaced the viewer from the privileged site of aestheticist vision—a place that stands for the ability to be nowhere in particular. The act of literally setting the spectator in motion corresponded, then, to his or her political mobilization. For *The Ludwig Brigade* suggested that, despite grandiose claims, the disinterested subject of traditional aesthetics is always involved in social conflicts.

In May 1985, about a year after *Broadness and Diversity of the Ludwig Brigade* appeared in Kreuzberg, Louise Lawler mounted an installation called *Interesting* in a gallery on the Lower East Side of New York City. Like Kreuzberg, the Lower East Side was then the scene of what the mass media and the art press called an "artistic renaissance."[83] And, like the Ludwig Foundation for Art and International Understanding, the "East Village art scene" helped create an atmosphere favorable to the interests of big capital. For the Lower East Side was also in the throes of gentrification, an upward change in the area's class composition that, replacing poor residents with members of the upper-middle class, was being celebrated as an "urban renaissance." Creating the material conditions to reproduce the city's new white-collar labor force, the gentrification process destroyed housing and services for a traditional working class that once held jobs in the city's quickly declining manufacturing industries. The displacement generated a crisis of survival for the redundant group, manifested in the tens of thousands of homeless people living on New York's streets. Part of a broader attack on working-class living standards—cutbacks in social services and relatively lower wages—gentrification also expedited the flight of capital from sectors where profits were falling to inflated areas such as investment in the built environment. A neighborhood whose primary function had been to reproduce a working-class community was, then, fast becoming the "East Village"—a spatial product of the real-estate market.[84]

As part of the unique packaging of this commodity, the new commercial art scene, emerging in its full outlines by 1982, helped facilitate gentrification.[85] The physical preconditions had been prepared years in advance by the abandonment or neglect of the area's existing housing stock and consequent devalorization of real estate. When galleries and artists, assuming the role of the proverbial "shock troops" of gentrification, moved into inexpensive storefronts and apartments, they aided the mechanism by driving up rents and displacing residents. Art journals, catalogues, videotapes, and museum exhibitions circulated images of the neighborhood that, in a manner resembling art-world representations of Kreuzberg, transformed poverty and "urban decay" into the ingredients of a romantic bohemia that permitted, it was said, the flourishing of individual freedom. Diverse kinds of art were shown in galleries in the East Village, but the art originally packaged under the East Village label and promoted by East Village critics wholeheartedly embraced the expressionist revival, consisting largely of paintings embodying a return to the artistic goal of liberation through the production of self-expressive, "transcendent" artworks.

Louise Lawler, by contrast, belongs to that group of artists whose work demonstrates that the identity of art is socially produced, inseparable from the conditions of its existence. To illuminate the contingency of aesthetic meaning, she calls attention to modes of artistic display, using the context of an exhibition as part of the material of her work. She generally locates her projects in the array of equipment used by art institutions to present objects as art—gallery invitations, installation photographs, press releases, wall labels. She thus employs elements of art's framing apparatus to question the institution's claim that it merely recognizes and displays, rather than constitutes, aesthetic values. Appropriating the institutional apparatus as both target and weapon, Lawler's gallery installations, as one critic succinctly put it, concentrate on presenting the gallery "rather than being passively presented by it."[86]

When Lawler presented an East Village gallery, she altered it "to infer," as she wrote in the show's press release, "another kind of space, one that is redolent with the institutionalization of self-interest, where money gets money." Redesigning the gallery's interior so that it looked like a bank lobby, she painted the walls with a commercial supergraphic and stenciled the logo "Interesting" in corporate typography on the gallery's rear partition. Segmented by the edge of a diagonal green stripe that divided the partition, the word *interest* became the installation's leitmotif. Lawler's conversion of the space did not ingenuously equate art galleries with financial institutions, suggesting that galleries are principal actors in the Lower East Side housing market. Neither did Lawler simplistically inform her audience that galleries deal in commodities, thereby reducing the meaning of artworks to the economic circumstances of their production. She did attempt to use the gallery to intervene in the dominant production of meanings taking place within East Village galleries and other art-world institutions. While these institutions deflected attention from the role they were playing in urban social conditions, Lawler's installation addressed that role, focusing first on the gallery's interior and then infiltrating it with allusions to the real-estate, housing, and art markets, which, though conventionally relegated to the gallery's "outside," were actually the conditions of its existence. The word *interest*—casting doubt on the notion of disinterested aesthetic contemplation—resonated in the redesigned space with

---

Louise Lawler, *Interesting,* installation view, Nature Morte Gallery, New York, 1985 (photo courtesy Louise Lawler and Metro Pictures).

implications of self-interest and references to the financial interests served by the East Village art scene. It hinted at the acquiescence of that scene in the activities of still more powerful economic interests.

With trenchant humor, Lawler also commented on the relation between contemporary urban spatial arrangements and the regressive ideas about aesthetic space embodied in neoexpressionism. On one side of the gallery she installed a shelf that resembled the counters where bank customers prepare transactions. Instead of deposit and withdrawal slips, however, this counter offered press releases referring to the exhibition's urban context and to what Lawler called the art scene's "use and abuse" of the Lower East Side neighborhood. Across the room hung three Cibachrome photographs accompanied by a wall text with the standard format and typography of museum or gallery labels. Instead of providing a pedigree

— GALLERY —

NATURE
MORTE

204 EAST TENTH STREET
NEW YORK CITY 10003
— 212·420·9544 —

Dear Reader,

A press release is written to inform and intrigue the press; wet their appetites and turn their heads in the right direction. It is sent to critics, newspapers, magazines, museums, and corporate advisors. For this exhibition I am taking this press release as an additional location of my work. It will be sent to the entire mailing list and will be part of the presentation in the gallery.

An exhibition entitled "Interesting" will be at Nature Morte for the month of May. Nature Morte is a gallery in the East Village—the recently formed "third" Art District. More than the "first" (uptown) and "second" (Soho), the "third" Art District is seen as a homogenous package. The neighborhood itself is used and abused as part of the art. The work, appropriately handmade souvenirs, attempts to embody the falsification that conflates 'wild,' 'free' and 'creative' with neglect and abandonment.

The gallery has been redesigned, altered to infer another kind of space, one that is redolent with the institutionalization of self interest, where money gets money. Three pictures are included in this installation—photographs of a contemporary object. These photographs represent an expressionism that has 'rolled-over.'

Louise Lawler, April 1985

An opening reception will be held at Nature Morte on Wednesday, May 1st from 6 to 8 p.m. and the show will continue until May 26th. Promotional photos are available from the gallery directors, Alan Belcher and Peter Nagy. Nature Morte is located on Tenth Street at Second Avenue and is open Wednesday through Sunday, 12 Noon to 6:30 p.m. and by appointment.

End

Louise Lawler, press release for *Interesting,* 1985.

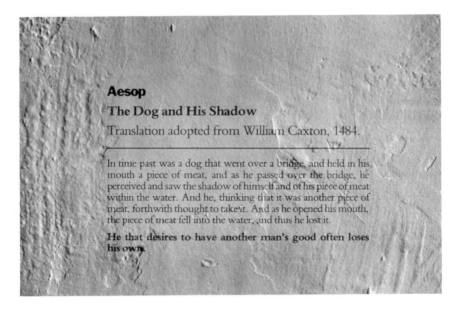

Aesop

The Dog and His Shadow

Translation adopted from William Caxton, 1484.

In time past was a dog that went over a bridge, and held in his mouth a piece of meat, and as he passed over the bridge, he perceived and saw the shadow of himself and of his piece of meat within the water. And he, thinking that it was another piece of meat, forthwith thought to take it. And as he opened his mouth, the piece of meat fell into the water, and thus he lost it.

He that desires to have another man's good often loses his own.

Louise Lawler, wall text accompanying photographs in *Interesting,* 1985 (photo courtesy Louise Lawler and Metro Pictures).

for an artwork, however, this label related an Aesop's fable. The fable, concerning responsibility and the wages of greed, narrates the adventures of a dog who carries a piece of meat in his mouth. Crossing a bridge, the dog is tricked by his reflection in the water below and, opening his mouth to snatch the meat that he thinks he sees there, drops his food into the water. Confused by an illusory image of himself, he loses his grip on reality.

Like the animals in Aesop's fable, the inanimate object in Lawler's photographs can also be used to tell a tale. This story, too, alludes to the consequences of illusions about the self. The object is drastically enlarged and dramatically lit against rich, deeply saturated monochromatic backgrounds—red, green, blue. The photographs were matted and framed like valuable art photography. But the photographed object itself is far from a precious commodity. It is, rather, an inexpen-

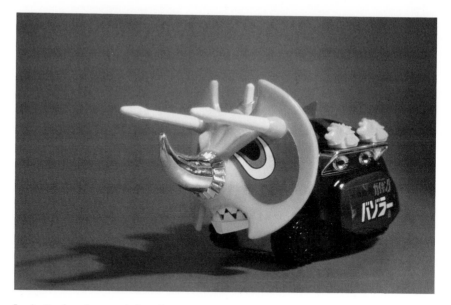

Louise Lawler, photograph from *Interesting*, 1985 (photo courtesy Louise Lawler and Metro Pictures).

sive Japanese toy called the Gaiking Bazoler. Mechanistic and aggressive little creatures, Gaiking Bazolers wear exaggerated, cartoonlike facial expressions that can be altered by attaching different noses selected from a supply of standardized parts. Different facets of their temperaments can also be emphasized, as Lawler did in her photographs, by viewing the toys from different angles.

Lawler had photographed the Gaiking Bazolers before her East Village show. But since her work argues against the contention that immutable meanings reside inside self-contained artworks, she continually reuses pictures in new contexts that inevitably change their meanings. In the *Interesting* installation, the sham ferocity of the commercial novelties, flaunting their "individual" expressions, functioned as spoofs of East Village art, a commodified and childish expressionism that strained to produce startling effects as it repeated habitual and outworn gestures. Lawler's photographic blowups—and her overblown handling of the Gaiking Bazolers—

Louise Lawler, photograph from *Interesting,* 1985
(photo courtesy Louise Lawler and Metro Pictures).

combined the seductive techniques of commercial photography with methods of artistic presentation that create an aura of sanctity around art objects. Her treatment mimicked the hyperbolic manner in which pseudo-expressionist products and the East Village art scene as a whole were artificially inflated by the marketplace and propped up by an art discourse that espoused transcendent values while capitulating to the conditions of the culture industry.[87] The photographs represented, in Lawler's words, an "expressionism that has 'rolled-over.'"

Lawler's parodic reenactment of this inflationary operation and her deployment of the Gaiking Bazolers in the East Village installation emphatically deflated the pretensions of such work. *Interesting* also punctured the widespread illusion that recycled urban expressionism confronts the harsh realities of "the urban situation." For, as Lawler's (de)fetishized objects suggested, in the context of devastation on New York's Lower East Side, solipsistic exercises in bombastic self-expression—products of "the urban personality"—gloss over the sources of urban brutality: the politics of space. They could only serve those powerful interests whose presence in our cities we have every reason to fear.

"Hans Haacke: Unfinished Business," presented at the New Museum of Contemporary Art in 1985–86, was the artist's first one-person exhibition at a New York City museum.[1] But it was not the first attempt to hold such a show. In 1971 the Guggenheim Museum had planned an exhibition of Haacke's work that was called off shortly before it was due to open. At issue then was Haacke's proposal to include what he termed "real-time social systems"—his two real-estate pieces in particular—which the Guggenheim judged to be incompatible with the functions of a prestigious art institution. Fifteen years later Haacke placed the real-estate pieces at the beginning of his New Museum installation and so invited a reconsideration of the circumstances that prompted the cancellation.

Shortly after the Guggenheim incident, describing the interventionist principles governing his new projects, Haacke speculated about the scope and duration of the works' influence: "Works operating in real time must not be geographically defined nor can one say when the work is completed. Conceivably the situation into which a new element was injected has passed when the process unleashed at that moment has gained its greatest potential."[2] For the real-estate pieces, this process presumably began with the Guggenheim's censorship, intensified in the course of the ensuing controversy, and concluded with the subsequent exhibition of the rejected works in other venues. What, then, was to be gained by extending that situation beyond the Guggenheim episode? In what sense were the real-estate pieces still "unfinished business" in 1985? What, on the other hand, were the dangers of such a retrospective investigation?

Paramount among the risks was the likelihood that, directed toward art history's traditional ends and undertaken according to the discipline's standard procedures, the inclusion of the real-estate pieces would further marginalize—this time through accommodation—works initially cast outside the official boundaries of art by authoritative decree. Conventionally, art-historical reexaminations try to vindicate repudiated works by assimilating them to art's ontological norm. If, in this spirit, Haacke's project had been submitted to the judgment seat of history by being referred back to normative criteria and stabilized aesthetic categories, it would consequently have been withdrawn from the historical conjuncture in which it arose as well as that in which it continued to survive.

Consigned, for instance, to a homogenized lineage of avant-garde art, the real-estate pieces could have been linked to a chain of nonconformist artistic ventures initiated by nineteenth-century salon scandals. But such an approach, which disavows the heterogeneity of avant-garde history and in which the very production of outrage becomes the normalizing standard for a work's eventual canonization, would have masked the impact of crucial historical changes in critical art practice. In equally invariant terms, Haacke's works could have been legitimated by absorbing them into a venerable tradition of realist artworks united by their objective presentations of unidealized, lower-class themes. Indeed, some of Haacke's advocates at the time of the Guggenheim cancellation based their defense of the real-estate pieces on the contention that they utilized the now fully respectable techniques of nineteenth-century realism. Whatever the tactical value during the struggle with the museum, this argument reduces realism to a mere commitment to subject matter and adheres to a long discredited belief in a transparent relationship between realistic representations and the empirical phenomena to which they refer. Today critical practices claiming the legacy of realism have extensively redefined that heritage. Among other pursuits, they explore the mediation of consciousness by representations and investigate the conditions of possibility of what is perceived to be "real" at a given historical moment.

Instead of subsuming the banned real-estate pieces under avant-garde or realist traditions, art historians could have authenticated them as art by utilizing the
discursive form of the monograph and placing the works within the artist's career.
This option, too, would have severed them from historical determination, for, as
Griselda Pollock writes, monographic conventions primarily define works of art as
the unique products of sovereign artistic subjects.[3] Although the specificity of
Haacke's work militates against such neutralization, the biographical form can incorporate widely divergent practices. Within its narrative of individualistic creative
development, the real-estate pieces could have been classified as "early political
works," their flaws or rhetorical errors indicated. In these works, historians could
have found the seeds of the artist's eventual stylistic mastery of techniques and
materials. In his "mature phase," Haacke could then have emerged, predictably, as
an "exemplary political artist," a new version of the "great artist" who is, in fact,
the real object produced by monographic study.[4]

These approaches resurrect precisely those transhistorical artistic conditions
and idealist aesthetic categories—author, style, oeuvre—that artists such as Haacke
challenged beginning in the late 1960s. Against the prevailing dogma that works of
art are self-contained entities possessing fixed, transcendent meanings, these artists
explored the cultural process of meaning production. They also investigated the
changing functions of art in relation to the contingencies of history that had previously been relegated in both formalist criticism and its purported adversary,
mainstream social art history, to a more or less distant backdrop." From the beginning," Haacke says, "the concept of change has been the ideological basis of my
work."[5] This concern is signaled in the titles of the real-estate pieces: *Shapolsky et
al. Manhattan Real Estate Holdings, a Real-Time Social System, as of May 1, 1971* and
*Sol Goldman and Alex DiLorenzo Manhattan Real Estate Holdings, a Real-Time Social
System, as of May 1, 1971.* The words *as of,* followed in each title by a precise date,
are significant for two reasons. First, they suggest something important about the
works' subject matter: the documented real-estate operations function elusively,
their activities and compositions continually altering. But the titles also allude to
the materialist premises informing Haacke's mode of artistic production: the belief
that a work's meaning is always incomplete, changing "as of" different temporal

situations, that the work includes the responses it evokes and mutates according to the uses to which it is put, and, finally, that this relativity of meaning depends on the position of viewing subjects themselves contingent within history.

Haacke assembled his real-estate pieces in 1971, several years after minimalist artists had initiated a critique of artistic autonomy by investigating the spatial and temporal conditions of aesthetic perception. The minimalists' temporary, site-specific installations incorporated the place of a work's perception into the work itself to demonstrate that perception depends on context.[6] But formalism reentered minimalist art in the assumption that the sites of aesthetic perception are politically and socially neutral. A more decisive shift in contemporary art occurred when artists broadened the concept of site to embrace not only the aesthetic context of a work's exhibition but the site's symbolic, social, and political meanings as well as the historical circumstances within which artwork, spectator, and place are situated.

These inquiries led in diverse directions. One group of artists pursued an investigation of the institutions that mediate between individual works of art and their public reception, developing strategies of intervention in institutional spaces and discourses. Occupying a key place in this critique of art institutions, Haacke's real-estate pieces—including the official reaction that they provoked—interrogated the museum as such a primary mediating agency, foregrounding how it determines and limits the reading of artistic texts. The works also confronted the broader social functions of the museum—its points of intersection with specific economic or political interests and its role in legitimating political realities in a society structured on relations of oppression and exploitation.

Attempts to reevaluate Haacke's real-estate pieces by removing them to a realm of sweeping continuities that repress evidence of rupture and multiplicity in contemporary art could only have seemed a betrayal of the shifts in aesthetic practice that the works themselves helped set in motion. Such interpretations distort the meaning of Haacke's rigorous investigation into the concrete historical factors that characterize his works' sites. There were, however, other imperatives that compelled a recollection of the real-estate pieces when they reappeared in 1985 at the artist's New Museum exhibition. Of overarching concern was the desire to retrieve a crucial moment in the development of contextualist art practice as part of a struggle for historical memory necessitated in the 1980s by a climate of artistic reaction and widely disseminated neoconservative reconstructions of contemporary art history. That period was marked by a return in the established art world to conventional forms and mediums of artistic production. An embrace of the conditions of the art market coupled with a resurgence of ideologies of aestheticism and self-expression accompanied a resurrection of the authority of traditional art institutions. The critical art practices developed during the previous twenty years and the contemporary art committed to elaborating their principles were frequently ignored, falsified, or absorbed under the rubric of a "pluralism" that proclaimed art's freedom from history and evacuated its past. An understanding of the stakes in the Guggenheim Museum's confrontation with Haacke's real-estate pieces could help restore the ability to apprehend genuine differences and conflicts in contemporary art discourse, conflicts with far-reaching ramifications in the political field.

In still another, more specific, sense Haacke's real-estate pieces shed light on the 1980s and could, reciprocally, be illuminated from the vantage point of that decade. They raised questions about a particular interface between economic and artistic concerns: the connection between dominant aesthetic discourses and the interests of real-estate capital in New York. During the years that had elapsed between the Guggenheim episode and the New Museum show, the problems embedded in Haacke's subject matter—real-estate dealings, deteriorated housing, and the role played by the needs of profit in determining New York's landscape—had acquired a new urgency. In the late 1970s, as a "solution" to the city's fiscal crisis and, moreover, as part of post-Fordist capitalism's reorganization of the domestic and international divisions of labor, the city entered a period of accelerated restructuring as a center for international corporations and corporate-related services. The restructuring entailed an attendant impoverishment and dispersal of the blue-collar laborers whose jobs in manufacturing industries had been disappearing from the city's economic base since the 1950s. The physical conditions to support the new economic structure and facilitate corporate domination of the city had been created by city planning policies that promoted privatized construction of corporate headquarters, office buildings, and luxury apartments that service white-collar industries and workers. Fostering gross speculation and enriching big real-estate developers, this phase of urban redevelopment also engineered the destruction of the material conditions of survival—housing and services—for residents no longer needed in the city's economy. Redevelopment was, then, one aspect of a more extensive and continuing crisis for this group, a crisis that included unemployment, attacks on unions, and cutbacks in social services.

New York's cultural apparatus played, sometimes unwittingly, a variety of instrumental roles in the redevelopment process. For example, commercial galleries moving into the Lower East Side facilitated gentrification by raising rents and upgrading the area's image for other members of the gentrifying class.[7] In addition, works of art, sometimes even entire museum branches, were routinely placed in "public" areas of new corporate buildings and luxury apartment complexes. Whether sponsored by the state or the private sector, they elevated property values and legitimated private speculation by presenting an image of new construction as beautification programs that furnish cultural benefits to New York's populace. As Walter Benjamin commented about another urban transformation—Haussmann's spatial reorganization of nineteenth-century Paris—such works were largely deployed to "ennoble technical necessities by artistic aims."[8] To a certain extent this collaboration was possible because a great deal of the public art produced for New York's redeveloped, corporate spaces was informed by academic notions of site-specificity that gave this art an aura of social responsibility but suppressed comprehension of the real character of its urban sites. City spaces were treated solely as aesthetic, physical, or functionalist environments; economic forces shaping them were obscured in an enforced distinction between spatial forms and social processes. Haacke's real-estate pieces, by contrast, spanned that artificially created gap, expanding the definition of site-specificity in relation to both urban and cultural sites. The works addressed two spaces—the city and the museum—and treated each spatial form not as a static physical or aesthetic entity but as the effect and context of specific social relations.

The issue of specificity lay at the heart of the Guggenheim's rejection of Haacke's work. Inadequately and contradictorily defined by the museum's spokesperson, the specificity of Haacke's art was nonetheless cited as the principal reason for its unacceptability. "It is well understood in this connection," the Guggenheim's director Thomas Messer wrote to Haacke, "that art may have social and political *consequences* but these, we believe, are furthered by indirection and by the generalized, exemplary force that works of art may exert upon the environment, not, as you proposed, by using political means to achieve political ends, no matter how desirable these may appear to be in themselves."[9] Within the terms of this stock argument, Haacke's work is positioned, on account of its specificity, as "political" in contrast to the "indirect" art authorized by museological discourse and constituted, by virtue of the comparison, as "neutral." The practical implications of this doctrine were readily apparent in New York in the late 1980s, when public art that addressed its urban environment in aestheticized or narrowly utilitarian terms reverted to art's official purposes. In so doing, it complied with the demand that artists remain ignorant of the specific forces shaping their works' locations and oblivious to the works' functions. But the usefulness of this work to the forces of urban redevelopment undermined the credibility of Messer's assertion that art yields purely beneficial consequences. In 1971 the notion of art's "generalized exemplary force" was rallied to evict real estate from a New York City museum by claiming that Haacke's detailed analysis of real-estate operations was "alien" to artistic purposes. By the following decade the same aesthetic notion was used to validate the participation of artists, critics, and museums in advancing the interests of the real-estate industry in New York, which was evicting residents from the city. This change does not represent a reversal but, rather, a continuity in dominant aesthetic practice. In both instances, existing economic relations are actively shielded from public exposure by disavowing their direct ties to the conditions of artistic production. Art is severed from economics. When Haacke's work attempted to heal this ideological breach in aesthetic ‚thought, the Guggenheim Museum unveiled its repressive powers.

The Guggenheim's director canceled the exhibition "Hans Haacke: Systems" a few weeks before its planned opening in April 1971. The decision followed a brief period of negotiation between Haacke and Messer about the problems that the director anticipated with those works dealing with social, as distinguished from Haacke's previous physical or biological, themes. On April 5, following Haacke's publication of a statement about the cancellation, Messer responded: "I did explain that by trustee directive this museum was not to engage in extra-artistic activities or sponsor social or political causes but was to accept the limitations inherent in the nature of an art museum." [10]

Haacke's "extra-artistic" works included a visitors' poll that expanded a type of work that the artist had invented two years earlier—the audience survey. In 1970 Haacke conducted such a survey at the Museum of Modern Art's "Information" exhibition. [11] The MoMA poll directed attention to conditions of aesthetic reception by casting museumgoers in an active role. It queried spectators about their opinions on a timely political issue, asking, "Would the fact that Governor Rockefeller has not denounced President Nixon's Indochina policy be a reason for you not to vote for him in November?" Since Rockefeller, his relatives, and his business and political associates were integrally connected to MoMA either as officers or members of the board of trustees, the question, mounted on the museum wall, not only interrogated spectators about their own political leanings but encouraged them to interrogate modernist assumptions about the museum's status as a neutral arena cleansed of social and political concerns. The museum's white walls, signifier of the art institution's supposed purity and purportedly a mere background for equally pure art objects, became instead part of the material of the work. Haacke converted an element of art's physical frame into a vehicle for revealing, rather than masking, art's social context in a work that provoked public scrutiny of the social structure of the art institution and the economic interests of those who control it. In his Guggenheim survey of the following year, Haacke planned to query viewers about current social and political issues and tabulate responses to demographic questions that would, like his earlier *Gallery-Goers' Residence Profile* (1969), have yielded sociological information about the status and class composition of the art world. Part of a critique of audience and reception that challenged the existence of an art public untroubled by social divisions, the residence profiles suggested that art audiences are composed not of universal "citizens of art" but of specific subjects of class and race. These works also implied that art museums do

Question:

Would the fact that Governor Rockefeller has not denounced President Nixon's Indochina policy be a reason for you not to vote for him in November?

Answer:

If 'yes'
please cast your ballot into the left box,
if 'no'
into the right box.

Hans Haacke, *MOMA-Poll,* installed as part of the exhibition "Information," Museum of Modern Art, New York, 1970 (photo courtesy Hans Haacke).

not preserve aesthetic truths transcending social conflicts but are, rather, social institutions that preserve privilege and are therefore immersed in conflict.

Although Messer expressed reservations about the poll, he named Haacke's other "social systems" works as the reason for the show's cancellation. Using material freely available in public records, these works documented the property holdings and investment activities of two separate real-estate groups. One piece provided information about various types of buildings owned by the association of Sol Goldman and Alex DiLorenzo. The other displayed the slum properties of the Shapolsky family organization. In a letter of March 19, preceding the final cancellation, Messer stated that the likelihood of legal consequences precluded the exhibition of these works:

> When we began our joint exhibition project, you outlined a three-fold investigation and proposed to devote several exhibits to physical, biological, and social systems. From subsequent detailed outlines, it appeared that the social category would include a real-estate survey pointing through word and picture to alleged social malpractices. You would name, and thereby publicly expose, individuals and companies whom you consider to be at fault. After consultation with the Foundation's president and with advice from our legal counsel, I must inform you that we cannot go along with such an exhibition outline.[12]

Having also conferred with lawyers who denied that legal suits would arise from the work, Haacke commented a few months later that Messer's written statement had not referred to the poll as a reason for refusing to mount the show "because it was impossible to generate a legal smoke-screen for its rejection; in a meeting with the curator and my lawyer, Mr. Messer demanded the elimination of all directly political questions, a demand with which I, naturally, could not comply."[13] Debating the cancellation in art journals and the mass media, both the museum's director and Haacke's supporters consistently concentrated on the Shapolsky real-estate piece. The emphasis on the Shapolsky work is probably best explained by the compelling social contradictions that it addresses and the consequent force of its confrontation with the museum's universalizing pretensions.

———

ns Haacke, *Shapolsky et al. Manhattan Real Estate Holdings, a Real-Time Social System, as of May 1, 1971,* installation
w (photo courtesy Hans Haacke).

This confrontation was ensured by the sheer magnitude of the purely factual data that comprised the work and by the display of this material in a format unalloyed by either expressionistic sentiments or traditional aesthetic arrangements. *Shapolsky et al. Manhattan Real Estate Holdings* gathers individual photographs of 142 buildings and vacant lots located primarily in New York slum neighborhoods as well as a number of typewritten sheets, charts, diagrams, and maps detailing real-estate transactions. The piece incorporates these documents into a complex presentation. Had it been installed in the Guggenheim, spectators willing to commit time to viewing the work might have perceived striking physical and sociological contrasts between the buildings in the photographs, on the one hand, and the museum building in which the work and its audience were located, on the other.

Such observations would have been encouraged because Haacke's organization of pictorial and textual material blocks traditional avenues of aesthetic escape from the social conditions portrayed. Similarly, the Shapolsky piece refuses to supply the means by which a museumgoer's attention is conventionally diverted from the conditions in which art is viewed. Engaging its public in an active reading process, the work decisively rejects the single-image form of the painted, photographic, or sculptural object accompanied by a discrete caption, a form historically invested with the task of promoting transcendent experiences of "presentness" and evoking contemplative responses from spectators purportedly abstracted from historical circumstances. Moreover, the deadpan, unrelieved factuality of the Shapolsky piece counteracts attempts to convert the concrete specificity of its subject matter into a tribute to the artist's expressiveness and compassion. The repetitive arrangement militates against the transformation of the social reality the work documents into an elegant aesthetic composition, a supposedly self-contained totality.

Shapolsky et al. deviates from the conventions of a genre in which a similar iconography of lower-class urban neighborhoods had previously entered the modern art museum—liberal social documentary, or what Allan Sekula calls the "find-a-bum school of concerned photography."[14] Haacke's photographs document the same kind of New York tenement buildings that had been the object of social reformers' attention for decades, but while the Guggenheim Museum repeatedly referred to Haacke's work as a deed of "social reform," the project differs fundamentally from the humanist photography associated with reformist traditions. "The subjective aspect of liberal esthetics," Sekula writes about concerned photography, "is compassion rather than collective struggle. Pity, mediated by an appreciation of 'great art,' supplants political understanding."[15] Because such work is informed by overwhelmingly subjectivist or aestheticist ideals, it has found shelter within the museum, where it can be united with other aesthetic objects defined as products of unique artistic subjects. Since the art institution pays homage to the sensibility that transposes wretched social conditions into the register of art, the social documentarian's—and, by extension, the viewer's—distinct position of privilege in relation to his or her subject matter is confirmed. But power and privilege are concealed even as they are reinforced since the aesthetic domain is proclaimed a universal public sphere unfissured by class, race, or gender.

The Shapolsky piece alters to the point of reversal the viewing dynamics of liberal aesthetics. "Political understanding" replaces "pity, mediated by an appreciation of 'great art.'" Exhibited in the Guggenheim, it would have precipitated inspection not only of Shapolsky's real-estate maneuvers but of the museum's physical space, social position, and ideological tenets. The Guggenheim, originating in a collection of early twentieth-century idealist abstractions and trading in equally abstracted concepts of spiritual liberation, individual expression, and purified aesthetic experience, would have confronted a work employing painstakingly researched, concrete information about the specific material reality of New York. A museum building renowned as an aesthetic monument of architectural history would have housed representations of buildings defined solely as economic entities. Other contrasts—between the pristine museum interior and the deteriorating tenement facades, between the social status of the viewers' space in a luxury enclave of Manhattan and that of the impoverished minority ghettos pictured—also threatened to erode the aura of isolation constructed around the museum and to dismantle its pretensions to represent universal interests. Instead, the museum might have emerged as a space occupying a position of material privilege in relation to other sites. Viewers might then have focused on the character and interrelationship of these spaces. The anticipated confrontation between the Shapolsky piece and the museum quickened into an open rupture when Haacke's show was canceled. Once the cancellation was publicized, however, it only intensified the work's effects.

While the Shapolsky work sets up tensions between the spaces it addresses— the city and the museum—it also suggests correspondences between the two sites. Explicitly, it documents the ownership and control of urban space, but the work implicitly raises questions about how proprietorial interests affect the cultural space as well. By expanding the work's context beyond the museum walls to encompass the city in which the museum is situated, Haacke did not merely extend the notion of site-specificity geographically. Neither did he simplistically attempt to surmount institutional boundaries by symbolically placing his artwork "outside" the museum and addressing "real" subject matter. Rather, he permitted the viewer to apprehend the institutional apparatus by questioning the twin fetishisms of two, equally real, sites. Both the city—constructed in mainstream architectural and urban discourses as a strictly physical, utilitarian, or aesthetic space—and the museum—

conceived in idealist art discourse as a pure aesthetic realm—appear as spatial forms marked by a political economy.

Wanting to expose the presence of power in sites that appear neutral or self-evident, Haacke investigated the urban site by concentrating on real estate as a force determining the shape of New York's environment. This investigation, which, it turned out, flagrantly violated the museum's rules of aesthetic propriety, explains why Haacke selected the Shapolsky group as his object of study. Searching public records in the office of New York's County Clerk, he identified those real-estate owners with the most extensive holdings in their particular categories of investment. Far from an arbitrary choice, this decision was crucial to the fulfillment of Haacke's objective—revealing the degree to which large-scale real-estate interests dominate New York's landscape. As Haacke explains in the notes accompanying his presentation, in 1971 the Shapolsky properties represented the largest concentration of real estate in Harlem and the Lower East Side under the control of a single group. After choosing Shapolsky, who appeared in the *Manhattan Real Estate Directory* as the principal of these substantial holdings, Haacke researched the publicly recorded deeds and mortgage agreements for each of Shapolsky's properties. A careful examination of the names and addresses of the parties to the real-estate transactions disclosed that Shapolsky was the key figure in a family group that possessed even more properties. Tracking additional connections among members of this group, Haacke uncovered 142 parcels of land owned by the group for which title was legally held by about seventy different corporations. Frequent sales and exchanges took place among the individuals and corporations comprising the system. Properties were sold and mortgages obtained, assigned, and cross-held.

Haacke photographed the individual properties and coupled each picture with a typewritten sheet providing data about the property: address; block and lot number; size; building type (its official code—predominantly old- and new-law tenements and apartment buildings); holder of mortgage; assessed land value and total assessed value. He then synthesized this data in a series of diagrams that chart the business transactions relating to the properties in the twenty-year period prior to 1971. Three charts list the corporations holding the real-estate parcels and trace connections among the corporations in the form of exchanges of mortgages or properties. A fourth reveals the large number of mortgages on Shapolsky proper-

212 E 3 St.
Block 385 Lot 11
5 story walk-up old law tenement

Owned by Harpmel Realty Inc., 608 E 11 St., NYC
Contracts signed by Harry J. Shapolsky, President('63)
                     Martin Shapolsky, President('64)
Principal Harry J. Shapolsky(according to Real Estate
Directory of Manhattan)

Acquired 8-21-1963 from John the Baptist Foundation,
c/o The Bank of New York, 48 Wall St., NYC,
for $237 600.- (also 7 other bldgs.)

$150 000.- mortgage at 6% interest, 8-19-1963, due
8-19-1968, held by The Ministers and Missionaries
Benefit Board of the American Baptist Convention,
475 Riverside Drive, NYC(also on 7 other bldgs.)

Assessed land value $25 000.- , total $75 000.- (including 214-16 E 3 St.)(1971)

214 E 3 St.
Block 385 Lot 11
5 story walk-up old law tenement

Owned by Harpmel Realty Inc., 608 E 11 St., NYC
Contracts signed by Harry J. Shapolsky, President('63)
                     Martin Shapolsky, President('64)
Principal Harry J. Shapolsky(according to Real Estate
Directory of Manhattan)

Acquired 8-21-1963 from John the Baptist Foundation,
c/o The Bank of New York, 48 Wall St., NYC,
for $237 600.- (also 7 other bldgs.)

$150 000.- mortgage at 6% interest, 8-19-1963, due
8-19-1968, held by The Ministers and Missionaries
Benefit Board of the American Baptist Convention,
475 Riverside Drive, NYC (also on 7 other bldgs.)

Assessed land value $25 000.- , total $75 000.- (including 212 and 216 E 3 St.) (1971)

Hans Haacke, photos of building facades and data sheets from *Shapolsky et al. Manhattan Real Estate Holdings, a Real-Time Social System, as of May 1, 1971* (photos courtesy Hans Haacke).

216 E 3 St.
Block 385 Lot 11
5 story walk-up old law tenement

Owned by Harpmel Realty Inc., 608 E 11 St., NYC
Contracts signed by Harry J. Shapolsky, President('63)
                     Martin Shapolsky, President('64)
Principal Harry J. Shapolsky(according to Real Estate
Directory of Manhattan)

Acquired 8-21-1963 from John the Baptist Foundation,
c/o The Bank of New York, 48 Wall St., NYC
for $237 600.-(also 7 other bldgs.)

$150 000.- mortgage at 6% interest, 8-19-1963, due
8-19-1968, held by The Ministers and Missionaries
Benefit Board of the American Baptist Convention,
475 Riverside Drive, NYC (also on 7 other bldgs.)

Assessed land value $25 000.-, total $75 000.- (including 212-14 E 3 St.) (1971)

228 E 3 St.
Block 385 Lot 19
24 x 105' 5 story walk-up old law tenement

Owned by Harpmel Realty Inc. 608 E 11 St. NYC
Contracts signed by Harry J. Shapolsky, President('63)
                     Martin Shapolsky, President('64)
Acquired from John The Baptist Foundation
c/o The Bank of New York, 48 Wall St. NYC
for $237 000.- (also 5 other properties) , 8-21-1963

$150 000.- mortgage (also on 5 other properties) at 6%
interest as of 8-19-1963 due 8-19-1968 .
held by The Ministers and Missionaries Benefit Board of
The American Baptist Convention, 475 Riverside Dr. NYC

Assessed land value $8 000.- total $28 000.-(1971)

292 E 3 St.
Block 372 Lot 19
22 x 105' 5 story walk-up semi-fireproof apt. bldg.

Owned by Broweir Realty Corp., 608 E 11 St., NYC
Contracts signed by Seymour Weinfeld, President
            Alfred Fayer, Vicepresident
Principal Harry J. Shapolsky(according to Real Estate
Directory of Manhattan)

Acquired 10-22-1965 from Apponaug Properties Inc.
475 Riverside Drive, NYC, Frank L.Taylor, President

$55 000.- mortgage at 6% interest, 10-22-1965, held by
The Ministers and Missionaries Benefit Board of The
American Baptist Convention, 475 Riverside Drive, NYC
(also on 312 E 3 St.)

Assessed land value $6 500.- , total $55 000.- (1971)

299 E 3 St.
Block 373 Lot 56
18 x 96' 5 story walk-up old law tenement

Owned by West No. 10 Realty Corp., 608 E 11 St., NYC
Contracts signed by Martin Shapolsky, Pres.('65)
            Donald Sherman, Pres.('68)
Principal Harry J. Shapolsky(according to Real Estate
Directory of Manhattan)

Acquired 3-11-1965 from 300 Realty Corp.,
608 E 11 St., NYC,
contracts signed by Harry J. Shapolsky, Pres.('66/67)
            Pearl Shapolsky, Pres.('64/65/67)
            Donald Sherman, Vicepres.('71)
Principal Harry J. Shapolsky(according to Real Estate
Directory of Manhattan)

Due $8 875.27 of mortgage at 6% interest, held through
assignment, 8-30-1967, by 428 Realty Corp., 608 E 11 St.,
NYC, Harry J. Shapolsky, Pres.('61/3/5/6), due 12-1-1967,

Due $8000.- of mortgage held through assignment, 7-30-1965,
by 428 Realty Corp.

Assessed land value $5 200.- , total $18 000.- (1971)

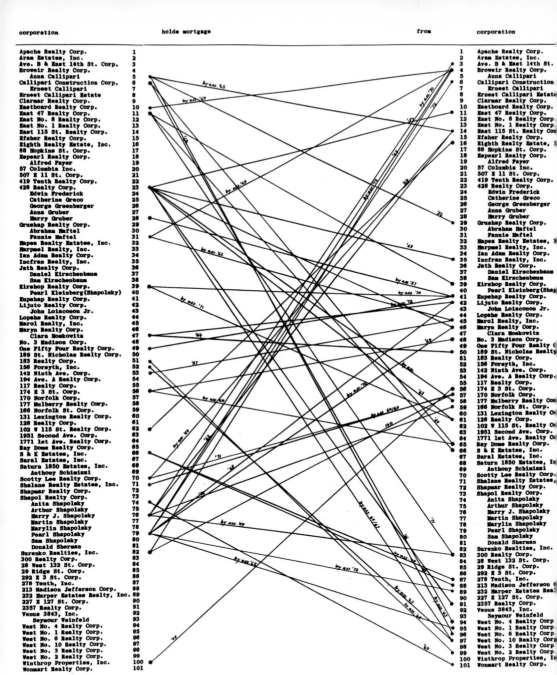

Hans Haacke, chart showing exchange of mortgages within Shapolsky group, from *Shapolsky et al. Manhattan Real Estate Ho a Real-Time Social System, as of May 1, 1971* (photo courtesy Hans Haacke).

ties held by two Baptist organizations. Finally, two charts inventory the corporation presidents and their addresses and juxtapose this material with the names of vice-presidents and secretaries as well as corporate addresses. These charts reveal that the Shapolsky real-estate system is a web of obscured family ties and dummy corporations that veil the identities of principal property owners. Completing Haacke's piece are enlarged maps of the Lower East Side and Harlem with the lots owned by the Shapolsky group circled.

The Shapolsky real-estate piece comprises, then, a dossier on an individual Manhattan slumlord, his family, and his associates. It identifies one kind of real-estate operation in the city and makes visible the complex mechanics of a profitable investment strategy. The photographs testify to the kinds of property in which the investments are made—housing in impoverished neighborhoods lucratively run at a low maintenance level. The data sheets and charts exhibit the myriad financial exchanges and the general investment organization that maximize the gains accruing from these manipulated properties. The Shapolsky system is open-ended. Following its various strands, the multiple relations among its individual and corporate components, one sees an even more labyrinthine and radiating network of real-estate power—a system that includes rental agents, city workers, city agencies, and religious groups, among others. The dispersal of functions within this "extended family" masks the system's interdependent operations. These operations appear random or discrete, rendering the system difficult to penetrate by tenants and the broader public, thereby enhancing its flexibility and control.

The full extent of the system's control emerged when, in addition to gathering and shaping the data, Haacke pursued research on the group in newspapers and other public sources of information. The results, some of which appear in the work's explanatory text, disclose that Shapolsky had been repeatedly investigated on a variety of criminal charges. These include concealing bank accounts and acting as a front for investments by members of the city's buildings department in properties he operated.[16] In 1959 Shapolsky was found guilty of rent gouging but was never imprisoned because the sentencing judge received numerous letters testifying to his good character from "very, very responsible people in the community."[17] Among Shapolsky's character witnesses was one of the Baptist organizations that Haacke's work reveals as the mortgage holder on many Shapolsky properties. In 1966, after an investigation by radio station WMCA, a bill was introduced into the state legislature requiring the publication of the names of slum owners who operate behind "the obscurity of corporate names."[18] The station cited Harry Shapolsky as one of about twelve real-estate operators who "had controlled 500 tenement buildings housing 50,000 persons buying and selling—or foreclosing—among each other in deals that increased rents and profits."[19] The bill proposed that a list of all true owners of any property declared "a public nuisance" be published in two newspapers. A liability clause would have made these owners—including mortgage holders—personally liable for repairs to buildings.[20]

The information gleaned from these news reports illuminates two strategies—self-dealing and corporate ownership—that, as Haacke's work makes clear, are central to Shapolsky's real-estate system. The frequent self-dealing maximizes profits. Multiple corporate ownership limits personal liability. Both strategies obscure the identities of the principal investors in individual buildings and conceal the full extent of the owners' holdings. Consequently, they limit public knowledge and, therefore, the owners' accountability for nondelivery of services to tenants as well as for tax payments. Using techniques that structure complex deals worked out by lawyers and accountants, such private speculation is, in reality, publicly supported.

But a knowledge of these techniques generates perceptions that extend beyond recognition of the mechanics of the Shapolsky strategy or even the system's comprehensive nature. Such knowledge underscores a fundamental contradiction in a larger real-estate system framing the Shapolsky operation: that between market requirements and the social needs of city residents. This contradiction may emerge most dramatically in the quasi-legal or criminal activities of unscrupulous landlords, yet it springs from the basic organization of housing as a private investment in capitalist society. Indifference to human needs cannot finally be attributed to the callousness of individual landlords but is, rather, structurally determined. Alluding to this contradiction—and Haacke always encourages viewers to explore his works' full implications—Haacke's piece, too, exceeds the limits of its investigation of Shapolsky family relations and becomes a critique of social relations of property.

This aspect of Haacke's critique raises questions about the real-estate pieces' "specificity"—which, as we have seen, was the main reason for the Guggenheim's refusal to show the works. When Messer defined specificity, he distinguished between the act of naming specific individuals, on the one hand, and the representation of an anonymous system, on the other. He claimed that the designation of actual people, not a social system, was impermissible in the museum. Repeatedly, however, he also stated that social issues should be engaged artistically only through symbolism, generalization, and metaphor, thereby disqualifying specificity about the identity of a system as well as of individuals. Equivocation on this point pervades Messer's justification for the cancellation. "Where do we draw the line?" he asked. "*With the revealed identities of private individuals and the clear intention to call their actions into question,* and by a concomitant reduction of the work of art from its potential metaphoric level to a form of photo journalism concerned with topical statements rather than with symbolic expression."[21] Questioned by an astute interviewer who tried to untangle Messer's definition of "particularity," he replied: "I don't know that I fully understood you. But I would say that in the motivation again what is acceptable is the general illustration of a system. What is for the purposes of this discussion inacceptable [sic] is that it is aimed at a specific situation. In other words, it no longer has a self-contained creative objective, but is something with an ulterior motive."[22]

From Messer's obfuscating explanations of what constitutes unacceptable specificity—naming individuals *only* and, simultaneously, *any* nongeneralized reference to a social situation—it is only reasonable to conclude that the real-estate pieces in fact contained two kinds of specificity that the museum found objectionable: first, the detailed identification of the activities of a landlord whose right to operate out of public view had to be protected and second, the implicit designation of a broader framework for this system in a historically specific structure of property relations.

Several elements of Haacke's work permit viewers to question this second system. The condition of the photographed buildings is linked to—indeed is regulated by—the financial operations documented in the data sheets and charts. Clearly neither a natural nor a random process, these operations are themselves directed by careful decisions dictated by the logic of an investment system. The juxtaposition of photographs of deteriorated housing with extensive calculations of large amounts of accumulating capital focuses the viewer's investigation. The investment activities do not serve the interests of poor tenants, nor does the provision of services to those tenants seem to provide a high rate of return on investment. Once the drive for profit through capital accumulation and appropriation of rents is seen as the principal factor governing the provision and condition of housing, serious doubts arise as to whether the needs of low-income residents can ever be met.[23]

In 1959, criticizing the suspension of Shapolsky's sentence for rent gouging Puerto Rican tenants, New York's assistant district attorney stated that Shapolsky had "ruthlessly exploited the shortage of housing."[24] Without minimizing the importance of this charge, it is crucial to recognize that when the housing problem is addressed exclusively in terms of the need to eliminate *abuses* of scarcity, this condition itself remains unexamined. Scarcity of housing is socially, not naturally, produced and is, moreover, a precondition of the market system. This fact has special ramifications for ghetto areas like those documented in Haacke's work. Given the institution of private ownership of real-estate parcels and the drive to increase profits by appropriating higher rents, coupled with the extremely limited choices of poor people in securing access to urban resources, it is difficult to escape the conclusion that, as David Harvey asserts, "the rich can command space whereas the poor are trapped in it."[25] Exploitative behavior by landlords only exacerbates the effects of normal entrepreneurial operations. Speculation in land and housing is an inevitable feature of capitalist urban development, resulting from forces at the core of our economic system.

Within this system, land and the structures on it assume the form of commodities. They do not, however, necessarily manifest this form with regularity. Real estate is likely to be in use for long periods of time and only rarely exchanged. The dialectical unity of use and exchange value embodied in the commodity appears with greatest frequency in the activities shown in the Shapolsky piece: the operation of rental housing and the frequent sale of properties. Haacke's mode of display emphasizes the commodity character of the buildings, neighborhoods, and city. The data sheets, for example, initially label each vacant lot or building by the conventional units—block and lot numbers—that classify it as real property. Subdivisions of Manhattan's grid structure, the spatial organization imposed on the city by the Commissioner's Plan of 1811, these units facilitate profit maximization and provide the infrastructure for real-estate speculation. Haacke's photographs reinforce at the level of individual structures the impression that the city itself is an economic product. Shot from street level, looking up at the buildings, the photographs have borders that coincide with property lines, emphatically refusing compositional devices that might identify the buildings as historically or aesthetically interesting urban structures rather than as real estate. The municipal maps represent the city in a similar manner, objectified as an assemblage of blocks with Shapolsky's lots indicated. This objectification is particularly striking in relation to the sociology of the areas represented—Harlem and the Lower East Side, two working-class sectors of Manhattan. In the past, ethnic and racial minorities have been directed to these ghettos, which retain strong identities as communities containing vital networks of social institutions. In Haacke's maps, photographs, and data sheets, however, they appear not as communities but as spatial terrains defined purely by the real-estate market, a collection of houses, physical structures, and vacant lots.

Real estate is a commodity with some unusual features. One is physical immobility: it cannot be moved at will. But fixity does not characterize the social processes that organize land and buildings into particular formations. These processes have the opposite quality: as human practices they can be transformed. While the substantial power of real estate is amply demonstrated in Haacke's Shapolsky piece, the land and buildings do not appear to be immutable. Their permanence is shaken, and not only because they are continually manipulated and transferred in the marketplace. Rather, seen as private property and commodities, they embody relationships of exploitation and domination open to change.

Similarly, Haacke's work jolted the fictitious air of stability surrounding the building in which it was to be installed and undermined that building's claim to represent eternal values. *Shapolsky et al.* created numerous comparisons between its subject matter and the Guggenheim—analogies between the ownership and control of properties and the ownership and control of culture, between houses collected by the Shapolsky family and art collected by the Guggenheim family, between the commodity form of both housing and art production, and, especially after the show's cancellation, between the concealment of power in the city and in the museum. Ultimately, the work highlighted the fact that the museum building, too, is no isolated architectural structure, container of static aesthetic objects, but a social institution existing within a wider system, a product and producer of mutable power relations.

Following the cancellation, Haacke enlarged the project initiated in the real-estate piece—submitting private actions to public scrutiny—by publicizing the museum's censorship of his exhibition and discussing it openly in newspapers and art magazines as well as on television and radio. Throughout the discussion, the museum's director repeated his initial explanation for the cancellation but added that, even without the fear of legal reprisal, Haacke's work "posed a direct threat to the museum's functioning within its stated and accepted premises."[26]

Should social malpractices be exposed if the evidence is dependable and reliable? Certainly, but not through the auspices of an art museum. It is freely admitted that this conclusion is self-protective, that is, protective of the museum's function as we currently understand it. Individuals and companies who would have suddenly found themselves the unsuspecting targets of a work of art could be expected to react against the artist as well as his museum sponsor. The possibility of a libel suit resulting from such a situation is therefore not farfetched. *But the museum's sponsorship would hardly seem defensible even if the legal effects proved to be containable* through the presumably unassailable nature of the assembled documentation—a rather large assumption on the part of the artist.

A precedent would, in any case, have been set for innumerable analogous presentations with predictably damaging effects upon the museum's central function. What would, for instance, prevent another artist from launching, again via a work of art, a pictorial documentation of police corruption in a particular precinct? What would stand in the way of a museum-sponsored attack upon a particular cigarette brand which the documentation assembled for this purpose would show to be a national health risk?[27]

What indeed? In a historical period marked in the United States by mass protests against governmental policy, police actions, and corporate endangerment of public safety at home and abroad, these possibilities could hardly have seemed absurd or even undesirable. What, for that matter, would prevent an artist from exposing "via a work of art" the threat to public interests posed by the activities of those who control art institutions?

Haacke did just that.[28] In 1974, his *Solomon R. Guggenheim Museum Board of Trustees* extended some of the parallels suggested in the Shapolsky work. A key step in Haacke's development of a type of artwork that interrogates, rather than deflects attention from, the economic and political structure of art institutions, *Guggenheim Trustees,* in a manner strikingly reminiscent of *Shapolsky et al.,* traces the connections among members of the Guggenheim family, other trustees of the museum, and several corporations that frequently shared addresses and officers. For the multinational Kennecott Copper Corporation—which counted a Guggenheim family member and two museum trustees on its board of directors—Haacke presented information about the company's investments in Chile and included a statement by the country's deposed and murdered president, Salvador Allende, that such transnational corporations were "not accountable to or representing the collective interest" of Chilean citizens. Kennecott was later named in hearings on the destabilization of the Allende democracy by United States interests.[29] Using the typography and layout of official trustee lists, *The Solomon R. Guggenheim Board of Trustees* referred pointedly to the museum's interest in concealing its own relationship to the operations of privatized property against "the collective interest," a concealment that parallels the Shapolsky strategy for avoiding public accountability.

Hans Haacke, *Solomon R. Guggenheim Museum Board of Trustees,* 1974, panel 1 (photo courtesy Hans Haacke).

Hans Haacke, *Solomon R. Guggenheim Museum Board of Trustees,* 1974, panel 2 (photo courtesy Hans Haacke).

Hans Haacke, *Solomon R. Guggenheim Museum Board of Trustees,* 1974, panel 3 (photo courtesy Hans Haacke).

Hans Haacke, *Solomon R. Guggenheim Museum Board of Trustees*, 1974, panel 4 (photo courtesy Hans Haacke).

Hans Haacke, *Solomon R. Guggenheim Museum Board of Trustees,* 1974, panel 5 (photo courtesy Hans Haacke).

Hans Haacke, *Solomon R. Guggenheim Museum Board of Trustees*, 1974, panel 6 (photo courtesy Hans Haacke).

Hans Haacke, *Solomon R. Guggenheim Museum Board of Trustees,* 1974, panel 7 (photo courtesy Hans Haacke).

Self-protectively, the Guggenheim's director repeatedly described the museum as a private domain and characterized Haacke's real-estate works as an invasion of the privacy of both individual entrepreneurs and the artistic "sanctuary." Designed to foster private experience, the museum was an inappropriate place to question publicly real-estate investors committed to limiting public awareness of their activities. "These individuals," Messer asserted, "would have been held up to public scrutiny and condemnation without their knowledge and consent."[30] By attacking their right to seclusion, he contended, Haacke was taking unfair advantage of the museum as a refuge to protect *himself* from repercussions:

> Haacke's work implicates certain individuals from the safety of its museum sanctuary. Protected by the armor of art, the work reaches out into the sociopolitical environment where it affects not the large conscience of humanity, but the mundane interest of particular parties. Upon the predictable reaction of society the work, turned weapon, would recede into its immune "art-self" to seek shelter within the museum's temporary custody.[31]

Willing, nonetheless—by canceling the exhibition—to offer the museum's protection to large-scale private property and individual slumlords, Messer rehearsed prevalent illusions about the art institution as a natural retreat from the exigencies of society. In so doing, he tacitly invoked a view of the museum consistent with its role as surrogate for the bourgeois domestic interior.

Far from a naturally given entity, however, the interior emerged in the nineteenth century to perform functions tied to concrete economic conditions. Analyzing the bourgeois living environment as a prismatic cultural object that refracts and illuminates these conditions, Walter Benjamin succinctly reconstructed its origins in bourgeois society's historical demarcation of public and private spheres, the latter representing the privilege of seclusion. There, private individuals were guaranteed protection and freedom to pursue their own self-interest. To the considerable extent that such freedom ensured the liberty of acquiring and disposing of property at will, the private sphere testified to the definitive withdrawal of resources from social control and served a crucial function in legitimating the bourgeois view of life.

Within the private sphere, the domestic interior was constituted as a separate domain where harmony was artificially achieved by expelling the conflicts that characterize economic society. Dependent for its comforts on gains in the economic realm, the illusions of the security of the interior were necessary precisely because the basis of capitalist society lies in a collision of interests. "The private person," wrote Benjamin, "who squares his accounts with reality in his office demands that the interior be maintained in his illusions. This need is all the more pressing since he has no intention of extending his commercial considerations into social ones. In shaping his private environment he represses both. From this spring the phantasmagorias of the interior."[32] "The interior is the retreat of art,"[33] Benjamin continued, describing the doomed attempts of the private owner of artworks to obliterate the commodity character of his collected objects.

The illusions of the interior as shelter and citadel, transferred to that other retreat of art—the museum—were severely shaken when Haacke proposed to bring texts and photographs of the exteriors of slum dwellings inside the Guggenheim's cloistered residence. The violent expulsion that this emblematic confrontation provoked suggests that economic and social conflicts are not, in reality, "alien" to the museum's harmonious space but—as Benjamin wrote about the interior—haunt it from the start.[34] At least that is what the museum itself intimated when, at an unusually telling moment, it articulated its ideology of autonomy and privacy through a literal defense of the rights of private property.

II

MEN IN SPACE

Men in Space

With the publication in 1989 of two books, both by geographers, urban studies decisively entered "the postmodern debate"—determined, apparently, to win. Indeed, Edward Soja's *Postmodern Geographies* and David Harvey's *The Condition of Postmodernity*[1] possess a winning combination: they bring together discourses about space, culture, and aesthetics within the framework of a critical social theory that purports to explain the postmodern world. This formula has been used before by a small group of disparate scholars who, over the last decade, have written not only about postmodern culture but about modernism as well.

For anyone in the art world eager to escape the control that traditional aesthetic categories exercise over how art is defined, such interdisciplinary approaches have a strong, even fatal, attraction. Strong for many reasons, but especially because they permit us to view art from previously excluded perspectives within which, linked to new elements, it modifies its very identity. That shift is illuminating not only for what it reveals about art but for what it suggests about knowledge. For an instant, all explanation appears uncertain, since objects of knowledge are themselves indeterminable, fixed only by discursive relationships and exclusions. Knowledge is "complete" only when it conceals this process. The interdisciplinary approach is appealing, then, because it momentarily undermines the authority of all knowledge that claims to know definitively the things it studies. But interdisciplinarity holds dangers, too, because it does not automatically become antidisciplinary. More often, disciplines unite in alliances that fortify an authoritarian epistemology—by adding to its appearance of completeness—instead of relinquishing it for a more democratic one. Is the current synthesis of urban and cultural studies such a defensive formation? If so, what are its casualties?

In 1985 sociologist Janet Wolff raised a similar question. Investigating the biases that have shaped her profession's definitions of both the modern urban experience and the culture of modernism, she drew a succinct conclusion: "The literature of modernity describes the experience of men."[2] Seconding Wolff's opinion and repeating her assertion that modernity is a product of the city, Griselda Pollock later extended Wolff's thesis to evaluate another discipline—art history—and, in particular, T. J. Clark's exemplary text of social art history, *The Painting of Modern Life: Paris in the Art of Manet and His Followers*.[3] Clark compares the spatial compositions and iconography of late-nineteenth-century modernist painting with the spaces of the modern city. He describes, with erudition, Baron Haussmann's architectural and social reorganization of Paris and analyzes the effects of Haussmannization using a sociological paradigm popularized in Marshall Berman's influential book *All That Is Solid Melts Into Air:* modernization is a process of capitalist socioeconomic restructuring; modernity, the experience produced by that process; and modernism, the culture developing from the modern experience.[4] Adhering to this model of society in which so-called levels—sets of relations and political practices—interact but are, in the end, hierarchically compartmentalized, Clark explains that, for him, economic life is not a given reality but, like the cultural realm, consists of representations. He does not, however, consider the politics of his own representation of society—which, in fact, he never examines as a representation at all. Instead, he feels free to "insist" unproblematically "on the determinate weight in society of those arrangements we call economic" and to state that "the class of an individual . . . is the determinant fact of social life."[5] Consequently, Clark interprets nineteenth-century modernist painting as an artistic response to the experience produced by Haussmann's spatial reorganization of Paris, which was determined, in turn, by the restructuring of capitalism during the Second Empire. Modernism "failed," in Clark's view, because it did not map the class divisions of modern Paris but rather obscured them by recreating in painting what Haussmann produced in the actual built environment—a mythologization of the city as "spectacle."

Not surprisingly, this account produces, as Pollock notes, "peculiar closures on the issue of sexuality."[6] Yet Clark's descriptions of cities and paintings do not entirely neglect women's "experience," nor do they completely ignore the topic of gender relations. What his book does dismiss is feminism, considered as a requisite, rather than expendable, mode of social critique. Clark's repression of feminism is not, as some commentators claim, necessitated by his interest in the category of class. Instead, it is authorized by his image of the social as a complete entity in which a single set of social relations are privileged as determinate—the absolute foundation of social totality.

Feminism, of course, has long challenged this kind of totalizing depiction. It has also made indispensable contributions to aesthetic thought precisely in relation to Clark's principal object of study: the visual image. Clark's book deals with both the city as a visual image and visual images of the city. For years, feminist theories have differentiated vision—pleasure in looking—from the notion of seeing as a process of perceiving the real world. The image and the act of looking are now understood to be relations highly mediated by fantasies that structure and are structured by sexual difference. Visual space is, *in the first instance,* a set of social relations; it is never innocent, nor does it merely reflect, either directly or through contrived mediations, "real" social relations located elsewhere—in, for example, the economic relations producing the built environment. From the moment this environment becomes an image—becomes what Raymond Ledrut calls "the locus of a certain 'investment' by the ego"[7]—its meaning is no longer reducible to nor fixed by the economic circumstances of its production. From the moment we try to understand the city as an image, feminist theories of visual space intersect with, and simultaneously problematize, the political economy of urban space, which, it is important to note, does not inherently exclude feminism. That exclusion is enforced in an epistemological field where grandiose claims are made on theoretical space, where only one theory is allowed to explain social relations of subordination. Refusing difference in social theory, the literature about modernity issuing from a synthesis of urban and cultural disciplines has, in this manner, constructed a coherent field by eliminating feminist criticism.

Will the same be true for urban postmodernity? This question has hovered at the margins of cultural criticism since 1984, when Fredric Jameson, drawing eclectically from spatial and aesthetic discourses, published his well-known article, "Postmodernism, or the Cultural Logic of Late Capitalism."[8] Jameson assesses postmodernism as a cultural "pathology." It is a condition produced by the multiple "fragmentations"—of space, society, the body, the subject—that Jameson attributes solely to the economic and spatial restructuring that constitute capitalism's third stage. To help overcome this condition, he issues a prescription for radical artists. They should engage, he says, in an "aesthetic of cognitive mapping"—the production of spatial images—by means of which inhabitants of "hyperspace" might overcome fragmentation, recover the ability to perceive the underlying totality, and consequently find their place in the world.

Jameson contends that he is suggesting a way for radical artists to participate in political battles over representation. Yet his proposal for analyzing space as a visual image begs, just as Clark's does, the political issues raised by feminist critiques of representation—most notably, the issue of positionality. A commanding position on the battleground of representation—one that denies the partial and fragmented condition of vision by claiming to perceive the foundation unifying social space—is an illusory place whose construction, motivated by wishes, entails hallucinations and blindness. It is analogous to a position created in styles of knowledge that seek to produce total—unfragmented—subjects. This cannot be wished away by stating, as Jameson has, that his concepts are, like all others, representations. This statement does not obviate the need to question the forms of our representations, which matter politically because representations are always constituted by acts of differentiation. If representations are social relationships, rather than reproductions of preexisting meanings, then the high ground of total knowledge can only be gained by an oppressive encounter with difference—the relegation of other subjectivities to positions of subordination or invisibility.

Jameson's image of society and his desire for accurate maps illustrate this mechanism. Fragmentation, in his account, is self-evidently a pathology, and our ability to find our places in the world has been destroyed by late capitalism alone. Diminishing the importance of social antagonisms other than those of class, Jameson conflates the disorienting effects of global capitalism with the rather different disorientations produced by recent challenges—from feminists, gays, postcolonials, antiracists—to the kinds of discourse that Jameson himself mobilizes: unitarian knowledge and foundationalist representation. These challenges expose Jameson's fragmented social unity and total subject position as fictions from the start, and he responds by silencing them. Accordingly, he has recently dispelled any doubts about the nature of "cognitive mapping" by revealing that what he actually means by this procedure for uncovering total reality is "class consciousness,"[9] thereby definitively wiping feminism off the map of radical social theory. How does it resurface? As just another force fragmenting our ability to apprehend the "real" unified political field.

The Jameson school of interdisciplinarity has yet to receive sustained attention from art critics. Its relationship to feminism has become more urgent with the appearance of Harvey's and Soja's books about postmodernism. Leaders in the field of Marxist geography, these authors have each made valuable contributions to theories of "the social production of space," which, as they make clear, is the very condition of late-capitalist restructuring. They have now turned to cultural theory in response to several developments: debates taking place within their own discipline about the epistemological basis and political stakes of geographical authority; the growth of a "postmodern" politics that diverges from the principles of traditional Marxism; and, perhaps, urban sociology's inability to address the built environment as a signifying practice. The seriousness of Harvey's and Soja's intentions to embrace the field of culture is called into question, however, when one examines their bibliographies. The literature that they have consulted is *very* exclusive, virtually restricted to texts by white, Western males and, of those, none that deal with feminism and postmodernism.

To note these similarities is not to equate the two books. Indeed, Soja is uncomfortable with Harvey's rigid economistic formulas for explaining the production of space and, to define space as social from the start, he advances concepts of a "socio-spatial dialectic" and a "spatialized ontology." He claims that he wants to disintegrate the boundaries between disciplines while respecting their specificity. But his readings of "postmodern landscapes" leave the cultural and economic fields curiously unmodified by their encounter; the identity of each remains intact. Moreover, by framing the city, and space in general, as a landscape surveyed by a transcendent viewer and by refusing to consider the politics of such a visualizing model of knowledge, Soja clings tenaciously to a belief in the total vantage point despite, as Liz Bondi points out, the interest that he expresses in postmodern decentering.[10]

Harvey sets out even more resolutely on the path forged by Clark and Jameson, defending "historical-geographical materialism" against postmodernism. Jameson is no longer alone in the strength of his negative evaluation of "fragmentation." For Harvey, too, postmodernism is monolithic and threatening, even apocalyptic. It mirrors fragmented, dislocated, compressed, and abstracted experiences of space and time, experiences wrought by post-Fordist capitalism's regime of flexible accumulation—"the condition of postmodernity." The concern for difference and specificity expressed in certain branches of postmodern thought, their skepticism about universalisms, "complies" with the concealment of capitalism's global penetration, which Harvey equates with all of social reality. Contemporary artists interested in what Harvey terms "image creation" are also complicit with capitalism. Their attention to images, he believes, is a turn away from the "real" social world because it fetishistically rejects "essential" social meanings: it fails to provide us with Jamesonian "mental maps" to "match current realities" or with a "trajectory out of the condition of postmodernity."[11]

Here, Harvey is seriously confused. It is certainly true that contemporary art has explored the image. But critical practices have done so neither to assert the status of the image as a container of universal, aesthetic meanings nor to celebrate the dominant images that circulate in our society. Rather, they have investigated visual images as part of a realm of representation where meanings and subjects are socially and hierarchically produced as, among other things, gendered. To the extent that this is their objective, postmodern artists' concentration on images is emphatically not a turn away from, but rather toward, the social—if, that is, relations of gender and sexuality count as more than epiphenomena of society. Harvey, ignorant of contemporary materialist discourses about images and blind to the fact that some of the art he criticizes *contests* the fetishistic representation of women, argues—in the name of antifetishism—for transparent images that reveal "essential" meanings. This—truly fetishistic—conception, in which representations are produced by subjects who discover, rather than project, meaning, corresponds to Harvey's own image of society: a metatheory that purports to perceive the absolute foundation of social coherence. Postmodernism interferes with that depiction. "Postmodernism," complains Harvey, "takes matters too far. It takes them beyond the point where any coherent politics are left. . . . Postmodernism has us . . . denying that kind of meta-theory which can grasp the political-economic processes." [12]

It is true that the term *postmodernism* means many different things and is surrounded by conflict. But this is no reason for reducing, as Harvey does, all critiques of totalization to an undifferentiated mass or for ignoring, in the process, the persistence of feminism within postmodern culture. Given the presence of feminism, what can it possibly mean to characterize postmodernity, *negatively*, as fragmented? Such assertions veer dangerously close to conservative tenets that feminists disrupt "our" unified heritage.

It would be a shame if urban studies intervened in cultural theory only to reinstate such ideas. Nonsubordinated feminisms would, then, be equated with political escapism and feminist contributions to analyses of the visual environment rejected as evasions of urban reality. If, unreceptive to the sexual politics of representation addressed in contemporary art, urban discourse continues to construct space as a feminized object surveyed by mastering subjects and if the effects of such discursive spatializations remain unexamined, the discipline will simply reproduce oppressive forms of knowledge.

Artists do not need more directives for the "cognitive mapping" of global space or exhortations to take the position of the totality. Postmodernists who problematize the image—artists like Cindy Sherman, Barbara Kruger, Silvia Kolbowski, Mary Kelly, Victor Burgin, Sherrie Levine, Laurie Simmons, Connie Hatch—reject such vanguard roles. They have been saying for years that, thanks to the recognition that representations are produced by situated—not universal—subjects, the world is not so easily mapped anymore. They do not seek to conquer this complexity but to multiply the fragmentations, mapping the configurations of fantasy that produce coherent images, including coherent images of politics. Geographers will have to examine that space.

BOYS TOWN

In the course of this work it became apparent that there were many empty rooms in the house of Marxian theory and that a lot of thought had to be given as to how best they might be furnished.

—David Harvey, *The Urban Experience*

Masculinity is not only erection but also enclosure, the logic of the house is as phallocentric as that of the tower.

—Mark Wigley, *The Architecture of Deconstruction: Derrida's Haunt*

Like most discussions of postmodernism, David Harvey's *The Condition of Post-modernity* aspires to a general theory of contemporary culture.[1] Harvey's ambitions, however, exceed the merely general. He seeks to unify all cultural events, all social relations, and all political practices by locating their origins in a single foundation. Harvey's claims to comprehensiveness are, therefore, grander than most. What, then, does it mean that in the book he completely ignores one of the most significant cultural developments of the past twenty years—the emergence of practices in art, film, literature, and criticism informed by feminist theories of representation? What, further, does it mean that Harvey disregards the presence of a feminist voice in postmodern aesthetics even though the work that he includes as an exemplar of postmodernism in the arts—the photography of Cindy Sherman—is just such a practice? Sherman's art raises questions about sexual difference and visual representation. Yet Harvey remains blind to this issue, among others, in Sherman's work, in the critical writing about her work and, more broadly, in the cultural discourse that is ostensibly his object of study. What motivates and legitimates such oversights in the work of a rigorous thinker?

And what are we to make of the numerous instances of carelessness or the outright errors, large and small, in Harvey's book? Is it meaningful, to take only one case, that Harvey accidentally changes the sex of the film theorist on whose writing he relies to analyze *Blade Runner,* one of his principal examples of postmodern film? Giuliana Bruno becomes Giuliano: she becomes he. This mistake signals still another transformation: Harvey brings Bruno's argument into conformity with his own point of view by appropriating only part of her essay on *Blade Runner,* overlooking its psychoanalytic and feminist dimensions. Bruno, like Harvey, criticizes the notion of history that permeates a certain idea of postmodern architecture. She characterizes as a fiction—"a dream of unity"—the belief that history is a homogeneous, continuous, or directly accessible reality. But unlike Harvey, she stresses the role that fantasy and desire play in constructions of the past. History, she writes, following Roland Barthes, "is the trace of the dream of unity, of its impossibility."[2] Bruno rejects not history but the idea that it possesses a coherence given by an absolute foundation. Her critique of "postmodern" architecture's appropriations of historical styles is not made in the name of an objective history whose meaning inheres in a basis existing independently of discourse. Harvey's dismissal of key aspects of Bruno's essay is, then, hardly neutral. It permits him to use her article to defend a position that she is casting into doubt: a belief in the authority of historical truths constituted apart from subjects. Does the sex change—Harvey's inadvertent transformation of Bruno into a man—correspond to, even emblematize, this more extensive operation—Harvey's metamorphosis of Bruno's ideas into the image of his own?

Other misperceptions pervade *The Condition of Postmodernity.* At one point, for instance, Harvey alludes to feminist ideas about difference. He briefly refers to Carol Gilligan's *In A Different Voice,* a book that affirms the relativity, rather than singularity, of moral development. Although Gilligan's book can scarcely be considered a model of all feminist critiques of universalizing thought—feminists frequently question the book's essentializing of women's experience—it serves as Harvey's token reference to feminism. It is one of only two or three citations of feminist literature in his bibliography of postmodernism, and the reference to Gilligan represents a rare moment—really, I think, the only one—when Harvey differentiates feminism from other items in a list of what he considers to be special interest groups: women, gays, blacks, ecologists, regional autonomists, etc.

Even this moment of interest is fleeting. Only a few sentences after mentioning Gilligan's ideas about difference, Harvey catalogues "women" within a typically homogenizing enumeration of new social movements. Most of these, he immediately adds, "pay scant attention to postmodernist arguments" and, he concludes, "some feminists are hostile" (48). Despite the apparent neutrality, this passage relies on a series of slippages that secure support for the author's own attitude toward postmodernism. Harvey fails to distinguish, first, among different social movements and then between academic theories, on the one hand, and social movements, on the other. Next, he neutralizes the heterogeneity of discourses about both feminism and postmodernism, and, finally, he ignores the diversity of current discussions about connections between the two. Harvey thus exploits feminism's complex relationship with postmodern discourses to defend his own, frequently different, hostilities. What accounts for these escalating failures to see the difference?

The answer, I think, is simple. Totalizing visions of society such as Harvey's are precisely, to borrow Giuliana Bruno's phrase, "dreams of unity." Harvey's discourse claims to observe, rather than construct, the absolute foundation of all social life. The subject of this discourse supposedly perceives society in its entirety and so seems to stand outside, not in, the world. His identity apparently owes nothing either to his real situation or to the object he studies—society. In denying the discursive character of that object, Harvey's account also denies that subjectivity is a partial and situated position. "Society," construed as an impartial object independent of all subjectivity, generates the illusion of an equally autonomous subject who views social conflicts from a privileged and unconflicted place. Since this total vantage point can be converted from fantasy into reality only by disavowing its contingent nature—its dependence on objects—and by relegating other viewpoints or different subjectivities to invisible, subordinate, or competing positions, foundationalist totalizations are systems that try to immunize themselves against uncertainty and difference.

They do so in different ways. The three examples cited from Harvey's book are all cases of mistaken identity. Mistaken not because Harvey misapprehends the true meaning of the art and texts that he describes but because he repeatedly represents difference as sameness: he does not dismiss Cindy Sherman's work, he ignores its specificity within postmodern art production; he disregards the distinction between Giuliana Bruno's argument about postmodernism and his own; and he homogenizes what are actually diverse positions on feminism and postmodernism to reconcile them with his own view. The subject of Harvey's discourse, the total subject, clearly thrives on mistaken identity.

Today, totalizing impulses are routinely manifested in indifference to feminism—to feminism's difference from other social analyses, its internal differences, and its theories of difference. This disregard survives—indeed it is even being revived—in some branches of cultural criticism despite feminism's decisive impact on cultural practices. It persists even more tenaciously in critical urban studies that, until recently, have granted feminist theories only the most marginal visibility. Now there is growing interest in interdisciplinary mergers of critical urban and cultural discourses. On the one hand, aesthetic practitioners—architects, urban planners, artists—have used the contributions of urban theory to examine how their work functions in urban social contexts. Urban scholars, on the other hand, have turned to cultural theory to study the city as a signifying object. Both groups hope that encounters between the two fields—themselves composed of several disciplines—will expand our ability to understand and intervene in what urban theorists call the politics of space.

Barbara Kruger, *Untitled (You thrive on mistaken identity)*, 1981
(photo courtesy Barbara Kruger).

Undertaking such a project means, however, that we must also reconfigure
the space of politics. What role does culture play in urban political struggle? What
is the relationship between cultural and economic conflict? Is not urban studies
itself a cultural activity? These questions require us to rearticulate the terms of
urban politics and rethink interdisciplinarity. For when the elements that constitute
the field of spatial politics are combined in truly new formations, without assuming that one is the essence of "the urban" and the others mere epiphenomena,

the elements themselves are altered and the boundaries that define disciplines undermined.

Radical interdisciplinary work, in other words, takes account of its own spatial relations. It interrogates the epistemological basis and political stakes of disciplinary authority. Less interdisciplinary than postdisciplinary, such work is based on the premise that objects of study are the effect rather than the ground of disciplinary knowledge. How these objects are constituted—through which exclusions or repressions—is itself a political question that conventional forms of interdisciplinarity disregard. Instead, they grant their objects of study an independent existence and therefore take for granted the existence of absolute foundations underlying distinct, specialized areas of knowledge. Mere exchanges of data, of course, leave disciplinary identities and authority intact. Sometimes, however, disciplines defend this authority more actively. They may turn to developments outside their borders only to expunge that exterior and reaffirm their own foundations. In this spirit, urban scholars might read cultural texts to resist the threat that cultural theory poses to the critical social sciences' claim to explain spatial organization or, for that matter, to define space. Still other, less overtly defensive possibilities jeopardize the creative potential of interdisciplinary work. Disciplines often unite to protect themselves against the intrusion of ideas traditionally perceived as common threats, or, given the presence of internal conflicts within each discipline, to repress differences within individual fields. If Harvey's book, the newest addition to a rapidly proliferating collection of urban-aesthetic literature, becomes a model for this newly popular interdisciplinary combination, it will simply consolidate itself as such a defensive formation: an alliance of the two fields that perpetuates the suppression of, among other things, feminist inquiry.

In this spirit of suppression, defenders of the total critique often try to belittle, even intimidate, anyone who questions totalizing discourses or builds less grandiose theories. Criticism of totalization is routinely equated with trivialized objects, most tiresomely, with fashion. It has even been suggested that the current rejection of "totalizing discourses" has no significance at all since the term itself designates nothing: it has only gained prominence because critics wield it to confuse issues and evade serious political discussion.

But if, as I have suggested, Harvey's account of postmodernism depends on feminism's absence, then his failure to acknowledge cultural production that uses feminist ideas and his neglect of feminist ideas as ways of understanding cultural production are no incidental by-products but rather structural components of his style of totalizing knowledge. The question that feminism introduces into urban studies, then, is not, as Harvey ultimately suggests, how to add something that is missing—either feminist analysis or the topic of gender relations—to existing social theory. The issues currently being examined by feminists—relations of representation and difference—are already present there. The real question is, what is being protected by resistance to feminist inquiry? Far from an instance of "me-too-ism," the assertion of feminism's significance for urban studies arises from the demand that the field examine its own politics and problems, problems that, I suspect, have led some urban scholars to turn to culture in the first place.

VISUALITY

Harvey's introduction to *The Urban Experience,* written in 1989, demonstrates the necessity, and inadvertently indicates the place, for feminist interventions in critical theories of the city and, especially, in the discussion about what urban studies conventionally calls "the image of the city." In fact, Harvey's introduction illustrates, again unknowingly, how the authority invested in particular urban theories that purport simply to be about urban images actually requires converting the city into an image. "The essays assembled in this book are about ways of seeing the city," Harvey writes and describes the thrill of ascending to the highest point in a city and looking down on what he believes to be "the city as a whole."[3] Citing Michel de Certeau's *The Practice of Everyday Life,* Harvey calls this elevated vantage point the perspective of the voyeur and contrasts it, as does de Certeau, with the condition of being immersed in the city's streets. Both perspectives, Harvey asserts, are "real enough," although unequal: the voyeuristic perspective offers a superior—because total—view of social reality.[4]

Shortly after making this distinction, Harvey equates the elevated form of vision with his preferred form of knowledge, metatheory, and describes metatheory as a voyeuristic way of seeing the city. Of course, Harvey concedes, seeming to acknowledge the role of subjectivity in knowledge production, any voyeur or metatheoretician is burdened by prejudices that may influence, even distort, his or her observations. Yet Harvey suggests that his preference is itself unprejudiced, determined solely by objective considerations of social justice and explanatory adequacy: "I find (and still find) it the most powerful of all the explanatory schemas available."[5]

Is the voyeur's city "real enough?" Harvey is confident that from the elevated vantage point "we" can see "the city as a whole," but de Certeau thinks that the coherent image of the city is more like an optical illusion. De Certeau supports practices that resist the leveling rationalities of established systems by forcing a recognition of particularities. He emphatically rejects the impulse to mastery implicit in aerial perspectives. Disembodied viewpoints, says de Certeau, yield "imaginary totalizations" such as the "panorama-city" and correspond to objectifying epistemologies that produce a "fiction of knowledge."[6] Harvey nonetheless characterizes the effort to "possess the city in imagination" as heroic—"the hardest of intellectual labors"—and innocent—"a basic human attribute,"[7] confounding de Certeau's critical appraisal of totalization with his own celebratory one. For de Certeau, forms of imagination and knowledge are never neutral but, instead, have social functions. Imaginary totalizations of the city—"'theoretical' (that is, visual)"—are constituted not only through relations of power but through a specific destructive act: "The panorama-city . . . is a picture whose condition of possibility is an oblivion and a misunderstanding of practices."[8]

De Certeau draws sharply different distinctions than Harvey. He does not really compare two "views" of the city—aerial and street-level. He socializes vision itself. True, he outlines two kinds of spatial activity—on the one hand, visualizing the city or arranging things into an image to be surveyed by distanced subjects and, on the other hand, inhabiting the city or creating ground-level practices or tactics of everyday life that elude the "cancerous growth of vision." But for him only the first activity yields a view, in the sense of an exterior perspective.[9] Moreover, looking down on the city as an image and what de Certeau calls "walking in the city" do not, as Harvey assumes, produce valid and mutually reinforcing pictures of reality. To begin with, de Certeau challenges as dogma the assertion that reality speaks directly through any representation; further, he holds that the two approaches are antithetical. Everyday life is differentiating, situated, and involved while visualizing social discourses produce coherent knowledge by withdrawing from society and claiming an exterior position.

Since de Certeau imputes such visualizing knowledge to the "lust to be a viewpoint and nothing more,"[10] we might ask whether the metatheoretician-voyeur himself is "real enough." Does he exist, as Harvey describes him, burdened by the weight of prejudices, prior to his sighting of the panorama-city? Or is he an illusion of a pure viewpoint, dependent on another fiction—a voyeur-god brought into existence with the image he sees?[11] A de Certeauian answer seems clear. Harvey's is not a neutral method of perceiving reality exercised by an autonomous viewer. It is a specifically modernist model of vision, a social visuality, with a function: establishing a binary opposition between subject and object, it makes the subject transcendent and the object inert, thus underpinning an entire regime of knowledge as mastery.

It is not surprising then that while Harvey does not question the pleasure of seeing the city as a whole, de Certeau asks at the outset: "To what *erotics* of knowledge does the ecstasy of reading such a cosmos belong?"[12] Indeed, the equation of voyeurism with metatheory—of vision with a form of knowledge—is considerably less innocent than Harvey suspects. Far from a colorful but neutral synonym for a real total perception of a real total reality, the term *voyeurism* itself suggests a critique of the very way of seeing that Harvey advocates—of its conception of, and pretensions to know, reality. For the designation of looking and knowledge as voyeuristic not only lifts them both out of the realm of objective perception but sets them down squarely within the domain of sexual pleasure.

In one sense, Harvey's choice of the term *voyeurism* simply emphasizes what is true of all vision: looking implies subjects who arrange things into images and who are themselves constituted by looking. While Harvey criticizes empiricist approaches in geography, his framing metaphor indicates an empiricist bias assuming

Barbara Kruger, *Untitled (You molest from afar)*, 1982
(photo courtesy Barbara Kruger).

the ultimate visibility, that is, knowability, of an autonomous reality. But voyeurism also announces that looking involves a psychic economy pursuing objectives indifferent to perceptual reality. Employed as a trope for knowledge and vision, it actually mocks empiricist claims, raising questions about how unconscious aims and fantasies structure representational and epistemological systems. Voyeurism denotes a scopophilia or pleasure in looking; specifically, it designates an act in which sexual gratification is obtained without proximity, through the secret observation of others as objects. Distancing, mastering, objectifying—the voyeuristic look exercises control through a visualization that merges with a victimization of its object. Harvey's misreading of de Certeau's visual metaphor for totalizing knowledge as positive, or at the very least neutral, deserves attention. For Harvey's blindness to the metaphor's most obvious implications only demonstrates de Certeau's premise: such knowledge, like vision, is highly mediated by fantasy, denial, and desire. Imaginary ascents to the top of the city express a desire for exteriority, and the image that they produce is not a reproduction of the world but a self-image.

To consider the full ramifications of Harvey's visual conceit is to call into question how urban discourse has conventionally formulated the topic of the image of the city. The conceit also sheds light on related issues yet to be confronted in recently popular analyses of "postmodern landscapes." These works, though critical, generally adopt a classic realist approach, treating the image of the city as a mere reflection or distortion of the "real" city or as an object that either reveals or disguises underlying spatial realities. A landscape, however, is an object framed for, and therefore inseparable from, a viewer. If the image of the city is indissolubly bound up with vision and therefore with the subjectivity of viewers and if, as the metaphor of voyeurism makes clear, vision is mediated by fantasy and implies relations of power and sexuality, then urban analyses can no longer ignore what are in fact the constitutive elements of images and landscapes—or they can ignore these issues only by relegating them to a nonpolitical arena. To confront the social and psychic relations of images and so extend the critique, urban scholars can, however, draw on well-developed theories of visual representation, including a sophisticated psychoanalytic feminist literature about vision and subjectivity.

As we have seen, critical geography itself is long overdue for such an analysis. Even the most cursory investigation reveals the degree to which its authoritative texts are permeated by a politics of vision while remaining oblivious to the extensive critique of that politics. Yet as early as 1973, in a famous article entitled "Visual Pleasure and Narrative Cinema," one of the first essays to inaugurate the feminist discourse about vision, British filmmaker Laura Mulvey explored precisely the poles of vision operating in Harvey's introduction to *The Urban Experience*—voyeurism and narcissistic looking. Mulvey addressed the role played by these types of vision in the construction of human subjectivity, which she analyzed not as a process of imprinting external social norms on individuals but as a complex and ambivalent procedure of psychic identifications, internalizations, and projections with political effects. While the voyeur erects rigid boundaries between himself and objects, the narcissistic viewer, Mulvey speculated, sees an idealized reflection of the self in the world: "Here, curiosity and the wish to look intermingle with a fascination with likeness and recognition: the human face, the human body, the relationship between the human form and its surroundings, the visible presence of the person in the world." [13]

Separation from the surrounding world and the imaginary merger with the world are not, however, independent operations. They are intimately connected aspects of the subject's relation to its images. For the subject "recognizes" an ideal self in its surroundings precisely by means of an image that is simultaneously alienating, a self-as-other. Assuming its own discrete image, which permits it to set up relationships among objects of the surrounding world, the subject simultaneously separates itself from and depends upon its objects. The self, then, is not a self-contained whole but an intersubjective relation with the other. The defining separation of the subject—its differentiation from its surroundings—entails a loss of immediacy and plenitude, but through the "perception" that external objects form a unified totality, the subject can try to secure its own wholeness and compensate for this loss. Because an external unity or state of completeness can be observed only from outside, alienation from objects becomes the precondition for recuperating wholeness by establishing the subject's unique connection to the world: severed from objects, the sovereign subject also enjoys unmediated access to them.

The paradoxical structure of narcissistic looking resembles that of social epistemologies deemed adequate because they purportedly uncover the absolute foundation of a social totality. Such representations of society not only position discrete and distanced subjects; by eliminating all lacunae in their pictures of the world, they seek to close the gap between the subject and the object of the representation. The act of granting an autonomous existence to objects of knowledge by disavowing subject-object or discourse-object relationships establishes the illusory basis of the subject's coherence, authority, and uniqueness. The subject of an adequate—or a potentially adequate—representation "sees" an objective reality that is wholly manifest and exists solely for him. He misses nothing. Unfragmented, sovereign, unsituated, he speaks implicitly in Harvey's description of metatheory as "a theoretical framework that has the potential to put all such partial views together not simply as a composite vision but as a cognitive map that shows how each view can itself be explained by and integrated into some grander conception of what the city as a whole, what the urban process in general, is all about."[14]

When Harvey mourns the abandonment of metatheories as a retreat into "emasculated and relatively powerless formats," he reveals the phallic pretensions of his visualizing epistemology.[15] Knowledge can only be perceived to be castrated against the background of a belief that it can be whole. But Harvey's totalizing representation of the social world does not transparently reveal the foundation of a unified structure of exploitation and oppression; it is itself a hierarchical structure of differentiation that situates an all-seeing subject. The objective theorist is a masculine being who makes himself complete by claiming to perceive the ground of an impartial totality but who actually occupies a position of threatened wholeness in a relation of difference. Through which mechanisms it maintains that position is a political question. What repressions enable the equation of voyeuristic models of knowledge with objectivity and adequacy? Whose subjectivities are the casualties of epistemologies that produce total beings? What violence is enacted by authors who speak and pretend that reality speaks for itself? Who signifies the threat of inadequacy so others can be complete? Whose expulsion and absence does completion demand? What positions are determined by relations of total knowledge, and who has historically occupied these positions? Addressed by feminists for decades, these questions are still evaded, through renewed claims to a scientific attitude, by those with little tolerance for the complications they introduce.

DEMOCRACY

"Postmodern," as everyone knows, is a complicated term. Attached to an array of objects, ideas, and practices, it means different things in different disciplines and to different people. Diverse, even opposing, ideological interests alternately claim and reject it. Instead of trying to disentangle the confusions surrounding postmodern culture by cataloguing and evaluating its numerous empirical manifestations, we might say that postmodernism is about complication: its critique of the abstract universalisms that have characterized modern Western thought disrupts the coherence of the social world. Such an assertion, avowedly partial in both senses of the term, is less concerned with defending postmodernism as a stable cultural category or with describing it as an embracing historical condition—and even less with defining it as an artistic style—than with emphasizing the antiessentialist stand shared today by many intellectual tendencies. Of course, not everyone agrees that the abandonment of universals is a good idea. Does the social complexity it fosters obscure political issues and paralyze political struggle? Or is that complexity the very condition of possibility—an opportunity—for social change? Is it, perhaps, a kind of social change itself?

These questions lie at the heart of the postmodern debate but they also express, more broadly, divergent reactions to a crisis of left politics. Answers depend, in turn, on a question of representation—the representation of society. Since the very notion of fragmentation presupposes a prior unity, assessments of postmodern "complications" vary with competing images of—and investments in—the sources of social coherence. For critics who understand the unity of the social field in a materialist sense, not as an impartial totality but as a fiction—a construction— from the start, fragmentation facilitates an awareness of the divisions, differences, and indeterminacy disavowed in the creation of unity. Others, presupposing that social unity derives from an absolute foundation—whether provided by God, nature, or historical necessity—argue that fragmentation obfuscates reality. Disturbed by the challenge that the critique of foundationalism initiates against claims to know reality fully, adherents of the second position fortify social theories that, as British cultural critic Stuart Hall once remarked, provide "a way of helping you sleep at night." Such theories, writes Hall, referring to conventional Marxism and its interpretation of culture, seek to "guarantee that although things don't look simple at the moment, they really are simple in the end. You can't see how the economy determines, but just have faith, it does determine in the last instance!" [16]

The title of Harvey's book announces such an agenda. Clearly a rejoinder to Jean-François Lyotard's *The Postmodern Condition* (1979), it reasserts, against Lyotard's famous critique of Marxist metatheory, that economic relations are the origin, and therefore determine the significance, of all changes in the structure of social life. Harvey challenges the positive appraisal of postmodern culture that he believes is wholly represented by Lyotard. Lyotard defines the postmodern condition—a condition of contemporary Western civilization—as one in which the metadiscourses that lent Western science and politics their authority and power have lost credibility. His principle targets in the realm of social theory are the Marxist metadiscourse of historical materialism and its "grand narrative" of the simultaneous development of society's productive forces and the class struggle. Authorized by the doctrine that relations of economic production constitute the foundation of the social totality, this narrative has privileged the role of class conflict in human emancipation. Allowing only one starting point for social theory, it legitimates the subordination of different analyses and different struggles to the imperatives of a unitary struggle and presupposes the existence of essential relations—products of the foundation—among social groups. For Lyotard, the apprehension of different and incommensurable struggles with no necessary relation defines the postmodern condition. Needless to say, Harvey's restoration of political economy to a privileged position in social theory and concomitant relegation of other approaches to subordinate places has been warmly received by critics who, locating politics primarily in the economic sphere, feel that Harvey has restored "reality" to cultural analysis.

But the equation of Lyotard's text with the entire body of postmodern thought exemplifies Harvey's reductive strategies. For many voices have objected, like Lyotard, to the denial of specificity and difference in modern metatheory without, as Lyotard is accused of doing, relinquishing social theory altogether. To be sure, many social theorists reject the notion that the Marxist metanarrative provides the essential foundation of relations among social groups, but not all theorists propose as an alternative an essential nonrelation among groups. Harvey, failing to draw such distinctions, reduces a multitude of diverse social theories to an undifferentiated mass presided over by Lyotard and so creates a straw man of postmodernism. He sets up a single difference in social philosophy: an opposition between a preconstituted unity of relations that is the basis for political action versus pure difference that is the basis for political escapism.

"After reading this book," scolds Terry Eagleton on the back cover, "those who fashionably scorn the idea of the 'total' critique had better think again." Why? Because, in Harvey's view, the postmodern condition—challenges to the authority of metanarratives—is actually a product of "the condition of postmodernity"—transformations in global capitalism, explainable only by Marxist metadiscourse. Since Harvey never seriously considers the possibility that new ideas might call into question his basic premises, "incredulity toward metanarratives" simply demonstrates their truth, much as atheists prove the existence of God. "The historical sketch I have here proposed," Harvey writes, "suggests that shifts of this sort [postmodernism] are by no means new, and that the most recent version of it is certainly within the grasp of historical materialist enquiry, even capable of theorization by way of the meta-narrative of capitalist development that Marx proposed." (328)

Briefly, Harvey's thesis goes like this. Contradictions and crises inherent in capital accumulation—especially tendencies toward overaccumulation—necessitate periodic transformations in the organization of the accumulation process. Late-twentieth-century capitalism is defined by such a change—from the rigid structures of Fordist organization to a system of flexible accumulation. The elements that form the post-Fordist regime of accumulation (geographic mobility, deindustrialization, a new international division of labor, flexible employment practices, a powerful and increasingly autonomous world financial system, advances in telecommunications and information technology) enhance capitalism's resilience and control. The post-Fordist metamorphosis, like earlier responses to crises in capitalism's quest for profits, entails a progressive increase in the pace of life and dissolution of spatial barriers, what Harvey calls "time-space compression." A new round of intensified time-space compression accompanies the current reorganization of space on urban, regional, and global scales. Capitalism's economic alterations thus produce new experiences of space and time that, because of their intensity, are "capable of sparking . . . a diversity of social, cultural, and political responses" (240). Postmodern aesthetic movements, the current cultural response, "reflect" and "intervene in" current spatiotemporal experience—"a collapse of time horizons and preoccupation with instantaneity" (59). In short, experience of space and time mediates between economic relations, on the one hand, and, culture, on the other.

In Harvey's view, postmodern culture conforms to this inexorable logic because, above all else, it valorizes fragmentation. "I begin," Harvey writes, "with what appears to be the most startling fact about postmodernism: its total acceptance of the ephemerality, fragmentation, discontinuity and the chaotic that formed the one half of Baudelaire's conception of modernity. . . . Postmodernism swims, even wallows, in the fragmentary and the chaotic currents of change as if that is all there is" (44). He attributes this change to the new regime of flexible accumulation: "The relatively stable aesthetic of Fordist modernism has given way to all the ferment, instability, and fleeting qualities of a postmodernist aesthetic that celebrates difference, ephemerality, spectacle, fashion, and the commodification of cultural forms" (156). Harvey's "Fordist modernism" expresses his certainty that aesthetic meaning is determined and subsumed by economics, a belief that, though it forms his principal thesis, is never really argued but merely asserted.

Still another sleight of hand can be detected in this passage. "Difference" has been smuggled into a list of temporary, trivial, even wicked things. Throughout Harvey's book, difference is itself undifferentiated. Does it mean variety? Incommensurability? Specificity? Injustice? The constitutive factor of meaning and identity? We are never told, although at one point Harvey does specify one kind of difference that has gained importance in postmodern politics: postmodernism acknowledges multiple sources of social oppression and multiple forms of resistance to domination. Relying largely on Andreas Huyssen's astute reading of postmodernism, Harvey describes "the opening given in postmodernism to understanding difference and otherness, as well as the liberatory potential it offers for a whole host of new social movements (women, gays, blacks, ecologists, regional autonomists, etc.)" (48). But since Harvey has suggested earlier that precisely the "liberative" concern for "otherness" makes postmodernism seductive, we are left with the impression that, for him, it is postmodern's most dangerous quality.[17]

When Harvey describes the specific aesthetic form in which postmodernism valorizes fragmentation, his logic becomes more capricious and his categories oddly constituted. He identifies depth with complexity and literalizes this identification by defining visual images—what he calls "depthless images"—as superficial reflections of a complex world. But the inherent lack that Harvey perceives in visual images is not, for him, a condition of all representation, or even, paradoxically, of all visual images. Rather, it contrasts with the potential adequacy to reality of other representations: historical materialism and, in the aesthetic realm, realist art, which, Harvey implies, transparently unveils the content of an empirically knowable reality.

For Harvey, the postmodern artist's preoccupation with forms—images and surfaces—is a fragmenting procedure that conceals "deeper" and "larger" realities. This distrust of visual images strikingly contradicts his earlier description of his own theory as a visualization. But leaving this problem aside for the moment, let us note that Harvey thinks only one reality is truly deep. Since the dispersal, mobility, decentralization, and flexibility of advanced capitalism—which produce experiences of time-space compression—only disguise the tightened organization and global expansion of capital and since culture mirrors this process, it follows that postmodern art's interest in images participates in the concealment of the underlying reality: the interconnected totality of capitalism. Postmodern aesthetics—embodied in the exploration of images—and what Harvey treats as its complement—a concern for difference in social movements—aid and abet late capitalism's masking of new structures of oppression, operations that Harvey identifies with fetishism. "Postmodern concerns for the signifier rather than the signified," he concludes, "the medium (money) rather than the message (social labor), the emphasis on fiction rather than function, on signs rather than things, on aesthetics rather than ethics, suggest a reinforcement rather than a transformation of the role of money as Marx depicts it" (102).

Needless to say, Harvey's assessment of the fragmentation that he believes is explored and engendered in postmodern art and culture is negative—postmodernism is a condition that we must escape. His judgment is twofold. Postmodern "superficiality," embodied in attention to images, conceals the underlying unity of capitalism. Likewise, granting conceptual autonomy to different social struggles or theories fragments the only body of knowledge—Marxist metatheory—capable of perceiving that unity. Postmodernism, Harvey concedes, exercises a degree of "positive influence" by bringing attention to race and gender, but it "takes matters too far" by not going far enough. "It takes them beyond the point where any coherent politics are left. . . . Postmodernism has us celebrating the activity of masking and cover-up, all the fetishisms of locality, place, or social grouping, while denying that kind of meta-theory which can grasp the political-economic processes . . . that are becoming ever more universalizing in their depth, intensity, reach and power over daily life" (117).

With this evaluation, Harvey adopts the position on postmodernism that, until now, has been most influentially expressed in Fredric Jameson's 1984 essay "Postmodernism, or the Cultural Logic of Late Capitalism." Jameson diagnoses postmodernism as a cultural "pathology," a symptom of the experiences of fragmentation initiated by the spatial restructuring that constitutes capitalism's third stage. What we need, Jameson prescribes, are new spatializations of the world— "cognitive maps"—to reveal the underlying totality and stabilize our position within it. Early in *The Condition of Postmodernity,* Harvey invokes what he calls Jameson's "daring thesis that postmodernism is nothing more than the cultural logic of late capitalism" (63).

Far from a new explanation of culture, however, Jameson's interpretation employs a popular model of society that has become familiar from numerous analyses of modernism: modernization is a socioeconomic process; modernity the experience of that process; and modernism the cultural expression of modernity. Such an image of the social as composed of clearly demarcated levels overseen by the economic one legitimates the refusal of difference in social theory. This image corresponds to a unitarian epistemology in which only one theory is authorized to explain social relations of domination. As a model for theorizing postmodernism, this epistemology validates Jameson's failure to differentiate among diverse kinds of fragmentation. Primarily addressing the fragmentations caused by economic restructuring, Jameson seems at first glance simply to disregard others. He appears, for one thing, to minimize the "fragmenting" effects of those political voices (feminist, gay, antiracist, postcolonial) that, by insisting that social subjects occupy situated rather than universal positions, challenge universalizing discourses. In addition, Jameson bypasses the "fragmenting" questions raised by recent psychoanalytic critiques of unitary subjectivity while himself reducing the psychic to a metaphor for a socioeconomic condition and so dismissing questions of sexuality.[18] In the end, however, Jameson does not really ignore these voices or critiques. Because he assesses fragmentation negatively and treats this assessment as a foregone conclusion, he defines these critiques as dangers to unified social struggles and stable subjects. His references to "homeopathic" methods of "undoing" postmodernism express a desire to restore the subject to a lost position of mastery, conceived of as a healthy place. Jameson, whose "Postmodernism" essay borrows from urban spatial theories, has paid his debt twice over: he sanctions Harvey's dismissal of new social movements as fragmenting forces and lends authority to Harvey's selective, indeed amateurish, treatment of culture.

The vagueness, even whimsy, that mark Harvey's approach to modern and postmodern art contrast vividly with the precision of his economic and spatial analyses—the book's most valuable contribution. Moving beyond mere eclecticism into the realm of error, Harvey's treatment of art is plagued by fallacies: equivocations (the failure to distinguish between aesthetics and aestheticism, for instance, or, for that matter, to recognize historical variations in definitions of art); inadequate information;[19] inconsistencies (the routine assertion that postmodernism is a diverse phenomenon and simultaneous reduction of postmodernism to a single entity with a monolithic voice); and the use of misleading contexts that transform isolated quotations from "authorities" into supports for Harvey's arguments.

The imbalance between Harvey's erudite treatment of political economy and geography, on the one hand, and his impoverished account of aesthetics, on the other, cannot be attributed to the inevitable perils that attend interdisciplinary scholarship. Rather, the book's reductive argument *engenders* an asymmetry that mirrors Harvey's premise that relations between economic and cultural practices are primarily a stable process of one-way determination. Within this deterministic framework, each practice retains an essential identity, constituted outside their interrelationship. "Aesthetic theory," Harvey declares in an attempt to distinguish it from social theory, "seeks out the rules that allow eternal and immutable truths to be conveyed in the midst of the maelstrom of flux and change" (205). A consummate expression of the tenets of mainstream idealist aesthetics, this statement takes no account, as we shall see, of recent materialist practices (site-specificity, institutional critique, critiques of representation) that explore art as a contingent relation rather than a container of "immutable truths." Harvey moves toward greater complexity when he states that aesthetic practice not only imitates but intervenes in social life; but, according to his definition of aesthetics, art intervenes only by affecting an exterior material world. "Changes in the way we imagine, think, plan and rationalize are bound," Harvey remarks, "to have material consequences" but themselves are not material (114).

We have heard this account of art and society before. No matter how much it parades as a daring thesis, it can only be sustained by ignoring decades of work in Western Marxism, cultural studies, art criticism, and film and feminist theory. This work has irrevocably altered how we define culture—as a social relation, a meaning-producing activity, a material practice—problematizing the traditional boundaries dividing the "social sciences" from cultural disciplines. Harvey's defense of these boundaries is consistent with his other hierarchical categorizations but disappointing in the context of current efforts to forge new interdisciplinary connections between urban and aesthetic discourses. For, in a sense, Harvey's rejection of critical aesthetic theory also repudiates the possibilities and questions raised by his own work, and that of other scholars, in critical urban studies.

The significance of materialist geography and of Harvey's role in its creation and development are, by now, well known. Indeed, it is difficult to overestimate either the impact that Harvey has had in his own field or the relevance of his work for professions that produce the built environment. His detailed theorization of the urban process under capitalism remains required reading for anyone seeking to understand how space is socially—not naturally, technologically, or biologically—produced. His contextualization of contemporary urbanization within a political framework of global restructuring has helped artists, planners, and architects question the political implications of their roles in the design or decoration of urban spaces.

But the idea that the built environment is a product of capitalism, while overcoming the essentialist biases of traditional urban theory, hardly exhausts the topic of space as a social construction. Rather, the social constructionist thesis poses difficult questions similar to those that have occupied critical aesthetics as, over the last twenty years, it has elaborated the concept of the social production of art. Once the city—like art—is no longer defined by transhistorical essences, is it social only insofar as it reflects "real" social relations that reside elsewhere—in, for instance, the economic circumstances of its production? An affirmative answer, much like the "solutions" to art-city relationships adopted in social art history, only reintroduces idealism: built form remains essentially nonsocial, and social relations are detached from the physical city.

This problem troubles critical urban studies, and many scholars have tried to escape the dilemma by proposing models of reciprocal determination or of interaction between space and other components of the social. But the built environment—and visual or textual images of the city—can only be rescued from idealist doctrines and analyzed as social in the first instance if, released from the grip of determinism, they are recognized, as other cultural objects have been, as representations. Neither autonomous in the aestheticist sense—embodiments of eternal aesthetic properties—nor social because produced by an external society, representations are not discrete objects at all but social relations, themselves productive of meaning and subjectivity. If urban discourse wants to take account of this kind of sociospatial relation, it can only benefit from encounters with critical aesthetic practice. For the critique of images as representations or signifying practices— rather than as objects transparent to empirical referents or social truths—necessary fully to politicize urban discourse has already been forged in some of the postmodern art that Harvey rejects and particularly in the feminist theories of representation that have played such a key role in contemporary aesthetic production.

In certain ways, Harvey's urban theory helped make it possible to understand the city as a representation. Space, he said, is produced in the image of capital. Were his ambitions more modest, this formulation would present fewer problems. It could help us analyze a crucial factor in the social organization of space. Compelled, however, to make it explain everything—not only the sole cause of global spatial production but also the political meaning of the built environment and now of art, architecture, and film in their entirety—Harvey positions all other factors, spatial discourses, and forms of knowledge as political escapism: they avoid "confronting the realities of political economy and the circumstances of global power"

(117). But to analyze the way in which space is produced in capital's image is not, as Harvey assumes, to analyze the city as an image. Eliding the difference between the two, *The Condition of Postmodernity* not only establishes a closure at the level of political economy but, warding off different explanations of spatial relations, simultaneously evades responsibility for the politics of its own representation.

The book defends Marxism as a foundational metatheory yet denies that such a position is a "statement of total truth" (355). Nonetheless, Harvey's discourse is a totalizing representation insofar as it explains human history and society as a whole unified by a single, fundamental antagonism. The claim to apprehend an objective and determinable reality underlying the apparent diversity of the social field removes this explanation and the intellectual operations of those who "perceive" it from the contingencies of any particular social situation. Such a representation produces universal knowledge, independent objects of knowledge, and all-seeing subjects of knowledge. This subject position—the total vantage point—created by relegating different perspectives to subordinate or competing positions, claims the power to harmonize conflicts by ordering them hierarchically and reducing them to a predetermined norm. Harvey exercises this power at the very moment he is most eager to demonstrate Marxism's capacity to tolerate differences. Metatheory, he concedes, has tended to "gloss over important differences" and "failed to pay attention to important disjunctions and details" (114). But, listing the areas in which Marxism requires "development," he asserts that "the importance of recuperating such aspects of social organization as race, gender, religion, *within the overall frame of historical materialist enquiry (with its emphasis upon the power of money and capital circulation) and class politics (with its emphasis upon the unity of the emancipatory struggle)* cannot be overestimated" (355, my emphasis).

This proposal integrates "various aspects of social organization" by trivializing them. Social struggles, groups, and theories become part of a hierarchically differentiated unity in which, denied autonomy, they are ruled by the privileged realm of political economy. Yet political economy does not demand such exclusions, nor is a totalizing perspective necessary to appreciate the totalizing ambitions of global capital. What overidentification with power does such a project betray? Should a critical theory mirror the system that it seeks to dismantle?

Many critics think otherwise. Linda Nicholson and Nancy Fraser, arguing for a postmodern feminism and fully aware—like all socialist feminists—of the significance of capitalism, suggest that attention to large-scale structures of domination need not be jettisoned along with metatheory.[20] Neither must economic realities be the starting point of every social analysis. Ernesto Laclau proposes that postmodernity is defined not by the disappearance of metanarratives but by a "weakening of their absolutist character" or their claim to be grounded in an objective presence that guarantees their truth.[21] Postmodernism, he suggests, is characterized by a new metanarrative of the absence of foundational guarantees and the need to construct new bases for unity. Others, skeptical even about reconstituted unities as the basis of political struggles, question whether change is mediated through the totality at all. Paul Patton, for example, maintains that it is crucial for specific-issue struggles to resist absorption into larger unities. For Patton, the radical potential of these movements lies precisely in their rejection of totalization, which he analyzes as an operation of power. He distinguishes between the "universalizability" of a perspective and the sense in which it may be called "totalizing." A universalizable perspective can be applied to the whole range of social phenomena, but

> A perspective is "of the totality" in a quite different sense to the extent that it purports to stand outside and oversee the different analyses of particular theories or to regulate the conflicting demands of particular social movements. . . . The injunction to adopt a global view, even if it is initially only in respect of the conflicting needs of other oppressed groups, is ultimately the injunction to govern a multiplicity of interests. The position of the totality is the position of power.[22]

The position of the totality differs from that of new social movements, and "the specificity and irreducibility of the minority position have to be defended against all attempts to abolish that difference."[23]

Harvey, disregarding these nuanced debates and refusing to relinquish the polarities of his social theory, in a remarkably circular argument tries to remedy his theory's errors by extending its grasp. "The task within the Marxian camp," he writes, "is to deepen and sharpen theory so that it can reach into realms that have hitherto remained opaque and define new social practices that can integrate in the socialist project" (16). The colonizing language with which Harvey describes his theory's purported openness is fitting. The "discovery" of social elements that are then granted a place within a predetermined totality is actually a formula for exclusion. This exclusion structures any discourse that aspires to know its object of study completely. For once it is allowed that discursive practices constitute social meaning and identity, we can no longer relegate representation to a sphere outside the social realm. Once it is recognized that, in the absence of a foundational presence, meaning emerges discursively (through the construction of relations, equivalences, and exclusions), we know that every totality is incomplete and can be "completed" only by denying these differentiating processes.

Harvey voices such a denial when he speaks of the empty rooms that have had to be furnished within "the house of Marxist theory."[24] The architectural metaphor—Marxism as a house—is apt. It expresses the stabilizing and unifying ambitions of Harvey's political discourse. As the classic image of a secure, enclosed interior, the house is also the paradigm of a self-contained order of meaning. Harvey's uncritical use of this metaphor demonstrates his habit of supporting arguments by reasserting the very principles that have been questioned as oppressive. He assumes that to compare Marxism to a house is to present it as a hospitable environment, but the comparison has less benevolent connotations. It makes domestic space the model of political space and, as a consequence, exposes the masculine force of Harvey's political theory. For one thing, the metaphorical house calls up images of the gender relationships that take place inside literal houses—the oppression of, and violence against, women. But architecture theorist Mark Wigley, who has analyzed the house as a figure of philosophy, argues that oppression and violence are not simply events occurring *in* the space of the house. The space of the house is constituted by—and therefore inseparable from—relationships themselves bound up with hierarchal constructions of sexual difference. In other words: Harvey uses the house as a metaphor for a space—Marxist theory—which, he says, is capable of explaining the politics of space. But he forgets that the house itself is a representation of a space already organized by spatial politics.

Harvey presents Marxism as an interior whose boundaries are secured by a foundational meaning, or presence, rather than by spatial relationships. Harvey's house is, then, what Wigley calls "a domestic space that attempts to domesticate space."[25] It attempts to repress the fact that it is a spatial construction. The house of Marxism functions as the image of presence only "by repressing something about houses"[26]—that their closure is not the stable effect of a foundation preceding representation but rather the unstable effect of representation. The house divides an inside from an outside, but since the "outside" is constitutive it can never really be excluded, only domesticated or enclosed. Wigley contends, moreover, that enclosure cannot be detached from subordination of the feminine: "The classical figure of the feminine is that which lacks its own secure boundaries, producing insecurity by disrupting boundaries, and which therefore must be housed by masculine force that is no more than the ability to maintain rigid limits or, more precisely, the effect of such limits, the representation of a space."[27] The house brings the feminine into accommodation with the home environment, with, that is, the phallic regime of enclosure and completion.

When the house in question is the house of Marxist political theory, one feminine element that must be domesticated is feminism itself. No wonder many feminists are reluctant to move into—let alone decorate—the Marxist house. They know what violence maintains its harmony. They do not necessarily reject the insights of Marxism but, questioning the epistemological basis and political stakes of a transcendental Marxism, recognize that its illusions are merely compounded by greater comprehensiveness and can only be dismantled by constructing more democratic forms of knowledge.

This project has been undertaken in new social theories to which Harvey's book remains, at least overtly, oblivious. Proponents of radical democracy such as Chantal Mouffe and Ernesto Laclau suggest that Marxism transform itself, rather than everything around it, into a component of the democratic revolution that, though initiated by modernity, is today thwarted by major tenets of Enlightenment philosophy: abstract universalism, essentialist concepts of totality, notions of unitary subjectivity. Mouffe and Laclau reverse Harvey's proposal: socialism, reduced to human size, is integrated within new social practices. Links between different social struggles must be articulated at given historical moments rather than presupposed to exist, determined by a fundamental social antagonism—class struggle. But individual social groups also have no essential identities. They, too, are formed only through relationships. The practice of articulating relationships—and simultaneously modifying the social identities formed through relations—offers yet another alternative to Harvey's political options: a priori unity or random fragmentation.[28]

The democratic project has also been fostered in postmodern art practices informed by feminist theories of vision. Harvey, as we have seen, ignores these practices, even though visual images are one of his principle objects of study and despite the fact that Cindy Sherman's photographs, which for him epitomize postmodernism, have figured prominently in critiques of visual representation. Harvey isolates work like Sherman's from its specific historical context: the contemporary development of politicized visual art production. Elsewhere, I have drawn a parallel between the trajectory followed by this art and by discourses about the social production of art, on the one hand, and the unfolding of a social production of space perspective in urban studies, on the other.[29] But the two developments may be less similar than I thought. Harvey's account of postmodernism establishes an antagonistic relationship between them, setting up the new aesthetic work as an opponent and using critical spatial discourse to build a protective formation against it. But Harvey's rejection of contemporary art does not represent a split between urban studies and cultural theory. Rather, it signals an interdisciplinary alliance between particular groups within each field. For certain left art critics also reject the complications that feminist and other critiques of representation have introduced into the social construction of art thesis.

Harvey's cavalier treatment of postmodern art cannot, then, be ascribed to his status as a stranger in a new discipline, although as a nonspecialist purporting to explain cultural developments he has abdicated the responsibility to learn about aesthetic discourse. Rather, Harvey's careless approach, including the manner in which it exempts itself from interdisciplinary obligations, issues from a defense of specialization inherent in a social theory that privileges the social-science disciplines. Moreover, Harvey's disapproval of contemporary culture stems not from a critical approach to art history but from acceptance of the mainstream assumptions informing that discipline. It is precisely these assumptions that much of the art he rejects has challenged.

Harvey recognizes that postmodern artists have directed their attention to a study of images, rather than to what he calls "social reality" or "social meanings" outside images, but he does not understand why. He could, however, have easily discovered the reasons by consulting the extensive body of literature about the politics of representation, a topic addressed in numerous fields over the last two decades. While critical work on images is far from monolithic, it generally shares at least one concern: it questions the assumption that reality and representation are given and discrete categories and rejects the definition of representations as mere appearances opposed to, and devalued by contrast with, "reality." Critical artists investigate representations precisely because what is commonly called reality—social meanings, relations, values, identities—is constituted in a complex of representations. This does not mean, as is frequently charged, that there is no world external to thought—only that no order of meaning exists in itself. No founding presence, unconditional source, or privileged ground guarantees the authority of meanings constituted apart from discursive interventions. Nor is the stress on representation a desertion of politics; it enlarges and recasts our conception of the political to include the forms of discourse. We might even say that it is thanks to the deconstruction of absolute grounds of meaning and exterior viewpoints that politics becomes a necessity. When such nonrelational grounds and viewpoints are questioned, references to meanings that precede representation emerge as an authoritarian form of representation deployed in battles to name reality. There is no unproblematic, simply given representation of politics but there is always a politics of representation.

Contemporary artists intervene in the politics of representation in diverse ways, which I can enumerate here only schematically, not even representatively. Recognizing the power of images, many artists contest the meanings and identities produced for oppressed groups by stereotypical or official depictions, and some seek to place the means of representation in the hands of groups marginalized by cultural institutions. Others analyze the instrumentality of aesthetic images for dominant political and economic forces. Some artists undermine the apparently natural relation between images and reality by calling attention to the socially coded nature of visual representation. They do so, however, not to uncover an authentic significance or empirical referent that lies beneath a false meaning but to problematize referentiality. They also question the power exercised through naturalizing representations that disguise the image's social character. These artists focus on the image's construction—its own political relations and relations to other practices. Perhaps the most radical challenge to beliefs in coherent and objective images has been leveled by artists who have used psychoanalytic theory to expose the repressed constructions that produce illusions of coherence. These artists stress the role played by vision in constituting the human subject and explore operations specific to visual images that, they hold, introduce us into the field of fantasy that Jacques Lacan calls "the imaginary," the register where the subject seeks to conjure an experience of immediacy and plenitude through complex mechanisms of identification and internalization.[30] Whether or not they address such issues, most artists explicitly engaged in the politics of representation call attention to the constructed character of their own images. They reflect critically on their own activity of meaning production instead of perpetuating the belief that, as vanguard figures, they transmit superior perceptions of preexisting aesthetic or political realities to others who cannot see them.

Harvey concludes that attention to images means that postmodern art forms "necessarily turn inward upon themselves" (323), but art involved with the politics of images does the opposite: precisely by acknowledging that the image is a social relation, it chooses to be openly in the world, intervening in diverse political spaces. Harvey misses the point for two reasons. On the one hand, he believes that visual representations are no problem. Images either reveal or conceal empirical referents—events, objects, social relations. They correspond, adequately or inadequately, to nondiscursive external objects. He describes his own social theory as precisely a visualization, comparing the perception of the social totality to sighting "the city as a whole." Insofar as adequacy is equated with the ability to "see" the foundation of totality, only the construction of society as an image is, for Harvey, an adequate representation.

Yet Harvey is ambivalent about visual images and, on the other hand, they present him with nothing but problems. He finds only insufficiency, absence, fragmentation. Something is always "missing" in the field of vision. If his introduction to *The Urban Experience* defined metatheory as visual, *The Condition of Postmodernity* defends its supremacy over the visual. Ignoring the contradiction between his distrust of visual images as inadequate and his preference for visualization as the only adequate method of social analysis, Harvey now wants to demonstrate the poverty of all visual images in comparison with other modes of representation. "Cinema," he writes, "is . . . the supreme maker and manipulator of images . . . and the very act of using it well always entails reducing the complex stories of daily life to a sequence of images upon a depthless screen." Bound to a depth model of meaning, Harvey does not acknowledge even the possibility of other spatial configurations—the complexity of cinematic space as the effect of montage, for example—or the existence of other discourses about space—such as film theory's complex analysis of film's intricate, highly structured spatial relation with viewers. Equating literal depthlessness with intellectual and political shallowness, Harvey concludes that images inevitably mask the underlying totality of the social field. Marx himself, Harvey says,

> would surely accuse those postmodernists who proclaim the "impenetrability of the other" as their creed, of overt complicity with the fact of fetishism and of indifference towards underlying social meanings. The interest of Cindy Sherman's photographs (or any postmodern novel for that matter) is that they focus on masks without commenting directly on social meanings other than on the activity of masking itself. (101)

FEMINISM: A SHORT HISTORY OF CONTEMPORARY ART

Harvey's accusation of fetishism, leveled against Sherman via Marx, is so seriously confused that it can be untangled only by surveying, no matter how briefly, the aesthetic context within which Sherman's work emerged. From 1978 to 1980,

Sherman produced a large number of photographs, each one called *Untitled (Film Still)*. The photos portray a woman—the model is always Sherman herself—in a variety of generic movie scenes. They appropriate and make visible the conventions that structure cinematic images of femininity: lighting, gesture, pose, camera angle, focus, framing, address to the viewer. Sherman's *Film Stills* were part of a group of works—by such artists as Barbara Kruger, Louise Lawler, Richard Prince, and Sherrie Levine, to name only a few—for which, nearly twenty years ago, many critics first used the term *postmodern*. In 1979 Douglas Crimp called these works, collectively, "pictures," a term that in retrospect conveys their most salient trait: they are culturally recognizable, often mass-media images.[31] They were pictures and they were postmodern, we felt, because they effected a break with the beliefs that officially defined artistic modernism, highly idealist and fetishistic beliefs.

Modernist doctrine was based on Kantian concepts of aesthetic disinterestedness—the perception of an object in and for itself—and was largely codified in the writings of American formalist critics, especially Clement Greenberg. But Greenberg's underlying assumptions embodied Western society's most treasured beliefs about its high culture and had long dominated writing about art, whether it appeared in scholarly literature or popular media. Victor Burgin has usefully outlined the axioms of modernism: Art is a self-referential and autonomous sphere of human activity. It characterizes humanity since the dawn of civilization. All art shares a universal, timeless aesthetic essence and expresses a universal, timeless human essence that is also the essence of civilization. The visual artist does so through forms that are purely visual and therefore separate from the everyday world of social and political life.[32]

Art's autonomy and universality purportedly inhere in the aesthetic form of the artwork—the relations among the work's internal elements—that, according to Greenbergian modernism, is essentially detached from the circumstances of the work's production, circulation, and reception. The art object, container of an irreducible and universal essence, is a self-governing totality generated by sovereign, universal artists and "beheld" by equally autonomous viewers. In the moment of aesthetic contemplation, object and viewer are elevated to a realm divorced from

Cindy Sherman, *Untitled Film Still #21,* 1978 (photo courtesy Cindy Sherman and Metro Pictures.

Cindy Sherman, *Untitled Film Still #32,* 1979 (photo courtesy Cindy Sherman and Metro Pictures).

Cindy Sherman, *Untitled Film Still #35,* 1979 (photo courtesy Cindy Sherman and Metro Pictures).

Cindy Sherman, *Untitled Film Still #48,* 1979 (photo courtesy Cindy Sherman and Metro Pictures).

society, at least society understood as a set of historical, conflictual, and mutable relations. Within the dominant story of modernism, social conditions might influence art but artworks ultimately transcend historical contingencies. Likewise, the history of art chronicles the unfolding of pure aesthetic ideas. Transcendence—ensured by the artwork's possession of a universal essence—harmonizes all art objects.

What else, after all, but the possession of intrinsic, universal qualities could bring objects from diverse historical periods and places into a single physical or discursive space—the art museum, let us say, or an art-history textbook? The question is not simply rhetorical. It was posed in the late 1960s as part of a radical shift from normative analyses of art to critiques of art's social functions. What else indeed? To assert that the meaning of art derives from absolute sources is to conceal art's social production—the discursive processes and political relations that position objects as art. As one conceptual artist remarked in 1974, echoing Marx's critique of the commodity form, objects do not transform themselves into works of art: "They cannot elevate themselves from the host of man-made objects simply on the basis of some inherent qualities."[33] Like the idealist paradigms that dominated explanations of spatial organization in urban sociology, the notion of art as the embodiment of absolute values obscured the historical conditions of art's existence—the specific social processes that endow objects with aesthetic value and produce them as art. Aesthetic meaning appeared as an ahistorical, spiritual property contained in objects themselves, and therefore the particular institutions that defined art assumed the semblance of universality.

In the late 1960s and 1970s artists challenged the dogma that aesthetic objects contain fixed meanings by exploring and revealing specific cultural processes of meaning production. In art discourse, the antiuniversalizing impulses of postmodernism took the form of a multifaceted investigation of art's social production. Postmodern practices include what is loosely called contextual art, a term that initially referred to art that incorporates its exhibition context—museum, gallery, corporation, urban space—into the artwork itself. Contextual practices attempted to erode the aura of isolation that aesthetic institutions have traditionally constructed around art and to draw attention to, rather than divert it from, the circumstances of aesthetic production and reception relegated to a space outside the artwork's frame. To demonstrate, for example, that aesthetic perception is not disinterested but contingent on the conditions in which art is viewed, artists made works designed specifically for and physically inseparable from their sites. Site-specific works demonstrated that the art object does not have an autonomous meaning that remains intact in changing spatial or temporal circumstances. The meaning of art is formed in relation to its framing conditions and, as a consequence, alters with the spaces it occupies and the positions of viewing subjects.

Contextual art insisted on the specificity rather than universality, contingency rather than autonomy, and fluidity rather than stability of perception and meaning, but essentialism often reentered early contextual art in the assumption that the spaces of aesthetic perception are politically and socially neutral. Eventually artists broadened the concept of site to embrace not only the physical or perceptual context of the work's exhibition but the site's symbolic, social, and political meanings as well as the historical circumstances within which artwork, spectator, and place are situated. Some artists explored connections between artworks and art institutions, on the one hand, and political contexts, on the other, exposing the relations between the two traditionally cloaked by illusions of aesthetic autonomy. For the authority and prestige that art enjoyed under modernism, based on its supposedly universal forms, actually allowed art to serve as an alibi for all kinds of powerful forces—colonial conquest, urban redevelopment projects, multinational corporations cum art sponsors.

But art is not simply an object susceptible to manipulation by preexisting interests or social forces. To draw this conclusion from the critique of artistic autonomy is to hand over contextual art to a new form of essentialism. Art per se remains socially neutral; art and society remain discrete identities. While the belief in art's isolation from a fundamentally and properly social sphere lingers in many current formulations of art's social character, other artists and critics have extended the materialist aesthetic critique. Those practices that I have identified under the rubric "the critique of representation" examine art as itself a social relation, a revision that recasts the identity of "the social" as well.

Feminist theory, in particular, amplified but also problematized the materialist practices of the 1970s and 1980s by introducing gender, and then sexual difference and representation, into aesthetic discussion. Feminists, of course, had been
arguing since the early 1960s that art's celebrated universality and its corollary, the
unitary aesthetic tradition, are myths. One had only to visit a museum or to open
H. W. Janson's *History of Art* to realize that women, who rarely figured in the canon
of "great artists," figured prominently—and differently from men—as the subject
matter of painting and sculpture. Something other than pure, disinterested vision,
we realized, must be taking place in art institutions.

During this period, some feminists tried to challenge dominant artistic portrayals of women by criticizing "negative" images and substituting "positive" ones.
While these efforts helped provoke awareness that women have been relegated to
circumscribed social roles in so-called universal art history, the discussion of images
as positive or negative poses its own problems. It assumes, for one thing, a consensus about what is negative and positive and, moreover, limits images to two categories: stereotypical (negative) or realistic (positive). More importantly, as film
theorist Teresa de Lauretis argues:

> Such discussions rely on an often crude opposition of positive and neg-
> ative, which is not only uncomfortably close to popular stereotypes
> such as the good guys versus the bad guys, or the nice girl versus the
> bad woman, but also contains a less obvious and more risky implica-
> tion. For it assumes that images are directly absorbed by the viewers,
> that each image is immediately readable and meaningful in and of
> itself, regardless of its context or of the circumstances of its produc-
> tion, circulation, and reception. Viewers, in turn, are presumed to be
> at once historically innocent and purely receptive, as if they too existed
> in the world immune from other social practices and discourses.[34]

This assumption, that the core identities of both images and viewers are
stable and absolute, united the otherwise conflicting realms of modernist criticism
and some of its early feminist opposition. The "positive/negative images" critique

sought to undermine modernism's concealment of art's social character by focusing on what Greenbergian criticism excluded, the subject matter—often referred to as the "content"—of aesthetic images. Yet because the critique restricted content to the iconography of images and form to the internal relation of elements within images, it actually preserved a modernist division between content and form and, like modernism, reduced visual meaning to what takes place within the borders of the image. Form per se remained politically innocent or was understood as social only insofar as it was the vehicle for an externally produced social message. But the politics of vision is not only about what happens inside the image. It is about the constitution of the image. The positive/negative critique evades a crucial feminist issue: the status of woman as an image when images are understood not as static containers of meaning but as positions produced in hierarchical relations with viewing subjects. The question of the role played by vision in producing and maintaining sexual difference emerged only when images and viewers were defined in a mutually constitutive relation. Form, including the artwork's connection to a viewer, and content, understood as the meanings produced in the viewing relationship, were not only indissolubly linked but ineluctably political.

In the 1970s feminists in numerous cultural fields mounted a critique of visual representation that investigated a problem newly broached as "woman as image" rather than "images of women."[35] The two formulations embody divergent theoretical assumptions, first about the relation between images and reality and second about the character of femininity. While the "images of women" approach measures images against real female identities forged outside representations, identities merely reflected in images, the "woman as image" approach treats visual images as part of a complex of representations producing femininity as a relational, rather than fixed, identity. The proposal that aesthetic images should be investigated to reveal how they mirror or distort the identities of real women is frequently offered as an alternative to aestheticism but does not radically challenge essentialist notions of aesthetic meaning: the ultimate source of the image's meaning is merely transferred from a neutral aesthetic sphere to a proper political one. "Society" substitutes for "nature" with the viewer now fixed by social, rather than spiritual, essences.

239

Two developments intersected, then, in feminist critiques of representation. One was the abandonment of notions of essential, fixed femininity—biological or social—and the concomitant examination of femininity as a social concept produced only in its difference from masculinity. The other was the postmodern rejection of the idea that representation is transparent to meanings and subjectivities. New feminist critiques still challenged, to be sure, the authoritarian impulses of biological determinism, but beyond that they excavated the less obvious dogmatism of certain social constructionist positions. We arrived, as Craig Owens wrote, "at an apparent crossing of the feminist critique of patriarchy and the postmodernist critique of representation."[36]

The conjuncture was more intricate than Owens's formulation suggests. For if sexual identity is engendered neither by nature nor by an extradiscursive social world, then femininity is produced in representation through differentiation. The image of man depends on the image of woman. At stake in defining femininity as a position in representation is not the revelation of true identities for men and women but an exploration of existing representations of sexual difference. Since relational approaches to identity entail the disappearance of exteriority, they introduce subjects who, never outside political conflicts, are always involved: Who speaks? From where? How is this position produced? The complete, masculine subject can only be produced as such by assuming the power to represent others in various forms of domination and conquest—as negative, complement, self-image.

The image of woman in patriarchal constructions of sexual difference cannot then simply be referred back to sociologically constituted women but is, rather, a signifier of femininity as incompleteness, inadequacy, lack. Using psychoanalysis as a discourse about the construction of sexual difference, feminists have explored the instrumentality of this image for constructions of masculine subjectivity. At an early stage in the investigation of woman as image, feminists turned to Freud's analysis of sexual fetishism, finding a model of a representational economy in which masculine desire achieves representation through the repression of difference. Freud's essays about fetishism, "Medusa's Head" and "Fetishism," made vision central to the establishment of sexual difference.[37] A fetish object, as Freud defined it, substitutes for something perceived as "missing," something whose absence threatens the desire for wholeness. It replaces in fantasy the penis, the "lack" of which woman's body represents to man. Castration fear is actualized, not initiated, by the male child's sight of an anatomical difference in which the female appears to be "castrated," and the fetish is set up to deny that sight, to ward off the knowledge of difference. An object of devotion, the fetish—the penis replacement—is a fragment that promises wholeness in place of lack, presence where absence has been "perceived." It is an idealized self-image testifying at once to the threat and denial of castration, to the recognition and disavowal of difference.

Raising fetishism from the level of a private perversion to a mass-cultural phenomenon, from a stage of individual development to a representational system, some theorists analyzed cultural images of woman as fetish objects: arrangements of the woman's body as a complete and pleasurable, rather than horrible, sight. Freud himself had discussed one example of such a collective, iconic representation of woman as image—the decapitated head of Medusa, her hair composed of snakes, that turns men to stone. Symbolizing the horror of castration, Medusa's head nevertheless offers multiple replacements of the penis as well as the promise of erection—petrification—and thereby soothes, by means of a sight, the anxiety produced by a sight.

The fetishistic representation of woman as an idealized image of man aims to reassure viewers of their own perfection, but not only the iconography of woman offers this illusory reassurance. The visual form of the self-contained artwork, unified by a transcendent property, is also designed to ensure the authority and wholeness of the viewing subject. The structure of the fetish, a fragment forming a self-contained whole, is also the structure of the so-called autonomous aesthetic object, which, unmodified by what lies outside its frame, "denies," as Victor Burgin puts it, "that there is anything lacking in the field of vision."[38] The understanding that images are relations of hierarchical differentiation taking place not only between objects depicted within images but between images and viewers strikes at the very heart of the belief that images are transparent pictures of the world with an intrinsic content discernible by stable viewers. Feminist explorations of vision suggested, on the contrary, that purportedly independent images universalize their subjects through the conquest of difference.

The materialist and feminist ideas about images briefly sketched here meet in their critique of the fetishism of aesthetic objects. Both maintain that images are constructed relationships whose meaning arises in a historical meeting of the image, the viewer, and the spatiotemporal circumstances of their existence and is therefore uncertain and mutable.

How, then, can we interpret David Harvey's charge that Cindy Sherman's photography is complicitous with fetishism and indifferent to underlying meanings? Work like Sherman's appropriates recognizable cultural images because it is grounded in the premise that meaning is culturally and conventionally—not individually, universally, and spontaneously—produced. Sherman uses or refers to reproducible and collectively received media such as film and photography. Since these media are less burdened with connotations of spirituality and individualism than traditional painting, sculpture, or "art photography," Sherman counteracts essentialist notions of art production. In addition, Sherman's overt recycling of cinematic and photographic codes sharply diverges from the conventions of documentary photography, which, at least in its traditional forms, promises unmediated referentiality and transparency to its object, suggesting that the "unmanipulated" photograph offers incontrovertible evidence of the reality it depicts. But critical photography, which foregrounds photographic construction, reveals that such truth claims are their own kinds of fictions: photographs are decontextualized fragments, constituted through the absence of their referents and themselves constituting, rather than simply reproducing, reality. Sherman's photographs address a specific reality—the production of woman as a cultural category. By highlighting and undermining the codes that construct feminine identity in a range of visual practices, by interfering with the smooth transmission of their messages, Sherman exposes the processes by which feminine identity is socially produced as natural.

In Harvey's view, fetishistic images conceal "underlying social meanings" behind the activity of "masking." Sherman's photographs, he says, "mask the person" (316). Harvey's criticism implies that images of women should unmask feminine identities that, although "social," precede representation, but Sherman's work locates fetishism precisely in this belief in preexisting and unambiguous meanings.

Sherman does not treat the image as an object that reveals or conceals the interior identity—or underlying social meaning—of the person depicted. She explores the image as a site where identity is produced *as an interior*. Interior identity, she reveals, is an effect of cinematic and photographic signifiers—or, by extension, of other material processes of representation. Her female characters do not "have" an interior character concealed by a mask. Interiority is, rather, a function of the mask—a social effect that marks the surface of the female body. Since the feminine is culturally coded as the very figure of the presence of interior truths, Sherman's *Film Stills* not only call into question specific images of women but disrupt the image of femininity itself.

To the extent that Sherman's work deals with masking in the sense of concealment, masking designates the illusion of fundamental meanings within or behind the image, an illusion that disguises—masks—the production of meaning by images and viewers. The "possession" of meaning by the image is as much a fantasy projection as the possession of value by the commodity, which, as Harvey knows, is a crucial component of fetishism. Fetishism of the image, referring to the "magical thinking" that separates meaning from projection, designates the search for, and devotion to, a real content behind the form and the concomitant erasure or denial of the signs of that search. Masking emerges in Sherman's work as the procedure of framing objects and endowing them with "independent" identities—objects in whose presence the controlling subject can develop.

The reference to Sherman's art as fetishistic is yet another example of the relations of difference that structure Harvey's discourse. It represses Sherman's specific object of investigation. It ignores particular cultural discourses about fetishism and does not distinguish among different forms of images. It fails to appreciate different theories of fetishism and, by positing a reality behind the image, disavows the author's own production of meaning. Most clearly, in other words, Harvey's accusation reveals the fetishism of his own representation.

Jean Baudrillard in his early work cautioned that such reversals would occur in all critiques of fetishism that deny fetishism's place in a structure of desire. "The term fetishism," he warned, with the exception of the Freudian concept of the fetish, "almost has a life of its own. . . . Instead of functioning as a metalanguage for the magical thinking of others, it turns against those who use it and surreptitiously exposes their own magical thinking."[39]

Sherman's *Film Stills* provoke an awareness of the psychic investments structuring fetishistic portrayals and so unmask the desires that propel quests for real meaning—in images, in "woman." British cultural critic Judith Williamson describes how the *Film Stills* both elicit and frustrate this search. Sherman exhibits multiple images, and her work consists not of the production of any single picture but of the relationship among them all. Individual photos depict mutually exclusive female identities. Each is Sherman herself and seems to convey a single, essential identity—the "real" Sherman—but none can actually be "the real thing" precisely because they all promise to be. They are always and never her. Sherman thus turns viewers' attention back on themselves and on their relation to the image, stressing the attempt to fix meaning. How do we look, and what are we looking for? "I think," writes Williamson, "that this false search for the 'real' her is exactly what the work is about, and it leads people . . . right up the garden path. The attempt to find the 'real' Cindy Sherman is unfulfillable, just as it is for anyone, but what's so interesting is the obsessive drive to find that identity."[40]

What Harvey cannot locate in Sherman's photographs and, more broadly, in postmodern culture—what he takes them to task for concealing—is not the real woman but another fantasy: a preexisting and directly accessible social reality behind the image. The quest for that meaning parallels Harvey's search for social unity behind fragmentation and behind what he considers to be the illusions of difference. He finds it not in the world but in his image of the world—his social theory. Feminist and other antiessentialist projects that assert the inadequacy of all representations are the casualty of that theory, but they also hold a key to its secrets. Harvey, in other words, may not consider feminism worth knowing about, but feminism, while it hardly knows everything, knows something about him.

CHINATOWN, PART FOUR? WHAT JAKE FORGETS
ABOUT DOWNTOWN

Lately, writers have been comparing the texts of critical urban studies with literary or film noir and describing urban spatial theorists as noir detectives, especially as hard-boiled private eyes. It is hardly surprising that some urban scholars feel an affinity for the tough-guy crime story. Given the centrality of the city as both scene and object of noir investigation, the analogy practically suggests itself. In 1934 Raymond Chandler wrote that the "mean" urban settings of early hard-boiled detective novels—by contrast with the genteel environments typical of classic whodunits—attest to the new genre's realism, bringing out the sociological implications of the theme of murder. "The realist in murder," says Chandler, "writes of a world in which gangsters can rule nations and almost rule cities . . . where the mayor of your town may have condoned murder as an instrument of money-making."[1] What, then, could be more obvious than the resemblance between noir detectives unmasking the power of money and critics of the capitalist city? Guided by a sense of geographic competence, they move warily through treacherous urban spaces—landscapes veiled by deceptive appearances, where almost no one speaks the truth—to trace the histories of violence that have unfolded in space and, moreover, in the economic production of space.

The depiction of urban scholars as streetwise sleuths differs from other references to noir sprinkled throughout recent urban analysis. Occasionally, for instance, critics have cited noir descriptions of cities—like Chandler's melancholic portrait of Los Angeles's Bunker Hill as "lost town, shabby town, crook town"—to enliven their own accounts of city neighborhoods and, more importantly, to counteract the optimistic rhetoric surrounding such brutal urban processes as the 1980s redevelopment of downtown Los Angeles. Perhaps such quotations, merely by their presence, associate urban analysis with the knowing stance of a Philip Marlowe, Chandler's model private investigator. Only recently, however, has the noir detective story been invoked expressly as an image of radical spatial theory's own activity.

In many respects, the metaphor is a natural. Yet it is only possible to assume that noir and urban theory easily share a vision of the city—and that, consequently, hard-boiled private eyes and urban scholars are kindred spirits—by ignoring at least one dissimilarity. While noir, notable for its images of women, routinely identifies the dangers of the city with the sexuality of its femme fatales, the new urban theory endowed with noir's mantle just as readily detaches space from sexuality and, for that matter, barely mentions women at all. Of course, this difference from noir on the level of overt content hardly means that urban analysis is innocent of either gender relations or constructions of sexual difference. The popularity of the tough-guy metaphor itself suggests that in urban theory precisely the absence of the topic of sexuality gives us the first clue to its presence. But if in film noir the femme fatale is conventionally killed off or otherwise punished as the narrative unfolds, in urban theory's version she meets her inevitable demise before the story begins. No matter how apparently transparent, then, the image of urban theorists as noir detectives entails—and in this way is, though unwittingly, noir-like—some mysterious disappearances themselves worthy of investigation.

It may seem fanciful to pursue an inquiry into the likelihood of a relationship between a fictional character and an urban scholar. Taken seriously, however, the conceit may prove more telling than its proponents suspect. For the trope of noir detection, which presents urban discourse as a disinterested search for the hidden truth of the city, also has the capacity to dismantle this claim. The comparison suggests, that is, that the subject of urban spatial discourse (as distinguished from the actual urban theorist) is itself a fiction. For Chandler, the supreme achievement of realistic crime stories is not the reproduction of urban reality but the invention

of the hard-boiled detective, the character who, undismayed by violence, embodies what Chandler considered the genre's essence—the quality of redemption in a
violent world. "Down these mean streets," Chandler famously wrote, "a man must
go who is not himself mean. . . . He is the hero; he is everything. He must be a
complete man and a common man and yet an unusual man."[2] A figure in a landscape, the detective is passionately bound up with, yet independent of, the space
of the city. Urban theory's embrace of this figure invites us to explore, by analogy,
the mutually constitutive and ambivalent relationship between the scholarly investigator and his object of scrutiny. How do images of the city, suppressing the evidence of this reciprocity and giving the impression that they simply offer access to
the real world, produce the "complete man?" How does "urban reality" invent
the hard-boiled urban theorist? With the help of noir, we might even begin to
connect sexuality with the desexualized spaces of the city as they so often appear
in new urban theory.

Geographer Derek Gregory has taken a step in this direction in an article
fittingly titled "*Chinatown*, Part Three? Soja and the Missing Spaces of Social Theory."[3] Gregory draws the detective-urban-theorist comparison satirically in order
to criticize Edward Soja's book, *Postmodern Geographies*.[4] Soja is a leading figure of
the neo-Marxist school of urban research located in Los Angeles—quintessential
noir territory—and Gregory's opening vignette casts him as a Southern California
operative bent on solving the dual mysteries of social theory and urban geography.
"I begin in this way," explains Gregory, "because it conveys . . . what I take to be
the essence of *Postmodern Geographies*."[5] Examining the geography of Soja's text,
Gregory concludes that, by adhering to a belief in the existence of a political-
economic foundation unifying social and urban space, Soja, despite his claim to
embrace postmodern "fragmentation," actually produces an imaginary totalization
of the city. This replete image of Los Angeles depends on the construction of an
external vantage point; the subject of Soja's representation exercises a disembodied,
controlling look, that of the detective. For Gregory, the detective represents the
subject who stands outside space, assuming a position of mastery.

But the title of Gregory's article is not only a parody. It is borrowed from,
and pays tribute to, the work of Mike Davis, an important urban theorist whose

earlier article, "*Chinatown, Part Two? The 'Internationalization' of Downtown Los Angeles,"* in turn pays homage to Roman Polanski's noir revival film set in 1920s Los Angeles.[6] Gregory uses Davis's essays on Los Angeles as a counterpoint to *Postmodern Geographies.* Like Soja, Davis stresses the political economy of socio-spatial restructuring. Unlike Soja, he also pays attention to the specific struggles and distinctive cultures of L.A.'s third world, struggles whose obliteration, Gregory argues, is the very condition of Soja's visualizing representation. For Gregory, these struggles and cultures exemplify what Michel de Certeau calls ground-level practices or "tactics of lived space," activities that resist the regulatory control implicit in aerial perspectives.[7] Gregory adopts de Certeau's influential streets/heights dualism as a framework for criticizing neo-Marxist geography's own discursive spatializations. By operating at street level, Gregory says, or, more exactly, by adding an account of local, resistant practices to an overarching political economic framework, Davis avoids arranging the city into an image and consequently relinquishes the position of the detective. Yet there is an incongruity in Gregory's trenchant critique—a contradiction that usefully undermines the streets/heights opposition. For the milieu of the noir investigator, Gregory's symbol of the controlling look, is precisely the "mean streets," the very site that Gregory privileges as a safeguard *against* voyeurism and so idealizes as simply real.

In fact, though Gregory portrays Davis as the antithesis of Soja's detective, no urban scholar is more regularly linked to noir than Davis. Both jacket endorsements and the press release for *City of Quartz,* Davis's forceful analysis of Los Angeles, make the comparison:

Mike Davis knows where a lot of bodies are buried. . . . This is fine history noir.

Davis is wild at heart yet brilliantly controlled. This book is as accessible and fast-paced as *film noir.*

Combining the rigor of a cultural theorist and historian with the hard-boiled clarity of a Philip Marlowe or a Jake Gittes, Davis uncovers extraordinary tales of greed, power, and prejudice.

No doubt, the book's candid fascination with noir sensibility inspires such descriptions. Stylistically, Davis's language recalls what noir criticism conventionally terms the "gritty realism" of the urban tough-guy novel. His atmospheric descriptions of Los Angeles rival film noir's celebrated high-contrast visual style. More to the point, noir is one pole of a thematic division within which Davis frames his picture of Los Angeles. The book's first chapter, "Sunshine or *Noir?*" examines how successive generations of intellectuals related to Los Angeles. Davis constructs a typology of cultural representations of L.A., a city that, he says, is "infinitely *envisioned.*" Indeed, "it has come to play the double role of utopia *and* dystopia for advanced capitalism" in cultural productions whose opposing outlooks Davis labels, respectively, "sunshine" and "*noir.*"[8] Davis carefully distinguishes among a variety of tendencies within the "complex corpus of . . . *noir,*" which exemplifies the "acute critiques" of late-capitalist culture generated in Los Angeles. In the hands of "leftish *auteurs noirs,*" he concludes, film noir, mirrored in 1940s hardboiled L.A. writing, "sometimes approached a kind of Marxist *cinema manqué*" (40–41). Over the years, it has even "come to function as a surrogate public history" that contests the powerful "city myth" constructed by L.A.'s "official dream machinery" (24).

Associating his own alternative history of L.A. with noir fictions, Davis seems to define urban theory as a discourse that not only analyzes representations of the city but, like noir, produces images of the city. Such a reading of urban scholarship as culture, not "social science," is a welcome departure from the field's traditional configuration of interdisciplinary space. Acknowledging the permeability of boundaries between disciplines, it promises to bring the insights of urban political economy into the arena of cultural studies while dislodging political economy from a privileged position as the ontological basis of all spatial politics. Yet Davis reneges on rearticulating the political field insofar as he interprets noir itself as a kind of social science. Into the sunshine-noir schema, he introduces a third category of L.A. representations: "We must avoid the idea that Los Angeles is ultimately just the mirror of Narcissus. . . . Beyond the myriad rhetorics and mirages, it can be presumed that the city actually exists. I thus treat, within the master dialectic of sunshine and *noir,* three attempts, in successive generations, to establish authentic epistemologies for Los Angeles" (23). Davis then outlines two current efforts to construct an authentic epistemology—the research into post-Fordist urbanism by "the neo-Marxist academics of the 'Los Angeles School'" and the interventions in popular culture by "the community intellectuals of 'Gangster Rap'" (24). In Davis's view, both projects have failed—for different reasons—to disengage themselves fully from today's "corporate celebration of 'postmodern' Los Angeles." Despite this failure, Davis says, "a radical structural analysis . . . can only acquire social force if it is embodied in an alternative experiential vision" (87).

City of Quartz accepts the mandate to create such a vision. As Gregory notes, Davis combines an economic analysis of the city's spatial organization with an account of the struggles of Los Angeles's third-world street cultures—at least, certain aspects of those struggles. He locates the meaning of the city in a terrain between global capitalist structures, on the one hand, and the use of urban space by specific social groups, on the other. But when, under the rubric of noir, Davis designates his achievement an "authentic epistemology," a representation governed by an independent, authenticating model—the L.A. that really exists—he does more than extricate urban scholarship from the city's official dream machinery. By disavowing the question of subjectivity in representations of the city, he disengages urban theory and, strangely, noir as well from any dream machinery whatsoever.

Consider "Chinatown, Part Two?" Foreshadowing City of Quartz, this essay explicitly equates radical urban analysis with a specific instance of noir detection, the investigation undertaken by private eye Jake Gittes in Chinatown, urban studies' archetypal film noir. "What Jake discovers about downtown," as Davis puts it— political corruption, landgrabs, the forced displacement of farmers during L.A.'s early-twentieth century aqueduct conspiracy—is the precursor of what Davis exposes about contemporary downtown: quiet municipal subsidization of super-profit speculation, conducted under the aegis of the Community Redevelopment Agency, as one consequence of post-Fordist restructuring. To be sure, these are crucial discoveries. Like Jake, Davis brings to light the links between violent activities taking place in urban space—the displacement of city residents, for instance— and the violence inherent in the uneven socioeconomic relations that produce advanced capitalist space.

Still, this is only part of the story. What Jake discovers about downtown is not only speculation and the murderous power of money. An investigator of illicit love affairs, he also finds domestic violence, ambiguous family identities, and—as he trails the mysterious Mrs. Mulwray through Los Angeles—a tale of incest and a father's sexual power. Nor are the violent spaces that Jake investigates strictly outside himself. Rather, as in countless noir scenarios, the qualities that make the city "realistic"—its meanness, decadence, violence—do not just mirror sociological conditions or, what amounts to the same thing, express psychological experiences engendered in sociologically constituted city dwellers by the real urban environment. These qualities also entangle the city with the protagonist's psychic geography, with the spatial processes that form his identity. Chinatown is the site of a traumatic loss in Jake's past—a woman's death—which he relives as the adventure unravels and which, with the film's final eruption of violence, he is destined to "forget" again. As Jake is repeatedly brutalized, as his own quest to probe Mrs. Mulwray's secrets grows more cruelly determined, his path leads beyond the discovery of political corruption and sexual scandals. He enters an area outside the law in another sense: the image of the city, like the image of the woman, is mediated by the detective's unconscious fantasies and so—whether lucid or confused—tied up with the mysteries of sexuality.

Overlooked in Davis's gloss on *Chinatown,* sexuality and subjectivity—and their intimacy with violence—have long been viewed by feminist critics as film noir's principal themes and, moreover, as the imperatives shaping its visual and narrative structures. Feminist readings have also theorized these problems in spatial terms, showing how the detective story mobilizes a distinctive spatial mise-enscène organized around an axis of sexual difference. The neglect of such ideas in urban cultural history that is nonetheless equated with noir corresponds to a general indifference to feminist perspectives in these texts' accounts of urban violence, an erasure paralleling, in turn, a troubling silence on gender. It is easy to understand the benefits of avoiding feminist cultural criticism. Making it possible to disregard the noir detective's ambivalent relationship to the city and to relegate the sources of violence to an independent socioeconomic realm—"the mean streets"—this avoidance facilitates an equally untroubled identification of the urban theorist with the private eye—who is not himself mean. By the same token, to acknowledge the reciprocity between subjects and objects of noir detection is to face the difficulties that plague urban studies' self-representation. The desire to render urban theorists in the image of noir investigators contradicts the equally strong impulse—embodied in espousals of authentic epistemologies—to believe that urban space as an object of knowledge can be specified externally to the space of the writer or reader. Doubting this inside-outside dichotomy is not the same as asserting that the city does not really exist. But insofar as urban spatial theory enforces a rigid separation of the two spaces in discourses about the city and, as a result, can push violence wholesale into the "outside" world, it is actually less like film noir and closer to the "unrealistic" whodunit that Raymond Chandler so despised.

According to Laura Mulvey, what distinguishes "the simple detectives of the whodunit" from "the modern, post-psychoanalytic, heroes-in-crisis of the *film noir*" is precisely the theme of internal transformation animating the latter: "The story [the noir detective] investigates is his own."[9] Mary Ann Doane also analyzes noir in terms of the construction of masculine identity. Film noir, she writes, following Christine Gledhill, abandons the usual goal of the detective film, "the comprehensible solution of crime." Instead, it "constitutes itself as a detour, a bending of the hermeneutic code from the questions connected with a crime to the difficulty posed by the woman as enigma (or crime)."[10] For Mulvey as well as for Teresa de Lauretis, the protagonist's effort to solve the enigma links noir to the structure of the detective narrative understood as a version of the Oedipal myth. The movement of the narrative, de Lauretis argues, establishes the difference between the sexes, an operation duplicated in the story's spatial structure, which "produces the masculine position as that of mythical subject and the feminine position as mythical obstacle or, simply, the space in which that movement occurs."[11] Within the visual relations of narrative cinema, the masculine position is also the place of the look, the feminine position, that of image—and landscape. It has become a critical commonplace to observe that in noir the figure of the femme fatale resists confinement in—or as—space and, crossing boundaries, threatens the protagonist's identity. The role of the urban detective and, some critics believe, the work of noir itself, is to repress her image, to master the feminine—how successfully is controversial—thereby restoring spatial order and, with it, the detective's own perceptual clarity and geographic proficiency.

This brief sketch is not meant to do justice to the complexity of *Chinatown,* noir, or feminist opinions about noir. Even less does it defend a psychic, rather than social, determinist explanation of urban violence or advocate "psychoanalytic" readings of urban theory that claim to find evidence of individual conflicts or a general sexual symbolism. But a critical glance at noir suggests that, with regard to sexual difference, the new urban studies may bear some resemblance to hard-boiled stories after all. In each case, an urban investigator sets out on a search that, presented as a quest for reality, is actually a way of articulating a vision of reality. In each case, an image of space plays a key role in a more intricate spatial production: the emergence of a subject whose integrity rests on an ability to detect what lies behind a facade of spatial uncertainties, identified in noir with the femme fatale, and in neo-Marxist spatial theory with post-Fordist capitalism. While in noir the detective's stability returns with the woman's downfall, in urban criticism it is gained by "discovering" an underlying economic foundation of spatial violence or by other externalizations of political space. These respective endings are connected, however, since the appeal to independent grounds of meaning, protecting the authority of a single reference point, cleanses sexuality and difference from urban discourse and from its picture of the city. For this reason, Davis's alternative vision of Los Angeles, despite its important opposition to official urban rhetoric, is still largely a masculine terrain. Will urban theory interrogate this space, or will it remain "just Chinatown"?

III

PUBLIC SPACE AND DEMOCRACY

Four years after a public hearing that many critics viewed as a show trial, the United States General Services Administration (GSA) dismantled Richard Serra's *Tilted Arc,* a public sculpture that the agency had installed a decade earlier in New York City's Federal Plaza. The government's action became a cause célèbre in some sectors of the art world, especially among certain left-wing critics who saw it as one episode in a neoconservative campaign to privatize culture, restrict rights, and censor critical art. Briefly, the *Tilted Arc* story unfolded like this:

1979: The GSA commissions Serra to conceive a sculpture for the Federal Plaza site.

1981: Following approval of the artist's concept, *Tilted Arc* is installed.

1985: William Diamond, the GSA's New York regional administrator, names himself chairman of a hearing to decide whether Serra's sculpture should be, as Diamond puts it, "relocated" in order "to increase public use of the plaza." Although the majority of speakers at the hearing testify in favor of retaining *Tilted Arc,* the hearing panel recommends relocation, and Dwight Ink, the GSA's acting administrator in Washington, tries in vain to find alternative sites for the sculpture.

1986 to 1989: Serra pursues several unsuccessful legal actions—based on breach of contract, violation of constitutional rights, and artists' moral rights claims[1]—to prevent *Tilted Arc*'s removal.

1989: *Tilted Arc* is removed.

Then, in 1991, *The Destruction of Tilted Arc: Documents* appeared, like an act of historic preservation.[2] By that time, of course, the book could do nothing to save the sculpture itself. But it does preserve the record—correspondence, official memos, press releases, hearing testimonies, and legal documents—of a key conflict in the growing controversy about the political functions of contemporary public art. Clara Weyergraf-Serra and Martha Buskirk carefully edited the papers generated in the course of the *Tilted Arc* proceedings, and the publication of this primary material provides a solid foundation for future art-historical and legal scholarship. Some readers will welcome the opportunity to weigh opposing arguments and determine, in retrospect, the merits of an individual public artwork. More importantly, however, *The Destruction of Tilted Arc: Documents* keeps alive—and public—debates about the political issues at stake in the *Tilted Arc* incident. The documents raise timely questions, whose implications extend far beyond arcane art-world matters, about what it means for art and space to be "public." Insofar as the GSA ostensibly dismantled *Tilted Arc* "to increase public use of the plaza," the documents pose related questions about current uses of urban space.

Despite claims to the contrary, the officials presiding over the *Tilted Arc* procedure were far from neutral on these questions. To suggest that the GSA had, in fact, answered them in advance is not to contend, as many of Serra's supporters did, that the sculpture's fate had been prejudged (though that may also be true). But the GSA *had* adopted prior decisions about the meaning of the terms "use," "public," and "public use" and had built these precedents into the structure of the *Tilted Arc* proceedings from the start. As the editors of *The Destruction of Tilted Arc* point out, official announcements of the hearing contained an implied value judgment, framing the proposed debate as a contest between, on the one hand, *Tilted Arc*'s continued presence in the Federal Plaza and, on the other hand, increased "public use of the plaza" (22). Clearly, it had been predetermined that the sculpture's presence detracted from "public use," but this judgment assumed that definitions of "public" and "use" are self-evident. "The public" was presumed to be a group of aggregated individuals unified by their adherence to fundamental, objective values or by their possession of essential needs and interests or, what amounts to the same thing, divided by equally essential conflicts. "Use" referred to the act of putting space into the service of fundamental pleasures and needs. Objects and practices in space were held to be of "public use" if they are uniformly beneficial, expressing common values or fulfilling universal needs.

Categories like "the public" can, of course, be construed as naturally or fundamentally coherent only by disavowing the conflicts, particularity, heterogeneity, and uncertainty that constitute social life. But when participants in a debate about the uses of public space remove the definitions of public and use to a realm of objectivity located not only outside the *Tilted Arc* debate but outside debate altogether, they threaten to erase public space itself. For what initiates debate about social questions if not the absence of absolute sources of meaning and the concomitant recognition that these questions—including the question of the meaning of public space—are decided only *in* a public space?

That words like "use" and "public"—employed as figures of universal accessibility—suppress conflict will hardly surprise anyone familiar with prevailing discourses about the built environment. The GSA's verdict, confirming its premise that *Tilted Arc* interfered with the use of a public plaza, was consistent with a host of other opinions handed down throughout the 1980s on the uses of public space and public art. The decision against *Tilted Arc* was not a ruling against public art in general. On the contrary, the verdict coincided and was perfectly consistent with a widespread movement by city governments, real-estate developers, and corporations to *promote* public art, especially something called the "new public art," which was celebrated precisely because of its "usefulness." The new public art was defined as art that takes the form of functional objects placed in urban spaces— plumbing, park benches, picnic tables—or as art that helps design urban spaces themselves. Official efforts to discredit *Tilted Arc* cannot be isolated from attempts to portray other kinds of public art as truly public and useful. Moreover, the promotion of the new public art itself took place within a broader context, accompanying a massive transformation in the uses of urban space—the redevelopment and gentrification of cities engineered throughout the 1980s as the local component of global spatioeconomic restructuring. The *Tilted Arc* proceedings were, then, part of a rhetoric of publicness and usefulness that surrounded the redevelopment of urban space to maximize profit and facilitate state control. *Tilted Arc,* represented by its opponents as elitist, useless, even dangerous to the public, became the standard foil against which conservative critics and city officials routinely measure the accessibility, usefulness, humaneness, and publicness of the new public art.[3]

Although Serra's most astute supporters generally remained detached from urban issues, some countered the accusation that *Tilted Arc* obstructed the use of public space by defending the sculpture precisely because, as Rosalind Krauss argued, it "invests a major portion of its site with a use we must call aesthetic." Because this use is aesthetic, Krauss implied, it is also public: "This aesthetic use is open to every person who enters and leaves the buildings of this complex, and it is open to each and every one of them every day" (81).

Relativizing use, Krauss's strategy challenged determinist notions that space has uses that are simply given and therefore indisputable. But Krauss also mobilized a conception of the aesthetic as a universally accessible sphere—which, coupled with notions of universal publics and uses, is the hallmark of mainstream treatments of public art. Precisely this universalizing vocabulary has made public art so effective as a means of portraying particular uses of space—to fulfill the needs of profit, for one—as advantageous to all. Simply proposing a plurality of equally universal uses of space leaves untouched the depoliticizing language of use that was the most powerful weapon wielded against *Tilted Arc.*

The Destruction of Tilted Arc: Documents invites us, by contrast, to examine the uses of language. Because the volume's title openly supports Serra's contention that "to remove" a work like *Tilted Arc* "is to destroy the work," it promises that the book will not merely report on but will engage in discursive struggles—beginning with the struggle over the meaning of site-specificity. Adopting Serra's terminology, Weyergraf-Serra and Buskirk implicitly defend the materialist approach to aesthetics historically invested in site-specific practices against current efforts to bring site-specificity into conformity with idealist concepts of art. Diamond, the GSA administrator, did not mention destruction. He referred to the sculpture's removal as a "relocation." In fact, Diamond portrayed himself as a virtual urban preservationist who, in keeping with conservative notions of preservation, was seeking to restore a fundamental sociospatial harmony that should have been preserved but was not. Diamond asserted that *Tilted Arc*'s relocation would "restore" and "reinstitute" the Federal Plaza's openness, coherence, and public usefulness.

But calling a site-specific sculpture's removal a relocation obscures a key difference between two aesthetic philosophies: on the one hand, the modernist doctrine that artworks are self-governing objects with stable, independent meanings and can therefore be relocated or moved intact from place to place, and, on the other hand, the idea, which gave rise to site-specific practice, that aesthetic meaning is formed in relation to an artwork's context and therefore changes with the circumstances in which the work is produced and displayed. Seemingly blind to the contradiction between these competing conceptions of art, the officials who opposed *Tilted Arc* did not acknowledge the incompatibility between site-specificity and the "truly public American art" described in the GSA's factsheet about the Art-in-Architecture Program for Federal Buildings. According to the factsheet, the objective of public art is "integration" with a "site," defined in turn as a "total architectural design." Consequently, the factsheet concludes that the Art-in-Architecture Program should sponsor art that "embellishes" federal buildings and "enhance[s] the building's environment for the occupants and the general public" (23).

But equating site-specific art with art that creates harmonious spatial totalities is so profoundly at odds with the impulse that historically motivated the development of site-specificity that it nearly amounts to a terminological abuse. For the invention of a new kind of artwork that neither diverts attention from nor merely decorates the spaces of its display emerged from the imperative to interrupt, rather than secure, the seeming coherence and closure of those spaces. Site-specific practice has two objectives that emerged in quick succession. Site-specificity sought first to criticize the modernist precept that works of art are autonomous entities and second to reveal how the construction of an apparent autonomy disavows art's social, economic, and political functions. But the politicization of art embodied in this attention to context is offset when artists adopt neutralizing definitions of context. Academic site-specificity, for instance, simply replaces the modernist aestheticization of the artwork with a similar aestheticization of art's architectural, spatial, or urban sites. Other artists and critics neutralize site-specificity by stressing the importance of art's social contexts but then defining society as a determinable object that, unified by a foundation external to art, governs and fixes aesthetic meaning. Both approaches reestablish, at the level of the site, the closure of meaning that site-specificity helped challenge.

Ignoring this challenge, many of *Tilted Arc*'s opponents advocated the sculpture's removal in order to restore the Federal Plaza's coherence. But proponents of a political site-specificity are skeptical about spatial coherence, viewing it not as an a priori condition subsequently disturbed by conflicts *in* space but as a fiction masking the conflicts that *produce* space. Henri Lefebvre, the urban theorist who coined the phrase "the production of space," refers to this homogenizing fiction when he describes late-capitalist space as "simultaneously the birthplace of contradictions, the milieu in which they are worked out and which they tear up, and, finally, the instrument which allows their suppression and *the substitution of an apparent coherence*."[4] Against this process, and in striking contrast to the GSA's notion of integration, site-specific works become part of their sites precisely by restructuring them, fostering—we might even say, restoring—the viewer's ability to apprehend the conflicts and indeterminacy repressed in the creation of supposedly coherent spatial totalities.

When Weyergraf-Serra and Buskirk use the term *destruction* to describe *Tilted Arc*'s fate, they take an avowedly partial stand consistent with the abandonment of totalizing perspectives implicit in site-specificity itself. After so many years of cultural critiques of objectivism, it should be unnecessary to point out that admitting partiality is not an abdication of responsibility for factual accuracy or fairness. *The Destruction of Tilted Arc* is scrupulously researched, the documents rigorously footnoted, and the chronology of events and texts painstakingly reconstructed. Far from a license to dissemble, the designation of *Tilted Arc*'s removal as a destruction frankly signals the editors' desire to support site-specificity as a critical art practice against the current implication that such work can merely affirm its sites. Affirmative site-specific art, endowed with an aura of social responsibility, naturalizes and thus validates the social relations of its sites, legitimating spaces as accessible to all when they may be privately owned or when, tolerating little resistance to corporate or state-approved uses, they exclude entire social groups. The editors' admission of partiality also diverges from the position taken by *Tilted Arc*'s most powerful antagonists who spoke in the name of certainties like "common sense," "reality," and "the people's interest." The appeal to such absolute grounds of meaning sheltered their arguments from political interrogation.

To support the book's argument in favor of *Tilted Arc,* the editors framed the chronologically arranged sections of documents with footnotes and brief introductions that summarize and interpret data, provide supplementary information, or point out inaccuracies and fallacies in opponents' statements. Most candidly declaring the book's partisanship, however, is the inclusion of a general introduction written by Serra himself, a detailed polemic against both the GSA's arguments and subsequent court decisions dismissing the artist's appeals. The frank abandonment of pretensions to documentary impartiality implicit in this choice could have turned the editors' and Serra's introductions into an opportunity not merely to preserve but also to amplify and transform the *Tilted Arc* debate.

But the editors missed this chance. The introductions reiterate the opinions expressed by Serra and his supporters in the documents themselves. As a consequence, the book's intervention in public art discourse stays firmly within the boundaries that shaped—and constrained—discussion in the thick of the *Tilted Arc* controversy. At that time, liberal and left members of the art world who unconditionally supported *Tilted Arc* forged their arguments primarily in opposition to the neoconservative rhetoric mobilized against the sculpture, a reactive position with some serious risks. For if the desire to defeat conservatism exhausts all political contests over the meaning of public art, the problems presented by traditional left ideas of aesthetic politics and of art's public functions will remain uninterrogated. Yet critical thought is hardly united in support of these ideas, nor, for that matter, did the left unanimously defend *Tilted Arc.* To give the impression of a self-evident unity of critical opinion that forms the proper basis for opposing conservatism (a strategy that comes close to mirroring that of *Tilted Arc*'s enemies) is to imply that different critical ideas are divisive forces, giving comfort to the enemy. Because it is important to extend, and reframe, current debates about public art—and not because the book should impart an aura of disinterestedness—the absence of a critical essay by someone other than Serra is regrettable.

———

This deficiency narrows the book's treatment of several important issues. Consider, for instance, the key issue of site-specificity, which Serra's introduction patiently explains and elaborates. He insists that, because a site-specific work incorporates its context as an essential component of the work, site-specificity denotes permanence. This provides a strategic basis for claiming that *Tilted Arc*'s removal breaches the government contract guaranteeing the sculpture's permanence and, moreover, for disputing Diamond's invention of definitions that make site-specificity compatible with relocation or adjustment. But the relationship between site-specificity and permanence is complex, and the simple equation of the two deviates in significant ways from the principles of contextualist art practice. Given that site-specific projects are based on the idea that meaning is contingent rather than absolute, they actually imply instability and impermanence.

The book's failure to differentiate among different senses of "permanence" repeats a slippage made repeatedly in the Serra camp throughout the hearing when unqualified references to the intrinsic permanence of site-specific works contributed to a blurring of distinctions between the antiessentialist tenets of site-specificity, on the one hand, and liberal platitudes that "great art" is eternal and possesses "enduring qualities," on the other. In the latter case, permanence is given the property of an essence. But the belief in art's timelessness, in its determination by an aesthetic essence and its independence from historical contingencies, is precisely what contextualist practices challenged in the first place. This is no trivial confusion. Allowing site-specific art to be swept into a realm of transhistorical continuities, it neutralizes—just as Diamond's relocation proposal does—the very shift in contemporary art that decisively opened the artwork to history, politics, and everyday life. This shift wrested art out of an eternal sphere superior to the rest of the social world. Not surprisingly, then, the effort to shore up *Tilted Arc*'s unconditional permanence and therefore its aesthetic privilege coincided with a tendency for *Tilted Arc*'s defenders to evade questions of elitism.

It has been traditional for some leftist voices in the art world to deal inadequately with the problem of elitism, even to dismiss it out of hand. This dismissal parallels a tendency prevalent until recently in broader left discourse, where discussions of democracy often concentrated on exposing the mystifications of formal bourgeois democracy and proposing "concrete" socialist alternatives while ignoring the undemocratic character not only of actually existing socialist regimes but of the left's own theories. Among artists and critics, the failure to take democracy seriously springs in part from the pressure that the left has felt to defend itself against attacks from conservative critics who routinely use anti-intellectual and populist strategies to give democratic legitimacy to authoritarian campaigns against critical art and theory.

These pressures were strong during the *Tilted Arc* hearing. A rhetoric of democracy pervaded the debate, demonstrating the degree to which public art discourse had become a site of struggle over the meaning of democracy. Government officials disparaged critical art under the banner of "antielitism," a stance consistent with a general tendency in neoconservative discourse to accuse art of arrogance or inaccessibility in order to champion privatization and justify state censorship in the name of the rights of "the people."

The *Tilted Arc* proceedings exemplified this inversion, combining talk of government's accountability to the public with action by the government in a role resembling that of a private economic actor. From the start, the GSA emphasized its responsibility to protect the people from what it called *Tilted Arc's* "private" encroachment on public space. Diamond mobilized this protectionist discourse on the day the sculpture was dismantled: "Now," he declared, "the plaza returns rightfully to the people." Later, however, when Serra tried to appeal the decision, the courts protected the government as a property-owning entity. Serra pleaded, first, that he had been denied due process in the form of a fair, impartial hearing and, second, that the GSA's decision violated his First Amendment rights, which prohibit the government from removing a medium of expression on the basis of its content once it has been publicly displayed. The courts dismissed both claims. The judge for the U.S. Court of Appeals for the Second Circuit argued that because the government owned both the sculpture and the Federal Plaza, Serra was never constitutionally entitled to a hearing. Due process in this case was called a "gratuitous benefit," not a right (253). There are parallels between this decision and a conservative legal tendency that, as constitutional scholar Laurence H. Tribe writes, has potentially staggering effects on the exercise of free speech rights. The distinction between "benefit" and "right" recalls the legal distinction between "privilege" and "right," which, says Tribe, can be used as a "tool for cutting off the free speech rights of those who rely on the government as an employer, provider of benefits, or property owner."[5] The basis of the distinction is the doctrine that a speaker's First Amendment rights are violated only if she is deprived of something to which she is independently entitled. But no one has the right to enter government property—only the "privilege." If strictly applied, warns Tribe, the right-privilege doctrine could "leave would-be speakers with a right to speak, but nowhere to exercise that right."[6]

Subsequently, Serra claimed, again unsuccessfully, that against the rights of private ownership, he has "moral rights" in the work as an artist. Artists' moral rights are frequently declared in opposition to the privileges of private property, but the GSA implicitly discredited this opposition when it suggested that the government owned the work and the plaza not as a private-property owner, but as "the people": "This space belongs to the government and to the public," said Diamond. "It doesn't belong to the artist. . . . Not if he sells [his work] to the government. . . . He doesn't have the right to force his art upon the public forever" (271). Claims of accountability to the public were articulated with action by the government as a property owner, tying the people's interest to the rights of private property in controlling public spaces.

Tilted Arc's proponents spoke for democracy, too. Some testified in favor of the right of free artistic expression or, like Abigail Solomon-Godeau, deplored the denial of due process inherent in Diamond's prejudgment of the case. Benjamin Buchloh stressed the democratic necessity of independent peer review as a guarantee against statism and collective prejudice. Clara Weyergraf-Serra cautioned against the totalitarian dangers of appeals to the people's "healthy instincts." *Tilted Arc*'s advocates thus argued persuasively, and I think justifiably, against a government intervention that could be a textbook example of what Stuart Hall terms "authoritarian populism": the mobilization of democratic discourses to sanction, indeed to pioneer, shifts toward state authoritarianism.[7] Serra's supporters insistently exposed the manner in which state officials used the language of democracy and such existing democratic procedures as public hearings and petitions to bind popular consent to the coercive pole of state power in so-called public spaces. The importance of this critique can hardly be overestimated. In New York, as in other cities, authoritarian populist measures, coupled with anticrime campaigns—the very strategies rallied against *Tilted Arc*—have authorized the relentless proliferation of pseudo- or private public spaces.

Yet beyond the challenge raised to authoritarian populist notions of public art and to the trivializing reduction of public spaces to harmonious leisure spots or places to eat lunch, and beyond the espousal of formal rights, Serra's supporters made few efforts to articulate democracy, public art, or public space in more radical directions. Insofar as *The Destruction of Tilted Arc: Documents* perpetuates this quiescence, it abandons public art discourse as a site of struggle over the meaning of democracy. Indeed, although Serra alludes briefly to the critical difference between "community" and "public," *The Destruction of Tilted Arc* does not try to define "publicness." The introductions do not, for instance, elaborate the suggestion, broached in Douglas Crimp's and Joel Kovel's hearing testimonies, that a distinction between public space and the state apparatus is essential to democracy. Nor do they amplify the implications for public art discourse of Kovel's crucial point that a democratic public space must be understood as a realm not of unity but of divisions, conflicts, and differences resistant to regulatory power. The *Tilted Arc* controversy is never linked to the efforts currently being made by artists, critics, and curators to recast public art as work that helps create a public space in the sense of a public sphere, an arena of political discourse. And although the word "public" might be applied to Serra's work not so much because *Tilted Arc* occupied a government plaza as because it explored how the viewer, far from a strictly private being, is formed in relation to an outside world, the book never extends this investigation of subjectivity to ask who the subject of a democratic public space is.

Given the neglect of this question, it is hardly accidental that throughout the Serra debate the left's neglect of critical issues about public space and democracy was coupled with a failure to challenge substantially either the myth of great art or its corollary, the myth of the great artist. In fact, *Tilted Arc's* radical supporters frequently relied, almost by default, on the standard left counterparts of these myths—political-aesthetic vanguardism and the exemplary political artist.

Consequently, Serra's proponents offered only a limited and problematic alternative to authoritarian populist conceptions of public art. For vanguardism implies the existence of sovereign subjects whose superior social vision can penetrate illusions and perceive the people's "true" interests, and this idea has itself been charged with authoritarianism—even with the attempt to eliminate public space. According to new theories of radical democracy, public space emerges with the abandonment of the belief in an absolute basis of social unity, a basis that gives "the people" an essential identity or true interest. Public space, in this view, is the uncertain social realm where, in the absence of an absolute foundation, the meaning of the people is simultaneously constituted and put at risk. The vanguard position—the external vantage point on society—is incompatible with a democratic public space.

The Destruction of Tilted Arc vigorously defends public space against neoconservatism, privatization, and state control and helps document the current state of public art discourse. But the book itself reveals that if we want to extend rather than close down public space, it is to questions of democracy that we should turn.

No return to the past is conceivable within the framework of democracy.

—Claude Lefort, "Human Rights and the Welfare State"

What does it mean for space to be "public"—the space of a city, building, exhibition, institution, or work of art? Over the last decade, this question has provoked vigorous debates among art, architecture, and urban critics. Important issues are at stake in these debates. How we define public space is intimately connected with ideas about what it means to be human, the nature of society, and the kind of political community we want. While there are sharp divisions over these ideas, on one point nearly everyone agrees: supporting things that are public promotes the survival and extension of democratic culture. Judging, then, by the number of references to public space in contemporary aesthetic discourse, the art world is taking democracy seriously.

When, for instance, arts administrators and city officials draft guidelines for putting "art in public places," they routinely use a vocabulary that invokes the principles of both direct and representative democracy: Are the artworks for "the people?" Do they encourage "participation?" Do they serve their "constituencies?" Public art terminology frequently alludes to democracy as a form of government but also to a general democratic spirit of egalitarianism: Do the works avoid "elitism?" Are they "accessible?"

When it comes to public art, even neoconservative critics—no strangers to elitism in artistic matters—are out there with the people. Historically, of course, neoconservatives have objected to what Samuel P. Huntington once called an "excess of democracy"—activism, demands for political participation, and challenges to governmental, moral, and cultural authority. Such demands, wrote Huntington, are the legacy of "the democratic surge of the 1960s," and they impede democratic rule by elites. They make society ungovernable by rendering government too accessible: "Democratic societies cannot work when the citizenry is not passive."[1] Today, however, neoconservatives call the government excessive and attack the "arrogance" and "egoism" of public art, especially critical public art, precisely in the name of democratic access—the people's access to public space.[2]

Opinions on the best-known recent controversy over public art—the removal of Richard Serra's *Tilted Arc* from New York's Federal Plaza—also focused, at least for opponents of the sculpture, on democratic access. "This is a day for the people to rejoice," declared William Diamond of the federal government's Art-in-Architecture Program on the day *Tilted Arc* was destroyed, "because now the plaza returns rightfully to the people." But supporters of the sculpture, testifying at the hearing convened to decide *Tilted Arc*'s fate, *defended* the work under the banner of democracy, upholding the artist's right to free expression or portraying the hearing itself as destructive of democratic processes.[3]

Others, equally committed to public art yet reluctant to take sides in such controversies, seek instead to resolve confrontations between artists and other users of space by creating procedures generally described as "democratic": "community involvement" in the selection of works of art or the "integration" of artworks with the spaces they occupy. Such procedures may be necessary, in some cases even fruitful, but to take for granted that they are democratic is to presume that the task of democracy is to settle, rather than sustain, conflict.

Yet no topic is itself more embattled than democracy, which, as even these few examples show, can be taken seriously in more ways than one. The emergence of this topic in the art world is part of a far more extensive eruption of debates about the meaning of democracy currently taking place in many arenas: political philosophy, new social movements, educational theory, legal studies, and mass-media and popular culture. As a site of such debates—and not, as critics frequently claim, because public art is located in universally accessible public sites—discourse about public art reaches beyond the boundaries of arcane art-world concerns.

The question of democracy has, of course, been raised internationally by challenges to racially oppressive African governments, Latin American dictator-ships, and Soviet-style state socialism. Widely touted as the "triumph of democ-racy" and equated with the supposed deaths of socialism and Marxism, these challenges have propelled the use of democracy as a catchword that glosses over the uncertainties of contemporary political life, but they have also cast doubt on such rhetoric, posing the question of democracy as, precisely, a question.

For critics on the left, sensitivity to and uncertainty about democracy stems not only from recent discredit brought upon totalitarian regimes. Leftists of various kinds have long been aware that totalitarianism is no mere betrayal of Marxism. They have been troubled by the failure of Marx himself and orthodox Marxists to appreciate fully ideas about freedom and human rights. The most ossified forms of Marxism have been so preoccupied with challenging bourgeois democracy as a mystified form of capitalist class rule and with insisting that economic equality guarantees true or "concrete" democracy that, as one writer says, they have been "unable to discern freedom in democracy" or "servitude in totalitarianism."[4] But the rejection of economistic notions of democracy and of totalitarianism is clearly no reason to remain content with anticommunism. For, as Nancy Fraser sensibly reminds us, "There is still quite a lot to object to in our own actually existing democracy."[5] Powerful voices in the United States often convert "freedom" and "equality" into slogans under which the liberal democracies of advanced capitalist countries are held up as exemplary social systems, the sole political model for socie-ties emerging from dictatorships and actually existing socialism. Yet the relentless escalation of economic inequality in Western democracies since the late 1970s—the U.S. taking the lead in this respect—the growth of corporate power, and fierce attacks on the rights of expendable groups of people reveal the dangers of adopting a celebratory attitude. Taking issue with Francis Fukuyama's thesis that human struggle against tyranny inevitably ends with capitalist democracy, Chantal Mouffe writes, "We have, in fact, to acknowledge that the victory of liberal democracy is due more to the collapse of its enemy than to its own successes."[6]

At the same time, a countervailing democratic force has also emerged—the proliferation of new political practices inspired by the idea of rights: movements for the right to housing, privacy, and freedom of movement for homeless residents, for instance, or declarations of the right of gays and lesbians to a public sexual culture. Aimed at gaining recognition for collective and marginalized particularities, these new movements defend—and extend—acquired rights, but they also propagate demands for new rights based on differentiated and contingent needs. Unlike purely abstract liberties, these rights do not eliminate from consideration the social conditions of the claimants' existence. Yet while such new movements challenge the exercise of state and corporate power in liberal democracies, they deviate from the principles informing traditional left political projects. Focusing on the construction of political identities within society and forming provisional coalitions with other groups, the new movements distance themselves from overall solutions to social problems. They also refuse to be governed by parties claiming to represent the people's essential interests.

Over the last two decades, certain left political thinkers have sought to make room for these new types of political struggle, on the one hand, and to confront the experience of totalitarianism, on the other. This dual objective has led scholars like Claude Lefort, Ernesto Laclau, Chantal Mouffe, Etienne Balibar, Jean-Luc Nancy, and Philippe Lacoue-Labarthe, among others, to renew theories of democracy. A generative participant in this project is Lefort, a French political philosopher who in the early 1980s framed ideas that have since emerged as key points in discussions about radical democracy. The hallmark of democracy, says Lefort, is the disappearance of certainty about the foundations of social life. Uncertainty makes democratic power the antithesis of the absolutist monarchical power it destroys. In Lefort's view, the French bourgeois political revolution of the eighteenth century inaugurated a radical mutation in the form of society, a mutation he calls, following Alexis de Tocqueville, "the democratic invention." The democratic invention was one and the same event with the Declaration of the Rights of Man, an event that shifted the location of power. All sovereign power, the declaration states, resides within "the people." Where had it previously lived? Under the monarchy, power was embodied in the person of the king who, in turn, incarnated the power of the state. But the power possessed by king and state ultimately derived from a transcendent source—God, Supreme Justice, or Reason. The transcendent source that guaranteed the king's and the state's power also guaranteed the meaning and unity of society—of the people. Society, then, was represented as a substantial unity, its hierarchical organization resting upon an absolute basis.

With the democratic revolution, however, state power was no longer referred to an external force. Now it derived from "the people" and was located inside the social. But with the disappearance of references to an outside origin of power, an unconditional origin of social unity vanished as well. The people are the source of power but they, too, are deprived in the democratic moment of their substantial identity. Like the state, the social order, too, has no basis. The unity of society can no longer be represented as an organic totality but is, rather, "purely social" and therefore a mystery. Unprecedented in democracy is the fact that the place from which power derives its legitimacy is what Lefort calls "the image of an empty place."[7] "In my view," he writes, "the important point is that democracy is instituted and sustained by the *dissolution of the markers of certainty.* It inaugurates a history in which people experience a fundamental indeterminacy as to the basis of power, law and knowledge, and as to the basis of relations between *self* and *other.*"[8]

Democracy, then, has a difficulty at its core. Power stems from the people but belongs to nobody. Democracy abolishes the external referent of power and refers power to society. But democratic power cannot appeal for its authority to a meaning immanent in the social. Instead, the democratic invention invents something else: the public space. The public space, in Lefort's account, is the social space where, in the absence of a foundation, the meaning and unity of the social is negotiated—at once constituted and put at risk. What is recognized in public space is the legitimacy of debate about what is legitimate and what is illegitimate. Like democracy and public space, debate is initiated with the declaration of rights, themselves deprived in the democratic moment of an unconditional source. The essence of democratic rights is to be declared, not simply possessed. Public space implies an institutionalization of conflict as, through an unending declaration of rights, the exercise of power is questioned, becoming, in Lefort's words, "the outcome of a controlled contest with permanent rules." [9]

Democracy and its corollary, public space, are brought into existence, then, when the idea that the social is founded on a substantial basis, a positivity, is abandoned. The identity of society becomes an enigma and is therefore open to contestation. But, as Laclau and Mouffe argue, this abandonment also means that society is "impossible"—which is to say, that the conception of society as a closed entity is impossible. [10] For without an underlying positivity, the social field is structured by relationships among elements that themselves have no essential identities. Negativity is thus part of any social identity, since identity comes into being only through a relationship with an "other" and, as a consequence, cannot be internally complete: "the presence of the 'Other' prevents me from being totally myself." [11] Identity is dislocated. Likewise, negativity is part of the identity of society as a whole; no complete element within society unifies it and determines its development. Laclau and Mouffe use the term *antagonism* to designate the relationship between a social identity and a "constitutive outside" that blocks its completion. Antagonism affirms and simultaneously prevents the closure of society, revealing the partiality and precariousness—the contingency—of every totality. Antagonism is "the 'experience' of the limit of the social." [12] The impossibility of society is not an invitation to political despair but the starting point—or "groundless 'ground'"—of a properly democratic politics. "There is politics," says Laclau, "because there is subversion and dislocation of the social." [13]

It will be the Lefortian contention of this essay that advocates of public art who want to foster the growth of a democratic culture must also start from this point. Linked to the image of an empty place, democracy is a concept capable of interrupting the dominant language of democracy that engulfs us today. But democracy retains the capacity continually to question power and put existing social orders into question only if we do not flee from the question—the unknowability of the social—that generates the public space at democracy's heart. Instituted by the declaration of the rights of man, public space extends to all humans the freedom that Hannah Arendt calls "a right to have rights."[14] Public space expresses, in the words of Etienne Balibar, "an essential limitlessness characteristic of democracy."[15] But when the question of democracy is replaced with a positive identity, when critics speak in the name of absolute rather than contingent—which is to say, political—meanings of the social, democracy can be mobilized to compel acquiescence in new forms of subordination.

Today, discourse about the problems of public spaces in American cities is dominated by the articulation of democracy in authoritarian directions. This movement is engineered in two interlocking steps. First, urban public spaces are endowed with substantive sources of unity. Particular uses of space are deemed self-evident and uniformly beneficial because they are said to be based on some absolute foundation—eternal human needs, the organic configuration and evolution of cities, inevitable technological progress, natural social arrangements, or objective moral values. Second, it is claimed that the foundation authorizes the exercise of state power in these spaces (or the power of such quasi-governmental entities as "business improvement districts").

But with this claim power becomes incompatible with democratic values, and public space is, to borrow a term from Lefort, "appropriated." When, that is, guardians of public space refer their power to a source of social unity outside the social, they attempt to occupy—in the senses of filling up, taking possession of, taking possession by filling up—the locus of power that in a democratic society is an empty place. Let us be clear. For Lefort, "appropriation" does not simply designate the exercise of power or the act of making a decision about the use of a space. Lefort does not deny the necessity of power or political decision making. Appropriation is a strategy deployed by a distinctly undemocratic power that legitimates itself by giving social space a "proper," hence incontestable, meaning, thereby closing down public space.[16]

A single example should suffice to illustrate the appropriative strategy in contemporary urban discourse, since this strategy has become so familiar. Today it travels under the slogan "the quality of urban life," a phrase that in its predominant usage embodies a profound antipathy to rights and pluralism. Formulated in the singular, "the quality of life" assumes a universal city dweller who is equated with "the public"—identities that the phrase actually invents. The universality of this urban resident is called into question when we note that those who champion a better quality of life do not defend all public institutions equally. While conservative journalists routinely seek to protect municipal parks, they do not necessarily support public education, for example, or public housing. Yet how strongly do they even defend the publicness of parks?

In 1991 the *New York Times,* endorsing "The Public's Right to Put a Padlock On a Public Space,"[17] reported the triumph of a public space—Jackson Park, a tiny triangle in Greenwich Village that had previously fallen into disorder. Nearly a year later, a special "Quality of Urban Life" issue of *City Journal,* the voice of neoconservative urban policy intellectuals, corroborated the *Times's* positive judgment and further inflated the little plaza into a symbol of progress in the ongoing struggle to restore public space.[18] Located on a traffic island, Jackson Park is surrounded by upper-middle-class houses and apartments and by a substantial number of residents without apartments. Following a $1.2-million reconstruction of the park, a neighborhood group, Friends of Jackson Park—a group the *Times* consistently mistakes for both "the community" and "the public"—decided to lock the newly installed park gates at night. The City Parks Department, lacking sufficient personnel to close the park, welcomed "public" help in protecting public space, a defense they equated with evicting homeless people from city parks. "The people who hold the keys," announced the *Times,* "are determined to keep a park a park."[19]

A preordained public space, the *Times* tells us, is being defended by its natural owners—a statement that inverts the real sequence of events. For it is only by resorting to an argument outside argumentation—"a park is a park"—and so decreeing in advance which uses of public space are legitimate that such a space first becomes the property of an owner—"the people who hold the keys." Increasingly, conservative urbanists promote the transformation of public space into proprietary space—the occupation of public space—by conceding that public spaces are conflictual not harmonious terrains yet denying the legitimacy of spatial contests. *City Journal,* for instance, joining the *Times* in celebrating the "Jackson Park solution," notes that while urban analysts frequently ignore such problems, "what the homeless crisis has made unavoidable, is the clash of values created around contested spaces."[20] Whereupon, the *City Journal* avoids conflict by representing the decision to lock Jackson Park as the "reclamation" of "our" public space from "undesirables." The *Journal* portrays contests over city space as a war between two absolute, rather than political, forces: the Friends of Jackson Park, who are conflated with "the public" and who, backed by the local state, represent the proper uses that will restore the original harmony of public space and the park's enemies—homeless people who disrupt harmony.

In this scenario, recognition of conflict reassures observers that society might be free of division. The homeless person, represented as an intruder in public space, supports the housed resident's fantasy that the city, and social space in general, is essentially an organic whole. The person without a home is constructed as an ideological figure, a negative image created to restore positivity and order to social life. To appreciate this ideological operation, we might recall Theodor Adorno's postwar speculations about negative, that is anti-Semitic, images of Jews. Responding to the then prevalent idea that persisting German anti-Semitism could be defeated by acquainting Germans with "real" Jews—by, for instance, emphasizing the historical contribution of Jews or arranging meetings between Germans and Israelis—Adorno wrote: "This sort of activity depends too much upon the assumption that anti-Semitism essentially has something to do with Jews and could be combatted through an actual knowledge of Jews."[21] On the contrary, stated Adorno, anti-Semitism has nothing to do with Jews and everything to do with the psychic economy of the anti-Semite. Efforts to counteract anti-Semitism cannot, then, rely on the purportedly beneficial effects of education about "real" Jews. Such efforts must, rather, *"turn toward the subject,"* scrutinizing the fantasies of the anti-Semite and the image of the Jew that he or she desires.[22]

Elaborating on Adorno's suggestion, Slavoj Žižek brilliantly analyzes the construction of the "Jew" as an ideological figure for fascism, a process that, though not identical to, has important parallels with current constructions of "the homeless person" as an ideological figure.[23] Disorder, unrest, and conflict in the social system are all attributed to this figure—properties that cannot be eliminated from the social system since, as Laclau and Mouffe argue, social space is structured around an impossibility and is therefore irrevocably split by antagonisms. But when public space is represented as an organic unity that the homeless person is seen to disrupt from the outside, the homeless person becomes a positive embodiment of the element that prevents society from achieving closure. The element thwarting society's ability to cohere is transformed from a negativity within the social itself into a presence whose elimination would restore social order. In this sense, negative images of the homeless person are images of a positivity. The homeless person becomes, as Žižek writes about the "Jew," "*a point at which social negativity as such assumes positive existence.*" [24] The vision of the homeless person as the source of conflict in public space denies that there is an obstacle to coherence at the very core of social life. The homeless person embodies the fantasy of a unified urban space that can—must—be retrieved. [25]

To challenge the image of the homeless person as a disruption of the normal urban order, it is crucial to recognize that this "intrusive" figure points to the city's true character. Conflict is not something that befalls an originally, or potentially, harmonious urban space. Urban space is the product of conflict. This is so in several, incommensurable senses. In the first place, the lack of absolute social foundations—"the disappearance of the markers of certainty"—makes conflict an ineradicable feature of all social space. Second, the unitary image of urban space constructed in conservative urban discourse is itself produced through division, constituted through the creation of an exterior. The perception of a coherent space cannot be separated from a sense of what threatens that space, of what it would like to exclude. Finally, urban space is produced by specific socioeconomic conflicts that should not simply be accepted, either wholeheartedly or regretfully, as evidence of the inevitability of conflict but, rather, politicized—opened to contestation as social and therefore mutable relations of oppression. For, as I have argued elsewhere, the presence of homeless people in New York's public places today is the most acute symptom of the uneven social relations that determined the shape of the city throughout the 1980s, when it was redeveloped not, as promoters of redevelopment claimed, to fulfill the natural needs of a unitary society but to facilitate the restructuring of global capitalism.[26] As the specific form of advanced capitalist urbanism, redevelopment destroyed the conditions of survival for residents no longer needed in the city's new economy. The gentrification of parks played a key role in this process.[27] Homeless people and new public spaces, such as parks, are not, then, distinct entities, the first disrupting the peace of the second. The two are, rather, dual products of the spatioeconomic conflicts that constitute the contemporary production of urban space.

Yet, as I have also argued elsewhere, public art programs, serving as an arm of urban redevelopment, helped produce the opposite impression. Under several unifying banners—historical continuity, preservation of cultural tradition, civic beautification, utilitarianism—official public art collaborated with architecture and urban design to create an image of new urban sites that suppressed their conflictual character. In so doing, they also constructed the homeless person—a product of conflict—as an ideological figure—the bringer of conflict.[28]

In this pervasive atmosphere of conservative democracy, it might be seen as an encouraging sign that today's widespread enthusiasm for "public art" has been tempered from the beginning by uncertainty about the definition of the term. Artists and critics have repeatedly asked what it means to bring the word *public* into proximity with *art*. Writers alert to the problems that plague conventional concepts of publicness often begin their explorations of public art by questioning the identity, even the existence, of their object of study. In 1985 Jerry Allen, director of the Cultural Affairs Division of the City of Dallas, voiced this bewilderment: "Nearly 26 years after the passage of the first Percent for Art ordinance in Philadelphia, we still are unable to define exactly what public art is or ought to be."[29] Three years later, the critic Patricia Phillips concurred: "Though public art in the late 20th century has emerged as a full-blown discipline, it is a field without clear definitions."[30] Recent anxieties over the category "public art" could serve as a textbook example of the postmodern idea that objects of study are the effect, rather than the ground, of disciplinary knowledge.

Critics dedicated to public art's democratic potential but dissatisfied with its traditional classifications and uses have turned their uncertainty into a mandate to redefine the category. By 1988, writers like Kathy Halbreich of the National Endowment for the Arts had begun to insist that as an essential part of this redefinition "equal stress be placed on the words 'public' and 'art.'"[31] Soon the balance shifted even further, in favor of the first word. By now, attention to the term *public* is the touchstone of redefinitions of public art. Some writers have coined names, like Suzanne Lacy's "new genre public art," to designate the work of public artists who, as Lacy puts it, "adopt 'public' as their operative concept and quest."[32] Doubtless, these are steps in the direction of democratizing public art discourse. But critics often propose definitions of "public" that circumvent or eliminate what I, following Lefort, have called the question that gives rise to public space. Instead of describing public space so that it escapes appropriation altogether, those who challenge the conservative domination of public art discourse have largely reappropriated the term.

This tendency clearly dominates the principal forms of liberal public art discourse. For Allen, to give only one example, public art is a problem not because the meanings of art and public are uncertain or even subject to historical variation; on the contrary, problems arise because the meanings of the two terms are fixed in advance and inevitably clash:

> The very notion of a "public art" is something of a contradiction in terms. In it, we join two words whose meanings are, in some ways, antithetical. We recognize "art" [in the 20th century] as the individual inquiry of the sculptor or painter, the epitome of self-assertion. To that we join "public," a reference to the collective, the social order, self-negation. Hence, we link the private and the public, in a single concept or object, from which we expect both coherence and integrity.[33]

This formulation ignores the forceful challenge that certain key branches of twentieth-century art and criticism have directed against individualistic notions of the artist as an autonomous self and of art as an expression grounded in this strictly private being. Individuals or artists may not be so securely private as Allen thinks. The dismissal of this possibility leads critics to support a rigid opposition between "art" and "public" that rephrases standard liberal dichotomies between individual and society, private and public. The public/private opposition has also been mobilized to unite, rather than polarize, "art" and "public." Critics often treat both art and the public as universal spheres that, harmonized by a common human essence, stand above the conflictual realm of atomized individuals, purely private differences, and special interests. In these cases, "public art" is not, as Allen assumes, a contradictory entity, but instead comes doubly burdened as a figure of universal accessibility.

Although the two formulations—art opposed to public, art united with public—place art on different sides of the public/private divide, they stay within the same polarizing framework. The failure to question this framework has led many critics to open and close the question of the public in a single gesture. While they note that public art is difficult to define and stress the incoherence of the contemporary public, they still equate public space with consensus, coherence, and universality and relegate pluralism, division, and difference to the realm of the private. They tacitly view the plurality and strife that characterize the public as problematic facts that supporters of public space must find procedures to reduce and finally eliminate. Allen, for instance, who offers a solution typically adopted by many public art advocates, initially acknowledges that art's "public context" is broad and heterogeneous. Public art cannot hope to express values held by everyone. Still, its goal should be to serve unified, if multiple, publics that, says Allen, can be found if artists suppress their individual egos and consult the people "immediately affected by the project"—preexisting groups or communities who use specific urban sites, distinct constituencies each defined by some common identification.[34]

Homogeneity and unanimity—frequently cast in the shape of "community"—become the object of quests for true publicness as some critics, while usefully documenting controversies fought over specific public artworks and even espousing controversy as a natural ingredient of the public art process, continue to associate public space and democracy with the goals of building consensus, consolidating communities, and soothing conflicts. At the same time they place the definition of democratic public space fundamentally outside controversy.

This dynamic is illustrated by a 1992 anthology titled *Critical Issues in Public Art: Content, Context, and Controversy.* In the book's opening sentence, the editors tie public art to democracy: "Public art with its built-in social focus would seem to be an ideal genre for a democracy."[35] They continue: "Yet, since its inception, issues surrounding its appropriate form and placement, as well as its funding, have made public art an object of controversy more often than consensus or celebration."[36] The conjunction *yet*, which links these two sentences, performs important ideological work. It joins democracy—introduced in the first sentence—and controversy—introduced in the second—in an adverse relationship. Public art would be democratic *except* that it is controversial, or—in a more optimistic reading— public art retains its democratic potential *despite* the fact that it is controversial. "Yet" signals a reversal. Public art would seem to be democratic but instead turns out to be controversial. Controversy, moreover, serves as a foil for consensus, which consequently emerges as democracy's proper goal and is, further, associated with celebration. While the book's editors and many authors of the essays stress, or even valorize, disunity and antagonism, the word "yet" reveals an indecision at the heart of accounts of public art that interrogate the meaning of public space only to beg the question. "Yet" dissociates democracy from the fact of conflict and binds democracy to consensus-oriented, homogenizing notions of public space and public art. Conflict is simultaneously acknowledged and disavowed, a fetishistic process whose repressions generate certitudes about the meaning of public space. Later in *Critical Issues in Public Art,* for example, the editors simply repeat their universalizing assumptions: "The very concept of public art, defined in any meaningful way, presupposes a fairly homogeneous public and a language of art that speaks to all."[37]

Conservative and liberal aesthetic discourses are by no means alone in finding ways simultaneously to open and close the question of public space. Some of the most influential radical critiques of those discourses also try to dispel uncertainty. Many leftist cultural critics, for instance, search history to discover the origin and essence of democratic civic life. In the Athenian polis, the Roman republic, late-eighteenth-century France, and the commons of early American towns, critics locate the spatial forms that supposedly embody such a life. This quest has become especially common among left urban and architecture theorists who, driven by opposition to the newly homogenized, privatized, and state-regulated public spaces created by advanced capitalist urbanization, have formed influential alliances. Michael Sorkin, for example, introduces his interdisciplinary anthology of critical essays, *Variations on a Theme Park: The New American City and the End of Public Space,* with a plea for a return to "the familiar spaces of traditional cities, the streets and squares, courtyards and parks," that are "our great scenes of the civic."[38] Sorkin concludes that in the new "'public' spaces of the theme park or the shopping mall, speech itself is restricted: there are no demonstrations in Disneyland. The effort to reclaim the city is the struggle of democracy itself."[39]

When Sorkin treats public space as the site of political activity rather than as a universal domain that must be protected from politics, he significantly redirects mainstream discourse about public space. He is right to link public space to the exercise of free speech rights and to challenge the current proliferation of sanitized urban spaces that tolerate little resistance to the most circumscribed uses.[40] But when Sorkin idealizes traditional city space as a "more authentic urbanity,"[41] a space essential to democratic politics, he avoids the politics of *its* historical constitution as well as the possibility of its political transformation. Within this idealizing perspective, departures from established spatial arrangements inevitably signal the "end of public space." Edge cities, shopping malls, mass media, electronic space (even, for the right, "bizarrely shaped" voting districts) become tantamount to democracy's demise.

The cover of *Variations on a Theme Park* discloses certain problems with this approach. It depicts a group of Renaissance figures, the men and women normally seen in quattro- and cinquecento paintings disposed throughout the perspectival, orthogonally ordered, and visually unified outdoor squares of Italian cities. But on the book jacket these inhabitants of a stable public realm are spatially and temporally displaced. With patrician gestures and flowing drapery intact, they find themselves riding an escalator in a new "antiurban" structure—perhaps it is an

---

Detail of jacket of *Variations on a Theme Park: The New American City and the End of Public Space*, edited by Michael Sorkin (photo Kevin Noble).

"inward-looking atrium hotel" or multilevel shopping mall—a structure which, according to the book's thesis, signifies "the end of public space." Appropriated to visualize this thesis, providing the literal background of the book's subtitle, the illustration links Sorkin's trenchant critique of contemporary urbanism to a strong current of urban nostalgia that indeed pervades many of the essays in the book.

There are good reasons for radical urban critics to eschew this connection. Most obviously, the turn to the past brings them uncomfortably close to conserva-

284

tive urban discourse. Throughout the boom years of redevelopment, nostalgic images of the city were employed by real-estate developers, historic preservationists,
and city officials to advertise individual redevelopment projects as advances in an
ongoing struggle to restore an ideal city from the more or less remote past. In
New York, these projects were promoted as piecemeal contributions to the city's
own "renaissance," the rebirth of a lost urban tradition. Redevelopment projects,
it was claimed, would help restore New York to its place in a lineage of earlier
cities that, centered on expansive public spaces, were harmonious in their entirety.[42] The tradition continues. For Paul Goldberger, the newly renovated Bryant
Park in midtown Manhattan is an "out-of-town experience." His appraisal, like so
many contemporary accounts of the city, implies that homeless people control
access to public space: Bryant Park, he says, is a place the poor have begun to
"share." Now it "feels as if it has been . . . dropped into some idyllic landscape far,
far away."[43]

Public space, these comments suggest, is not only something we do not have.
Rather, it is what we once had—a lost state of plenitude. Since it is lost, however,
and not simply dead, we can recover it. "Whatever Became of the Public Square?"
asked *Harper's Magazine*'s lead article in 1990 as a prelude to a search for new urban
designs that will restore the public square—what *Harper's* calls "that great good
place."[44] What is pictured on the cover of *Variations on a Theme Park* if not a loss?
We see, in absentia, a zone of safety, a great good place from which we have been
banished—at least those of us who identify with Renaissance city dwellers as exiled
inhabitants of a democratic public space.

This qualification should give us pause. Pursuing specificity, it raises two sets
of questions that can help sharpen currently hazy images of public space. The first
inquires into the concrete identity of the sketchy people who exemplify supposedly
true publicness on the cover of Sorkin's book. Which social groups were actually
included, and which excluded, in the purportedly fully inclusive, or at least more
inclusive, urban public spaces of the near or distant past? Who counted as a citizen
in the "great scenes of the civic" figured as missing? "*For whom,*" as cultural critic
Bruce Robbins asks, "was the city once more public than now? Was it ever open
to the scrutiny and participation, let alone under the control, of the majority?

. . . If so, where were the workers, the women, the lesbians, the gay men, the African Americans?"[45]

Raising the issue of who identifies with the displaced residents of a classical urban square not only urges us to consider the attributes of the figures in an image of public space; it also turns our attention to the viewers of the image. It broaches a second question, one largely neglected, sometimes actively repudiated, in aesthetic discussions about public space: the question of subjectivity in representation. How do images of public space create the public identities they seem merely to depict? How do they constitute the viewer into these identities? How, that is, do they invite viewers to take up a position that then defines them as public beings? How do these images create a "we," a public, and who do we imagine ourselves to be when we occupy the prescribed site? If, as I have claimed, the cover of *Variations on a Theme Park* depicts a Renaissance square as the archetype of public space, then whose identity, in the present, is produced and reinforced by an image of public space tied to the traditional spaces of perspectival representation? What is publicness, if it is equated with the fixed, all-seeing viewpoint that is the real subject of these Renaissance spaces? Who must be displaced to guarantee the authority of the single reference point? Is the possessor of this viewpoint really a public being—the individual who can remain safely behind the rectangular frame of its "window on the world," who can, like the figures in the image, walk into public space and just as easily walk out? Or is it possible that the displacement of this secure subject is not, as Sorkin's cover suggests, "the end of public space" but precisely the effect of being *in* public space, the realm of our "being-in-common" where, it is often said, we encounter others and are presented with our existence outside ourselves?

The same questions apply to another discourse about public space, closely related to *Variations on a Theme Park,* that has recently been embraced by left art critics. Like architecture and urban scholars, sometimes joining forces with them, critical sectors of the art world have tried to rescue the term *public* from conservative depoliticizations by defining public space as an arena of political activity and redefining public art as art that participates in or creates a space of politics. For this purpose, critics have found a valuable resource in the category of the "public sphere." This term is used loosely to designate a realm of discursive interaction about political issues. In the public sphere, people assume political identities.

The term inevitably conjures Jürgen Habermas, whose book *The Structural Transformation of the Public Sphere: An Inquiry into a Category of Bourgeois Society* provides the archetypal account of the public sphere as a lost democratic ideal.[46] Written in 1962, Habermas's study first appeared in English in 1989, but its basic tenets were already familiar to many English-speaking readers, partly through a 1974 translation of his brief encyclopedia article on the public sphere.[47] Habermas describes the public sphere as a specific historical formation first elaborated as an idea in Kant's definition of "enlightenment"—the use of reason for public criticism.[48] The public sphere, according to Habermas, arose with the advent of bourgeois society, which inaugurated a strict division between the private and the political realms. In the safety of the private sphere, the bourgeoisie could pursue financial gain unimpeded by society or the state. But bourgeois society, says Habermas, also gave rise to a set of institutions—the public sphere—through which the bourgeoisie could exercise control over the actions of the state while renouncing the claim to rule. In the public sphere—a realm between society and the state—a sphere in principle open and accessible to all, the state was held accountable to citizens. There people emerged from privacy and, casting aside private interests to commit themselves to matters of common concern, constituted themselves into a public by engaging in rational-critical political discussion. But in Habermas's view the public sphere declined with the entry of nonbourgeois groups, the growth of mass media, and the rise of the welfare state. These phenomena eroded the secure border between public and private life that for Habermas is the origin and remains the condition of the public sphere's existence.

One may question the homogenizing tendency glimpsed even in this brief description of Habermas's ideal of a singular, unified public sphere that transcends concrete particularities and reaches a rational—noncoercive—consensus. For now, however, let us emphasize that there are other conceptions of the public sphere less hostile to differences or conflict, less eager to turn their backs on critiques of modernity, and more skeptical about the innocence of either reason or language and note the strong impact that any conception of a public sphere exerts on conventional assumptions about public art. For the interpretation of public art as art operating in or as a public sphere—whether it follows or rejects the Habermasian model—means that an art public, by contrast with an art audience, is not a preexisting entity but rather emerges through, is produced by, its participation in political activity.

The introduction of the concept of the public sphere into art criticism shatters mainstream categorizations of public art. It also helps circumvent confusions plaguing some critical discussions. Transgressing the boundaries that conventionally divide public from nonpublic art—divisions drawn, for example, between indoor and outdoor art, between artworks shown in conventional institutions and those displayed in "the city," between state-sponsored and privately funded art—the public sphere excavates other distinctions that, neutralized by prevailing definitions of public space, are crucial to democratic practice. By differentiating public space from the realm of the state, for instance, the concept of the public sphere counteracts public art discourse that defines the public as state administration and confines democracy to a form of government. The public sphere idea locates democracy in society to which state authority is accountable. With public space linked to political decision making and to rights and social legitimacy, arts administrators can less easily ignore the displacement of social groups from urban public spaces while continuing to describe these sites as "accessible." In addition, and perhaps preeminently, the public sphere replaces definitions of public art as work that occupies or designs physical spaces and addresses preexisting audiences with a conception of public art as a practice that constitutes a public, by engaging people in political discussion or by entering a political struggle. Since any site has the potential to be transformed into a public or, for that matter, a private space, public art can be viewed as an instrument that either helps produce a public space or questions a dominated space that has been officially ordained as public. The function of public art becomes, as Vito Acconci put it, "to make or break a public space."[49]

But one effect of introducing the idea of the public sphere into debates about public art overwhelms all others in the strength of its challenge to neutralizing definitions: when critics redefine public art as work operating in or as a public sphere, the by now unanimous admonition to make art public becomes virtually synonymous with a demand for art's politicization. Art that is "public" participates in, or creates, a political space and is itself a space where we assume political identities.

Yet, offered as a response to the question of public space, the idea of the public sphere does not by itself fulfill the mandate to safeguard democracy as a question. In fact, the assertion that public space is the site of democratic political activity can repeat the very evasion of politics that such an assertion seeks to challenge. For, like the urban critic's defense of traditional city space as a terrain in which political discourse takes place, this assertion does not require us to recognize, indeed it can prevent us from recognizing, that the political public sphere is not only a site of discourse; it is also a discursively constructed site. From the standpoint of radical democracy, politics cannot be reduced to something that happens inside the limits of a public space or political community that is simply accepted as "real." Politics, as Chantal Mouffe writes, is about the constitution of the political community.[50] It is about the spatializing operations that produce a space of politics. If democracy means that the political community—the public, "we, the people"—has no absolute basis, then laying down the foundations that mark off a political public space, deciding what is legitimate and illegitimate there, is an ineluctably political process. Distinctions and similarities are drawn, exclusions enacted, decisions made. However much the democratic public sphere promises openness and accessibility, it can never be a fully inclusive or fully constituted political community. It is, from the start, a strategy of distinction, dependent on constitutive exclusions, the attempt to place something outside.[51] Conflict, division, and instability, then, do not ruin the democratic public sphere; they are the conditions of its existence. The threat arises with efforts to supersede conflict, for the public sphere remains democratic only insofar as its exclusions are taken into account and open to contestation. When the exclusions governing the constitution of political public space are naturalized and contests erased by declaring particular forms of space inherently, eternally, or self-evidently public, public space is appropriated. Although it is equated with political space, public space is given a prepolitical source of political meaning and becomes a weapon against, rather than a means of, political struggle.

To undo this appropriation, the question of public space might be approached in a more genealogical spirit than has hitherto animated left aesthetic or urban discussions. We will not capture the truth of public space by recovering its origins. According to Friedrich Nietzsche, who conceived the term *genealogy* in opposition to nineteenth-century conceptions of history, the recovery of origins does not reveal the essential, unchanging meaning of a concept; it shows, on the contrary, that meanings are conditional, formed out of struggles. Precisely because the "essence" of publicness is a historically constituted figure that grows and changes, the public is a rhetorical instrument open to diverse, even antagonistic, uses that vary with widely differing contexts. The origin and purpose of an object of knowledge, Nietzsche warns, are two separate problems that are frequently confused: "The cause of the origin of a thing and its eventual utility, its actual employment and place in a system of purposes, lie worlds apart; whatever exists, having somehow come into being, is again and again reinterpreted to new ends, taken over, transformed, and redirected by some power superior to it."[52] Concealing a particular "system of purposes" by appealing to essential truths contained in the origins of the public is a ruse of authoritarian power that, glossing over the disjunction between a term's beginnings and its subsequent uses, renders "the public" invulnerable to transformation. In short, stories about the beginning of public space are not really about the past; they tell us about the concerns and anxieties inhabiting our present social arrangements. From a genealogical perspective, the question of what it means for art to be public may still be worth asking, but it calls for another question: What political functions does the exhortation to make art public—that is, political—currently fulfill?

PUBLIC VISIONS

Questions about the constitution, transformation, and uses of the public are, of course, not new in public art discourse, but directing them at critical redefinitions of public art is. Since the 1980s, art critics on the left have tried to reframe aesthetic debates about public space by abandoning normative evaluations of the word *public* in favor of functional analyses that examine its uses in particular historical circumstances. In 1987, for example, Craig Owens noted "how malleable the concept of the public can be" and concluded that "the question of who is to define, manipulate and profit from 'the public' is . . . the central issue of any discussion of the public function of art today."[53] Owens examined the way in which rhetoric about "the public good" and "the protection of culture for the public" has historically provided an alibi for modern imperialism. Using Nelson Rockefeller's cultural and economic investments in Latin America as an example, Owens argued that individuals who represent the economic interests most deeply implicated in *destroying* other cultures in order to bring them into the sphere of capitalist social relations have also collected the artifacts of those cultures in the name of *preserving* culture for the public.

In the 1980s I criticized a similar rhetoric of the public good that provided an alibi for urban redevelopment.[54] Owens's and my arguments were part of a far broader effort in critical sectors of the art world to redefine the public so that the concept might be marshalled against two developments in art: first, massive economic privatization—the art-market explosion, attacks on public funding, growing corporate influence on exhibition policies—and second, the growth of a new public art industry serving as the aesthetic arm of oppressive urban policies. Owens and I each invoked the concept of art as a political public sphere to counteract the inversion we identified as the hallmark of conservative discourse about the public—forces that profit from the destruction of public spaces and cultures pose as their protectors.[55] "If culture is to be protected," Owens asked, "is it not precisely from those whose business it is to protect culture?"[56]

Today, however, critical voices in the art world cannot afford to formulate ideas about "real" public art solely by exposing the relations of domination concealed by liberal or conservative notions—any more than leftists have been able to confine their critique of democracy to uncovering the mystifications of bourgeois democracy while ignoring the authoritarian potential of some of their own ideas about "real" democracy. To do so is to claim that public space can simply be liberated from conservatives and liberals who have hijacked it from its rightful owners. The history of radical social thought cautions against making this claim—itself an appropriation of the public. Leftists do not simply represent the true meaning of public space. They, too, define and have, moreover, "manipulated and profited from 'the public.'" In critical social theory, as Nancy Fraser writes, "private" and "public" have long been powerful terms "frequently deployed to delegitimate some interests, views, and topics and to valorize others . . . to restrict the universe of legitimate public contestation."[57] Left art criticism needs to take a closer look at what—and at whom—its use of the term *public* forces into privacy. Setting critical conceptions of "art in/as a public sphere" against celebratory conceptions of "art in public places" or "the new public art" is by now a commonplace that hardly exhausts all contests over what it means to bring the word *public* into proximity with *art*.

Without in any way relinquishing this earlier critique, but in the interest of extending the scope of a genealogical inquiry into the meaning of the public in art, I would like to stage a different yet, to my mind, no less urgent confrontation: not the customary meeting between celebratory and critical conceptions of public space but an encounter between two critical events that took place in the New York art world during the 1980s. The adjective *public* figures prominently in both events but describes divergent concepts of space. The first is an exhibition entitled "Public Vision" held in 1982; the second, a talk delivered in 1987 by the art historian Thomas Crow at a panel on "The Cultural Public Sphere." Through this juxtaposition, I hope to bring to light certain suppressed terms of the current debate about art's publicness. The work exhibited in "Public Vision" represents a type of art that many consider irrelevant, even inimical, to the project of making art public. This judgment is implicit in the concept of an artistic public sphere that Crow espouses as the fulfillment of art's public functions. I will argue that the reverse is closer to the truth. As the exhibition's title suggests, art like that shown in "Public Vision" has long been part of the project of extending, not endangering, public space. The questions that this art raises are vital to democracy, and definitions of a political public sphere that reject these questions reveal a hostility toward a richly agonistic public life.

"Public Vision," organized by Gretchen Bender, Nancy Dwyer, and Cindy Sherman, was presented at White Columns, a small alternative space then on the edge of Soho in Lower Manhattan.[58] The exhibition brought together a group of

Public Vision, poster, designed by Jo Bonney, 1982 (photo Kevin Noble).

women artists whose work is associated with what would soon become known as the feminist critique of visual representation. The show was small, brief, and undocumented. In retrospect, however, it has the quality of a manifesto. Mounted at the height of an internationally proclaimed, male-dominated neoexpressionist revival of traditional aesthetic values, it announced the arrival of a new feminist politics of the image destined to unsettle established aesthetic paradigms. "Public Vision" also promised that art informed by feminist theories of representation would change the course of what was then the most radical critique of traditional paradigms: the discourse about postmodernism. In the early 1980s theories of postmodernism in art remained indifferent to sexuality and gender.[59] "Public Vision" was a feminist intervention in both mainstream and radical aesthetic discourses—a little-known forerunner of "The Revolutionary Power of Women's Laughter" (1983),[60] the highly influential "Difference: On Representation and Sexuality" (1985),[61] both originating in New York, and a host of later exhibitions that combined postmodern challenges to the universalizing premises of modernism and postmodern declarations of "the birth of the viewer" with feminist critiques of phallic visual regimes. "Public Vision" was less programmatic than subsequent exhibitions on these themes but, composed only of women artists, signaled a feminist agenda, even if the type of feminism informing the show was ultimately not gender-exclusive. Placing the work of artists who had already figured prominently in discussions of postmodernism—Barbara Kruger, Louise Lawler, Sherrie Levine, Cindy Sherman, Laurie Simmons—in a manifestly feminist context, the show promoted a rereading of this work.

"Public Vision" challenged the official modernist doctrine that vision is a superior means of access to authentic and universal truths because it is supposedly detached from its objects. The idea of visual detachment and related concepts of disinterested judgment and impartial contemplation depend on the belief that an order of meaning exists in itself, in things themselves, as presence. Within the modernist scenario of disinterested aesthetic vision, a self-sufficient viewer contemplates an equally autonomous art object that possesses meanings independent of the particular circumstances of its production or reception. Clement Greenberg's influential writings about modernism had defined modernist painting as the very figure of such a fully constituted truth—a self-contained totality—and treated visual experience as a pure, irreducible category isolated from other orders of experience. Vision was given the property of an essence.[62] The prestige enjoyed by traditional art rested on this doctrine of visual purity. Museums and galleries, it was held, simply discover and preserve timeless, transcendent values present in art objects.

In the late 1960s and 1970s certain artists launched a critique of art institutions that challenged the claim of aesthetic transcendence. Artists like Hans Haacke, Martha Rosler, Adrian Piper, Daniel Buren, and Marcel Broodthaers demonstrated that the meaning of a work of art does not reside permanently within the work itself but is formed only in relation to an outside—to the manner of the work's presentation—and therefore changes with circumstances. Indeed, the very designation of an object as a work of art depends on the work's framing conditions—including the physical apparatus that supports it, prevailing discourses about art, and the presence of viewers. The significance of an artwork is not simply given or discovered, it is produced. Artists engaged in what became known as "institutional critique" investigated this process of production by making the context of art's exhibition the subject matter of their work, thereby demonstrating the inseparability of the artwork from its conditions of existence. They transformed the exhibition spaces and museological apparatus through which illusions of aesthetic detachment are constructed. Sometimes they drew attention to the specific social and economic interests that "detachment" has historically served.

At the same time, feminist artists and critics were undermining claims of aesthetic neutrality by calling attention to the asymmetrical positions occupied by men and women in the history of art. As an important part of this project, feminists criticized the stereotypical, idealized, or degraded depictions of women—the so-called negative images—that abound in works of art. They held "transcendent" art and "universal" aesthetic vision accountable for the reproduction of what were in fact oppressive, social gender norms.

The work in "Public Vision" drew on the strategies of early critiques of institutions and early feminist critiques of aesthetic images but revised these strategies by challenging their presuppositions about the viewer. Institutional critiques often stressed the activity of the viewer but sometimes treated this as the accomplishment of a determinate task. Hans Haacke's work, for instance, invited viewers to decipher relations and find content already inscribed in images but did not ask them to examine their own role and investments in producing images. Likewise, feminist analysis of images of women in terms of positive or negative content presumed that images contain stable meanings simply perceived by preconstituted viewers. Some images are false and deficient; others, true and adequate. This analysis thus lapses into a positivist fiction. By contrast, artists in "Public Vision" went beyond the positive-negative approach to produce what might be called "critical images." They unsettled the modernist model of visual neutrality at its core by proposing that meaning arises only in an interactive space between viewer and image—but not between preexisting viewers or images. Rather, these artists explored the role played by vision in constituting the human subject and, moreover, in the continuous reproduction of this subject by social forms of visuality. They did not confine their analysis of the politics of the image to what appears inside the borders of a picture, within the visual field. Instead, they turned their attention to what is invisible there—the operations that generate the seemingly natural spaces of the image and the viewer. In so doing, these artists treated the image itself as a social relationship and the viewer as a subject constructed by the very object from which it formerly claimed detachment. Visual detachment and its corollary, the autonomous art object, emerged as a constructed, rather than given, relationship of externality, a relationship that produces—is not produced by—its terms: discrete objects, on the one hand, and complete subjects, on the other. These subjects are no harmless fictions. They are, rather, relationships of power— masculinist fantasies of completion achieved by repressing different subjectivities, transforming difference into otherness, or subordinating actual others to the authority of a universal viewpoint presupposed to be, like the traditional art viewer, uninflected by sex, race, an unconscious, or history.

The works in "Public Vision" intervened in the subject constructed by modernist painting, disrupting and reconfiguring the traditional space of aesthetic vision. In diverse ways—I will give three examples—these works advanced toward viewers, disengaging them from habitual modes of aesthetic reception, turning their attention away from the image and back on themselves—or, more precisely, on their relationship with the image.

In one respect, Sherrie Levine's contribution, *After Egon Schiele* (1982), provided the exhibition's keynote. Levine displayed framed photographs of the sexually graphic drawings executed in the early twentieth century by Viennese expressionist Egon Schiele. Levine's display, like "Public Vision" as a whole, was a site-specific intervention in the early 1980s art world. She commented directly on the expressionist ethos then being celebrated in a widespread neoexpressionist revival of traditional artistic media—oil painting, drawing, bronze sculpture. In the expressionist model, a sovereign individual struggles heroically against the constraints imposed by a society that is strictly external and inevitably alienating. The artist registers his presence—embodied in painterly brushstrokes, traces of the touch of the hand—in unique works of art that are subjective protests against, and victories over, social alienation. The artwork is conceived of as an expression grounded in a preexisting, autonomous self—the artist and, by extension, the viewer who identifies with the expression.

Levine's reframing of Schiele's drawings ironically reenacted neoexpressionism's own reenactment of original German expressionism, exposing both expressionisms to scrutiny. Recontextualizing Schiele's drawings and presenting them as socially coded, reproducible forms of visual culture rather than unmediated, painterly expressions, Levine generated a moment of unrecognizability for the viewer. In this moment, the viewer's identification with the image—solicited by images whose meanings appear to be simply natural—was arrested. Viewer and image were displaced. Rather than an autonomous identity expressed in artworks, the expressionist self appeared as a construction produced through visual representation. Levine's re-presentation of Schiele pointed to an ambivalence in this construction, an ambivalence that further unsettles the idea that the subject is self-contained. The expressionist artist seeks to "express" himself, in the sense of recording emotional and sexual impulses, in images presented as evidence of an authentic, interior identity that cannot be alienated. At the same time, the expressionist artist tries to "express," in the sense of emptying himself of, dissonant impulses, which he controls precisely by alienating or projecting them onto an exteriorized image or other.

Cindy Sherman's contribution to "Public Vision" was an image from her

Sherrie Levine, *After Egon Schiele: 2,* 1982 (photo
courtesy Marian Goodman Gallery).

then ongoing project of photographing herself as a model acting out a range of
female character types drawn from mass-media images—movies, magazines, and
television (see pages 234–235). Sherman explored these characters not as reproductions of real identities but as effects produced by such visual signifiers as framing, lighting, distance, focus, and camera angle. In this way she drew attention to
the material process of identity formation that takes place in culturally coded but
seemingly natural images of women. Sherman's photographs both elicit and frustrate the viewer's search for an inner, hidden truth of a character to which the

viewer might penetrate, an essential identity around which the meaning of the image might reach closure. Rosalind Krauss reminds us that this search for truth is the hallmark of the hermeneutic idea of art, an idea with, moreover, a gendered subtext: "The female body itself has been made to serve as a metaphor for hermeneutics . . . all those meanings to which analysis reaches as it seeks the meaning behind the surface flood of incident, all of them, are culturally coded as feminine."[63]

Sherman's photographs thwart this interpretive grasp by replacing the seeming transparency of the image with the opacity of cinematic and photographic signifiers. Interiority emerges, then, not as a property of the female character but as a social effect that marks the surface of the female body. And, as Judith Williamson writes, while each of Sherman's photographs calls forth the expectation that it will disclose a coherent, inner identity, none can actually be the "real" Sherman precisely because they all promise to be.[64] The viewer's attention is thus focused on the search itself, on the desire for interior depth, coherence, and presence in the picture, for an object that might ensure the viewer's own coherent identity. This desire for wholeness drives the unfulfillable search to find a unifying meaning in or behind the image, a search linked, moreover, to the establishment of the difference between the sexes. The masculine viewer can construct himself as whole only by finding a fixed femininity, a truth of the feminine that precedes representation. In this sense, the image of "woman" is an instrument for producing and maintaining a fantasy of masculine identity.

In Barbara Kruger's contribution to "Public Vision," *Untitled (You delight in the loss of others),* a written text superimposed on a radically cropped photograph of a woman's outstretched hand dropping a glass of milk, is the vehicle for interrupting the rhetoric of the image—the strategies whereby the image imposes its messages on viewers. Bluntly addressing the viewer, the words "You delight in the loss of others" invoke the sadistic pleasures of voyeuristic looking, the pole of vision directly linked to the ideal of visual detachment: the voyeuristic look frames objects as images, sets them at a distance, encloses them in a separate space, and places the viewer in a position of control. Simultaneously, however, Kruger's text speaks as a feminist voice that undercuts the security of this arrangement. Her

Barbara Kruger, *Untitled (You delight in the loss of others)*, 1981–83 (photo courtesy Barbara Kruger).

image "sees" the viewer, collapsing the distance between the two. Kruger's acknowledgment of the viewer's presence asserts that receivership is an essential component of the image and erodes the invisibility that protects the purportedly neutral viewing subject from interrogation. It does so, however, not to finger an actual viewer but to call the spectator's identity into question. The personal pronoun *you* does not indicate a real person; it has no stable or absolute referent.[65] "You" denotes a position in a relationship with "others," a viewer constituted by its images. Kruger's photomontage also suggests that the spaces assigned to viewer and image in voyeuristic structures are bound up with hierarchical structures of sexual difference—not just because women have historically occupied the space of the visual object and are literally looked at but because the voyeuristic look renders whatever it looks at "feminine"—if, as Mark Wigley writes, the feminine is understood as that which disrupts the security of the boundaries separating spaces and must therefore be controlled by masculine force. Masculinity in this sense "is no more than the ability to maintain rigid limits or, more precisely, the effect of such limits."[66] It has been argued that the iconographic figure of woman in images of women is less a reproduction of real women than a cultural sign producing femininity as the object of such masculine containment, as what Laura Mulvey famously calls "to-be-looked-at-ness."[67]

Kruger's "you" is counterposed to a photograph whose status as a feminized object is underscored by the fact that it depicts a woman: a woman's hand and, moreover, a part-object or symbolic equivalent of the maternal woman—the spiller of milk. "You" thus acquires a gender. It designates a masculine viewer who delights in an idealized self-image—whole, universal, without loss. Far from an essential identity, however, this masculine "you" is a site of representation, a subject, who emerges through two procedures, each designed to disavow incompleteness and each, therefore, pertaining to loss. This "you" renders different subjectivities absent—it overlooks them, loses them, and, of course, they lose. But it does so precisely by keeping the woman in sight, framing her as an image distanced from, but existing for, itself. This "you" tries to ensure its own coherence by setting itself in opposition to the feminine, transforming difference into a subordinated otherness, into a sign of incompleteness, into loss itself. The quintessential example of both procedures—and of their connection to vision—is the fetishistic disavowal of sexual difference inherent in the "perception" that woman, in contrast to man, is "castrated." The fact that woman does not have the phallus can only be translated into the perception that she has "lost" the phallus if, as Slavoj Žižek reminds us, it is presupposed that she should have it—if, that is, it is believed that there is a state of wholeness, signified by the possession of the phallus, from which it is possible to fall. The transformation of difference into castration disavows the fact that this lost state does not exist.[68] Rather, as Kruger's work suggests, the complete, self-possessed identity is from the start a contingent relationship, a "you" produced by inflicting loss on others.

But Kruger's work does not cry over spilt milk. The drive to control by looking cannot be abolished, but the visual image can resist taking shape as an object in whose presence the controlling look can develop. "You" can be undone as the image's hierarchies are weakened and its violences exposed. Indeed, Kruger's text and manipulations of the image imbue the photograph with an atmosphere of violence. It takes on the appearance of a cinematic close-up and acquires narrative implications. What has caused the woman's hand suddenly to open and the glass to fall? In movies, such partial images may tell the audience that a climactic and brutal event is occurring. Read in this way, as a film still, the photograph in Kruger's work suggests that an attack is being perpetrated against a woman; she is being stilled. The center of the action is displaced; it remains outside the frame. So does the assailant. At this point in the story, his identity may still be unknown to the moviegoer. Interpreted as the scene of an assault, the iconography of Kruger's photograph gives literal form to the artist's principal subject matter: the scene of vision. The offscreen aggressor is analogous to the masculine viewer who "delights in the loss of others." The victim corresponds to the woman immobilized in the image or, more broadly, to the feminine domesticated as an image. Visualization merges with victimization of its object. The viewer, like his cinematic counterpart, stays outside the borders of the image—at least until Kruger investigates his identity and, in so doing, unravels it. For this "you," Kruger's text reveals, is no independent and complete self. It cannot stand alone. Neither is the image a self-contained object. The autonomous subject is produced only by positioning others as objects of the look. Kruger's work finally suggests that the claim of visual detachment is not only an illusion but, as Kate Linker writes, a tool of aggression.[69]

Works such as those by Levine, Sherman, and Kruger opened up the modernist space of pure vision. Built into the architecture of modernist looking is an injunction to recognize images and viewers as given, rather than produced, spaces and therefore as interiors closed in on themselves. But art informed by feminist ideas about representation disrupts this closure by staging vision as a process that mutually constitutes image and viewer. Pure interiority, these works reveal, is an effect of the subject's disavowed dependence on the visual field. By exposing the repressed relationships through which vision produces the sense of autonomy—

by, in other words, exploring the viewer's noncontinuity with itself—this work also disturbs the sense that otherness is purely external. The opening of modernist vision creates a space where the boundaries between self and other, inside and outside, are challenged.

What is the point of calling this troubled space "public?" The phrase *public vision* has several connotations. It suggests that vision is shaped by social and historical structures; that the meaning of visual images is culturally, not individually, produced; and that images signify in social frameworks. In these respects, the term *public* implies that viewers and images are socially constructed, that meaning is public, not private. Used in the title of an exhibition that explored vision as an uncertain process in which viewers and images are not only constructed by a fixed social realm external to vision but also construct each other, the adjective *public* has more complex implications. It describes a space in which the meanings of images and the identities of subjects are radically open, contingent, and incomplete. "Public Vision" associated public space with a set of relations that exceed the individual level but are not strictly outside the individual. Publicness emerges as a quality that constitutes, inhabits, and also breaches the interior of social subjects. It is a condition of exposure to an outside that is also an instability within, a condition, as Thomas Keenan says, "of vulnerability."[70] "Public Vision" implied that the masculinist viewer's claim of disinterest and impartiality is a shield erected against this vulnerability, a denial of the subject's immersion in the openness of public space.

Yet it is just this impartial subject who, five years later, the art historian Thomas Crow described as the authentic occupant of public space and, moreover, as the possessor of a truly "public vision." Crow made these assertions as a participant on a panel about "The Cultural Public Sphere," one of two sessions devoted to this topic in a series of weekly discussions on critical issues in contemporary art organized by Hal Foster at the Dia Art Foundation. In the preface to the book that documents the Dia symposium, *Discussions in Contemporary Culture,* Foster explains that one such issue is "the definition of public and audience, historical and present."[71] Indeed, the Dia panels remain one of the most serious efforts to date to redefine public art in terms of its involvement in a political public sphere. As the first speaker at the opening session, Crow inaugurated the effort. Both his original talk and a revised version published in *Discussions in Contemporary Culture* begin by voicing the popular sentiment that the public sphere, in this case the public sphere of art, is lost.[72] Recently, however, in the years around 1968, it had been found. At that time, a group of "dematerializing" art practices sprang up, all involved in the singular project of criticizing the autonomy of the modernist art object. These practices—conceptualism, site-specificity, performance, installation art—promised, Crow says, to produce "a new art public which would be a microcosm, either actual or anticipatory, of a larger public."[73] They "are the ones we recall when we lament the loss of a public dimension and commitment for art. . . . As we look back, these practices feel as if they constituted a unity, a resurgent public sphere that seems diminished and marginal now."[74] Crow notes that "women's politics" found space "within" these practices (1). Later, he makes another feminist point, even questioning the rhetoric of loss pervading his own discussion: "One absence being registered in the sense of loss is the bygone unity provided by modernism, that is, by white-male-dominated elitist art and criticism" (2).

In his talk, however, Crow pursued a somewhat different line of argument. There, he suggested that the growth of women's politics and other new social movements was not part of the artistic public sphere but was responsible for its loss. The new movements, he said, had "balkanized" the art audience into separate groups, which, he thus implied, shattered the post-1968, coherent art public into ineffectual, frequently conflicting units. This does not mean that in Crow's view the public sphere was lost because the so-called balkanization created a disparity between actual art audiences and the ideal of a unified art public. For Crow, this disparity always exists. It is what defines the public as an ideal: "'The public' represented a standard against which the various inadequacies of art's actual consumers could be measured and criticized" (2). The public sphere was lost because new social movements no longer felt beholden to the unifying ideal. When they abandoned the attempt to approximate the ideal, Crow assumes, they simultaneously abandoned the attempt to create an artistic public sphere.

Crow's published essay deletes his earlier reference to the destructive effect of women's groups on the artistic public sphere, no doubt because he took seriously the objections raised during the discussion period by people such as Martha Rosler: "I'm shocked by your suggestion that it was somehow groups like women who dragged the discourse away from the pursuit of some imaginary high public."[75] Crow took less seriously criticisms of the pursuit itself. If he no longer blames women for the decline of an art public and now even includes them as part of the resurgent artistic public sphere of the late 1960s, he does not alter, or even question, his model of the political public sphere or his conviction that it has vanished. He thus leaves the feminist challenge unanswered. For it is precisely this model that recent feminist analyses have questioned as a masculinist structure built on the conquest of differences.

Crow constructs a politicized history of modern and contemporary art based on the civic humanist ideals of modern political theory. A key element of this theory is a conception of the public sphere—a democratic realm where individuals take on identities as citizens and participate in political life. By treating the art public as a microcosm of this larger public, Crow tries to integrate modern aesthetics into a theory and practice of the public sphere that stands at the beginning of the democratization of political institutions. The art viewer, in Crow's account, becomes part of an art public in the same way that private individuals become citizens. When the individual emerges as a member of the public, or, by extension, when a viewer of art joins an art public, he relinquishes his particularity and special interests in favor of the universal interest. He becomes, to use Crow's term, "adequate," in the sense of impartial.

Crow takes these ideas from Enlightenment writers on art. In the eighteenth century, English and French aestheticians envisioned an art public based on a new model of citizenship. They wanted to establish a "republic of taste," a democratic citizenry of art that replicated the structure of a political republic composed of free and active citizens. The security of both republics, it was believed, was founded on solid, universal principles. Both represented the common good and were therefore deemed capable, as Crow suggests, of counteracting the division of labor, self-interest, occupational specialization, and individualism that divided large, modern commercial nations. Indeed, Enlightenment writers turned to civic humanism because they, too, felt that public space was lost and in need of restoration.[76] For enlightened men like Joshua Reynolds, the analogy between the republic of taste and the civic public of citizenship had concrete, historical origins in earlier democratic civic formations. The republics of ancient Greece and Rome and Renaissance Italy provided these thinkers with a fertile source of examples of a once unified public sphere. For Enlightenment aestheticians, writes Crow, "The public of the Greek *polis* . . . had been ultimately responsible for the exemplary artistic achievements of antiquity. Similarly, the successful revival of the antique during the Renaissance was traced to the encouragement and scrutiny of the circumscribed citizenry of the Italian city-state" (2).

Prior to its current loss, Crow argues, the ancient civic humanist project of constructing an ideal public for art was rediscovered at three key periods of modern art history. Their differences notwithstanding, each period kept alive the ideal of a unifying—hence, public—aesthetic. Civic humanist aesthetics was first revived, as we have seen, in Enlightenment art discourse. Enlightenment theorists proposed that concentration on the unity of a pictorial composition elevated the art viewer above the private, material interests that, Crow says, were enshrined by the growth of capitalism. Then, in the late nineteenth and early twentieth centuries, "civic humanist aesthetics" reappeared as a kind of unconscious subtext of modernist abstraction. Modernism, says Crow, citing Clement Greenberg, also sought to create an abstract pictorial unity in the contemplation of which the viewer's "private, contentious self would be set aside" (7). True, Crow concedes, the political origins of the search for a unified art public were repressed in modernism. Still, by aspiring to create transcendent aesthetic form, modernist artists also tried, as Greenberg famously claims, to oppose the rise of commercial culture and so registered their antipathy to capitalism. Finally, civic humanism resurfaced in a newly politicized form in the "dematerializing practices" of the late 1960s. These practices, says Crow, once again sought to unify viewers, only this time in opposition to the modernist fetishization of the art object, a process originating in commodity fetishism and invading all aspects of life in capitalist society.

Crow unites these three periods as moments in the history of the formation of an artistic public sphere.[77] He suggests further that at each moment conceptions of the art public and the political public fused around a common idea of vision. The aesthetic vision supposedly cultivated at all three moments is akin to the political vision possessed by the ideal citizen of the civic public. Crow projects onto nineteenth- and twentieth-century art a similarity between aesthetic contemplation and membership in a political community—between taste and "the more serious duties of life"—that is inherent in Enlightenment aesthetics. John Barrell, author of an important critical study of eighteenth-century British art criticism, observes that for Reynolds, who consistently combined visual and political terminology, "the exercise of taste was . . . a mode of exercising the same faculties as were exercised in the contemplation of society and its interest."[78] The criteria for membership in the republic of taste and in the political republic were identical: the ability to comprehend a whole.[79] Citing Reynolds, Crow notes with approval that for Enlightenment writers on art public vision "meant to see beyond particular local contingencies and merely individual interests." It was "a gaze that consistently registered what united rather than what divided the members of the political community." It guaranteed "the ability to generalize or abstract from particulars," reflected a "consciousness . . . undivided by private, material appetites," and expressed "a transcendent unity of mind" (3).

Crow embraces the civic humanist idea of public vision as a criterion to measure contemporary art and finds that it lacks a public dimension. This embrace has two important consequences. First, it places Crow squarely within a political camp whose membership extends far beyond the boundaries of art discourse. It aligns him with writers like, most famously, Habermas who hold that an emancipatory democratic politics must be based on a recovery of the unrealized ideals of modern political theory. At the same time, Crow's espousal of an Enlightenment concept of public vision places him just as squarely, though less overtly, against the feminist critique of vision that was first manifested in events like the "Public Vision" show and that had made a decisive impact on art criticism by the time of the Dia symposium. Crow does not concede the existence, let alone the influence, of art informed by feminist theories of vision. Nonetheless, indeed for that very reason, he tacitly opposes it. Omitting this work from the field of contemporary art, from his own aesthetic vision, Crow presents as an absolute a model of public vision compatible with the modernist ideal of disinterested contemplation—the very ideal identified by the "Public Vision" show as nonpublic. "Public Vision" agreed with Crow's premise that modernist aesthetics positions a disinterested viewing subject but strongly opposed the idea that this position is located in a public space. On the contrary, "Public Vision" suggested that the production of an impartial viewer is an effort to escape from, rather than to enter, public space, which it associated with openness, contingency, incompletion—in other words, with partiality.

For Crow, however, the idea that public vision is impartial vision is a foregone conclusion. Within the borders of his vision, skepticism toward impartial vision cannot nourish a public space but can only be implicated in its loss. "Public Vision" cannot perform a political critique; it only jeopardizes politics. Crow's periodization of contemporary art confirms this judgment: art's public dimension falls into decline at the precise moment—the late 1970s and 1980s—when art informed by feminist ideas about vision begins to rise.

Feminist ideas about subjectivity in representation cannot be so easily expelled from the public sphere, for they, too, are part of a larger political discourse. The confrontation that I have staged between Crow's talk and the "Public Vision" show rephrases the terms of an important current debate about the meaning of public space and citizenship. Crow, as noted, joins the side of writers who hold that the modern idea of the citizen, based on an abstract concept of "man," is a necessary element of democratic politics. He applies this idea to aesthetic politics, likening the art viewer to the abstract citizen and invoking disinterested vision as a model of democratic citizenship. But art like that in "Public Vision" exposes the hierarchical relations of difference that produce the abstract subject of modernist vision, thus corresponding to critiques of modern political theory undertaken from the point of view that the modern idea of the citizen, although crucial for the democratic revolution, must be reworked if democracy is to be extended. The political philosopher Etienne Balibar comments that in the postmodern epoch, politics is being born "within and against" modern politics. The universalizing discourse of modern democracy, says Balibar, opened the right to politics to all humans. But postmodern politics poses "the question of going beyond the abstract or generic concept of man on the basis of generalized citizenship" and of "inscribing" the modern democratic program of general equality and liberty in singularities and differences.[80]

Insofar as postmodern politics is born "against" modern politics, one stake in the contest between the two is the ideal of impartiality, which Crow treats as self-evident but which others have challenged as "both illusory and oppressive."[81] The modern notion of the citizen depends on a strict opposition between an abstract, universalist public and a private realm of conflicting, partial interests. The opposition stabilizes the identities of both the political public sphere and its occupant, the citizen. But since the opposition generates the impression that the public and the private are discrete, enclosed spaces, it makes it seem as if these identities stabilize themselves. The public/private dichotomy performs other conjuring tricks. While it produces the public sphere as a privileged political realm, it also produces a privileged space *outside* political debate from which the citizen can observe the social world in its entirety. It produces, that is, the very private subject whose existence it presupposes.

In the civic public of citizenship, writes political philosopher Iris Marion Young, political discussion is confined to talk framed from the standpoint of a single, all encompassing "we." Members of the political community adopt a universal point of view, seek to discover the common good, and commit themselves to impartiality. As the hallmark of the public subject, impartiality does not mean simple fairness or consideration of other people's needs. It is equivalent to Reason:

> Impartiality names a point of view of reason that stands apart from any interests and desires. Not to be partial means being able to see the whole, how all the particular perspectives and interests in a given moral situation relate to one another in a way that, because of its partiality, each perspective cannot see itself. The impartial moral reasoner thus stands outside of and above the situation about which he or she reasons, with no stake in it, or is supposed to adopt an attitude toward a situation as though he or she were outside and above it.[82]

Civic republicanism, Young continues, constructs the ideal of a total, sovereign self "abstracted from the context of any real persons." This self "is not committed to any particular ends, has no particular history, is a member of no communities, has no body."[83] But this universal subject is neither the essential being nor the irreproachable public individual of the civic humanist imagination. It achieves completion by mastering and ultimately negating plurality and difference. Mobilizing a logic of identity that reduces objects of thought to universal principles, the impartial self seeks to eliminate otherness, which Young defines in three ways: the irreducible specificity of situations; differences among subjects; and desire, emotions, the body.

Young ultimately proposes an alternative to the modern view of citizenship that itself reduces difference to identity and thus retreats from some of the most radical implications of her own critique. This does not lessen the value of her contention that the impartial citizen is produced, like the detached viewer, through the loss of others—otherness in the self and others in the world. Hannah Arendt deplored the effects of this process three decades earlier. If, wrote Arendt, the "attempt to overcome the consequences of plurality were successful, the result would be not so much sovereign domination of one's self as arbitrary domination of all others, or . . . the exchange of the real world for an imaginary one where these others would simply not exist."[84] In a small but exemplary way, Crow's essay fulfills Arendt's predictions: it describes a contemporary art world from which feminist critiques of vision have simply vanished.

The positioning of a subject able to perform intellectual operations that give it information *about* the social world but owe nothing to its involvement *in* the social world has a corollary in the desire to objectify society. Impartial vision is possible only in the presence of an object that itself transcends partiality and is thus independent of all subjectivity.[85] Impartial social vision is possible only in the presence of "society" or "social space" as such an object. Construed as an entity with a positivity of its own, this object—"society"—serves as the basis of rational discussions and as a guarantee that social conflicts can be resolved objectively. The failure to acknowledge the spatializations that generate "social space" attests to a desire both to control conflict and to secure a stable position for the self. With the social world in its entirety set before it as an independent object—as what Martin Heidegger calls "a picture"[86]—the subject stands at a point outside social space from which it can purportedly discover the laws or conflicts governing that space.

Indeed, the subject becomes that external point, a pure viewpoint capable of penetrating beneath deceptive appearances to the fundamental relations underlying the apparent fragmentation and diversity of the social field.

Crow's discussion of the public sphere presupposes such an objectivist epistemology. He writes about social unity as if it is an empirical referent and speaks of the common interest as a substantive good. The public gaze "registers" what unites the community. What unifying element does it record? Crow does not answer this question directly, but he leaves clues. The unity of each of the three art-historical movements he designates as attempts to form an art public is ultimately given in each movement's opposition to capitalist economic relations. Moreover, antipathy to social division, which in Crow's account is attributed solely to capitalism, unites the three moments in a historical formation. Although Crow contends that public unity is an imaginary construct, public vision emerges in his text as a gaze able to perceive the foundation of an a priori social unity. His account of the public sphere thus mobilizes a fundamentalist logic that refers to a single antagonism—relations of economic production and class—that possesses an ontological priority to govern all other social antagonisms.

As many commentators have pointed out, feminist and other social movements that want to resist subordination to a privileged political struggle have a clear stake in disputing conceptions of public space based on such fundamentalist logic. For feminists, theories about art and public space that conform to this logic are problematic not just because, as Crow suggests, previous efforts to realize an art public have been dominated by white men. The problem cannot, moreover, be limited to the oppressive gender relations of civic humanist ideas. It is true, as John Barrell is careful to emphasize, that women were "denied citizenship, and denied it absolutely in the republic of taste as well as in the political republic" because they were believed incapable of generalizing from particulars and therefore of exercising public vision.[87] To be sure, discrimination against women is an important problem, but simply to protest the exclusion of women is to support the contention, routinely put forth by contemporary proponents of modern political theory, that the civic public ideal should be realized by including formerly marginalized groups. Leaving the ideal itself untouched, such a protest does not address the more intractable sexual politics in which laments for impartiality and dreams of a substantively unified public sphere are caught. These laments evince regret at the passing of a fantasy of a masculine self and attempt to restore what Homi Bhabha in another context calls "masculinism as a position of social authority"—a position historically occupied by men but with which women can also identify. "Masculinism as a position of social authority," writes Bhaba, "is not simply about the power invested in the recognizable 'persons' of men. It is about the subsumption or sublation of social antagonism; it is about the repression of social division; it is about the power to authorize an "impersonal" holistic or universal discourse on the representation of the social."[88] Masculinism as a position of social authority is also about the authority of traditional left intellectuals to account for the political condition of the entire world. What measures does it take to reestablish this authority in the name of the public? The foundations of society, the public, and the political subject—the citizen—must be treated as certainties. Feminist and other interrogations of the exclusions that constitute such certainties must be implicated in the loss of politics and banished from the public sphere.

Something, then, is in danger of getting lost in the art world's redefinition of public space as political space, something that champions of lost public spheres seem bent on, even to delight in, losing. For the polarization of art informed by feminist explorations of subjectivity in representation, on the one hand, and a left criticism that forces this art into privacy, on the other, is no isolated occurrence. Discussions of public art often betray a suspicion of art practices that question subjectivity, as if this question has no bearing on art's publicness, distracts from public concerns, or, worse, jeopardizes political struggle, diverting attention from "real" problems of public space—homelessness, for example. Certain art critics define public art and public space by ignoring or trivializing the issues raised by such work.[89] Writers like Crow, their eyes trained on an image of the public totality, simply overlook feminist critiques of vision. Other advocates of art's public functions, even those otherwise receptive to new political projects, explicitly disparage feminist critiques of vision as nonpublic, a position held by some critics who support "activist" art. Take, for instance, those writers who hold that art's public status is ensured by the willingness, as critic David Trend puts it, of "progressive artists" to engage in "practical aesthetics." Practical artists, according to Trend, respond to the necessity of supporting the goals and identities of community movements and of all forms of social struggle that can be grouped under the heading "new social movements." [90] These activities, he says, promote "civic consciousness" through "political education" and, moreover, represent the "recovery of the public function of art." [91] Cultural scholar George Yudice agrees: by "serving the needs of particular communities and simultaneously publicizing their practice for wider access," artists are "recovering the public function of art." [92]

Yudice makes these remarks in an article that begins by opposing neoconservative proposals to eliminate public arts funding. Yudice's broader purpose, however, is to appropriate the definition of what makes art public from conservatives. How, he asks, has the art world most effectively disputed conservative mandates to privatize art production, reverse recent cultural gains made by oppressed social groups, and censor critical art that, conservatives assume, affronts public values? First, Yudice rejects liberal responses that merely defend the abstract freedom of the artist. Such responses, he says, reinforce depoliticizing ideas that art is autonomous and public values are universal. More viable contestations of the conservative agenda, he continues, have come from artists who politicize art practice by working within new social movements. At this point Yudice takes a significant, and questionable, step: he asserts that artists who work within new social movements "dispense with the frame." [93] By this he means that they operate outside conventional art institutions and have thereby "recovered the public function of art."

In today's political climate, there is, I think, every reason to support the contention that art involved with new social movements is a crucial public practice. Naming such "activist" work "public art" challenges an authoritarian aesthetic discourse that claims to protect both "the public" and "the aesthetic" and supports this claim by presupposing that each category rests on unquestionable criteria: standards of "decency" and of "taste" or "quality." These standards are alternatively characterized as transcendent, natural, or consensual. Because they are attributed to an objective source, anyone who questions them is automatically placed outside the boundaries of the public and the aesthetic—indeed, outside "civilization." Yudice rightly points out that such references to absolute criteria are predicated on exclusions. Absolutist definitions of public space generate two kinds of privatization: they cast dissenting voices into privacy and appropriate—thus privatize— the public sphere itself.

A problem arises, however, when critics like Yudice, who want to take a stand against the authoritarian definitions of the public put forth by Jesse Helms and Hilton Kramer, redefine public art by erecting new public/private dichotomies—such as that between the inside and outside of art institutions. This division generates its own privileged public space and its own privatizations. As a consequence, proposals to redefine public art as art engaged in "practical aesthetics" themselves serve a practical function, one we have seen before: mapping a rigid "inside the institution/outside the institution" opposition onto an equally rigid public/private opposition, these proposals expel feminist politics of representation from the artistic public sphere. Listen, for example, to the first critic quoted above. Critiques of representation, says Trend, have no practical function because they are located in a space "outside social functioning." "Regrettably," he writes, "the art world is separated from social functioning by a complex mechanism that defines 'disciplines' in the arts and humanities" and that, "fragmenting knowledge, while distancing it from practical circumstances . . . drains the aesthetic of any practical dimension."[94] Work on the "politics of representation," if situated in an art institution and directed toward an art audience, "promotes an illusion of cultural practice that is socially disinterested and nonpolitical."[95]

Yudice agrees: "The 'politics of representation' engaged in by this type of art . . . this play on the constructedness of images . . . does not necessarily lead to changing the conditions that produced them in the first place."[96] Like Crow—but explicitly—Yudice measures art's publicness against work like that presented in "Public Vision": "Take, for example, Cindy Sherman's deconstruction of socially constructed representations of women in patriarchal society," he writes. "Despite the challenge to the authority of representation, her work is easily accommodated within the art world."[97] Sherman's work, in other words, performs no public function—it is private—because it does not "dispense with the frame."

In the name of the political public sphere, Yudice resurrects the very polar-ization that feminist critiques challenged for the express purpose of demonstrating that images are, precisely, public and political—the polarization between the for-mal operations of images and a politics exerted from the outside. When feminist critiques established a constitutive link between hierarchies of vision and hierar-chies of sexual difference, they made it clear that images per se are neither private nor politically neutral. As a result, we can no longer take it for granted that art institutions are secure interiors, isolated from social space. The intimate relation-ship between vision and sexual politics shows that this isolation is a fiction. Far from nourishing the institutional frame, work on the sexual politics of the image undermines the boundaries that supposedly sequester the inside of the institution from its outside, the private from the public. The doctrine that aesthetic vision is the disinterested perception of pure form and universal truths, the doctrine under-lying the illusion of the art institution's neutrality, is unsettled by the implication of pure form in the sexual pleasures of looking. And, as Jacqueline Rose writes, these pleasures are in turn part of an aesthetically extraneous political space.[98] To accept Rose's contention that work on images and sexed subjectivity threatens the closure—that is, the privacy—secured by the institutional frame one must accept, of course, that vision and sexuality are public matters.

Crow's and Yudice's redefinitions of the artistic public sphere produce the same casualty—feminist critiques of vision. This does not mean, however, that the two writers hold identical political positions. On the contrary: Yudice places new social movements at the heart of the artistic public sphere while Crow holds these movements responsible for the public sphere's demise. But the shared casualty is not a pure coincidence. Yudice and Trend can relegate art informed by feminist work on visual representation to a private space because they adhere, if inadver-tently, to a foundationalist vision of a unified public sphere. What other vision makes it possible to assume with confidence that a so-called fragmentation of spaces inevitably destroys the public sphere or separates art from any public func-tion? Critics who distrust fragmentation sometimes support their objections to art institutions by citing scholars who have analyzed the role of academic expertise and disciplinary specialization in depoliticizing knowledge. These art critics equate disciplinary specialization with the "isolation" of art institutions. Trend, for instance, refers to Edward Said's essay "Opponents, Audiences, Constituencies, and Community."[99] He mistakenly concludes, however, that the objective of politicized knowledge is not, as Said argues, to make visible the connections between scholarship and power but to restore the ultimate coherence of all political life and to do so, moreover, simply by abandoning the space of a discipline or, by extension, an art institution. With this abandonment, Trend implies, art enters an all-embracing social space and simultaneously recovers its public function. The public is turned, as Bruce Robbins writes, "into a mythic plenitude from which disciplines must then ceaselessly and vainly lament their impoverished exile."[100]

A similar logic underpins the idea that the politics of images can be reduced to the "conditions that produced them in the first place" and that changing these conditions is the sine qua non of public activity in the realm of visual culture. This reduction of an image's meaning to strictly external conditions echoes social theories that presuppose the existence of a foundation that not only forms the basis of but successfully governs all social meaning. Accordingly, meaning is localized in basic objective structures that become the principal objects of political struggle. Used to explain the meaning of images, these social theories smuggle back into art discourse an image of their own: a unique or privileged space of politics that feminist theories of representation have long rejected. Feminisms have contested this image of politics since it has been mobilized historically to relegate gender and sexuality to mere auxiliaries of social relations thought to be more fundamentally political. Now, with stubborn circularity, this image of politics subordinates the feminist politics of images to a public space assumed to precede representation. When critics who endorse a practical aesthetics uphold this image, they diverge from the premise on which feminist critiques of representation helped extend what I have called a democratic public space—the absence of absolute sources of social meaning.

Abandoning this premise, advocates of activist art also diverge from the more radical aspects of their own position. When they separate the politics of aligning art with new social movements, on the one hand, from the politics of vision, on the other, they do not appreciate that new social movements and feminist ideas about subjectivity in representation have something important in common. Both challenge foundationalist social theories and question, among other ideas, the tenet that class antagonism ensures the unity of emancipatory struggles. Is it not inconsistent to assert that an absolute foundation determines the meaning of images—a foundation that must be changed before art can be public—while supporting new social movements that declare their independence from such a foundation? These movements represent new forms of political identity that challenge traditional left political projects. They refuse to submit to the regulatory authority of political parties that exclude specificity and difference in the name of an essential political interest. Irreducible to a predetermined norm, new social practices offer the promise of more democratic kinds of political association.

Critics who support art's involvement with new social movements yet attack feminist work on representation as fragmenting and private undermine the very concern for difference that, in other ways, they vigorously defend. Though committed to plurality and opposed to conservative homogenizations of the public, they unintentionally align themselves with more influential critics who reject difference, especially those like David Harvey and Fredric Jameson who advance theories of postmodern culture based on neo-Marxist discourses about space. In earlier essays, I have criticized these theories.[101] Here I will simply add that Harvey and Jameson share today's widespread sensitivity to public space, seeking to appropriate space from capitalist domination and return it to the public. For them, too, public space is lost. Unlike Yudice, however, they acknowledge the similarity between the growth of new social movements and postmodern explorations of images and, instead of counterposing the two, reject both. Both developments, Harvey argues, spring from the fragmenting effects produced by post-Fordist restructuring of capitalism. Both also perpetuate fragmentation. The sheer immensity of late capitalism's spatioeconomic network precipitates a crisis of representation for the subject. It overwhelms our ability to perceive the interconnected social totality underlying apparent fragmentation and prevents us from apprehending our place—our class position—in the totality. This blindness keeps us from initiating the political action required to transform society. According to Harvey, the "confusion" of our perceptual apparatus is confounded by postmodern politics and postmodern aesthetics. Politically, fragmentation is manifested in the proliferation of new political identities that do not conform to a norm. Aesthetically, fragmentation occurs when artists concern themselves with images rather than a "reality" supposedly underlying images.

The notion that there is a crisis of, and inadequacy in, representations of the social world is only possible against the background of a belief in previously stable, univocal, and impartial—that is, adequate—representations, an illusion that justifies efforts to reinstate traditional authority. In the name of restoring public space, scholars who imagine, and identify with, a former golden age of total knowledge elevate themselves to a position outside the world. Others are demoted to secondary rank or worse. Within Harvey's spatial discourse, for instance, political reality is equated with uneven spatioeconomic arrangements. Homeless people, the most visible product of these arrangements, emerge as the privileged figures of political space. Efforts to talk about urban space from different starting points—or to address different spaces—are considered escapist, quietist, complicitous. Anyone who analyzes representations of the city not as objects tested against external reality but as sites where images are set up as reality and where subjects are produced is accused of callousness toward poor city residents and denounced as an enemy of the homeless. From a political point of view, this accusation is counterproductive for two reasons. First, precisely because we want to understand and change current representations of, and attitudes toward, homeless people, we must—to use Adorno's words—"turn toward the subject." [102] Second, the dismissal of questions of subjectivity often leads critics to invoke "the homeless person" less to promote social justice than to prove the sharper penetration of their own social vision.

COVER STORY

Earlier I asked what political functions are performed by the call in left art discourse to make art "public." One answer is that advocacy of an artistic public sphere has become a means of safeguarding the traditional space of left political projects. Under the protection of the word *public,* some critics return to unproblematized, precritical uses of the adjective *real*—real people, real space, real social problems, all presented as the ground of real political struggle. But art practices that question the exclusions that ground these "realities" do not, as their detractors claim, fall into privacy. On the contrary, these practices nurture the gestation of a different kind of public sphere that emerges precisely because our commonality is uncertain and therefore open to debate. Indeed, with new political formations taking shape before our eyes—with the propagation of demands for contingent rights, the proliferation of political projects based on partial critiques and aims, the growth of intellectual tendencies creating new objects of political analysis and toppling subjects of knowledge from their unsituated high grounds—public space has begun to look less like a "lost" entity than like what Bruce Robbins so compellingly calls a "phantom."

Robbins edited an anthology called *The Phantom Public Sphere*. In the introduction, he questions and stretches the meaning of the phrase "the phantom public," adopted from Walter Lippmann, who coined it in 1925.[103] In Lippmann's view, the public is a phantom because the democratic ideal of a responsible, unified electorate capable of participating in the machinery of government and able to supervise the state is unattainable. Modern citizens, he says, simply have no time to be sufficiently informed about all issues pertaining to the common good. Because the public is a phantom, Lippmann concludes, tasks of government should be relegated to educated social elites.

Like Lippmann, Robbins uses the idea that the public is a phantom to cast doubt on the existence of a unified public. But he does so to pursue different ends—not to relinquish the public sphere but to challenge the Habermasian ideal of a singular public sphere that has supposedly fallen into decline. For proponents of this ideal, recovery of a traditional critical public sphere is an alternative to proposals, like Lippmann's, for an elite management of democracy. For Robbins, the Habermasian ideal is itself a phantom because the very quality that supposedly makes the public sphere public—its inclusiveness and accessibility—has always been illusory. The lost public sphere was actually the possession of particular privileged social groups. On this point, Habermas would not disagree. While he knows that in practice the bourgeois public sphere was always exclusionary, Habermas wants to rescue the ideal from both its imperfect realization in its inaugural years and its later contamination by consumerism, mass media, and the welfare state. Far

319

from criticizing the principle of a singular public sphere, he calls for its rebirth in an uncontaminated form. Robbins, drawing on Alexander Kluge and Oskar Negt, argues that the traditional public sphere is a phantom less because it was never fully realized than because the ideal of social coherence, for which the term *public* has always stood, is itself irremediably deceptive and, moreover, oppressive. The ideal of a noncoercive consensus reached through reason is an illusion maintained by repressing differences and particularities. To contrast a "contaminated" public sphere with either an earlier or a potentially pure public is to sustain the illusion. "What needs to be done, rather, is to investigate the ideal history of the public sphere together with the history of its decay in order to highlight their identical mechanisms." [104]

For Robbins, the idea of the public as a phantom has beneficial effects. It counters appeals to lost publics that he rightly fears can lead to authoritarianism. At the same time, Robbins finds the public's phantomlike quality unsettling because he recognizes that some conception of a public sphere is essential to democracy. Robbins invokes Lippmann's suspicion that the public is a phantom as an impetus to the left not only to examine its own preconceptions about the meaning of the public but to rethink its commitment to the protection and extension of a democratic public space. "In radical struggles over architecture, urban planning, sculpture, political theory, ecology, economics, education, the media, and public health, to mention only a few sites among others," writes Robbins,

> the public has long served as a rallying cry against private greed, a demand for attention to the general welfare as against propertied interests, an appeal for openness to scrutiny as opposed to corporate and bureaucratic secrecy, an arena in which disenfranchised minorities struggle to express their cultural identity, a code word for socialism. Without this discursive weapon, we seem to enter such struggles inadequately armed. [105]

The phrase "phantom public" can be disorienting, then, because we cannot do without a concept of public space and are therefore reluctant "to see the public melt conclusively into air." [106]

Robbins uses the term "phantom" in multiple and ambiguous ways. First, he employs it to name—and criticize—ideals of a unitary public sphere that, he says, is not lost and cannot be retrieved. Robbins claims instead that this public sphere is a phantom, an illusion. When he associates the public's status as a phantom with its disappearance into thin air, he extends the term, representing the phantom as a danger to the public sphere. Later, however, Robbins transforms "the phantom public" into an alternative to (not just a critique of) "the lost public." His purpose, he concludes, is to push "the topic of the phantom public and its problems into a less backward-looking conversation."[107]

Latent in Robbins's text is the suggestion that while the lost public sphere is a phantom in one sense, more radical possibilities for democracy may lie in a public sphere that is precisely a phantom. Robbins's account leaves important questions in its wake. Taking the symbol of the phantom one step farther, we might ask if the lost public is constructed to deny that a democratic public sphere must, in some sense, be a phantom. Does the public's phantomlike quality hinder or promote democracy? Do we want to conjure *away* the phantom public, or rethink the public *as* a phantom? Which attitude—and which corresponding definitions of a phantom—should we adopt as we accept Robbins's mandate to rethink the public sphere? In short: Is the public sphere crucial to democracy *despite* or *because* of the fact that it is a phantom?

Some authors who have rethought the public sphere choose the first option. Iris Young, for instance, follows her trenchant critique of civic republicanism with a proposal to ground the meaning of the public sphere in difference rather than singularity. The civic ideal, she suggests, should be replaced with a heterogeneous public composed of multiple social groups. Citizenship should be differentiated by group. From a radical democratic perspective, her proposal to proliferate political identities and multiply political spaces is promising. Asserting that group differences are relational rather than substantive, Young argues persuasively against the universalizing civic ideal that marks only oppressed groups as different.[108] But even though she maintains that a group is differentiated by "affinity," not by any intrinsic identity, the politics of difference that she recommends ultimately consists of negotiating among preexisting demands of social groups already in place. Difference is reduced to identity, and Young seems to forget what she stressed earlier:

that every difference is an interdependence. Consequently, she avoids some of the most important questions facing a politics of pluralism: Which conception of plurality can counteract the fact that the drive to identity may be tempted to stabilize itself by condemning differences? Which concept of plurality can work against the aggressive reactions of established identities as they are destabilized by new ones?[109] Such questions are beyond the scope of this essay. Let us simply note that Young's politics of difference glosses over them, defining difference as the "particularity of entities," although she says that particularity is socially constructed.[110] As a result, Young does not consider the productive role that can be played by disruption, rather than consolidation, in the construction of identity, a disruption in which groups encounter their own uncertainty. Her concept of a pluralistic politics disintegrates the public sphere as a monolithic space but resolidifies it as an array of positive identities. This pluralism does not pursue the most radical implications of the uncertainty that Young herself introduced into the concept of the public when she questioned the logic of identity and metaphysics of presence underpinning the modern ideal. Stepping back from the complexity of her earlier critique and falling into a discourse of entities rather than relationships, Young presents an alternative whose objective, it appears, is to realize the public sphere as a fully inclusive, fully constituted realm and to dispel the phantom public, which she construes only as the illusion of a singular public.

Critical theorist Thomas Keenan approaches the question of public space differently. He, too, challenges the notion of a lost public sphere, considering it an illusion. But his contribution to Robbins's book recasts the democratic public sphere in the shape of a phantom.[111] Keenan links the public's ghostly aspect to the appearance, not disappearance, of public space. More precisely, he suggests that the public sphere rises as a phantom only at the moment of a disappearance.

Keenan's essay, "Windows: of vulnerability," uses an architectural element, the window, as a figure of the differentiation between private and public realms. Drawing on the pioneering work of Beatriz Colomina, Keenan connects historical architectural debates about the form and meaning of windows to current debates about the form and meaning of the political public sphere. "Any concept of the window," writes Colomina, "implies a notion of the relationship between inside and outside, between private and public space."[112] Does the window ensure or menace the rigor of the public/private divide? Does the window secure or erode the closure of the public and private realms generated by this divide? Like Colomina (though making different distinctions), Keenan links these questions to the status of the human subject. Do windows, as in traditional perspectival models, ground the subject by allowing its detached gaze to pass through the window and master a world framed as a discrete, external object? Or do windows let light—the exterior world—in and, interfering with vision, interrupt the subject's control of its surroundings and disturb the security of the interior? As Keenan remarks, "The more light, the less sight, and the less there is in the interior that allows 'man' to find comfort and protection, to find a ground from which to look."[113]

Light coming through the window is Keenan's conceit for a public sphere that he has rethought on the model of language. The public sphere, Keenan suggests, is not, as in traditional conceptions, an exterior space that we enter as private beings simply to use language impartially. It is "structured like a language" and thus makes impartiality inconceivable. Keenan's public sphere surpasses the level of the single individual and is more than a mere collection of other individuals. In this sense, the idea of a public sphere that is like language is no different from any other conception of the public. But, unlike classical notions of the public sphere, the public sphere modeled on language is not strictly opposed to the individual. Instead, it problematizes the possibility of a clear separation between public and private realms. For just as light comes through the window, language reaches us from a distance but cannot be kept at a safe distance, nor does it violate previously closed subjects. Rather, we are realized as subjects only by entering language, the preexisting social field where meaning is produced. The entry into language alienates us from ourselves, estranging us, as Freud said of the unconscious, from "our own house."[114] Language makes us present as subjects by dividing us and opening us to an outside. The inhabitant of Keenan's public sphere is not the unitary, private subject of classical public space. Language undermines our self-possession—depriving us of a basis inside ourselves—and it, too, is inadequate. Words do not equal "reality"; they do not give adequate expression to things as they are. There is no preexisting meaning in language—only differences between elements.

Composed of signifiers that acquire meaning only in relation to other signifiers—without a final term and therefore always in need of additions and open to disruptions—language is a singularly public and singularly unstable medium. "What if the peculiarity of the public," Keenan asks,

> were—not exactly (its) absence, but—the rupture in and of the subject's presence to itself that we have come to associate with writing or language in general? . . . In this sense, all those books and articles mourning the loss or disappearance of the public sphere in fact respond to, if in the mode of misrecognition, something important about the public—that it is not here. The public sphere is structurally elsewhere, neither lost nor in need of recovery or rebuilding but defined by its resistance to being made present.[115]

And what if this peculiarity of the public—that it is not here—is not inimical to, but the condition of, democracy? This, of course, is exactly what Lefort asserts when he defines public space as the open, contingent space that emerges with the disappearance of the thought of presence—the presence of an absolute foundation unifying society and making it coincide harmoniously with itself. If "the dissolution of the markers of certainty" calls us into public space, then public space is crucial to democracy not despite but because it is a phantom—though not in the sense of pure delusion, false impression, or misleading appearance. As Joan Copjec and Michael Sorkin argue, the "phantom public sphere is no mere illusion, but a powerful regulative idea."[116] Democratic public space might, rather, be called a phantom because while it appears, it has no substantive identity and is, as a consequence, enigmatic. It emerges when society is instituted as a society with no basis, a society, as Lefort writes, "without a body . . . a society which undermines the representation of an organic totality."[117] With this mutation, the unity of society becomes purely social and susceptible to contestation. If the public space of debate appears with the disappearance of an absolute social basis, public space is where meaning continuously appears and continuously fades. The phantom public sphere is thus inaccessible to political theories that refuse to recognize events—like new social movements—that cannot be grasped in preconceived conceptual terms or without recourse to final intentions. The phantom public sphere is invisible from political viewpoints that limit social reality to the contents that fill social space but ignore the principles generating that space. If democracy is a form of society that is destroyed if it is positivized, a democratic public space cannot be a lost state of political plenitude that we want but do not at present have. "We never had what we have lost," says Žižek, for society was always ruptured by antagonisms.[118] Produced instead by the loss of the idea of plenitude, a loss that founds democratic political life, public space may be the space that we as social beings are in but do not particularly want.

If so, all those books and articles mourning the lost beginning of the public sphere are not mere responses to the fact that the public is not here. Taking the form of what Keenan calls misrecognition, they are, rather, panicked reactions to the openness and indeterminacy of the democratic public as a phantom—a kind of agoraphobic behavior adopted in the face of a public space that has a loss at its beginning. From a sociological perspective, agoraphobia is primarily an affliction of women. In city streets and squares, where men have greater rights, women devise strategies to avoid the threats that present themselves in public spaces. The phobic woman may try to define, and stay within, what she considers a zone of safety. She invents "cover stories": explanations for her actions that, as one sociologist writes, "do not reveal that she is what she is, a person afraid of public places."[119] For instance, an agoraphobic who walks in the gutter, which she feels is safer than the sidewalk, may tell people that she is looking for something she has lost.[120]

The phantom public sphere is, of course, a different kind of space. It is not coextensive with empirically identifiable urban terrains—although it is no less real.[121] It, too, harbors threats and arouses anxieties. For, as Keenan writes, the democratic public sphere "belongs by rights to others, and to no one in particular."[122] It thus threatens the identity of "man"—the modern subject—who in this space can no longer construe the entire social world as a meaning for itself, as "mine." In the phantom public sphere, man is deprived of the objectified, distanced, knowable world on whose existence he depends and is presented instead with unknowability, the proximity of otherness, and, consequently, uncertainty in the self. No wonder this public sphere confronts the modern human type as an object of dread. Like the images in "Public Vision," it comes too close for comfort.

In this situation, the story of the lost public sphere might function in a manner analogous to an agoraphobic's cover story. The story of the lost public makes its narrator appear to be someone who is comfortable in, even devoted to, public space—someone who, akin to the figures on the cover of *Variations on a Theme Park,* is ill at ease when exiled from the public square. But while the story gives the impression that its speaker is unafraid of public space, it also transforms public space into a safe zone. The lost public sphere is a place where private individuals gather and, from the point of view of reason, seek to know the social world objectively. There, as citizens, they "find" the object—"society"—that transcends particularities and differences. There, society becomes possible. Founded, like all impartial totalities, on the loss of others, the lost public sphere closes the borders of the very space that to be democratic must remain incomplete.

Lefort analyzes totalitarianism as an attempt to reach solid social ground. Totalitarianism, he says, originates in a hatred of the question at the heart of democracy—the question that generates public space but also ensures that it remain forever in gestation. Totalitarianism ruins democracy by attempting to fill the void created by the democratic revolution and banish the indeterminacy of the social. It invests "the people" with an essential interest, a "oneness" with which the state identifies itself, thus closing down the public space, encircling it in what Lefort calls "the loving grip of the good society."[123] The grip of the totalitarian state closes the gap between state and society, suffocating the public space where state power is questioned and where our common humanity—the "basis of relations between *self* and *other*"—is settled and unsettled.[124]

"The loving grip of the good society" warns us of the dangers inherent in the seemingly benign fantasy of social completion, a fantasy that negates plurality and conflict because it depends on an image of social space closed by an authoritative ground. This image is linked to a rigid public/private dichotomy that consigns differences to the private realm and sets up the public as a universal or consensual sphere—the privileged space of politics. But the public/private dichotomy produces another privileged site outside social space and therefore immune from political interrogation: the total vantage point or, in Lefort's words, "that point of view on everything and everybody," the "phantasy of omnipotence." [125] It is the security of this public/private divide, which shelters the subject from public space, that art informed by a feminist critique of the image has so forcefully challenged by insisting that identity and meaning are formed *in* public space and so questioning the possibility of external viewpoints. Laclau has written that the main task of postmodern culture in democratic struggles is "to transform the forms of identification and construction of subjectivity that exist in our civilization." [126] When art intervenes in the forms of representation through which subjects construct themselves as universal and flee from difference, should we not welcome it—along with art involved in new social movements—as a contribution to the deepening and extension of public space? Especially if we hope to prevent the conversion of the public sphere into a private possession, which is so often attempted today in the name of democracy.

NOTES

INTRODUCTION

1. In order to preserve the independence and specificity of each essay, I retained some repetitions of material, particularly descriptions of urban redevelopment, site-specific art, and feminist critiques of vision. Wherever possible, I have condensed these descriptions and referred readers to more detailed accounts in other essays.

2. Rosalyn Deutsche and Cara Gendel Ryan, "The Fine Art of Gentrification," *October* 31 (Winter 1984): 91–111.

3. Another pioneering artwork that brings together discourses about urban and aesthetic spaces is Martha Rosler's phototext piece of 1974–75, *The Bowery in Two Inadequate Descriptive Systems.* *The Bowery* questions the representational conventions of liberal documentary photography, whose practitioners frequently photograph poor urban neighborhoods and city residents, especially homeless men. It examines how the messages about poverty conveyed by such photographs are inseparable from the institutional spaces in which they are exhibited. For documentation of Rosler's work and for her related essay, "In, Around, and Afterthoughts (On Documentary Photography)," see *Martha Rosler, 3 Works,* the Nova Scotia Pamphlets (Halifax: The Press of the Nova Scotia College of Art and Design, 1981). For a brief discussion of *The Bowery in Two Inadequate Descriptive Systems* in the context of Rosler's later project about the city, see my "Alternative Space," in Brian Wallis, ed., *If You Lived Here/The City in Art, Theory, and Social Activism: A Project by Martha Rosler,* Dia Art Foundation, Discussions in Contemporary Culture, no. 6 (Seattle: Bay Press, 1991), 45–66.

4. For this version of "Boys Town," I have added to my original comments about Harvey's use of the house as a metaphor for Marxist theory, drawing on Mark Wigley's innovative analysis of the house as a figure of presence in Western philosophy. See Wigley, *The Architecture of Deconstruction: Derrida's Haunt* (Cambridge: MIT Press, 1993).

KRZYSZTOF WODICZKO'S *HOMELESS PROJECTION* AND THE SITE OF URBAN "REVITALIZATION"

1. Paul Goldberger, *The City Observed—New York: A Guide to the Architecture of Manhattan* (New York: Vintage, 1979), 92 (my emphasis).

2. In 1986, reviewing an exhibition of Hugh Ferriss's architectural drawings held at the Whitney Museum's new branch at the Equitable Center, a building that itself represented a threat to the city's poor, Goldberger claimed that Ferriss "offers the greatest key to the problems of the skyscraper city that we face today" because he demonstrates "that a love of the skyscraper's power and romance need not be incompatible with a heavy dose of urban planning." Paul Goldberger, "Architecture: Renderings of Skyscrapers by Ferriss," *New York Times,* June 24, 1986, C13.

3. Paul Goldberger, "Defining Luxury in New York's New Apartments," *New York Times,* August 16, 1984, C1.

4. Observing the omission of social or economic history in Goldberger's "history" of the skyscraper, one reviewer wrote:

> The building process is born of economics. . . . Some of these factors might be: the state of the national and regional economies; the nature of the local transportation systems; the conditions of local market supply-and-demand; the relationship to desirable local geographic features or elements, such as proximity to a park; the perceived or actual quality of building services and image; and the economies of new construction techniques that reduce building costs or enhance efficiency—*all of which are factors that cannot be seen simply by looking at the building's skin.*

Michael Parley, "On Paul Goldberger's *The Skyscraper,*" *Skyline* (March 1982): 10 [my emphasis]. The factors that Parley listed indicate some of the most serious omissions in Goldberger's aesthetic history, although these factors, in turn, need to be placed within the framework of a broader social structure.

5. The designation appears in Department of City Planning, *Union Square Special Zoning District Proposal* (originally released November 1983; revised June 1984), 3.

6. Goldberger, *The City Observed,* 91.

7. Department of City Planning, *Union Square: Street Revitalization* (January 1976), 28.

8. For a history of the economic factors—the needs of business—that determined the development of Ladies' Mile, see M. Christine Boyer, *Manhattan Manners: Architecture and Style 1850–1900* (New York: Rizzoli International, 1985).

9. "The making of compositions, the making of streets, and the making of theater—it is these things that define the architecture of New York far more than does any single style." Goldberger, *The City Observed,* xv.

10. Krzysztof Wodiczko, "Public Projection," *Canadian Journal of Political and Social Theory* 7 (Winter/Spring 1983): 186.

11. Ibid.

12. Krzysztof Wodiczko, *The Homeless Projection: A Proposal for the City of New York,* installation (New York: 49th Parallel, Centre for Contemporary Canadian Art, 1986). Unless otherwise noted, this and subsequent quotations by Wodiczko are from the brochure titled "The Homeless Projection: A Proposal for the City of New York" that was distributed at the installation. The installation is documented and the brochure reprinted in Krzysztof Wodiczko, "Public Projections," *October* 38 (Fall 1986): 3–20.

13. Bernardo Secchi, "La forma del discourse urbanistico," *Casabella* 48 (November 1984): 14.

14. When this essay was first written, the shops along Fourteenth Street from First to Eighth avenues, including Mays department store facing Union Square, made up the largest shopping district south of Spanish Harlem for Manhattan's Hispanic residents. Some of the stores' sites had already been purchased for future redevelopment. Known as La Calle Catorse, this street has traditionally provided the link between the concentrations of Hispanics on the Lower East Side and in Chelsea; both neighborhoods have recently undergone redevelopment, resulting in large displacements of those populations.

15. Bruce London and J. John Palen, "Introduction: Some Theoretical and Practical Issues Regarding Inner-City Revitalization," in *Gentrification, Displacement and Neighborhood Revitalization,* ed. J. John Palen and Bruce London (Albany: State University of New York Press, 1984), 10.

16. Roger Starr, *The Rise and Fall of New York City* (New York: Basic Books, 1985), 36.

17. Neil Smith and Michele LeFaivre, "A Class Analysis of Gentrification," in *Gentrification, Displacement and Neighborhood Revitalization,* 43–63.

18. Ibid., 50.

19. See in particular David Harvey, "The Urban Process Under Capitalism: A Framework for Analysis," in *Urbanization and Urban Planning in Capitalist Society*, ed. Michael Dear and Allen J. Scott (London: Methuen, 1981), 91–121. Other works by Harvey include *Social Justice and the City* (Baltimore: The Johns Hopkins University Press, 1973) and *The Urbanization of Capital: Studies in the History and Theory of Capitalist Urbanization* (Baltimore: The Johns Hopkins University Press, 1985).

20. Harvey, "The Urban Process Under Capitalism," 108. For another analysis of the contemporary construction boom as a response to capitalist economic crisis, see Mike Davis, "Urban Renaissance and the Spirit of Postmodernism," *New Left Review* 151 (May/June 1985): 106–16.

21. Smith and LeFaivre, "A Class Analysis of Gentrification," 54.

22. Ibid., 46.

23. Rosalyn Deutsche and Cara Gendel Ryan, "The Fine Art of Gentrification," *October* 31 (Winter 1984): 91–111.

24. R. B. Cohen devised a "multinational index" for quantifying the status of U.S. cities as international business centers. See Cohen, "The New International Division of Labor, Multinational Corporations and Urban Hierarchy," in *Urbanization and Urban Planning,* 287–315.

25. Ibid., 305.

26. Ibid., 306.

27. Department of City Planning, Manhattan Office, *Union Square Special Zoning District Proposal* (originally released November 1983; revised June 1984), p. 17.

28. Thomas J. Lueck, "Rich and Poor: Widening Gap Seen for Area," *New York Times,* May 2, 1986, B1.

29. "How Many Will Share New York's Prosperity?" *New York Times,* January 20, 1985, E5.

30. Lueck, "Rich and Poor," B1.

31. Michael Kwartler, "Zoning as Architect and Urban Designer," *New York Affairs* 8, no. 4 (1985): 118 (my emphasis).

32. This process can be observed in the role that architecture and urban design played in the creation of Battery Park City, one of the country's largest real-estate developments. For an ac-

count of Battery Park City's housing and design history, see "Uneven Development: Public Art in New York City," in this volume.

33. Victor Marrero, chairman, Department of City Planning, preface, in *Union Square: Street Revitalization,* 3.

34. *Union Square: Street Revitalization,* 33.

35. Ibid., 37.

36. Benson J. Lossing, "History of New York City," in I. N. Phelps Stokes, *The Iconography of Manhattan Island 1498–1909* (1926; reprint, New York: Arno Press, 1967), 1896.

37. Robert H. Wiebe, *The Search for Order 1877–1920* (New York: Hill and Wang, 1967), 11–12.

38. Albert Halper, *Union Square* (New York: Viking, 1933).

39. M. Christine Boyer, *Dreaming the Rational City: The Myth of American City Planning* (Cambridge: MIT Press, 1983), 50.

40. See Wiebe, *The Search for Order;* Paul Boyer, *Urban Masses and Moral Order in America 1820–1920* (Cambridge: Harvard University Press, 1978); Mario Manieri-Elia, "Toward an 'Imperial City': Daniel H. Burnham and the City Beautiful Movement," in Giorgio Ciucci et al., *The American City: From the Civil War to the New Deal* (Cambridge: MIT Press, 1979); and M. Christine Boyer, *Dreaming the Rational City.*

41. Harvey, "The Urban Process Under Capitalism," 117.

42. Charles Mulford Robinson, *Modern Civic Art or, The City Made Beautiful* (New York and London: G. P. Putnam's Sons, 1903).

43. J. F. Harder, "The City's Plan," *Municipal Affairs* 2 (1898): 25–43.

44. Karl Bitter, "Municipal Sculpture," *Municipal Affairs* 2 (1898): 73–97.

45. Robinson, *Modern Civic Art,* 170.

46. Boyer, *Dreaming the Rational City,* 50.

47. Robinson, *Modern Civic Art,* 262.

48. Kurt W. Forster has examined current architectural attitudes toward history and preservation using Alois Riegl's 1903 study of monuments, undertaken to direct the Austrian government's

policy of protecting the country's historic monuments. Riegl's efforts to understand the nature of what he calls the unintentional monument—the landmark of art or architectural history—led him to conclude that relative and changing values determine the course and management of preservation programs. Riegl devotes much of his essay to an attempt to identify and categorize these conflicting values. To establish unintentional monuments as landmarks is to extract art and architecture from their original contexts and assign new roles in new circumstances. Relating Riegl's insights to current architectural attitudes, Forster has designated the unintentional monument "the homeless of history, entrusted to public and private guardians." He points out that Riegl's study fundamentally undermines the notion that architectural monuments possess stable meanings (Kurt W. Forster, "Monument/Memory and the Mortality of Architecture," and Alois Riegl, "The Modern Cult of Monuments: Its Character and Its Origins," *Oppositions* 25 [Fall 1982]: 2–19 and 21–51, respectively).

49. For a discussion of urban fiscal crisis and its relation to redevelopment, see "Uneven Development: Public Art in New York City," in this volume.

50. *Union Square: Street Revitalization,* 30.

51. Ibid., 40.

52. William K. Tabb, "The New York City Fiscal Crisis," in *Marxism and the Metropolis: New Perspectives in Urban Political Economy,* ed. William K. Tabb and Larry Sawers (New York: Oxford University Press, 1984), 336.

53. Roger Starr, "Making New York Smaller," *New York Times Sunday Magazine,* 14 November 1976, 105.

54. *Union Square Special Zoning District Proposal,* 2.

55. Ibid., 3.

56. Ibid.

57. Ibid.

58. *Union Square Street Revitalization,* 30.

59. Oscar Newman, *Defensible Space: Crime Prevention through Urban Design* (New York: Collier, 1972).

60. Michel Foucault, *Discipline and Punish: The Birth of the Prison* (New York: Vintage, 1977), 187. Boyer analyzes urban planning as a disciplinary technology in *Dreaming the Rational City.*

61. Newman, *Defensible Space,* 2–3.

62. Ibid., 114.

63. *Union Square Park Phase I,* statement by the design department of the City Park Commission (1986).

64. Quoted in Dierdre Carmody, "New Day is Celebrated for Union Square Park," *New York Times,* April 20, 1984, B3.

65. Edward I. Koch, "The Mugger and His Genes," *Policy Review* 35 (Winter 1986): 87–89. For other reviews by scientists who condemn the authors' methods and conclusions, see Leon J. Kamin, "Books: *Crime and Human Nature,*" *Scientific American* 254 (February 1986): 22–27; and Steven Rose, "Stalking the Criminal Chromosome," *The Nation* 242, May 24, 1986, 732–36.

66. Koch, "The Mugger and His Genes," 89.

67. *Union Square Special Zoning District Proposal,* 23.

68. Friedrich Engels, *The Housing Question* (Moscow: Progress Publishers, 1979), 71. First published as three newspaper articles in *Volksstaat,* Leipzig, Germany, in 1872–73.

69. Ibid., 74.

70. Keith Schneider, "As Night Falls, Crime Moves into Stuyvesant Square," *New York Times,* October 12, 1985, 29.

71. Ibid., 31.

72. Foucault, *Discipline and Punish,* 198.

73. Walter Benjamin, "What is Epic Theater?" in *Illuminations,* trans. Harry Zohn (New York: Schocken, 1969), 150.

74. "Speaking Up for Union Square," *New York Times,* August 16, 1984, A22.

75. Paul Goldberger, "The Statue of Liberty: Transcending the Trivial," *New York Times,* July 17, 1986, C18.

76. Wodiczko, "The Homeless Projection: A Proposal for the City of New York," reprinted in *October* 38 (Fall 1986).

77. Karl Marx, "On the Jewish Question," in *Karl Marx: Early Writings,* trans. Rodney Livingstone and Gregor Benton (New York: Vintage, 1975), 211–41.

78. Ibid., 229.

79. See Claude Lefort, "The Question of Democracy" and "Human Rights and the Welfare State," in *Democracy and Political Theory* (Minneapolis: University of Minnesota, 1988) and idem, "Politics and Human Rights," in *The Political Forms of Modern Society: Bureaucracy, Democracy, Totalitarianism* (Cambridge: MIT Press, 1986). For a more detailed account of Lefort's ideas about democracy and public space, see "Agoraphobia," in this volume.

80. Claude Lefort, "Human Rights and the Welfare State," 23.

81. "Glossary: Selected planning terms applicable to New York City real estate development," *New York Affairs* 8, no. 4 (1985): 15.

82. Kwartler, "Zoning as Architect and Urban Designer," 115.

83. Ibid., 113.

84. *Union Square Special Zoning District Proposal*, 1.

85. Ibid., 6.

86. Quoted in Lee A. Daniels, "A Plan to Revitalize Union Square," *New York Times*, July 1, 1984, 6R.

87. "Speaking Up for Union Square," A22.

88. "Glossary," 13.

89. New York State Department of Social Services, *Homelessness in New York State: A Report to the Governor and the Legislature* (October 1984), 3.

90. See the statement of Nancy E. Biberman, director, Eastside Legal Services Project, MFY Legal Services, Inc., to the City Planning Commission, October 17, 1984.

91. Ellen Baxter and Kim Hopper, *Private Lives/Public Spaces: Homeless Adults on the Streets of New York* (New York: Community Services Society, Institute for Social Welfare Research, 1981): 8–9, cited in Michael H. Schill and Richard P. Nathan, *Revitalizing America's Cities* (Albany: State University of New York Press, 1983), 170, note 120. Schill and Nathan quote Baxter and Hopper's statement only to discount it and to justify government policies that encourage redevelopment. *Revitalizing America's Cities* concludes that the displacement resulting from these policies does not justify stopping redevelopment. The authors' credibility is compromised by the fact that their methodology included "an effort . . . to avoid neighborhoods that contained high

concentrations of SROs or transient accommodations" and that "the survey of outmovers does not describe the rate of displacement among the most transient households or examine the problems faced by the homeless," 67.

92. *Homelessness in New York State,* 33.

93. Nancy Biberman, a lawyer from MFY Legal Services who at the time this essay was first written was doing private housing consulting, represented the tenants of 1 Irving Place. She was able to obtain a good settlement for the potential victims of direct displacement. Since Zeckendorf was eager to begin construction before December 1985 in order to be eligible for 421-a tax abatements and since legal problems could have held him up past the deadlines, he was pressured into offering these tenants the option of living in the Zeckendorf Towers themselves at the price of the tenants' old rents. For the victims of secondary displacement, Zeckendorf assumed little responsibility. He was required only to purchase and renovate forty-eight units of SRO housing.

94. Ernest Mandel, *Late Capitalism* (London: Verso, 1975), 509.

UNEVEN DEVELOPMENT: PUBLIC ART IN NEW YORK CITY

1. Peter Marcuse, "Neutralizing Homelessness," *Socialist Review* 18, no. 1 (January/March 1988): 83. Marcuse's premise—that the sight of homeless people is shocking to viewers but that this initial shock is subsequently counteracted or neutralized by ideological portrayals—implies that viewers' responses to the presence of homeless people in New York today are direct and natural. It thus fails to acknowledge that current experience of beggars and "vagrants" by housed city residents is always mediated by existing representations, including the naming of such people as "the homeless" in the first place. The form and iconography of such representations not only produce complex, even contradictory, meanings about the homeless—the object of the representation—but also, in setting up the homeless as an image, construct positions in social relations. It is important to question these relationships as well as the content of representations of the homeless. Despite Marcuse's ingenuous approach to the issue of representation, his description of official attempts to neutralize the effects of homelessness and his effective efforts to contest these neutralizations are extremely useful. This is especially true now, as, encouraged by the final years of the Koch administration, the media seem determined to depict homeless people as predators, to encourage New Yorkers to refuse donations to street beggars, and to create the impression that adequate city services exist to serve the needs of the poor and homeless.

2. *New York Ascendant: The Report of the Commission on the Year 2000* (New York: Harper and Row, 1988), 167.

3. David W. Dunlap, "Koch, the 'Entertainer,' Gets Mixed Review," *New York Times,* May 19, 1988, B4.

4. Raymond Ledrut, "Speech and the Silence of the City," in M. Gottdeiner and Alexandros Ph. Lagopoulos, ed., *The City and the Sign: An Introduction to Urban Semiotics* (New York: Columbia University Press, 1986), 122.

5. Henri Lefebvre, "Space: Social Product and Use Value," in J. W. Freiberg, ed., *Critical Sociology: European Perspectives* (New York: Irvington Publishers, 1979), 293.

6. Manuel Castells, *The City and the Grassroots: A Cross-Cultural Theory of Urban Social Movements* (Berkeley: University of California Press, 1983), 302.

7. For a more complete definition of "exclusionary displacement," see Peter Marcuse, "Abandonment, Gentrification, and Displacement: The Linkages in New York City," in Neil Smith and Peter Williams, eds., *Gentrification of the City* (Boston: Allen & Unwin, 1986), 153–77.

8. Attila Kotanyi and Raoul Veneigem, "Elementary Program of the Bureau of Unitary Urbanism," in Ken Knabb, ed., *Situationist International Anthology* (Berkeley: Bureau of Public Secrets, 1981), 65.

9. Ibid.

10. Neil Smith, *Uneven Development: Nature, Capital and the Production of Space* (Oxford: Basil Blackwell, 1984), 54.

11. Jean Baudrillard, "The Ideological Genesis of Needs," in *For a Critique of the Political Economy of the Sign* (Saint Louis: Telos Press, 1981), 86.

12. Ibid.

13. "Remarks by Mayor Edward I. Koch at Awards Luncheon of the American Institute of Architects," May 18, 1988, 7.

14. For a discussion of one example of this process, see "Krzysztof Wodiczko's *Homeless Projection* and the Site of Urban 'Revitalization,'" in this volume.

15. Alexander Kluge, "On Film and the Public Sphere," *New German Critique,* nos. 24–25 (Fall/Winter 1981–82): 212.

16. An especially patronizing depiction of the public as consumers of mass spectacle appeared in a 1980 *New York Times* editorial about New York's public spaces. "New Yorkers," the editorial

began, "love parades, festivals, celebrations, demonstrations and entertainments, particularly when such occasions bring large numbers of them together outdoors." The conflation of political demonstrations (rallies in Union Square were cited as a historical example) and patriotic celebrations (the 1976 bicentennial celebration, for one) and the reduction of both to an opportunity to enjoy the weather ("The finer the weather, the greater the urge to gather, the sweeter the siren call of causes") support the use of public funds and land to create public parks for a luxury redevelopment project—Battery Park City. Needless to say, by the end of the editorial any reference to political demonstrations had been dropped. "What better place for New Yorkers to do their public thing?" the editorial concludes ("A Public Plaza for New York," *New York Times,* June 16, 1980, A22).

17. Craig Owens, "The Yen for Art," contribution to a discussion entitled "The Birth and Death of the Viewer: On the Public Function of Art," in Hal Foster, ed., *Discussions in Contemporary Culture* (Seattle: Bay Press, 1987), 18.

18. Ibid., 23.

19. For a discussion of the concept of "the urban" that informs art history, see "Representing Berlin," in this volume, and my essay "Alternative Space," in Brian Wallis, ed., *If You Lived Here: The City in Art, Theory, and Social Activism: A Project by Martha Rosler* (Seattle: Bay Press, 1991), 45–66.

20. Douglas Crimp, "Serra's Public Sculpture: Redefining Site Specificity," in Rosalind Krauss, *Richard Serra: Sculpture* (New York: Museum of Modern Art, 1986), 53.

21. Ibid., 53–55.

22. For a lengthier account of the controversy about *Tilted Arc* and the rhetoric of "use" that pervaded the debate about the sculpture, see *"Tilted Arc* and the Uses of Democracy," in this volume.

23. Raymond Ledrut, *Les images de la ville* (Paris: Anthropos, 1973), 28.

24. Eric Gibson, "Public Art and the Public Realm," *Sculpture* 7 (January/February 1988): 32.

25. Douglas C. McGill, "Sculpture Goes Public," *New York Times Magazine,* April 27, 1986, 45.

26. Nancy Princenthal, "On the Waterfront: South Cove Project at Battery Park City," *Village Voice,* June 7, 1988, 99.

27. Nancy Holt, as quoted in McGill, "Sculpture Goes Public."

28. Robert Jensen, "Commentary," in *Architectural Art: Affirming the Design Relationship* (New York: American Craft Museum, 1988), 3.

29. See Gibson, "Public Art and the Public Realm."

30. Kate Linker, "Public Sculpture: The Pursuit of the Pleasurable and the Profitable Paradise," *Artforum* 19 (March 1981): 66. Linker acknowledges the function of the new public art in raising the economic value of its sites, but perhaps because the article was written early in the contemporary redevelopment process, it remains uncritical and fails to address the social consequences of this economic function.

31. As quoted in McGill, "Sculpture Goes Public," 63.

32. Ibid., 67.

33. As quoted in Princenthal, "Social Seating," *Art in America* 75 (June 1987): 131.

34. Ibid.

35. McGill, "Sculpture Goes Public," 66.

36. Diane Shamash, "The A Team, Artists and Architects: Can They Work Together?" *Stroll: The Magazine of Outdoor Art and Street Culture,* nos. 6–7 (June 1988): 60.

37. John Beardsley, *Art in Public Places: A Survey of Community-Sponsored Art Projects Supported by the National Endowment for the Arts* (Washington, D.C.: Partners for Livable Places, 1981), 81.

38. Michael Brenson, "Outdoor Sculptures Reflect Struggles of Life in the City," *New York Times,* July 15, 1988, C1, C28.

39. Beardsley, *Art in Public Places,* 90.

40. Kay Larson, "Combat Zone," *New York* (May 13, 1985): 118.

41. Neil Smith, "Gentrification, the Frontier, and the Restructuring of Urban Space," in *Gentrification of the City,* ed. Neil Smith and Peter Williams (Boston: Allen and Unwin, 1986), 18–19.

42. Jonathan Barnett, *An Introduction to Urban Design* (New York: Harper & Row), 46.

43. For critiques of traditional urban studies see, among others, Manuel Castells, *The Urban Question: A Marxist Approach* (Cambridge: MIT Press, 1977); M. Gottdeiner, *The Social Production of Urban Space* (Austin: University of Texas Press, 1985); Peter Saunders, *Social Theory and the Urban*

Question (London: Hutchinson, 1981); Edward W. Soja, "The Spatiality of Social Life: Towards a Transformative Retheorisation," in *Social Relations and Spatial Structures,* ed. Derek Gregory and John Urry (New York: St. Martin's Press, 1985), 90–127.

44. Gottdeiner, *The Social Production of Urban Space,* 264.

45. For a more detailed discussion of urban ecology and its parallels with treatments of the city in aesthetic discourse, see "Representing Berlin," in this volume.

46. Smith, *Uneven Development,* 77.

47. Summaries of these debates and histories of spatial theories are included in Gottdeiner, *The Social Production of Space;* Edward W. Soja, "The Socio-Spatial Dialectic," *Annals of the Association of American Geographers* 70 (1980): 207–25; Saunders, *Social Theory and the Urban Question.*

48. Lefebvre, "Space: Social Product and Use Value," 285.

49. Ibid., 286.

50. For a discussion of the international urban hierarchy, see R. B. Cohen, "The New International Division of Labor, Multinational Corporations and Urban Hierarchy," in Michael Dear and Allen J. Scott, eds., *Urbanization and Urban Planning in Capitalist Society* (London: Methuen, 1981), 287–315.

51. Smith, *Uneven Development,* xi.

52. Ernest Mandel, *Late Capitalism* (London: Verso, 1975), 102.

53. For explanations of the "rent gap," see Neil Smith and Michele LeFaivre, "A Class Analysis of Gentrification," in J. John Palen and Bruce London, eds., *Gentrification, Displacement and Neighborhood Revitalization* (Albany: State University of New York Press, 1984), 43–63; and Smith, "Gentrification, the Frontier, and the Restructuring of Urban Space."

54. Lefebvre, "Space: Social Product and Use Value," 286.

55. Ibid., 290.

56. Henri Lefebvre, *The Production of Space,* trans. Donald Nicholson-Smith (Oxford: Blackwell, 1991), 373. Originally published as *La production de l'espace* (Paris: Anthropos, 1974).

57. Henri Lefebvre, *Le droit à la ville* (Paris: Anthropos, 1968).

58. Manuel Castells, "From Urban Society to Urban Revolution," in *The Urban Question*, 86–95.

59. Michel de Certeau, *The Practice of Everyday Life* (Berkeley: University of California Press, 1984).

60. Lefebvre, *La production de l'espace*, 420. Translated in Gottdeiner, "Culture, Ideology, and the Sign of the City," in *The City and the Sign*, 215.

61. Soja, "The Spatiality of Social Life: Towards a Transformative Retheorisation," 90–127.

62. Walter Benjamin, "Theses on the Philosophy of History," in *Illuminations*, trans. Harry Zohn (New York: Schocken, 1969), 257.

63. Claudia Gould, "Mary Miss Covers the Waterfront," *Stroll: The Magazine of Outdoor Art and Street Culture*, nos. 4–5 (October 1987): 55.

64. Robin Karson, "Battery Park City: South Cove," *Landscape Architecture* (May/June 1988), 50–52.

65. Albert Scarino, "Big Battery Park City Dreams," *New York Times*, December 1, 1986, D1.

66. Nancy Princenthal, "On the Waterfront," *Art in America* 75 (April 1987): 239.

67. John Russell, "Where City Meets Sea To Become Art," *New York Times*, December 11, 1983, sec. 2, p. 1.

68. Ibid., p. 31.

69. Ibid.

70. Winston Williams, "Finally, the Debut of Wall Street West," *New York Times*, August 25, 1985, sec. 3, p. 1.

71. Paul Goldberger, "Public Space Gets a New Cachet in New York," *New York Times*, May 22 1988, H35.

72. Paul Goldberger, "Battery Park City is a Triumph of Urban Design," *New York Times*, August 31, 1986, H1.

73. Meyer S. Frucher, as quoted in Martin Gottlieb, "Battery Project Reflects Changing City Priorities," *New York Times*, October 18, 1985, B1. Gottlieb's article is the only account in the

Times's extensive coverage of all aspects of Battery Park City's current state that raises critical questions about the project's social history and conditions.

74. Michael deCourcy Hinds, "Vast Project Heads for '93 Finish," *New York Times*, March 23, 1986, R18.

75. As quoted in Gottlieb, "Battery Project Reflects Changing City Priorities," B2.

76. Ada Louise Huxtable, "Plan's 'Total' Concept is Hailed," *New York Times*, April 17, 1969, 49.

77. Alexander Cooper Associates, *Battery Park City: Draft Summary Report and 1979 Master Plan* (1979), 67.

78. Huxtable, "Plan's 'Total' Concept is Hailed," 49.

79. Maynard T. Robison, "Vacant Ninety Acres, Well Located, River View," in Vernon Boggs et al., eds., *The Apple Sliced: Sociological Studies of New York City* (South Hadley, Mass.: Bergin and Garvey Publishers, 1984), 180.

80. David K. Shipler, "Battery Park Plan Is Shown," *New York Times*, April 17, 1969, 49.

81. Ibid.

82. Ibid.

83. David K. Shipler, "Lindsay Will Get Housing Demands," *New York Times*, April 17, 1969, 49.

84. Robison, "Vacant Ninety Acres," 189.

85. Shipler, "Battery Park Plan Is Shown," *New York Times*, April 17, 1969, 49.

86. David K. Shipler, "Lindsay Reverses Stand on Housing," *New York Times*, August 15, 1969, 33.

87. Ibid.

88. "Battery Park City Is Given Approval," *New York Times*, October 10, 1969, 55.

89. "Amendments to the Master Lease," Battery Park City Annual Report (1972).

90. Ibid.

91. Ibid.

92. Robison, "Vacant Ninety Acres," 183.

93. Ibid., 192.

94. Edward Schumacher, "13 Years Later, Battery Park City's an Empty Dream," *New York Times,* October 26, 1979, B3.

95. Ada Louise Huxtable, "Is This the Last Chance for Battery Park City," *New York Times,* December 9, 1979, sec. 2, p. 39.

96. For critical analyses of urban fiscal crisis, see William K. Tabb, *The Long Default: New York City and the Urban Fiscal Crisis* (New York: Monthly Review Press, 1982); Eric Lichten, *Class, Power and Austerity: The New York City Fiscal Crisis* (South Hadley, Mass.: Bergin & Garvey Publishers, 1986); Michael D. Kennedy, "The Fiscal Crisis of the City," in *Cities in Transformation: Class Capital and the State,* ed. Michael Peter Smith (Beverly Hills: Sage Publications, 1984), 91–110; John Shutt, "Rescuing New York City, 1975–78," in *Urban Political Economy and Social Theory: Critical Essays in Urban Studies,* ed. Ray Forrest, Jeff Henderson, and Peter Williams (Hampshire, England: Gower Publishing, 1982), 51–77; Manuel Castells, *City, Class, and Power* (New York: St. Martin's Press, 1972); M. Gottdiener, "Retrospect and Prospect in Urban Crisis Theory," in *Cities in Stress: A New Look at the Urban Crisis,* ed. M. Gottdiener (Beverly Hills: Sage Publications, 1986), 277–91.

97. Peter Marcuse, "The Targeted Crisis: On the Ideology of the Urban Fiscal Crisis and Its Uses," *International Journal of Urban and Regional Research* 5 (September 1981): 330–55.

98. "Last Chance for Battery Park City," editorial, *New York Times,* November 17, 1979.

99. Richard J. Meislin, "Attempt to Revive Battery Park Plan is Readied by Carey," *New York Times,* October 28, 1979, 1.

100. Ibid.

101. Annmarie Hauck Walsh, *The Public's Business: The Politics and Practices of Government Corporations,* A Twentieth Century Fund Study (Cambridge: MIT Press, 1978), 4.

102. Michael Goodwin, "Construction of Battery Park City is Now Scheduled to Begin in June," *New York Times,* May 16, 1980, B4.

103. Alan S. Oser, "Battery Park City: The Newest Prestige Address," *New York Times,* April 18, 1982, sec. 8, p. 7.

104. Ibid.

105. Alexander Cooper Associates, *Battery Park City: Draft Summary Report and 1979 Master Plan.*

106. David K. Shipler, "Battery Park City Plans Scored and Praised at Public Hearing," *New York Times,* November 9, 1969, B4.

107. *Battery Park City,* leaflet distributed by Battery Park City Authority.

108. Paul Goldberger, "A Realist's Battery Park City," *New York Times,* November 9, 1979, B4.

109. "Esplanade Recalls Old New York," *New York Times,* July 3, 1986, C3.

110. For an analysis of the discourse of "preservation" used in New York redevelopment, see my "Architecture of the Evicted," *Strategies,* no. 3 (1990): 159–83.

111. Alexander Cooper Associates, *Battery Park City: Draft and Summary Report and 1979 Master Plan,* 18.

112. Ibid.

113. Brian Sullivan, Pratt Center for Community and Environmental Development, as quoted in Gottlieb, "Battery Park Project Reflects Changing City Priorities," B2.

114. Gould, "Mary Miss Covers the Waterfront," 54.

115. Roland Barthes, "The Great Family of Man," in *Mythologies* (New York: Hill and Wang, 1972), 101.

116. Ibid., 102.

117. "A Public Plaza for New York," *New York Times,* June 16, 1980, A22.

118. David V. Lurie and Krzysztof Wodiczko, *Homeless Vehicle Project,* installation (New York: The Clocktower, January 1988). This installation is documented in *October* 47 (Winter 1988): 53–76.

119. The *Homeless Vehicle Project* builds on and revises the strategies of Wodiczko's earlier public projects about homelessness in New York City, such as *The Homeless Projection: A Proposal for the City of New York* (1986), discussed in "Krzysztof Wodiczko's *Homeless Projection* and the Site of Urban 'Revitalization,'" in this volume. In these earlier works, which also include *The New Museum/Astor Building Projection* (1984) and *The Real-Estate Projection* (1988), Wodiczko projected

slide images onto the surfaces of individual buildings and monuments located in Lower Manhattan neighborhoods that had been slated for redevelopment, infiltrating these architectural structures with images that reveal the repressed social conflicts and effects of redevelopment. Like the slide projections, the *Homeless Vehicle* symbolically disrupts the city's architecture, but the *Homeless Vehicle*'s mobility extends the work's target to urban space as a whole, defining architecture as the construction of the city. Just as *The Homeless Projection* challenged the meanings that were being projected *onto* the statues in Union Square Park during the area's gentrification and countered the meanings projected *by* the statues, the *Homeless Vehicle* challenged the meanings projected onto urban space by real estate and state aesthetics and countered the meanings projected by the redeveloped spaces themselves.

As a description of Wodiczko's activity, the word *projection* refers, of course, to exhibiting slides on a screen—in Wodiczko's case, on the surfaces of buildings, monuments, or spaces—but "projection" has multiple definitions and denotes more than a technical mechanism. It is also a symbolic operation whereby concepts are visualized as external realities, and it is a rhetorical device for speaking with clarity at a distance. In these senses, "projection" refers to the procedural dimension of language. Indeed, Wodiczko treats architecture as itself a projection. The impact of his work depends on the degree to which it mobilizes in its audience an awareness that the architecture onto which it projects images is not merely a group of beautiful or functional objects. Rather, Wodiczko treats these objects as speech acts—one might say performers—transmitting messages about the meaning of the city. He challenges the rhetoric of these architectural images, the tactics whereby they impose their messages on spectators. To be effective against dominant architecture Wodiczko's projections must disengage viewers from habitual modes of perceiving and inhabiting the city, of receiving its messages. Calling attention to and manipulating architectural language, Wodiczko's works disrupt the city's speech. But they do not only interfere with the conscious perceptions of sociologically constituted spectators; they also subvert the fantasy projections of viewing subjects who, through modes of identification solicited by traditional architecture, seek an imaginary self-coherence by looking at images of a city apparently free of social division. In multiple ways, then, Wodiczko's works are projections onto projections.

The *Homeless Vehicle Project* expanded the artist's earlier projection techniques in order to confront a situation in which redevelopment threatened to occupy space entirely. The *Homeless Vehicle* treated the spatial organization of the city as itself a monument, if, to borrow a term from Alois Riegl, an "unintentional" one. (Alois Riegl, "The Modern Cult of Monuments: Its Character and Its Origin," trans. Kurt W. Forster and Diane Ghirardo, *Oppositions* [Fall 1982]: 21–51.) A landmark of history, New York's spatial design is a memorial to urban events. With redevelopment, it became a monument to the eviction of city residents. Like individual "intentional" monuments, such as the Union Square statues, the city's official spatial organization tries to project an image of the city as a stable entity. To do so, however, it must suppress conflicts and relegate whole social groups to oblivion. The architecture of redevelopment is truly an evicting architecture, commemorating the city's spatial violence. Applying architectural principles to an object designed to support the activities of the evicted, the *Homeless Vehicle Project* projected onto the city the condition of a monument and, like Wodiczko's other New York works, projected onto this monument the city's social contradictions.

For a discussion of the relationship between the *Homeless Vehicle Project* and Wodiczko's other New York works about homelessness and real estate, the multiple meanings of the term *projection,* and the ideology of historic preservation, see my "Architecture of the Evicted," *Strategies* 3 (1990): 159–83.

120. Theresa Funiciello, reply to letters, *The Nation* (June 18, 1988): 876.

121. "Homeless at Home" (New York: Storefront for Art and Architecture, 1986).

122. David V. Lurie and Krzysztof Wodiczko, "Homeless Vehicle Project," *October* 47 (Winter 1988): 61.

123. Henri Lefebvre, "The Everyday and Everydayness," *Yale French Studies,* no. 73 (1988): 11. Translation by Christine Levich, Alice Kaplan, and Kristin Ross of "Quotidien et Quotidienneté," *Encyclopaedia Universalis.*

REPRESENTING BERLIN

1. "German Art in the 20th Century, Painting and Sculpture 1905–1985," organized by Christos M. Joachimides, Norman Rosenthal, and Wieland Schmied (London: Royal Academy of Arts, 1985).

2. Richard Hülsenbeck, "Dada Forward," (1920–21), in Lucy Lippard, ed., *Dadas on Art,* (Englewood Cliffs, N.J.: Prentice-Hall, 1971), 45–54.

3. Raoul Hausmann, "New Painting and Photomontage," in *Dadas on Art,* 60.

4. Ibid., 61.

5. Christos M. Joachimides, "A Gash of Fire Across the World," in *German Art in the 20th Century: Painting and Sculpture 1905–1985,* 11.

6. In the early 1980s several critics suggested that the term *neoexpressionism* is a misnomer and should be replaced by *pseudoexpressionism.* Craig Owens, for example, wrote: "In 'Neo-

expressionism,' however—but this is why this designation must be rejected—Expressionism is reduced to convention, to a standard repertoire of abstract, strictly codified signs for expression. Everything is bracketed in quotation marks; as a result, what was (supposedly) spontaneous congeals into a signified: 'spontaneity,' 'immediacy'. . . . The pseudo-Expressionists retreat to the pre-Expressionist simulation of passion; they create illusions of spontaneity and immediacy, or rather expose the spontaneity and immediacy sought by the Expressionists as illusions, as a construct of preexisting forms." Craig Owens, "Honor, Power and the Love of Women," *Art in America* 71 (January 1983): 9–10.

7. The emblematic status of Rainer Fetting's many versions of *Van Gogh and the Wall* became a cliché in articles on Berlin's "violent painters." See, for example, Ernst Busche, "Van Gogh an der Mauer: Die neue Malerei in Berlin—Tradition und Gegenwart," *Kunstforum* (December 1981/January 1982): 108–16.

8. Quoted from an interview with Helke Sander by Ulla Ziemann in *Berlin: A Critical View. Ugly Realism 20s–70s,* exhib. cat. (London: Institute of Contemporary Arts, 1978), 174.

9. When this essay was first written, the Museum of Modern Art in New York City was preparing the exhibition "Berlinart," which opened in 1987. The exhibition's emphasis on establishing a relationship between expressionism and Berlin, its exclusion of artists such as Hans Haacke (despite the inclusion of the work of nonresident artists working in Berlin), and its mythologization of the urban social conditions of West Berlin confirm the conclusions drawn in this essay. "Berlinart" complemented and extended the thesis of "German Art in the Twentieth Century," emphasizing the painting of younger neoexpressionists not included in (although valorized by) the Royal Academy show because, according to Joachimides, the contemporaneity of their production precluded the possibility of "a comprehensive assessment."

10. Nicholas Serota, "Culture is not made by the Ministries of Culture," in *13° E: Eleven Artists Working in Berlin* exhib. cat. (London: Whitechapel Art Gallery, 1979), 5.

11. Ibid.

12. Hans Haacke, catalogue text accompanying *Solomon R. Guggenheim Museum Board of Trustees* in *Art into Society—Society into Art: Seven German Artists* (London: Institute of Contemporary Arts, 1974), 63.

13. Serota, "Culture is not made by the Ministries of Culture," 5.

14. Ibid.

15. Christos M. Joachimides, "Achilles and Hector before the Walls of Troy," in Joachimides and Norman Rosenthal, eds., *Zeitgeist* (New York: George Braziller, 1983), 10.

16. Ibid.

17. Wolfgang Max Faust, "Zeitgest-Fragen: Ein Interview mit Christos M. Joachimides," *Kunstforum* 56 (December 1982): 25.

18. Benjamin H. D. Buchloh, "Formalism and historicity—changing concepts in American and European art since 1945," in *Europe in the Seventies: Aspects of Recent Art,* exhib. cat. (Chicago: Art Institute of Chicago, 1977).

19. Ibid.

20. Busche, "Van Gogh an der Mauer," 109.

21. Erika Billeter, "Kreuzberg—das Soho von Berlin," *DU* 1 (1983): 23.

22. Burton Pike, *The Image of the City in Modern Literature* (Princeton: Princeton University Press, 1981), 14.

23. An important exception to art history's superficial treatment of city paintings is T. J. Clark's, *The Painting of Modern Life: Paris in the Art of Manet and His Followers* (New York: Alfred A. Knopf, 1986), published after this essay was first written. Clark's study of the image of Paris in nineteenth-century French modernist painting is the most sophisticated art-historical analysis of the modern city from a Marxist perspective. Its description of the Haussmannization of Paris is masterful. Marxist social art history differs from mainstream social art history by virtue of both its critical theory of society and its political analysis of culture. In Marxist discussions of city paintings, the paintings' subject matter—the city—is inseparable from capitalist social relations, and the paintings are often interpreted as a form of ideology. So far, however, Marxist accounts of art and the city have remained grounded in traditional ideas of social totality. They treat economic relations as the origin and governing factor of all social meaning, both urban and aesthetic. In this way, they replace mainstream social art history's separation of art and the city with a predetermined reduction of both to the economic level. Consequently, images of the city emerge as epiphenomena—no matter how elaborately mediated—of a more fundamental social realm. These interpretations thus trivialize the sociospatial relations of images and vision themselves. And, adopting a unitarian epistemology that allows only a single starting point of social analysis, they treat the relationship between urban space and sexuality or gender as subordinate social issues, tending, moreover, to disregard feminist social theories. See Griselda Pollock's important feminist response

to Clark, "Modernity and the Spaces of Femininity," in Pollock, *Vision and Difference: Femininity, Feminism and the Histories of Art* (London: Routledge, 1988). See also "Men in Space," in this volume, where I argue that the failure of Marxist historians of city paintings to consider the social relations of visual space is intimately related to their neglect of feminist thought, since feminism has developed a critique of the sexual politics of images.

24. Theda Shapiro, "The Metropolis in the Visual Arts, 1890–1940," in Anthony Sutcliffe, ed., *Metropolis 1890–1940* (Chicago: The University of Chicago Press, 1984), 95.

25. Manuel Castells, *The Urban Question* (Cambridge: MIT Press, 1977), 73.

26. Manfredo Tafuri, *Architecture and Utopia: Design and Capitalist Development* (Cambridge: MIT Press, 1976).

27. Walter Benjamin, "On Some Motifs in Baudelaire," in *Illuminations,* ed. Hannah Arendt, trans. Harry Zohn (New York: Schocken Books, 1955), 155–200.

28. Tafuri, 81.

29. Ibid., 84.

30. Ibid., 89.

31. Ibid., 86.

32. Eberhard Roters, "Big-City Expressionism: Berlin and German Expressionism," in *Expressionism: A German Intuition 1905–1920* (New York and San Francisco: Solomon R. Guggenheim Museum and San Francisco Museum of Modern Art, 1980), 238–51.

33. Eberhard Roters, *Berlin, 1910–1933* (New York: Rizzoli, 1982), 56.

34. Ibid.

35. Georg Simmel, "The Metropolis and Mental Life," in *The Sociology of Georg Simmel,* ed. and trans. Kurt H. Wolff (New York: The Free Press, 1950), 409–24.

36. Donald E. Gordon, *Ernst Ludwig Kirchner* (Cambridge: Harvard University Press, 1968), 86.

37. For a discussion of the urban problem that elevates this presupposition to the status of an unconditional fact, see Donald B. Kuspit, "Individual and Mass Identity in Urban Art: The New York Case," *Art in America* 65, no. 5 (September–October 1977): 66–77.

38. Ian Jeffrey, "Concerning Images of the Metropolis," in *Cityscape 1910–39: Urban themes in American, German and British Art* (London: Arts Council of Great Britain, 1977).

39. Ibid.

40. Ibid.

41. Ibid.

42. Simmel, "The Metropolis and Mental Life," 413.

43. Ibid., 414.

44. Ibid., 415.

45. Louis Wirth, "A Bibliography of the Urban Community," in Robert E. Park and Ernest W. Burgess, eds., *The City: Suggestions for Investigation of Human Behavior in the Urban Environment* (Chicago: The University of Chicago Press, 1967; Midway reprint ed., Chicago: The University of Chicago, 1925), 219.

46. Writings of the Chicago School are collected in Richard Sennett, ed., *Classic Essays on the Culture of Cities* (Englewood Cliffs, N.J.: Prentice-Hall, 1969) and Park and Burgess, eds., *The City: Suggestions for Investigation of Human Behavior in the Urban Environment*. Critical histories of urban ecology can be found in Peter Saunders, *Social Theory and the Urban Question* (London: Hutchinson, 1981) and M. Gottdiener, *The Social Production of Urban Space* (Austin: University of Texas Press, 1985).

47. Robert E. Park, "The City: Suggestions for the Investigation of Human Behavior in the Urban Environment," in Park and Burgess, eds., *The City: Suggestions for the Investigation of Human Behavior in the Urban Environment*, 1.

48. See R. D. McKenzie, "The Ecological Approach to the Study of the Human Community," in Park and Burgess, eds., *The City: Suggestions for the Investigation of Human Behavior in the Urban Environment*, 63–79.

49. For an analysis of the role played by urban ecology in naturalizing the contemporary spatial organization of New York, part of an extensive cultural critique of biological determinism, see Andrew Ross, "Bombing the Big Apple," in *The Chicago Gangster Theory of Life: Nature's Debt to Society* (London: Verso, 1994), 99–158.

50. McKenzie, "The Ecological Approach," 64.

51. Louis Wirth, "Urbanism as a Way of Life," in Sennett, ed., *Classic Essays on the Culture of Cities,* 148.

52. Saunders, *Social Theory and the Urban Question,* 92.

53. For a critique of art-historical interpretations of Kirchner's Berlin paintings, see Rosalyn Deutsche, "Alienation in Berlin: Kirchner's Street Scenes," *Art in America* 71, no. 1 (January 1983): 64–72.

54. Henri Lefebvre, *The Production of Space,* trans. Donald Nicholson-Smith (Oxford: Blackwell, 1991), 92.

55. For a more detailed account of these new theories of space, see "Uneven Development: Public Art in New York City," in this volume.

56. David Harvey, "Revolutionary and Counter-revolutionary Theory in Geography and the Problem of Ghetto Formation," in *Social Justice and the City* (Baltimore: The Johns Hopkins University Press, 1973), 120–52. For an analysis of how Harvey and other neo-Marxist geographers have repeated at another level the essentializing move they criticize, see "Boys Town," in this volume.

57. Ibid., 137.

58. Castells, *The Urban Question,* 83.

59. Ibid., 73.

60. Ibid., 85.

61. For a discussion of the parallels between politicized art and urban discourses, see "Uneven Development: Public Art in New York City," in this volume.

62. Harry Zellweger, "Im Westen nichts Neues," *Kunstwerk* 35, no. 1 (1982): 28.

63. "Berlin über alles," *Connaissance des arts,* no. 372 (February 1983): 15.

64. Helmut Middendorf, "Interview with Wolfgang Max Faust," *Flash Art* (Summer 1984): 36.

65. Donald B. Kuspit, "Flak from the 'Radicals': The American Case Against Current German Painting," in Jack Cowart, ed., *Expressions: New Art from Germany,* exhib. cat. (St. Louis and Munich: Saint Louis Art Museum and Prestel-Verlag, 1983), 43–55.

66. Theodor W. Adorno, "What does Coming to Terms with the Past Mean?" in Geoffrey H. Hartman, ed., *Bitburg in Moral and Political Perspective,* trans. Geoffrey H. Hartman (Bloomington: Indiana University Press, 1986), 114–29.

67. Gertrud Koch, "Torments of the Flesh, Coldness of the Spirit: Jewish Figures in the Films of Rainer Werner Fassbinder," *New German Critique* 38 (Spring–Summer 1986): 30–31.

68. Adorno, "What Does Coming to Terms with the Past Mean?" 124.

69. Billeter, "Kreuzberg—das Soho von Berlin," 23.

70. Other articles that describe Kreuzberg in similar terms include: Ursula Prinza, "Einführung," in *Gefühl & Härte: Neue Kunst aus Berlin,* exhib. cat. (Munich: Kunstverein München, 1982); Harry Zellweger, "'Im Westen nichts Neues,'" *Kunstwerk* 35, no. 1 (1982): 27–28; Armin Wildermuth, "City of the Red Nights: Helmut Middendorf's nächtliche Grosstadtbilder," *DU* 3 (1983): 84–85; Johannes Halder, "Helmut Middendorf 'Die Umarmung der Nacht,'" *Kunstwerk* 36 (September 1983): 169–70; John Russell, "The New European Painters," *The New York Times Magazine* (April 24, 1983): 42.

71. Wolfgang Max Faust, "'Du hast keine Chance. Nuze sie!' With It and Against It: Tendencies in Recent German Art," *Artforum* 20 (September 1981): 36.

72. For a history of the European guest-worker system, see Stephen Castles (with Heather Booth and Tina Wallace), *Here for Good: Western Europe's new ethnic minorities* (London: Pluto Press, 1984).

73. Armin Wildermuth, "The Crisis of Interpretation," *Flash Art* 116 (March 1984): 8–18.

74. Ernst Busche, "Van Gogh an der Mauer: Die neue Malerei in Berlin—Tradition und Gegenwart," *Kunstforum* 47 (December 1981/January 1982): 108.

75. Cleve Gray, "Report from Berlin: Wall Painters," *Art in America* 73, no. 10 (October 1985): 39–43.

76. Robert Storr, "'Tilted Arc': Enemy of the People?" *Art in America* 73, no. 9 (September 1985): 97. Clara Weyergraf-Serra later refuted Storr's assertion of the political effectiveness of Borofsky's work, citing in particular Borofsky's painting on the Berlin Wall. See "Letter," *Art in America* 73, no. 11 (November 1985): 5.

77. Walter Grasskamp, "An Unpublished Text for an Unpainted Picture," *October* 30 (Fall 1984): 19. *October* 30 is devoted primarily to Haacke's work. The issue contains documentation of *The Broadness and Diversity of the Ludwig Brigade,* Grasskamp's essay on the installation, and "A

Conversation with Hans Haacke," by Yves-Alain Bois, Douglas Crimp, and Rosalind Krauss. The text for *The Ludwig Brigade* is updated in Brian Wallis, ed., *Hans Haacke: Unfinished Business* (New York and Cambridge: New Museum of Contemporary Art and MIT Press, 1986), 266–71.

78. In 1986, after this essay was written, the Leonard Monheim AG was sold to a Swiss corporation. Ludwig retains his interests in the Trumpf and other labels. See Wallis, ed., *Hans Haacke: Unfinished Business*, 226.

79. Ludwig's posture, clothes, and attributes are partially modeled on a 1928 photograph of a confectioner by August Sander.

80. Haacke's painting of Ludwig recalls John Heartfield's photomontage *Mimicry* (1934), which shows Goebbels attaching a fake beard to Hitler so that, transformed into Karl Marx, he will be able to "win over for the regime any workers tending to opposition." Heartfield's photomontage appeared on the cover of the April 19, 1934 issue of *AIZ*.

81. Grasskamp, "An Unpublished Text," 19.

82. Bois et. al., "A Conversation with Hans Haacke," 23.

83. For analyses of the East Village art scene see Craig Owens, "Commentary: The Problem with Puerilism," *Art in America* 72, no. 6 (Summer 1984): 162–63; and Rosalyn Deutsche and Cara Gendel Ryan, "The Fine Art of Gentrification," *October* 31 (Winter 1984): 91–111.

84. For analyses of gentrification see "Krzysztof Wodiczko's *Homeless Projection* and the Site of Urban 'Revitalization'" and "Uneven Development: Public Art in New York City," in this volume.

85. See Deutsche and Ryan, "The Fine Art of Gentrification."

86. Andrea Fraser, "In and Out of Place," *Art in America* 73, no. 6 (June 1985): 125.

87. Craig Owens interprets the East Village art scene as an outpost of the culture industry in "The Problem with Puerilism."

PROPERTY VALUES: HANS HAACKE, REAL ESTATE, AND THE MUSEUM

1. "Hans Haacke: Unfinished Business," organized by Brian Wallis (New York: New Museum of Contemporary Art, 1986–87).

2. Hans Haacke, "Provisorische Bemerkungen zur Absage meiner Ausstellung im Guggenheim Museum, New York," in Edward F. Fry, ed., *Hans Haacke: Werkmonographie* (Cologne: Verlag M. Dumont Schauberg, 1972), 65.

3. Griselda Pollock, "Artists, Mythologies and Media—Genius, Madness and Art History," *Screen* 21, no. 3 (1980): 57–96.

4. For an example of these neutralizing approaches to Haacke's work, see Leo Steinberg, "Some of Hans Haacke's Works Considered as Fine Art," which was included in the catalogue of the New Museum exhibition where my essay also first appeared. See Brian Wallis, ed., *Hans Haacke: Unfinished Business* (New York and Cambridge: New Museum of Contemporary Art and MIT Press, 1986), 8–19.

5. Jeanne Siegel, "An Interview with Hans Haacke," *Arts* 45, no. 7 (May 1971): 19.

6. For an account of the changing political meanings of site-specific art since the mid-1960s, see Douglas Crimp, "Serra's Public Sculpture: Redefining Site Specificity," in Laura Rosenstock, ed., *Richard Serra/Sculpture* (New York: Museum of Modern Art, 1986), 41–56. A history of contemporary art practices that address the site of artistic display is contained in Benjamin H. D. Buchloh, "Allegorical Procedures: Appropriation and Montage in Contemporary Art," *Artforum* 21, no. 1 (September 1982): 43–56.

7. Rosalyn Deutsche and Cara Gendel Ryan, "The Fine Art of Gentrification," *October* 31 (Winter 1984): 91–111.

8. Walter Benjamin, "Paris, Capital of the Nineteenth Century," in *Reflections,* trans. Edmund Jephcott (New York: Harcourt Brace Jovanovich, 1978), 146–62.

9. Thomas M. Messer, letter to Hans Haacke of March 19, 1971, in "Gurgles around the Guggenheim," *Studio International* 181, no. 934 (June 1971): 249.

10. Thomas M. Messer, statement of April 5, 1971, in "Gurgles around the Guggenheim," 249.

11. "Information" (New York: Museum of Modern Art, 1970).

12. Messer, statement of April 5, 1971, 248.

13. Hans Haacke, "Editorial: Artists vs. Museums, Continued," *Art News* 70, no. 5 (September 1971): 21.

14. Allan Sekula, "Dismantling Modernism, Reinventing Documentary (Notes on the Politics of Representation)," in *Photography Against the Grain: Essays and Photo Works 1972–1983* (Halifax: The Press of the Nova Scotia College of Art and Design, 1984), 62.

15. Ibid., 67. On social documentary photography, see also Martha Rosler, "In, Around, and Afterthoughts (On Documentary Photography)," in *Martha Rosler: 3 Works* (Halifax: The Press of the Nova Scotia College of Art and Design, 1981), 59–86.

16. "Ex-Buildings Aid Held in Perjury," *New York Times,* April 24, 1958.

17. Jack Roth, "Shapolsky Found as Rent Gouger," *New York Times,* May 2, 1959.

18. Peter Kihss, "Liability is Fixed in New Slum Bill," *New York Times,* February 10, 1966.

19. Ibid.

20. Ibid.

21. Thomas M. Messer, "Guest Editorial," *Arts* 45, no. 8 (Summer 1971): 5 (My emphasis).

22. Barbara Reise, interview with Thomas M. Messer, "Which is in fact what happened," *Studio International* 182, no. 935 (July–August 1971): 37.

23. These doubts are not allayed by the fact that by 1986 one-third of the Shapolsky properties were owned by the city of New York. Most city-owned residential buildings were acquired through tax-delinquency proceedings. Once the city acquired such buildings, its intervention in the housing market consisted largely throughout the 1980s of selling parcels to private developers. This action helped clear the way for gentrification and the consequent displacement of large numbers of low-income residents in an unprecedented number of New York's neighborhoods. These include the Lower East Side, which has undergone a particularly brutal gentrification. (This information is based on research by Jennifer Freda.)

24. Roth, "Shapolsky Found as Rent Gouger."

25. David Harvey, *Social Justice and the City* (Baltimore: Johns Hopkins University Press, 1973), 171.

26. Messer, "Guest Editorial," 4.

27. Ibid. (My emphasis).

28. Four years after this essay was first written, Haacke did mount a critique of a "particular cigarette brand" (*Helmsboro Country* [New York: John Weber Gallery, 1990]). Messer's assertion that such a show would naturally have "damaging effects" on the purity of art institutions presumes that there is no existing relationship between art and cigarette brands. Haacke's exhibition indicated otherwise, exploring Philip Morris Companies' role as a sponsor of art exhibitions that serve as a smoke screen for its financial interests. Haacke juxtaposed the company's self-image as a promoter of pure artistic expression—which, as Messer had asserted, exerts a "generalized, exemplary force . . . upon the environment"—with, among other things, facts about the health risks posed by cigarettes' pollution of the environment. Haacke's work was prophetic. In 1994 Philip Morris pressured the art organizations it has funded—and from which it derives both tax and public relations benefits—to speak out against proposed legislation to ban smoking in public places in New York.

29. Jeanne Siegel, interview with Hans Haacke, "Leon Golub/Hans Haacke: What Makes Art Political?" *Arts* 58, no. 8 (April 1984): 111.

30. Thomas M. Messer, statement published in *Studio International* 181, no. 934 (June 1971): 250.

31. Messer, "Guest Editorial," 5.

32. Benjamin, "Paris, Capital of the Nineteenth Century," 154.

33. Ibid., 155.

34. "Eventually," wrote Messer, "the choice was between the acceptance or rejection of an alien substance that had entered the art museum organism." Messer, "Guest Editorial," 5.

MEN IN SPACE

1. Edward W. Soja, *Postmodern Geographies: The Reassertion of Space in Critical Social Theory* (London: Verso, 1989); David Harvey, *The Condition of Postmodernity: An Enquiry into the Origins of Cultural Change* (Oxford: Basil Blackwell, 1989).

2. Janet Wolff, "The Invisible *Flâneuse:* Women and the Literature of Modernity," *Theory, Culture and Society* 2, no. 3 (1985): 37.

3. T. J. Clark, *The Painting of Modern Life: Paris in the Art of Manet and His Followers* (New York, Alfred A. Knopf, 1985).

4. Marshall Berman, *All That Is Solid Melts into Air: The Experience of Modernity* (New York: Simon and Schuster, 1982).

5. Clark, *The Painting of Modern Life,* 6–7.

6. Griselda Pollock, *Vision and Difference: Femininity, Feminism and the Histories of Art* (London: Routledge, 1988), 53.

7. Raymond Ledrut, *Les images de la ville* (Paris: Anthropos, 1973), 21; translated in Mark Gott-diener and Alexandros Ph. Lagopoulous, eds., *The City and the Sign: An Introduction to Urban Semiotics* (New York: Columbia University Press, 1986), 223.

8. Fredric Jameson, "Postmodernism, or the Cultural Logic of Late Capitalism," *New Left Review* 146 (July/August 1984): 53–92.

9. Jameson, "Marxism and Postmodernism," *New Left Review* 176 (July/August 1989): 44.

10. Liz Bondi, "On Gender Tourism in the Space Age: A Feminist Response to *Postmodern Geographies,*" paper presented at the annual meeting of the Association of American Geographers Conference, Toronto, 1990.

11. Harvey, *The Condition of Postmodernity,* 116–17, 305.

12. Ibid.

Boys Town

1. David Harvey, *The Condition of Postmodernity: An Enquiry into the Origins of Cultural Change* (Oxford: Basil Blackwell, 1989). Subsequent references to this book appear in parentheses in the text.

2. Giuliana Bruno, "Ramble City: Postmodernism and *Blade Runner,*" *October* 41 (Summer 1987): 72.

3. David Harvey, *The Urban Experience* (Baltimore: Johns Hopkins University Press, 1989), 1.

4. Ibid., 3–4.

5. Ibid., 3.

6. Michel de Certeau, *The Practice of Everyday Life* (Berkeley: University of California Press, 1984), 92.

7. Harvey, *The Urban Experience,* 2.

8. De Certeau, *The Practice of Everyday Life,* 93.

9. Ibid., xxi.

10. Ibid., 92.

11. Ibid., 93.

12. Ibid., 92 (my emphasis).

13. Laura Mulvey, "Visual Pleasure and Narrative Cinema," in *Visual and Other Pleasures* (Bloomington: Indiana University Press, 1989), 16.

14. Harvey, *The Condition of Postmodernity,* 2.

15. Harvey, *The Urban Experience,* 4.

16. Stuart Hall, "The Toad in the Garden: Thatcherism among the Theorists," in *Marxism and the Interpretation of Culture,* ed. Cary Nelson and Lawrence Grossberg (Urbana: University of Illinois Press, 1988), 72.

17. Referring to Stanley Aronowitz's *The Crisis of Historical Materialism,* Harvey writes: "Aronowitz is here *seduced,* I suspect, by the most liberative and therefore most appealing aspect of postmodern thought—its concern with 'otherness'" (47, my emphasis).

18. For a critique of Jameson's use of the psychic as a metaphor for the social, see Jacqueline Rose, "*The Man Who Mistook His Wife for a Hat* or *A Wife Is Like an Umbrella*—Fantasies of the Modern and Postmodern," in Andrew Ross, ed., *Universal Abandon? The Politics of Postmodernism* (Minneapolis: University of Minnesota Press, 1988), 237–50.

19. Harvey's bibliography omits basic texts about postmodernism—Craig Owens, "The Discourse of Others: Feminists and Postmodernism," in Hal Foster, ed., *The Anti-Aesthetic: Essays on Postmodern Culture* (Port Townsend, Wash.: Bay Press, 1983), 57–82; Brian Wallis, ed., *Art after Modernism: Rethinking Representation* (New York: New Museum of Contemporary Art, 1984); Andrew Ross, ed., *Universal Abandon? The Politics of Postmodernism* (Minneapolis: University of Minnesota Press, 1988); Victor Burgin, *The End of Art Theory: Criticism and Postmodernity* (Atlantic Highlands, N.J.: Humanities Press International, 1986); Meaghan Morris, *The Pirate's Fiancée: Feminism, Reading, Postmodernism* (London: Verso, 1988)—as well as film theory and the multidisciplinary literature of cultural studies.

20. Nancy Fraser and Linda Nicholson, "Social Criticism without Philosophy: An Encounter between Feminism and Postmodernism," in Ross, ed., *Universal Abandon? The Politics of Postmodernism,* 83–104.

21. Ernesto Laclau, "Postmodernism and Politics," in Ross, ed., *Universal Abandon? The Politics of Postmodernism,* 67.

22. Paul Patton, "Marxism and Beyond: Strategies of Reterritorialization," in Cary Nelson and Lawrence Grossberg, eds., *Marxism and the Interpretation of Culture* (Urbana: University of Illinois Press, 1988), 133.

23. Ibid.

24. Harvey, introduction, in *The Urban Experience,* 15.

25. Mark Wigley, *The Architecture of Deconstruction: Derrida's Haunt* (Cambridge: MIT Press, 1993), 129. Wigley is analyzing the use of the house as a figure of presence in the philosophical tradition of metaphysics.

26. Ibid., 134.

27. Ibid., 137–38.

28. Ernesto Laclau and Chantal Mouffe, *Hegemony and Socialist Strategy: Towards a Radical Democratic Politics* (London: Verso, 1985).

29. See "Uneven Development: Public Art in New York City," in this volume.

30. Raymond Ledrut refers to the constitutive role of fantasy in relation to "the image of the city" when he says that the city is an image "only from the moment when it becomes the locus of a certain 'investment' by the ego." See Raymond Ledrut, "Speech and the Silence of the City," in *The City and the Sign: An Introduction to Urban Semiotics* (New York: Columbia University Press, 1986), 223.

31. Douglas Crimp, "Pictures," *October* 8 (Spring 1979): 74–88.

32. Victor Burgin, "The Absence of Presence: Conceptualism and Postmodernisms," in *The End of Art Theory: Criticism and Postmodernity* (Atlantic Highlands, N.J.: Humanities Press International, 1986), 30.

33. Hans Haacke, catalogue text accompanying *Solomon R. Guggenheim Museum Board of Trustees,* in *Art into Society—Society into Art: Seven German Artists* (London: Institute of Contemporary Arts, 1974), 63.

34. Teresa de Lauretis, *Alice Doesn't: Feminism, Semiotics, Cinema* (Bloomington: Indiana University Press, 1984), 38.

---

35. See Griselda Pollock, "What's Wrong with 'Images of Women'?" *Screen Education* 24 (1977): 123–36.

36. Craig Owens, "The Discourse of Others: Feminists and Postmodernism," in Hal Foster, ed., *The Anti-Aesthetic: Essays on Postmodern Culture* (Port Townsend, Wash.: Bay Press, 1983), 59.

37. Sigmund Freud, "Medusa's Head" (1922) and "Fetishism" (1927), in *Sexuality and the Psychology of Love* (New York: Collier Books, 1963), 212–19.

38. Burgin, "The Absence of Presence," 46.

39. Jean Baudrillard, "Fetishism and Ideology: The Semiological Reduction," in *For a Critique of the Political Economy of the Sign* (Saint Louis: Telos Press, 1981), 90.

40. Judith Williamson, "A Piece of the Action: Images of 'Woman' in the Photography of Cindy Sherman," in *Consuming Passions: The Dynamics of Popular Culture* (London: Marion Boyars, 1986), 103.

CHINATOWN, PART FOUR? WHAT JAKE FORGETS ABOUT DOWNTOWN

1. Raymond Chandler, "The Simple Art of Murder," in *The Simple Art of Murder* (New York: Vintage Books, 1934), 17.

2. Ibid., 18.

3. Derek Gregory, "*Chinatown*, Part Three? Soja and the Missing Spaces of Social Theory," *Strategies,* no. 3 (1990): 40–104.

4. Edward W. Soja, *Postmodern Geographies: The Reassertion of Space in Critical Urban Theory* (London: Verso, 1989).

5. Gregory, "*Chinatown,* Part Three?" 41.

6. Mike Davis, "*Chinatown*, Part Two? The 'Internationalization' of Downtown Los Angeles," *New Left Review* 164 (July/August 1987): 65–86.

7. Michel de Certeau, *The Practice of Everyday Life* (Berkeley: University of California Press, 1984).

8. Mike Davis, *City of Quartz: Excavating the Future in Los Angeles* (London: Verso, 1990), 18. Subsequent references to this book appear in parentheses in the text.

---

9. Laura Mulvey, "The Oedipus Myth: Beyond the Riddles of the Sphinx," in *Visual and Other Pleasures* (Bloomington: Indiana University Press, 1989), 190.

10. Mary Ann Doane, "*Gilda:* Epistemology as Striptease," in *Femmes Fatales: Feminism, Film Theory, Psychoanalysis* (New York: Routledge, 1991), 102.

11. Teresa de Lauretis, "Desire in Narrative," in *Alice Doesn't: Feminism, Semiotics, Cinema* (Bloomington: Indiana University Press, 1984), 143.

TILTED ARC AND THE USES OF DEMOCRACY

1. For a discussion of moral rights, see Martha Buskirk, "Moral Rights: First Step or False Start?" *Art in America* 79, no. 7 (July 1991): 37–45.

2. Clara Weyergraf-Serra and Martha Buskirk, *The Destruction of Tilted Arc: Documents* (Cambridge: MIT Press, 1991). Subsequent references to this volume are indicated in the text.

3. For an analysis of relationships between discourses of utility and urban redevelopment and a discussion of the "new public art" see "Uneven Development: Public Art in New York City," in this volume.

4. Henri Lefebvre, *La production de l'espace* (Paris: Anthropos, 1974), 420 (my emphasis).

5. Laurence Tribe, *Constitutional Choices* (Cambridge: Harvard University Press, 1985), 189.

6. Ibid., 203–4.

7. Stuart Hall, "Popular-Democratic vs Authoritarian Populism: Two Ways of 'Taking Democracy Seriously,'" in *The Hard Road to Renewal: Thatcherism and the Crisis of the Left* (London: Verso, 1988), 123–49.

AGORAPHOBIA

1. Huntington is the author of the American section of *The Crisis of Democracy,* a report issued by the Trilateral Commission, a private organization founded in 1973 to engineer a new world order controlled by the liberal democracies of North America, Western Europe, and Japan. The commission included prominent government, business, academic, and professional figures. For a discussion of "The Crisis of Democracy," see Alan Wolfe, "Capitalism Shows Its Face: Giving Up on Democracy," in *Trilateralism: The Trilateral Commission and Elite Planning for World Manage-*

ment, ed. Holly Sklar (Boston: South End Press, 1980), 295–306. Recently, neoconservatives have adopted a new rhetoric of democracy that diverges from the overt authoritarianism of the Huntington report. Claiming to defend public space, they have begun to celebrate what neoconservative journalists and political scholars call "the new community activism" or "the new citizenship." The new citizenship consists precisely of people making demands on government, which is itself now deemed "excessive." What makes the new activists acceptable, of course, is that they agitate against the placement of social services—homeless shelters, AIDS or mental health facilities—in their neighborhoods and, more broadly, against what conservatives call "the tyrannies of the therapeutic state." William A. Schambra, "By The People: The Old Values of the New Citizenship," *Policy Review,* no. 69 (Summer 1994): 38.

The concerns of the new activists—no matter how diverse the socioeconomic status of the neighborhoods they seek to protect—can therefore be grouped together to support three elements of conservative urban policy discourse: advocacy of cutbacks in social spending; the call for reliance on the resources of civil society—the capitalist economy as well as other nongovernmental institutions—rather than the state; denigration of government protection of civil rights, which are blamed for the "breakdown of public order" and decline in "the quality of life." "The project to restore civil society," writes Schambra, "is a bridge over one of the most troubling chasms in American society today—between conservatives and the inner city." *City Journal* agrees: "Citizens are rising to demand that the government stop dumping social problems onto their streets and start demonstrating a commonsense concern with the quality of life in the city's neighborhoods." Heather MacDonald, "The New Community Activism: Social Justice Comes Full Circle," *City Journal* 3, no. 4 (Autumn 1993): 44.

2. See, for instance, Eric Gibson, "Jennifer Bartlett and the Crisis of Public Art," *New Criterion* 9, no. 1 (September 1990): 62–64. Neoconservative devotion to the right of access to public space generally serves, of course, as a rationale for censoring critical art, eliminating government funding of the arts, and privatizing art production—a position outlined in Edward C. Banfield, *The Democratic Muse: Visual Arts and the Public Interest* (New York: Basic Books, 1984).

3. For a discussion of the language of democracy used during the *Tilted Arc* debate, see *"Tilted Arc:* The Uses of Democracy," in this volume.

4. Claude Lefort, "The Question of Democracy," in *Democracy and Political Theory* (Minneapolis: University of Minnesota Press, 1988), 10.

5. Nancy Fraser, "Rethinking the Public Sphere: A Contribution to the Critique of Actually Existing Democracy," in Craig Calhoun, ed., *Habermas and the Public Sphere* (Cambridge: MIT Press, 1992), 109.

6. Chantal Mouffe, "Pluralism and Modern Democracy: Around Carl Schmitt," in *The Return of the Political* (London: Verso, 1993), 117.

7. Lefort, "The Logic of Totalitarianism," in *The Political Forms of Modern Society: Bureaucracy, Democracy, Totalitarianism* (Cambridge: MIT Press, 1986), 279.

8. Claude Lefort, "The Question of Democracy," in *Democracy and Political Theory* (Minneapolis: University of Minnesota Press, 1988), 19.

9. Ibid., 17.

10. Ernesto Laclau and Chantal Mouffe, *Hegemony and Socialist Strategy: Toward a Radical Democratic Politics,* trans. Winston Moore and Paul Cammack (London: Verso, 1985), 122.

11. Ibid., 125.

12. Ibid. Mouffe and Laclau formulate their concept of "antagonism" in distinction from both "contradiction" and "opposition," which designate relationships between objects—conceptual or real—that are full identities. Antagonism, by contrast, is a relationship that prevents the fullness of any identity. See Laclau and Mouffe, *Hegemony and Socialist Strategy,* 124. Mouffe and Laclau also distinguish the negativity inherent in the concept of antagonism from negativity in the dialectical sense of the term. The negative, for them, is not a moment in the unfolding of a concept that is then reabsorbed in a higher unity. It is an outside that affirms an identity but reveals its contingency. Antagonism is not negation in the service of totality but the negation of a closed totality. Laclau, "New Reflections on the Revolution of Our Time," in *New Reflections on the Revolution of Our Time* (London: Verso, 1990), 26.

13. Laclau, "New Reflections on the Revolution of Our Time," 61.

14. Hannah Arendt, *The Origins of Totalitarianism* (San Diego: Harcourt Brace & Company, 1948), 296.

15. Etienne Balibar, "What Is a Politics of the Rights of Man?" in *Masses, Classes, Ideas: Studies on Politics and Philosophy Before and After Marx,* trans. James Swenson (New York: Routledge, 1994), 211.

16. Since I am applying Lefort's ideas to a discussion of contemporary urban discourse, it is important to note that Lefort uses the term *appropriation* in an opposite sense from Henri Lefebvre, whose concept of appropriation has been so compelling for critical urban thought. For Lefort, appropriation refers to an action of state power; for Lefebvre, it denotes an action against such

power. This terminological difference does not mean that the ideas of the two writers are polarized. On the contrary, they have certain affinities. Although Lefort is not writing specifically about urban space, his appropriation—the occupation of public space by giving it an absolute meaning—resembles what Henri Lefebvre calls the domination of space—the technocratic designation of objective uses that bestow an ideological coherence on space. Moreover, Lefort's appropriation and Lefebvre's domination are similar to Michel de Certeau's notion of "strategy" as the relationship that becomes possible when a subject with power postulates a *place* that can be delimited as its *own*. See Henri Lefebvre, *The Production of Space*, trans. Donald Nicholson-Smith (Oxford: Basil Blackwell, 1991) and Michel de Certeau, *The Practice of Everyday Life* (Berkeley: University of California Press, 1984), 36. All three endow space with proper meanings and uses and, in this proprietary manner, set up a relation with an exterior that threatens those uses. In fact, de Certeau uses the adjective *appropriated* to delineate a space—"a place appropriated as one's own"—that serves from inception "as a base from which relations with an exteriority composed of targets or threats . . . can be managed."

The actions described by Lefort, Lefebvre, and de Certeau call for countervailing democratic procedures: "depropriation" (a term that, as far as I am aware, Lefort does not explicitly use), Lefebvre's "appropriation," and what de Certeau calls "making do." In this context, depropriation and Lefebvre's appropriation have similar (though not identical) meanings. Like de Certeau's making do, they imply some kind of undoing by the outside of a space that has been made proper, a taking account of exclusions and differences, and consequent exposure of power where it has been naturalized and obscured.

17. Sam Roberts, "The Public's Right to Put a Padlock on a Public Space," *New York Times,* June 3, 1991, B1.

18. Fred Siegel, "Reclaiming Our Public Spaces," *The City Journal* 2, no. 2 (Spring 1992): 35–45.

19. Roberts, "The Public's Right," B1.

20. Siegel, "Reclaiming Our Public Spaces," 41.

21. Theodor Adorno, "What Does Coming to Terms with the Past Mean?" in *Bitburg in Moral and Political Perspective,* ed. Geoffrey H. Hartman (Bloomington: Indiana University Press, 1986), 127–28; translated from *Gesammelte Schriften* 10, pt. 2 (Frankfurt am Main: Suhrkamp 1977), 555–72. Adorno continues: "So long as one wants to struggle against anti-Semitism within individual persons, one shouldn't expect too much from recourse to facts, for they'll often either not be admitted or be neutralized as exceptions. One should rather turn the argument toward the people whom one is addressing. It is they who should be made conscious of the mechanisms that provoke their racial prejudice."

22. Ibid., 128.

23. Slavoj Žižek, *The Sublime Object of Ideology* (London: Verso, 1989), 128.

24. Ibid., 127.

25. The idea that the visibility of homeless people might reinforce the image of a unified urban space casts doubt on the more common assumption of critical urban discourse—that the mere presence of homeless people in public spaces challenges the appearance of harmony that official representations try to impose on dominated urban sites (I make this claim, for example, at the beginning of "Uneven Development: Public Art in New York City," in this volume). The visibility of homeless people neither guarantees the social recognition of homeless people nor legitimates conflicts over public space; it is just as likely to strengthen the image of an essentially harmonious public space, which legitimates the eviction of homeless people.

But raising questions about the conditions and consequences of visibility does not negate the importance of maintaining the visibility of homelessness, where visibility implies resistance to efforts to expel homeless people from public space and coercively assign them to shelters. The demand for visibility, understood as the declaration of the right of homeless people to live and work in public spaces, differs from a specular model of visibility, in which homeless people are constructed as objects for a viewing subject. The first demand challenges established legitimacy, questioning the legality of state power in evicting people from public spaces. The presence of homeless people can, then, reveal the presence of power in places, like parks, where it was formerly obscured. As power becomes visible and drops its veil of anonymity, the homeless person also emerges from her consignment to an ideological image into a new kind of visibility. It is, then, imperative to struggle against the possibility that, as the state exercises its monopoly on legitimate violence and evicts the homeless from public spaces, both state power and homeless people will fade into invisibility.

26. See "Krzysztof Wodiczko's *Homeless Projection* and the Site of Urban 'Revitalization,'" and "Uneven Development: Public Art in New York City," in this volume.

27. For a case study of the role played by parks in gentrification and redevelopment, see "Krzysztof Wodiczko's *Homeless Projection* and the Site of Urban 'Revitalization,'" in this volume.

28. See "Uneven Development: Public Art in New York City," in this volume.

29. Jerry Allen, "How Art Becomes Public," 1985; reprinted in *Going Public: A Field Guide to Developments in Art in Public Places* (Arts Extension Service and the Visual Arts Program of the National Endowment for the Arts, 1988), 246.

30. Patricia Phillips, "The Public Art Machine: Out of Order," *Artforum* 27 (December 1988): 93.

31. Kathy Halbreich, "Stretching the Terrain: Sketching Twenty Years of Public Art," in *Going Public: A Field Guide to Developments in Art in Public Places*, 9.

32. Suzanne Lacy, "Cultural Pilgrimages and Metaphoric Journeys," in Suzanne Lacy, ed., *Mapping the Terrain: New Genre Public Art* (Seattle: Bay Press, 1995), 20.

33. Allen, "How Art Becomes Public," 246.

34. Ibid., 250.

35. Harriet F. Senie and Sally Webster, ed., *Critical Issues in Public Art: Content, Context, and Controversy* (New York: HarperCollins, 1992), xi.

36. Ibid.

37. Ibid., 171.

38. Michael Sorkin, "Introduction: Variations on a Theme Park," in Michael Sorkin, ed., *Variations on a Theme Park: The New American City and the End of Public Space* (New York: The Noonday Press, 1992), xv.

39. Ibid.

40. The combination of profit-maximizing and desexualizing tendencies in contemporary urban planning is manifest both in the use of Disneyland as a model for contemporary urbanism and in the role played by the Disney Development Company in actual urban redevelopment. Since the publication of Sorkin's book, Disney has become financially and symbolically useful to the current partnership being forged in New York between real-estate interests and moral crusaders who want to repress urban sexual cultures. Disney's instrumentality emerged clearly in a recent *New York Times* article that announced the city's choice of the Disney Development Company and the Tishman Urban Development Corporation to rebuild the corner of 42nd Street and Eighth Avenue as part of the redevelopment of Times Square: "The $303 million project is the centerpiece of state and city efforts to transform 42nd Street between Seventh and Eighth Avenues from a seedy strip with its ever-present hustlers and sex shops into a glitzy family-oriented entertainment center. . . . But perhaps of even more value is the Disney name. In its effort to turn around a neighborhood long synonymous with urban danger and degradation, the city now has a partner that is a symbol of wholesome entertainment worldwide." Shawn G. Kennedy, "Disney and Developer Are Chosen To Build 42nd Street Hotel Complex," *New York Times,* May 12, 1995, B1.

41. Sorkin, "Introduction: Variations on a Theme Park," xv.

42. For an analysis of the functions of the preservationist rhetoric that accompanied redevelopment, see my "Architecture of the Evicted," in *Krzysztof Wodiczko: New York City Tableaux and The Homeless Vehicle Project,* exhib. cat. (New York: Exit Art, 1989), 28–37, reprinted in *Strategies* 3 (1990): 159–83; and "Krzysztof Wodiczko's *Homeless Projection* and the Site of Urban 'Revitalization,'" in this volume.

43. Paul Goldberger, "Bryant Park, An Out-of-Town Experience," *New York Times,* May 3, 1992, H34.

44. "Whatever Became of the Public Square? New Designs for a Great Good Place," *Harper's* (July 1990): 49–60.

45. Bruce Robbins, "Introduction: The Public as Phantom," in Bruce Robbins, ed., *The Phantom Public Sphere,* Cultural Politics 5 (Minneapolis: University of Minnesota Press, 1993), viii.

46. Jürgen Habermas, *The Structural Transformation of the Public Sphere: An Inquiry into a Category of Bourgeois Society,* trans. Thomas Burger with the assistance of Frederick Lawrence (Cambridge: MIT Press, 1989); originally published as *Strukturwandel der Öffentlichkeit* (Darmstadt: Hermann Luchterhand Verlag, 1962).

47. Jürgen Habermas, "The Public Sphere: An Encyclopedia Article (1964)," *New German Critique* (Fall 1974): 44–55.

48. Immanuel Kant, "An Answer to the Question: 'What is Enlightenment?'" in *Kant: Political Writings,* introd. Hans Reiss, trans. H. B. Nisbet (Cambridge: Cambridge University Press, 1970), 54–60.

49. Vito Acconci, *Making Public: The Writing and Reading of Public Space* (The Hague: Uitgever, 1993), 16. This publication accompanied "Vito Acconci: Models, Projects for Streets, Squares, and Parks," an exhibition at Stroom: The Hague's Center for Visual Arts, 1993.

50. Chantal Mouffe, "Democratic Citizenship and the Political Community," in Chantal Mouffe, ed., *Dimensions of Radical Democracy: Pluralism, Citizenship, Community* (London: Verso, 1992), 234.

51. Ibid., 235.

52. Friedrich Nietzsche, "On the Genealogy of Morals," in *On the Genealogy of Morals and Ecce Homo,* trans. Walter Kaufmann and R. J. Hollingdale (New York: Random House, 1967), 77.

53. See Craig Owens, "The Yen for Art," in Hal Foster, ed., *Discussions in Contemporary Culture,* Discussions in Contemporary Culture, no. 1 (Seattle: Bay Press, 1987), 23.

54. See "Uneven Development: Public Art in New York City," in this volume.

55. Owens discussed Alexander Kluge and Oskar Negt's notion of an oppositional public sphere in the talk he delivered in 1987 as a member of a panel on the "The Birth and Death of the Viewer: On the Public Function of Art" at the Dia Art Foundation but published a completely different essay in *Discussions in Contemporary Culture,* the book that documents the panel.

56. Owens, "The Yen for Art," 20.

57. Fraser, "Rethinking the Public Sphere: A Contribution to the Critique of Actually Existing Democracy," 131.

58. "Public Vision," an exhibition of the work of Gretchen Bender, Jennifer Bolande, Diane Buckler, Ellen Carey, Nancy Dwyer, Barbara Kruger, Louise Lawler, Sherrie Levine, Diane Shea, Cindy Sherman, Laurie Simmons, and Peggy Yunque, organized by Gretchen Bender, Nancy Dwyer, and Cindy Sherman at White Columns, New York, 1982. White Columns, during this innovative period in its history, was directed by Josh Baer. I would like to thank Gretchen Bender for help in reconstructing "Public Vision."

59. For accounts of early postmodern theory's blindness to feminism, see Jane Weinstock, "A Laugh, A Lass and a Lad," *Art in America,* 71, no. 6 (Summer 1983): 8; and Craig Owens, "The Discourse of Others: Feminists and Postmodernism," in Hal Foster, ed., *The Anti-Aesthetic: Essays on Postmodern Culture* (Port Townsend, Wash.: Bay Press, 1983), 57–82.

60. "The Revolutionary Power of Women's Laughter," organized by Jo Anna Isaak at Protetch McNeil, New York, 1983.

61. "Difference: On Representation and Sexuality," organized by Kate Linker and Jane Weinstock at the New Museum of Contemporary Art, New York, 1985.

62. Clement Greenberg, "Modernist Painting," in Gregory Battcock, ed., *The New Art* (New York: E. P. Dutton & Co., 1966), 66–77.

63. Rosalind Krauss, *Cindy Sherman 1975–1993* (New York: Rizzoli, 1993), 192.

64. Judith Williamson, "A Piece of the Action: Images of 'Woman' in the Photography of Cindy Sherman," in *Consuming Passions: The Dynamics of Popular Culture* (London: Marion Boyars, 1986), 103.

65. For an excellent discussion of Kruger's early work, especially of her use of the pronoun *you,* see Jane Weinstock, "What she means, to you," in *Barbara Kruger: We Won't Play Nature to Your Culture,* exhib. cat. (London: Institute of Contemporary Art, 1983), 12–16.

66. Mark Wigley, *The Architecture of Deconstruction: Derrida's Haunt* (Cambridge: MIT Press, 1993), 138.

67. Laura Mulvey, "Visual Pleasure and Narrative Cinema," in Brian Wallis, ed., *Art After Modernism: Rethinking Representation* (New York: New Museum of Contemporary Art and David R. Godine, 1984), 366.

68. Slavoj Žižek, *For They Know Not What They Do: Enjoyment as a Political Factor* (London: Verso, 1991), 174 n. 38.

69. *Love for Sale: The Words and Pictures of Barbara Kruger,* text by Kate Linker (New York: Harry N. Abrams), 61.

70. Thomas Keenan, "Windows: of vulnerability," in Bruce Robbins, ed., *The Phantom Public Sphere* (Minneapolis: University of Minnesota Press, 1993), 121–41.

71. Hal Foster, preface, in Hal Foster, ed., *Discussions in Contemporary Culture,* Dia Art Foundation Discussions in Contemporary Culture, no. 1 (Seattle: Bay Press, 1987).

72. Following the strong critical response that Crow's talk provoked from other speakers and members of the audience, he substantially rewrote the text for the book documenting the Dia discussions. The published essay leaves his concept of the public sphere essentially unaltered, however, so that, by coupling the essay with the transcript of the original discussion that followed the panel and is included in the book, Crow's initial position can be reconstructed.

73. "Discussion, The Birth and Death of the Viewer: On the Public Function of Art," in Hal Foster, ed., *Discussions in Contemporary Culture,* Dia Art Foundation Discussions in Contemporary Culture, no. 1 (Seattle: Bay Press, 1987), 24.

74. Thomas Crow, "These Collectors, They Talk about Baudrillard Now," in Foster, ed., *Discussions in Contemporary Culture,* 1–2. Subsequent references to this essay are indicated in the text.

75. "Discussion, The Birth and Death of the Viewer," 26.

76. John Barrell, *The Political Theory of Painting from Reynolds to Hazlitt: 'The Body of the Public'* (New Haven: Yale University Press, 1986), 3.

77. Crow's use of civic humanism to create a unity between modernism and the "dematerializing practices" of the late 1960s is odd. The latter practices were, after all, opposed to the very aspect of modernism—the claim of transcendence—through which Crow relates modernism to civic humanist aesthetics in the first place. Crow can only overcome this contradiction by treating as a given his contention that the dematerializing practices sought, albeit differently from modernism, to unify the art audience. But this contention—and Crow's consequent assimilation of the critique of autonomy mounted in the 1960s and 1970s to the ideals of civic humanism—is itself highly problematic. In the 1960s and 1970s many of the artists undertaking a critique of modernism did so precisely to challenge, not to support, the notion that in museums or galleries, viewers are united as "citizens of art." For example, Martha Rosler's artwork *The Bowery in Two Inadequate Descriptive Systems* and her essays "In, Around, and Afterthoughts (On Documentary Photography)" and "Lookers, Buyers, Dealers, and Makers: Thoughts on Audience" as well as Hans Haacke's various *Gallery-Goers' Residence Profiles* drew attention to the class, gender, or racial compositions of art audiences. Unlike Crow, Rosler and Haacke did not focus on the disparity between the social identity of actual viewers, on the one hand, and the supposedly transcendent viewer addressed by traditional aesthetic institutions, on the other, in order to set up the ideal viewer as "a standard against which the various inadequacies of art's actual consumers could be measured and criticized." Rather, these artists wanted to demonstrate that the transcendent viewer addressed by modernist aesthetic discourse is an imaginary entity, a disavowal of the fact that aesthetic space is itself immersed in conflictual social relations. Rosler and Haacke therefore challenged the illusion, perpetuated in aestheticism and civic humanism, of a higher, abstract unity among people who might really belong on different sides.

78. Barrell, *The Political Theory of Painting*, 79.

79. Robert R. Wark, ed., *Reynolds's Discourses on Art*, 2nd ed. (New Haven: Yale University Press, 1975), 202.

80. Etienne Balibar, "'Rights of Man' and 'Rights of the Citizen': The Modern Dialectic of Equality and Freedom" in *Masses, Classes, Ideas: Studies on Politics and Philosophy Before and After Marx*, trans. James Swenson (New York: Routledge, 1994), 59.

81. Iris Marion Young, "Impartiality and the Civic Public: Some Implications of Feminist Critiques of Moral and Political Theory," in *Feminism as Critique*, ed. Seyla Benhabib and Drucilla Cornell (Minneapolis: University of Minnesota Press, 1987), 60.

82. Ibid.

83. Ibid. Here Young is citing Michael Sandel's critique of the radically unsituated subject. See Michael Sandel, *Liberalism and the Limits of Justice* (Cambridge: Cambridge University Press, 1982).

84. Hannah Arendt, *The Human Condition* (Chicago: The University of Chicago Press, 1958), 234.

85. See Samuel Weber's discussion of objectivity in "Objectivity Otherwise," in *Objectivity and Its Other,* ed. Wolfgang Natter et. al. (New York: Guilford Press, 1995), 36–37.

86. Martin Heidegger, "The Age of the World Picture," in *The Question Concerning Technology and Other Essays* (New York: Harper and Row, 1977), 115–54.

87. Barrell, *The Political Theory of Painting,* 65–66.

88. Homi K. Bhabha, "A Good Judge of Character: Men, Metaphors, and the Common Culture," in Toni Morrison, ed., *Race-ing Justice, En-gendering Power: Essays on Anita Hill, Clarence Thomas, and the Construction of Social Reality* (New York: Pantheon Books, 1992), 242.

89. This denigration of questions of subjectivity in public art discourse is frequently supported by urban and architecture discourses—the very discourses introduced into the left art world in the 1980s in tandem with discussions of "the public" to forge more democratic concepts of public art.

90. David Trend, "Beyond Resistance: Notes on Community Counter-Practice," *Afterimage* (April 1989): 6.

91. Ibid.

92. George Yudice, "For a Practical Aesthetics," *Social Text* 25/26 (1990): 135.

93. Ibid., 134.

94. Trend, "Beyond Resistance," 4.

95. Ibid.

96. Yudice, "For a Practical Aesthetics," 135.

97. Ibid., 134.

98. Jacqueline Rose, "Sexuality in the Field of Vision," in *Sexuality in the Field of Vision* (London: Verso, 1986), 231. Barbara Kruger cited this passage as an epigraph to her contribution to the second Dia panel discussion on "The Cultural Public Sphere," where, the week after Crow's presentation, Kruger and Douglas Crimp insisted, in different ways, on the relevance of issues of sexuality to the public sphere.

99. Edward W. Said, "Opponents, Audiences, Constituencies, and Community," in Hal Foster, ed., *The Anti-Aesthetic: Essays on Postmodern Culture* (Port Townsend, Wash.: Bay Press, 1983), 135–59.

100. Bruce Robbins, "Interdisciplinarity in Public: The Rhetoric of Rhetoric," *Social Text* 25/26 (1990): 115.

101. See "Men in Space" and "Boys Town," in this volume.

102. Adorno, "What Does Coming to Terms with the Past Mean?" 129.

103. Bruce Robbins, "Introduction: The Public as Phantom," in Bruce Robbins, ed., *The Phantom Public Sphere,* Social Text Series on Cultural Politics 5 (Minneapolis: University of Minnesota Press, 1993).

104. Oskar Negt and Alexander Kluge, *Public Sphere and Experience: Toward an Analysis of the Bourgeois and Proletarian Public Sphere,* trans. Peter Labanyi, Jamie Owen Daniel, and Assenka Oksiloff (Minneapolis: University of Minnesota Press, 1993), 3; originally published as *Öffentlichkeit und Erfahrung: Zur Organisationsanalyse von bürgerlicher und proletarischer Öffentlichkeit* (Frankfurt: Suhrkamp, 1972).

105. Robbins, "Introduction: The Public as Phantom," x.

106. Ibid.

107. Ibid., xxiv.

108. Iris Marion Young, "Social Movements and the Politics of Difference," in *Justice and the Politics of Difference* (Princeton: Princeton University Press, 1990), 171.

109. The reminder that difference is interdependence and thus raises these questions was made by William E. Connolly in "Pluralism and Multiculturalism," a paper presented at the conference "Cultural Diversities: On Democracy, Community, and Citizenship," held at the Bohen Foundation, New York, in February 1994.

110. Iris Marion Young, "The Ideal of Community and the Politics of Difference," in Linda J. Nicholson, ed., *Feminism/Postmodernism,* Thinking Gender Series (New York: Routledge), 304.

111. Thomas Keenan, "Windows: Of Vulnerability," in Robbins, ed., *The Phantom Public Sphere,* 121–41.

112. Beatriz Colomina, *Privacy and Publicity: Modern Architecture as Mass Media* (Cambridge: MIT Press, 1994), 134.

113. Keenan, "Windows: Of Vulnerability," 127.

114. Sigmund Freud, *A General Introduction to Psychoanalysis,* trans. Joan Riviere (New York: Simon and Schuster, 1935), 252.

115. Keenan, "Windows: Of Vulnerability," 135.

116. Joan Copjec and Michael Sorkin, "Shrooms: East New York," *Assemblage* 24 (August 1994): 97.

117. Lefort, "The Question of Democracy," 18.

118. Žižek, *For They Know Not What They Do,* 168.

119. Carol Brooks Gardner, "Out of Place: Gender, Public Places, and Situational Disadvantage," in Roger Friedland and Deirdre Boden, eds., *NowHere: Space, Time and Modernity* (Berkeley: University of California Press, 1994), 349.

120. Ibid., 350.

121. In the course of this essay, as I examine current debates about "public space," I not only question the meaning of the term *public* but problematize the word *space.* As I tried to suggest from the opening sentence, space is not an obvious or monolithic category. It can be a city or a building, but it can also be, among other things, an identity or a discourse. Some critics try to keep these spaces separate, transforming the difference between them into an opposition, treating the first kind of space as more "real" than the second. In other words, these critics accept a classical opposition between the extradiscursive and the discursive—hence, between reality and thought—and map this opposition onto different categories of space. A democratic critique of space must, I think, break with these dichotomies. For no space, insofar as it is social, is a simply given, secure, self-contained entity that precedes representation; its very identity as a space, its appearance of closure, is constituted and maintained through discursive relationships that are themselves material and spatial—differentiations, repressions, subordinations, domestications, at- tempted exclusions. In short, space is relational, and consequently, as Mark Wigley writes, "There is no space without violence and no violence that is not spatial." Editorial, *Assemblage* 20 (April 1993): 7.

When critics draw an opposition between "real" or "concrete" spaces, which are suppos- edly constituted by extradiscursive processes, and other spaces that are held to be merely "meta- phorical" or "discursive," they not only drastically restrict the field of "reality"; they also conceal the politics through which the space of their own categories is constructed, presupposing that the object of their discourse is a purely objective field constituted outside any discursive intervention.

Unproblematized references to real spaces seal off the spaces in question from contestation precisely by repressing the fact that spaces are produced. More than that, to draw a hierarchical opposition between spaces is to produce space, a political activity masked by the claim that one is simply addressing a real spatial object. If our goal is to reveal and intervene in the political struggles producing spaces, we should not focus on distinguishing hierarchically among heterogeneous spaces, on pronouncing one space inherently more political than another, calling some real and others metaphorical, or on defending traditional spaces—urban squares, for example—against the supposed dangers to reality of new spatial arrangements—such as the media, information systems, and computer networks. These approaches deter us from investigating the real political struggles inherent in the production of *all* spaces and from enlarging the field of struggles to make many different kinds of spaces public.

122. Keenan, "Windows: Of Vulnerability," 133.

123. Claude Lefort, "Politics and Human Rights," in *The Political Forms of Modern Society: Bureaucracy, Democracy, Totalitarianism* (Cambridge: MIT Press, 1986), 270.

124. Recently, Jacques Derrida has written something similar about totalitarianism when, in another context, he speculated that totalitarianism originates in the terror inspired by a phantom. Jacques Derrida, *Specters of Marx: The State of the Debt, the Work of Mourning, and the New International*, trans. Peggy Kamuf (New York: Routledge, 1994).

Derrida refers to a different phantom—not the phantom public sphere but "the specter of communism." In defining communism as a specter, Derrida recalls the famous opening line of *The Communist Manifesto*: "A specter is haunting Europe—the specter of communism." Unlike Marx and Engels, however, speaking from a different historical conjuncture, Derrida writes about the fear that this specter called forth not in communism's adversaries but in its proponents. Derrida gives the *Manifesto*'s announcement a deconstructive inflection. For him, spectrality is a constitutive feature of communism. Communism is destroyed by being realized because it exists only in a disjointed space and time; it is never fully present but "always still to come." In this sense, communism stands for a destabilizing force that makes a fully constituted society impossible and therefore promises different solutions to social problems. This promise is not, however, directed toward and therefore beholden to an ideal—something known but not yet present. Rather, it exists only when society itself is a problem—open to unknown futures, unable to reach any real closure. Totalitarianism is the attempt to have closure. It is the consequence of an effort to escape society's essential incompletion and to bring about "the real presence of the specter, thus the end of the spectral." Totalitarianism, says Derrida, is "the monstrous realization" of a specter. By the same token, however, the collapse of totalitarianisms does not mean that communism is finished. Rather, it is freed from its monstrous realization to rise as a ghost and haunt capitalist societies.

Derrida likens the specter of communism to democracy. Communism, he writes, "is distinguished *like democracy itself,* from every living present understood as plenitude of a presence-to-itself, as totality of a presence effectively identical to itself." At this point Derrida's analysis seems to parallel that of Lefort: totalitarianism, an attempt to conjure away democracy, springs from discomfort with the idea that democracy's uncertainties cannot be finally resolved without its destruction. Slavoj Žižek has recently argued, however, that Derrida conceives of the specter as a "'higher' stratum of reality . . . that persists in its Beyond" and is thus itself a positivization. For Žižek, Derrida's specter gives "quasi-being" to a void and is therefore an attempt to escape something even more terrifying—"the abyss of freedom." See Slavoj Žižek, introduction, in Slavoj Žižek, ed., *Mapping Ideology* (London: Verso, 1994), 1–33.

125. Lefort, "Politics and Human Rights," 270.

126. Ernesto Laclau, "Building a New Left," in *New Reflections on the Revolution of Our Time* (London: Verso, 1990), 190.

CREDITS

Versions of these essays have appeared previously:

"Krzysztof Wodiczko's *Homeless Projection* and the Site of Urban 'Revitalization,'" *October* 38 (Fall 1986).

"Uneven Development: Public Art in New York City," *October* 47 (Winter 1988).

"Representing Berlin: Urban Ideology and Aesthetic Practice," in Irit Rogoff, ed., *The Divided Heritage: Themes and Problems in German Modernism* (Cambridge: Cambridge University Press, 1991).

"Property Values: Hans Haacke, Real Estate, and the Museum," in Brian Wallis, ed., *Hans Haacke: Unfinished Business* (New York: New Museum of Contemporary Art and MIT Press, 1986).

"Men in Space," *Artforum* 28, no. 6 (February 1990).

"Boys Town," *Environment and Planning D: Society and Space* 9 (1991), Pion Limited, London.

"*Chinatown*, Part Four? What Jake Forgets about Downtown," *Assemblage* 20 (April 1993).

"*Tilted Arc* and the Uses of Democracy," *Design Book Review* 23 (Winter 1992).

"Art and Public Space: Questions of Democracy," *Social Text* 33 (1993).

INDEX

Note: Illustrations are indicated by page numbers in italics.